The Presidency of

RICHARD

NIXON

AMERICAN PRESIDENCY SERIES

Clifford S. Griffin and Donald R. McCoy, Founding Editors
Homer E. Socolofsky, General Editor

George Washington, Forrest McDonald
John Adams, Ralph Adams Brown
Thomas Jefferson, Forrest McDonald
James Madison, Robert Allen Rutland
James Monroe, Noble E. Cunningham, Jr.
John Quincy Adams, Mary W. M. Hargreaves
Andrew Jackson, Donald B. Cole
Martin Van Buren, Major L. Wilson
William Henry Harrison & John Tyler, Norma Lois Peterson
James K. Polk, Paul H. Bergeron
Zachary Taylor & Millard Fillmore, Elbert B. Smith
Franklin Pierce, Larry Gara
James Buchanan, Elbert B. Smith
Abraham Lincoln, Phillip Shaw Paludan
Andrew Johnson, Albert Castel
Rutherford B. Hayes, Ari Hoogenboom
James A. Garfield & Chester A. Arthur, Justus D. Doenecke
Grover Cleveland, Richard E. Welch, Jr.
Benjamin Harrison, Homer B. Socolofsky & Allan B. Spetter
William McKinley, Lewis L. Gould
Theodore Roosevelt, Lewis L. Gould
William Howard Taft, Paolo E. Coletta
Woodrow Wilson, Kendrick A. Clements
Warren G. Harding, Eugene P. Trani & David L. Wilson
Calvin Coolidge, Robert H. Ferrell
Herbert C. Hoover, Martin L. Fausold
Harry S. Truman, Donald R. McCoy
Dwight D. Eisenhower, Chester J. Pach, Jr., & Elmo Richardson
John F. Kennedy, James N. Giglio
Lyndon B. Johnson, Vaughn Davis Bornet
Richard Nixon, Melvin Small
Gerald R. Ford, John Robert Greene
James Earl Carter, Jr., Burton I. Kaufman
George Bush, John Robert Greene

Richard Nixon in the characteristic "V" pose, 28 January 1970. (National Archives)

The Presidency of

RICHARD
NIXON

Melvin Small

UNIVERSITY PRESS OF KANSAS

Published by the University Press of Kansas (Lawrence,
Kansas 66049), which was organized by the Kansas
Board of Regents and is operated and funded by Emporia
State University, Fort Hays State University,
Kansas State University, Pittsburgh State University, the University
of Kansas, and Wichita State University.

Library of Congress Cataloging-in-Publication Data

Small, Melvin.
The presidency of Richard Nixon / Melvin Small.
  p.   cm. — (American presidency series)
Includes bibliographical references and index.
ISBN 0-7006-0973-3 (cloth : alk. paper)
ISBN 0-7006-1255-6 (pbk. : alk. paper)
1. Nixon, Richard M. (Richard Milhous), 1913–1994.   2. United
States—Politics and government—1969–1974.   I. Title.   II. Series.
E855.S63   1999
973.924'092—dc21   99-13148

British Library Cataloguing in Publication Data is available.

Printed in the United States of America

10 9 8 7 6 5 4

For the amazing triplets,
Aaron, Samantha, and Brendan,
who have a century of
presidents ahead of them

CONTENTS

Photo insert follows page 204.

FOREWORD

The aim of the American Presidency Series is to present historians and the general reading public with interesting, scholarly assessments of the various presidential administrations. These interpretive surveys are intended to cover the broad ground between biographies, specialized monographs, and journalistic accounts. As such, each is a comprehensive work that draws on original sources and pertinent secondary literature yet leaves room for the author's own analysis and interpretation.

Volumes in the series present the data essential to understanding the administration under consideration. Particularly, each book treats the then-current problems facing the United States and its people and how the president and his associates felt about, thought about, and worked to cope with these problems. Attention is given to how the office developed and operated during the president's tenure. Equally important is consideration of the vital relationships among the president, his staff, the executive officers, Congress, foreign representatives, the judiciary, state officials, the public, political parties, the press, and influential private citizens. The series is also concerned with how this unique American institution—the presidency—was viewed by the presidents, and with what results.

All this is set, insofar as possible, in the context not only of contemporary politics but also of economics, international relations, law, morals, public administration, religion, and thought. Such a broad approach is necessary to understanding, for a presidential administration is more than the elected and appointed officers composing it, since its work so often reflects the major problems, anxieties, and glories of the nation. In short, the authors in this series strive to recount and evaluate the record of each administration and to identify its distinctiveness and relationships to the past, its own time, and the future.

The General Editor

PREFACE

Richard Nixon once predicted that by the time the year 2000 rolled around and the passions surrounding Watergate and his controversial career had subsided, scholars would begin to evaluate his presidency more favorably. As we approach the millennium, with the cold war over for a decade and the Republican Party and conservative values ascendant, it is indeed an appropriate time to consider how Nixon's administration contributed to these astonishing developments. Twenty-five years after he became the first president to resign from office and after the release of mountains of documents and hundreds of hours of tape recordings, we should now be able to place his political legacy in historical perspective.

Nixon was an unpleasant human being. When he made his prediction about the year 2000, he could not have taken into account the impact of the release of a second round of tapes in 1996. For historians of his presidency, as distinct from biographers, the challenge is to pay attention not just to what he stated in public or murmured in private but to what he accomplished in domestic and foreign politics and his broader influence on American political institutions and culture.

The problem of evaluating Nixon fairly is compounded by his last political campaign—his relentless run for the ex-presidency from 1974 to his death in 1994. By the time prominent Americans delivered their fulsome eulogies, he had achieved his goal. He was again among America's most admired leaders, a wise elder statesman whose life's work drew praise from Republicans and Democrats alike.

As he watched the disgraced former president's approval ratings rise in the polls, historian Stanley Kutler warned, "Richard Nixon has struggled mightily for the soul of history and the soul of historians. Historians *ought* to worry about theirs."[1] Concerned about my own soul, I tried to steer a path between the legion of unreconstructed Nixon haters who have not forgotten his opportunistic and thuggish performance as an anticommunist during the early cold war and the growing number of Nixon revisionists who view Watergate and other dark deeds as aberrations in an otherwise productive, if hard-hitting, political career.

The unprecedented wealth of archival materials and the scores of valuable memoirs of administration officials that I pored over after my own passions had subsided enabled me to take a fresh look at the Nixon presidency. Although that presidency remains colored by Nixon's unattractive personality and immoral and illegal political practices, I found more solid achievements in his domestic programs than I expected. Conversely, I found his acclaimed foreign policies less admirable than have many other observers. Nixon's was a complex, inconsistent presidency that played itself out during one of the most turbulent and consequential periods in American history. A quarter of a century after he left Washington under the darkest cloud in presidential history, many of the ideas and policies that he advocated have been accepted by a majority of Americans. Few presidents have left such a legacy.

Historians of presidential administrations are always torn between adopting a chronological or a topical approach. The former enables the reader to understand how various policies related to one another from day to day, illustrating the difficulties inherent in having to deal with several major issues at the same time and how the resolution of one issue may have affected or been affected by the resolution of several other issues. The topical approach, the one I selected, permits the reader to observe the development of an entire domestic program or international relationship over an extended period. By employing this approach, I found it easier to make understandable the complicated policies, such as ending the Vietnam War or reforming welfare, that engaged Nixon during most of his tenure. Consequently, after dealing with Nixon's career through the 1968 election and the organization of the White House in the first two chapters, I examine foreign policy throughout Nixon's term in office in the next three chapters and then turn to domestic policy and Watergate.

I have been exceedingly fortunate to have the assistance of friends and colleagues who read all or parts of the manuscript. Stephen Ambrose, Peter Carroll, George Herring, Jeffrey Kimball, Stanley Kutler, Richard P. Nathan,

Keith Nelson, Lynn Parsons, Alan Raucher, Robert Schulzinger, Michael Small, and Athan Theoharis all made important contributions to the final product. Chester Pach, a reader for the University Press of Kansas, offered an especially useful critique. At the press, fine copy editor Linda Lotz, Mike Briggs, Rebecca Knight Giusti, and especially Fred Woodward were always thoughtful and encouraging.

Archivists at the Nixon Presidential Materials Project at the National Archives in College Park, Maryland; the Hoover Institution Archives in Stanford, California; the Gerald R. Ford Presidential Library in Ann Arbor, Michigan; the National Security Archive in Washington; and the Richard M. Nixon Presidential Library and Birthplace in Yorba Linda, California, were most helpful during my visits. Wayne State University provided me with a sabbatical and travel grants for the research and, as usual, with splendid assistance from the History Department staff, particularly Amie Meixner.

As has been the case with all my projects, both personal and professional, I owe the greatest debt to my wife, Sarajane Miller-Small, a Eugene McCarthy precinct delegate in 1968, who read the manuscript in all its stages, making substantive and stylistic suggestions that improved the final product immeasurably.

When referring to materials from the Nixon Presidential Materials Project, I used citations from accessible printed sources rather than the archive itself. However, in 1997, a new release of contested documents that few other historians had used necessitated more archival citations than I would have preferred. To simplify notes citing the various archives, I omitted folder numbers. In addition, all quotations from presidents, unless otherwise indicated, come from the *Public Papers of the President of the United States* series.

ABBREVIATIONS

ABA	American Bar Association
ABM	Antiballistic missile
ACDA	Arms Control and Disarmament Agency
ADC	Aid to Dependent Children
AFL	American Federation of Labor
AIM	American Indian Movement
AMA	American Medical Association
AVF	all-volunteer force
BIA	Bureau of Indian Affairs
BLS	Bureau of Labor Statistics
BNDD	Bureau of Narcotics and Dangerous Drugs
CAP	Community Action Program
CBO	Congressional Budget Office
CCEP	Cabinet Committee on Economic Policy
CEA	Council of Economic Advisors
CEQ	Council on Environmental Quality
CETA	Comprehensive Employment and Training Act
CIA	Central Intelligence Agency
CIEP	Committee on International Economic Policy
CIO	Congress of Industrial Organizations
CORE	Congress of Racial Equality
COSVN	Central Office for South Vietnam
CPB	Corporation for Public Broadcasting
CREEP	Committee to Reelect the President

CSCE	Conference on Security and Cooperation in Europe
DEA	Drug Enforcement Agency
DNC	Democratic National Committee
DOD	Department of Defense
EEOC	Equal Employment Opportunity Commission
EOB	Executive Office Building
EPA	Environmental Protection Agency
EQC	Environmental Quality Council
ERA	Equal Rights Amendment
FAP	Family Assistance Plan
FBI	Federal Bureau of Investigation
FCC	Federal Communications Commission
FOIA	Freedom of Information Act
FY	fiscal year
GNP	gross national product
GRS	general revenue sharing
HEW	Health, Education, and Welfare
HMO	health maintenance organization
HUAC	House Committee on Un-American Activities
HUD	Housing and Urban Development
ICBM	intercontinental ballistic missile
IDF	Israeli Defense Force
IG	interdepartmental group
IRS	Internal Revenue Service
MAD	mutually assured destruction
MBFR	mutual and balanced force reduction
MESBIC	minority enterprise small business investment company
MFN	most favored nation
MIA	missing in action
MIRV	multiple independently targeted reentry vehicle
NAACP	National Association for the Advancement of Colored People
NATO	North Atlantic Treaty Organization
NEA	National Endowment for the Arts
NEH	National Endowment for the Humanities
NEP	New Economic Policy
NLF	National Liberation Front
NOAA	National Oceanic and Atmospheric Administration
NOW	National Organization for Women
NSA	National Security Agency
NSC	National Security Council
NSDM	national security decision memorandum

NSSM	national security study memorandum
NWRO	National Welfare Rights Organization
OEO	Office of Economic Opportunity
OMB	Office of Management and Budget
OMBE	Office of Minority Business Enterprise
OPA	Office of Price Administration
OPEC	Organization of Petroleum Exporting Countries
OSHA	Occupational Safety and Health Administration
PAC	political action committee
PBS	Public Broadcasting System
PFLP	Popular Front for the Liberation of Palestine
PLO	Palestine Liberation Organization
POW	prisoner of war
PRC	People's Republic of China
RICO	Racketeer Influenced and Corrupt Organizations (Act)
RNC	Republican National Committee
ROTC	Reserve Officers' Training Corps
SALT	Strategic Arms Limitation Talks
SBA	Small Business Administration
SDS	Students for a Democratic Society
SEAL	sea, air, land (team)
SLBM	submarine-launched ballistic missile
SSI	supplemental security income
SSS	Selective Service System
SST	supersonic transport
UAC	Urban Affairs Council
UAW	United Auto Workers
UN	United Nations
UNESCO	United Nations Educational, Scientific, and Cultural Organization
VC	Vietcong
VMC	Vietnam Moratorium Committee
VVAW	Vietnam Veterans Against the War
WSAG	Washington special action group

1

★ ★ ★ ★ ★

TRAIN WHISTLES IN THE NIGHT

When a distinguished bipartisan panel of thirty-two historians, political scientists, and other experts was asked in 1996 to rank the presidents, Richard M. Nixon finished dead last. That result would not have surprised Nixon, who predicted that "History will treat me fairly. Historians probably won't because most historians are on the left."[1]

At first glance, it seems hard to believe that a president with so many dramatic accomplishments abroad—and even at home—could lag behind such abject failures as Andrew Johnson, Ulysses S. Grant, and Warren G. Harding. Of course, for many observers, Nixon's astounding presidential "firsts," from traveling to China to talking to astronauts on the moon to calling for the first welfare reform program, are overshadowed by his even more astounding first—being the only president to resign from office.

Of all American presidents, Richard Nixon remains the most controversial. This is partly a product of his tough partisanship in the political trenches, where he believed in "giving as good as you get."[2] He ran for national office in every presidential election year from 1952 through 1972, except for 1964. He also ran for the House in 1946 and 1948, for the Senate in 1950, and for the California state house in 1962. Senator Bob Dole (R-Kans.), in a eulogy for his friend and political mentor, proclaimed the second half of the twentieth century the "age of Nixon."[3] *Time* magazine apparently agreed, featuring Nixon on its celebrated cover fifty-six times during his lifetime.

Evaluating Nixon's presidency is made more difficult by his controversial personality and character. Noted presidential chronicler Theodore H.

1

White admitted in 1984 "that I have spent the greatest portion of my adult life writing about Richard Nixon and I still don't understand him." Economist Arthur Burns, a prominent Nixon adviser, warned another chronicler that he would never "fully understand" his former boss, and a Soviet diplomat reported that as late as 1972, his colleagues found "Nixon's personality . . . so impenetrable that we had no idea what would please him."[4]

Paradoxically, the task of understanding Nixon and what went on in his White House should be made easier, given the availability of several hundred hours of the infamous tapes, millions of documents, and scores of first-rate memoirs, including ten volumes of Nixon's own reminiscences. Unfortunately, these documentary riches make things more difficult, since Nixon appeared to be many different people at many different times to many different friends, associates, and journalists. William Safire, one of his speechwriters, saw him as an "amalgam of Woodrow Wilson, Nicholas Machiavelli, Teddy Roosevelt, and Shakespeare's Cassius, an idealistic conniver evoking the strenuous life while he thinks too much."[5]

However one evaluates Richard Nixon, all his biographers, including an unusual number of psychobiographers, have focused on his formative years. It was there, in southern California during World War I and the years after, that Richard Nixon developed the complex and contradictory, perhaps even schizophrenic, character traits that so affected his career and fateful presidency.

Richard Milhous Nixon weighed a hefty eleven pounds when he was born on 9 January 1913 to Francis Anthony (Frank) Nixon and Hannah Milhous Nixon in Yorba Linda, California, a town of 200 in Orange County. His mother named him after Richard the Lionhearted; Nixon in Gaelic means "he falleth not." He was the second of five brothers. Harold was born in 1909, Francis Donald in 1915, Arthur in 1918, and Edward in 1930. Arthur died of tubercular encephalitis in 1925, and Harold died in 1933 after a ten-year struggle with tuberculosis. Richard later reported that these traumatic events helped make him "a liberal on health issues."[6]

Frank Nixon was born in Ohio in 1878 in poor circumstances. His family, of Scots-Irish origin, had come to the United States before the Revolution, and one of its members, Sheriff John Nixon of Philadelphia, was the first official to read the Declaration of Independence in public. After a minimal education, Frank ran away from home when he was thirteen and worked at a variety of jobs until he ended up as a motorman in California in 1907, where he met Hannah Milhous.

Hannah, a cousin of the novelist Jessamyn West, was born in 1885 in Indiana in a much more stable middle-class milieu. She moved with her family and servants to Whittier, California, in 1897. The Milhouses, who were of German and Irish Quaker stock, had also come to the United States before the Revolution. Hannah had completed two years at Whittier College before she married Frank in 1908 following a whirlwind courtship. Her family did not approve of the match, believing that she had married beneath her station.

Frank was boisterous, crude, and often angry and argumentative. In contrast, the fastidious and courteous Hannah was cerebral, serene, and deeply spiritual. Richard and the rest of his siblings had a difficult time earning the approval of their father, a "very competitive man" and "a real disciplinarian."[7] They often turned to their mother for comfort and support, but she, being undemonstrative and shy, did not always satisfy their needs. Nonetheless, on the day he left office in 1974, Nixon looked back on them fondly: "I remember my old man. I think that they would have called him sort of a little man, a common man. . . . he did his job and every job counts up to the hilt regardless of what happens." As for his mother, "She will have no books written about her, but she's a saint."

Richard grew up in Yorba Linda in a 700-square-foot Sears kit house, which originally had no electricity or running water. His father ran a lemon orchard. When that project failed in 1919, Frank worked as a roustabout in an oil field, while Hannah labored at a Sunkist packing factory. A serious young boy, Nixon talked of the "hard but happy" days in Yorba Linda, where "sometimes at night I was awakened by the whistle of a train, and then I dreamed of the far-off places I wanted to visit someday."[8]

Much has been made of the Nixon family's difficult financial condition, particularly in Yorba Linda. Nixon himself noted, "It's been said our family was poor, and maybe it was, but we never thought of ourselves as poor."[9] They owned a car, and Frank and Hannah subscribed to the *Los Angeles Times*, the *Saturday Evening Post*, and *Ladies Home Journal*, over which their bookish son pored.

In 1922, the family moved to East Whittier, a town dominated by Quakers, where Frank opened a service station and grocery store. The Whittier Quakers, who belonged to the California Yearly Meeting, had pastors, were somewhat more evangelical and less liberal than eastern Quakers, and were not all pacifists. Religion was an important part of the Nixons' life, with the family going to church on Wednesday nights and several times on Sunday. Never one to make much of a display about his faith, Nixon claimed to be a deeply religious person whose devotions were "intensely personal and private."[10] He had something of a born-again experience in 1926.

The Nixon children worked hard to help support the family. When Hannah took Harold to Prescott, Arizona, for treatment for tuberculosis,

Richard and his brothers assumed her chores. In the summers of 1928 and 1929, he joined her in Arizona, where he found employment as a chicken plucker, swimming-pool boy, and carnival barker. At home in Whittier, he helped out at the grocery store, which sometimes meant driving at four in the morning to pick up produce in Los Angeles. In addition, he held jobs as a sweeper in a packing house and as a janitor, and at night he tended smudge pots in orange groves.

Nixon, who learned to read before he entered first grade in 1919, excelled in school, in part because he had a remarkable, almost photographic memory, a quality that contributed significantly to his success in politics. An "ambulatory computer," he could remember the names of thousands of politicians throughout the country and, even more importantly, could memorize long speeches, making it appear that he was talking extemporaneously.[11]

Generally a straight-A student, he was the valedictorian and president of his eighth-grade class, finished third in his high school class in 1930, was second in his college class in 1934, and was third in his law school class in 1937. In his senior year in college, he won the Southern California Intercollegiate Extemporaneous Speaking competition.

Never a hail-fellow-well-met sort, he was nonetheless a respected if not especially popular student leader who won almost all the elections he entered. He failed only once in his student political career when, in 1929, he lost the race for high school student-body president. That was the last election he lost until the presidential race in 1960.

Impressed by his musical talent, his mother sent him to study the piano with her sister, Jane Beeson, 200 miles away in Lindsay for five months in 1925. But Richard preferred sports, even though, according to one friend, "he had no athletic ability whatsoever."[12]

Although he had the grades and awards to attend a more prestigious college, financial necessity caused him to stay at home and attend Whittier College in 1930. When he enrolled, the college had a student body of 400, of whom less than 20 percent were Quakers. Whittier provided him with a classical education, dominated by courses in history and English. Early in his collegiate career, he led a successful challenge against the Franklins, a group of well-to-do students who ran most of the institutions at Whittier. This battle against an upper-class establishment was the first of many in his career.

Nixon talked often about Wallace Newman's influence on his character and development. "Chief" Newman was the inspirational coach of Whittier's football team, where Nixon was a tireless, courageous, but untalented last-stringer who failed to letter. Despite his attempts to be a regular guy in college, Nixon was awkward and ill at ease. One of his classmates later observed, "In today's terms we kids would have called him a nerd."[13] During his college years, he dated and ultimately became informally engaged to Ola Florine Welch, the daughter of the Whittier police chief. He had first met her during his senior year in high school when both acted in the *Aeneid*. The fun-loving and spontaneous Welch, who broke off the relationship in 1935, explained, "Most of the time I just couldn't figure him out."[14]

Nixon attended the highly competitive Duke University Law School from 1934 through 1937. The recipient of only a partial scholarship, he had to hustle to make ends meet, working part-time for the National Youth Authority. Successful once again in scholarship and campus politics, the extremely hardworking and serious Nixon, who never had a date while in law school, earned the sobriquet "Gloomy Gus." He proudly remembered being told that he had "what it takes to learn the law—an iron butt."[15] His heroes were Supreme Court Justices Louis Brandeis, Benjamin Cardozo, and Charles Evans Hughes.

At Duke, Nixon became something of a liberal on racial issues. Appalled by the system of segregation he experienced in North Carolina, he was especially distressed by the racist views of many of his classmates. At Duke, he also participated in his first office break-in. Concerned about his performance on final exams at the end of his second year (performance was linked to future financial assistance), he and several classmates broke into the dean's office to obtain an advance peek at the grade lists. No one discovered their minor transgression at the time.

Many of his peers at Duke thought that Nixon was destined for the scholarly life, considering his powerful intellect and remote personality. He certainly appeared suited for the contemplative career of an academic, where he could work relatively independently without having to interact very much with colleagues.

Although a good law school, Duke was not as prestigious as the older East Coast schools, a fact that frustrated Nixon when he sought employment at several New York law firms in the midst of the depression in 1937. He was also turned down for a job by the FBI. Much later, FBI director J. Edgar Hoover, by then a friend, told him that he had been approved for employment but that his line had been eliminated because of budget cuts. Another FBI official claims that Nixon was not hired because an interviewer found him "lacking in aggression."[16]

This early failure to obtain the law positions he wanted was just another one of the many self-perceived disappointments and humiliations Nixon confronted. Despite his many accomplishments during his school years, he remained a cold and shy young man who could not make friends easily, whose only girlfriend deserted him, who sat on the end of the football bench, who could not attend the college of his choice, and who grew up on the other side of the tracks in a cold, dysfunctional family that suffered grave losses.

Returning to Whittier in the summer of 1937, Nixon accepted a position with the small Wingert and Bewley law firm. His mother, who had gone to college with Tom Bewley, helped him obtain the job. He passed the California bar that year, which was an accomplishment in itself, since less than half of those who took the exam passed. Most of his cases for the three-person firm involved probate and estate work. He became a partner in 1939 and earned close to $4,000 in 1940, not an insignificant sum, although he lost a good deal of his money in a failed frozen orange juice venture. He also served as deputy city attorney for Whittier and president of the Whittier College Alumni Association and the Duke Alumni Association of California. He became so involved in Whittier campus politics that he was a serious candidate for the college's presidency in 1940.

That same year, he contemplated running for the California Assembly. Having registered as a Republican in 1938, he supported Wendell Willkie in the 1940 presidential campaign. Nixon's politics diverged from those of his parents. Frank was a populist who had voted for William Jennings Bryan, Theodore Roosevelt, Robert M. LaFollette, and Franklin Roosevelt. Hannah had supported Woodrow Wilson. Until the late 1930s, Richard had not been actively involved in politics; at this point in his career he was something of a nonideological centrist.

Far more important than his developing political and legal career was his love life. Nixon met Patricia Ryan when both appeared in a play with the Whittier Community Players in January 1938. For Nixon, it was "love at first sight"; immediately after their first meeting, he told the incredulous Pat that he was going to marry her.[17] It was not love at first sight for Pat, as she continued to date others, with the hapless Nixon volunteering to chauffeur her and her dates around town.

Pat had changed her name in 1930, having been born Thelma Catherine Ryan in impoverished circumstances in a miner's shack in Ely, Nevada, on 16 March 1912. She grew up in Artesia (now Cerritos), California, eight miles from Whittier. After her mother died, fourteen-year-old Pat assumed the family's female duties for her father and two brothers. She attended Fullerton Junior College in 1930 and then worked in New York City. Returning to California in 1934, Pat obtained employment as a bank teller in Artesia and occasionally as a film extra in Hollywood. After working her way through the University of Southern California, where she graduated cum laude with a B.A. in 1937, Pat obtained a post at Whittier High School teaching commercial courses. A Republican and also an agnostic, she became secretary of the Whittier branch of the American Association of University Women.

Dick pursued Pat for more than two years until, in March 1940, she accepted his proposal. He proposed at one of their favorite spots, the beach at Dana Point, California, near San Clemente, later the locale of their summer White House. They were married at the Mission Inn in Riverside on 21 June 1940 and honeymooned in Mexico.

When a Duke professor recommended Nixon for a job in the Office of Price Administration (OPA) in Washington, the young lawyer accepted the appointment, eager to escape the confines of his hometown. He and Pat arrived in the capital in January 1942 and took up residence in Alexandria. The OPA was full of liberals at the time Nixon came on board to deal with tire rationing. His boss, Thomas Emerson, who went on to Yale Law School, later headed the left-leaning National Lawyers Guild.

Although Nixon performed well at the OPA, his experiences there soured him on rationing and price controls and government bureaucracy in general. He liked some of his colleagues but felt that "others became obsessed with their own power and seemed to delight in kicking people around, particularly those in the private sector."[18] When, in April 1942, the navy issued a call for lawyers, a bored and disillusioned Nixon enlisted as a lieutenant, a commission to which his degree entitled him. This was not an easy decision, because he feared offending pacifist relatives.

In August 1942, he attended Officers' Candidate School at Quonset Point, Rhode Island, where a classmate was William Rogers, later his secretary of state. At the same time, Pat accepted employment as an assistant business analyst at the OPA. In October, she joined her husband for his six-month tour in Ottumwa, Iowa. He shipped off from San Francisco on 31 May 1943 for New Caledonia in the South Pacific, where he was an operations officer at an airstrip. From New Caledonia, Nixon moved to Bougainville in the Solomons in January 1944 and on to Green Island in March. Each of these moves brought him closer to the front, but he never saw combat. Nonetheless, he adopted the nickname the "Fighting Quaker" when running for Congress in 1946.

Nixon's experience in the Pacific brought him into contact with a wide variety of Americans for the first time. There he discovered a special rapport with working-class men, who knew him on Green Island as the proprietor of "Nick's Snack Shop." He spent a good deal of time reading serious books and magazines but also playing poker, where he developed a reputation for being a cautious and shrewd player who knew when and how to bluff. His poker winnings later helped finance his first campaign for office. Reflecting on his military experiences in his memoirs, Nixon attributed his successes in diplomacy, in part, to the skills he honed during the war over the card table.

He returned to San Diego in July 1944 for a posting at Alameda Naval Air Station and then moved to Philadelphia, New York, and finally Middle River, Maryland, where he worked on terminating wartime contracts. By the time he resigned from the navy in October 1945, he had achieved the rank of lieutenant commander.

Nixon left the service to run for Congress as a Republican from his old Twelfth Congressional District. In August 1945, the Committee of One Hundred, a group of Republican politicians and small businesspeople, ran an advertisement in twenty-six newspapers seeking to recruit a candidate to take on incumbent Democratic representative Horace Jeremiah (Jerry) Voorhis: "Wanted: Congressman candidate with no previous political experience to defeat a man who has represented the district in House for ten years."[19] Because the popular Voorhis seemed a shoo-in, despite the fact that his district had recently been gerrymandered, only eight people answered this unusual advertisement. A socialist as a young man, Voorhis, by 1946, was well within the Democratic Party and had earned credit for his honesty and diligence as a legislator. A member of the House Un-American Activities Committee (HUAC), he introduced Public Law 870, or the Voorhis Act, to require the registration of any organization controlled by a foreign government.

Disappointed with the candidates who had volunteered to challenge Voorhis, Herman Perry, one of the leaders of the Committee of One Hundred and head of the Whittier branch of the Bank of America, contacted his old acquaintance Richard Nixon in Washington to see if he was interested. For Perry, Nixon had "the personal appeal, the legal qualifications. He had been in Washington and around the world. He was a natural."[20]

On 1 October 1945, Nixon informed Perry that he would accept the challenge. Announcing his candidacy in newspaper advertisements in December, Nixon emphasized his opposition to the "economic dictatorship by irresponsible governmental agencies" and his support for "a progressive and constructive program . . . as opposed to class hatred and economic warfare."[21] In a private letter to Perry that month, Nixon conceded that Voorhis was "honest, conscientious and able," but he "votes with the most radical element of the New Deal group. He is definitely lined up with Congressman Vito Marcantonio of New York," as well as Helen Gahagan Douglas of California. Nixon intended to appeal especially to young people, Republicans, veterans, and the "so-called liberal wing" of the GOP.[22] Nixon told Perry that he would run in support of *practical* liberalism" as an "antidote to . . . New Deal idealism."[23]

Nixon hired Murray Chotiner to assist in his campaign. A lawyer and political operative, Chotiner had a reputation for being a gut fighter. He was not directly involved in Nixon's attack on Voorhis's alleged support from the CIO's Political Action Committee (PAC). In fact, the committee had endorsed Voorhis in 1944 but not in 1946. Voorhis did, however, receive the endorsement of the National Citizen's PAC, a more moderate organization. Voorhis blundered in agreeing to five debates with Nixon, a master debater. In the first one, on 13 September 1946, he became confused when Nixon came to the stage with a piece of paper containing alleged "proof" of Voorhis's endorsement by the CIO's PAC. Nixon later disingenuously claimed that there was "a distinction without a difference" between the two PACs.[24]

During the rest of the campaign, Republican operatives accused Voorhis of being a communist or fellow traveler; others, perhaps not directly related to Nixon, made anti-Semitic charges against Voorhis's supporters and positions. For his part, Nixon complained that someone from the Voorhis camp broke into his campaign headquarters and stole expensive pamphlets. As for the general nature of the campaign, Nixon later wrote, "If some of my rhetoric seems overstated now, it was nonetheless in keeping with the approach that seasoned Republican politicians were using that year."[25]

Nixon received the support of almost all the newspapers in his district, most notably the powerful *Los Angeles Times* and its publisher Norman Chandler and political editor Kyle Palmer, a kingmaker in the Republican Party. He was also supported in the *Alhambra Post-Advocate* by campaign reporter Herbert Klein, who had been one of the first to pick up the line that Voorhis's votes paralleled those of fellow-traveling Representative Marcantonio. Klein, who later worked on Nixon's campaigns, became his director of communications in 1969.

Nixon conducted a well-financed campaign, supported in part by contributions from outside the district, including one from Herbert Hoover, whose wife had been on the Whittier College board with Nixon. He ran one of the first California campaigns that was candidate and not party centered and in which independent professional political operatives controlled the candidate's media and fund-raising operations.

He beat Voorhis by a 57 to 43 percent margin, one of seven California Republicans to defeat incumbent Democrats in what was a big year nationwide for the GOP. The Republicans captured the House by 246 to 158 and the Senate by 51 to 45. Thus it was that Nixon, along with Pat and their first child, Tricia, who had been born the previous February, journeyed to Washington to join the historic 80th Congress. (Julie was born in July 1948.) Pat, whose secretarial skills proved useful to her husband during the campaign and in Washington, was not pleased with the rough-and-tumble nature of the Voorhis campaign. In Washington, she never really enjoyed being the wife of a highly controversial politician who worked at his job around the clock. Although the *Washington Post* labeled him "the greenest congressman in town," Nixon and some of his friends early on talked about the possibility of this hardworking, intelligent, attractive young veteran with a highly photogenic family someday becoming president.[26]

During his first term he served on HUAC, the Education and Labor Committee, and the House Select Committee on Foreign Aid, popularly known as the (Christian A.) Herter committee. Although a moderate in an extremely conservative Republican majority on HUAC, he chose anticommunism as the subject for his maiden speech in Congress on 18 February 1947. Commenting on the HUAC investigation of communist Gerhart Eisler, he later noted, "This was really the first time I had brought home to me the character of the Communist Party and the threat it presented to the country."[27] In 1948, he cosponsored the Mundt-Nixon Bill that called for the registration of Communist Party members. The bill died in the Senate but reappeared in another form in 1950 as the McCarran Act. On one occasion he complained about the stonewalling of the White House on an issue relating to subversion: "When Cong. can't get information from Exec. dept./info which is bandied about to press/then high time Congress did something about it."[28]

As a member of the House Education and Labor Committee, he helped draft the Taft-Hartley Act, which, he maintained, protected workers from corrupt and undemocratic unions. In April 1947, Nixon traveled with John F. Kennedy, a young Democratic member of the committee and another former navy man who had been elected in 1946, to debate the merits of the bill in McKeesport, Pennsylvania. He and Kennedy got along quite well during their years together in the House—so well, in fact, that Jack felt comfortable passing Dick a campaign contribution from his father, Joseph P. Kennedy, for Nixon's 1950 Senate race.

Of all his activities during his first term, Nixon's service on the Herter committee proved to be the most important in the long run. In the summer of 1947, he traveled to Europe to examine the desperate political and economic situation there. He returned a confirmed internationalist and free trader, convinced that the United States had to do more to rebuild and protect Western democracies. According to Herb Klein, that trip was "a major influence on his whole career in Congress."[29] It was also on that trip that he met Rose Mary Woods, the committee's bookkeeper. In February 1951, Woods joined Nixon's staff and remained one of his most important and loyal assistants throughout his career.

He made long-lasting political allies when he joined the Chowder and Marching Society, an informal group of fifteen young Republicans impatient with the pace of conservative change in Congress. Among the members were Kenneth Keating from New York, Thruston Morton from Kentucky, and Gerald R. Ford from Michigan. Here, among his "best and most intimate friends" in Washington, Ford recalled that Nixon, who struck many as a cold fish, could let his hair down and be a "regular guy."[30]

He certainly was a regular Republican during his first term, voting 91 percent of the time with his party, a figure that fell to 74 percent during his second term. Since Nixon won both the Democratic and Republican primaries in 1948, he ran unopposed for reelection, after having been catapulted to national prominence because of the Alger Hiss case. Nixon virtually single-handedly took up the cause of Whittaker Chambers, a former Communist who accused Alger Hiss, a former State Department official and then president of the Carnegie Endowment for International Peace, of having been a fellow Communist. For a while, it looked as if Nixon had bet on the wrong horse. During the preliminary stages of the hearings, the smooth and elegant Hiss had the best of it over the rumpled, admitted Communist. But Nixon, the only lawyer on the committee, had been fed information from the FBI and was later assisted by a new friend, Bert Andrews of the *New York Herald Tribune*. Nixon was convinced that Chambers (coincidentally, also a Quaker) was telling the truth and that Hiss was bluffing. At the eleventh hour, Chambers produced incriminating microfilms hidden in a pumpkin patch on his farm that clinched the case for HUAC and the FBI, and Nixon triumphed. After his first trial ended in a hung jury, Hiss was found guilty of perjury and sentenced to a five-year prison term.

The Hiss case became an obsession with Nixon. It was here that he learned about the media, leaks, cover-ups, and the fact that the Justice Department often operated as a partisan agency. During his greatest crisis in 1973–1974, he constantly returned to the lessons of the Hiss case and urged his colleagues to read and reread his account of it in his best-selling book *Six Crises*. That account, in which Nixon takes center stage, was challenged by HUAC's chief investigator Robert Stripling, who called it "pure bullshit."[31] Stripling was correct to call attention to the way Nixon had exaggerated his role in bringing Hiss to justice.

The case not only catapulted Nixon to national prominence but also made him a polarizing national figure, a paladin of anticommunist conservatives and an enemy of eastern liberals and especially, as he contended for the rest of his life, the eastern media. In 1969, he complained about the media, "Seventy-five percent of those guys hate my guts. They don't like to be beaten" as they were on the Hiss case.[32] George Reedy, who worked for United Press International during the era and was President Lyndon B. Johnson's press secretary, later agreed that "none of us wanted him [Hiss]

11

to be guilty. We didn't want that committee to be right about anything. It was a committee that really made you cringe, it was so bad."[33]

Nixon claimed that because of the eastern establishment's hostility, which began over the Hiss case, he lost the 1960 election. But he also admitted that had it not been for the case, he never would have obtained the vice-presidential nomination in 1952. Dwight David Eisenhower allegedly told Nixon in 1951, "The thing that impressed me most was that you not only got Hiss, but you got him fairly."[34] Aside from its impact on his political career, Nixon contended, with some exaggeration, that the case "aroused the nation for the first time to the existence and character of the Communist conspiracy in the United States."[35]

The case demonstrated Nixon's willingness to take dramatic risks to pursue his goals. When at one point it appeared that the "Pumpkin Papers" might be forgeries, he exclaimed, "Oh my God, This is the end of my political career. My whole career is ruined!"[36] As things turned out, the Hiss case served as a launching pad for his 1950 Senate race against Representative Helen Gahagan Douglas.

It was during that race that Americans first heard of "Tricky Dick" Nixon. His campaign manager was Chotiner, an early practitioner of negative campaigning who subsequently worked in every one of Nixon's campaigns until 1968. His Democratic opponent, a former singer and actress, was a liberal whom the *Book of Knowledge* ranked as one of the twelve smartest women in the world. Although a critic of HUAC and anticommunism, Douglas had moved toward the center of her party in recent years. Yet communism became the chief issue for the Nixon camp. This focus was not exceptional, as the 1950 campaign coincided with Senator Joseph McCarthy's (R-Wisc.) emergence on the national scene and his charges of "Communists in the State Department." McCarthy campaigned in California for Nixon. McCarthy's charges received further impetus following the outbreak of the Korean War in June.

Douglas had already been wounded during a tough primary campaign when her conservative opponent first brought up the "Pink Lady" charge, suggesting that she was a communist sympathizer. In addition, she blundered when she compared Nixon's voting record with that of Vito Marcantonio. Nixon turned that charge around, comparing her voting record with Marcantonio's on pink-sheet broadsides, and labeled her "pink right down to her underwear."[37]

Throughout his career, Nixon was never comfortable with women in politics. The outspoken Douglas had even irritated Marcantonio, who urged Nixon to defeat the "bitch."[38] But Speaker of the House Sam Rayburn (D-Tex.) told Douglas, "Take that young man out in the finals. His is the most devious face of all those who have served in Congress all the years I've been here."[39]

As in the Voorhis campaign, apparently freelance Nixon supporters made anti-Semitic phone calls, calling attention to Douglas's husband, the actor Melvyn Douglas, one of whose parents was Jewish. In another scurrilous ploy, Nixon supporters mailed thousands of postcards reading, "Vote for our Helen for Senator. We are with you 100%. The Communist League of Negro Women Voters."[40]

Nixon later defended his own inflammatory rhetoric against the "extremist" Douglas, whose campaign was one of "stridency, ineptness, or self righteousness" matched only by George McGovern in 1972.[41] In 1958, however, he confided to a British publisher, "I'm sorry about that episode. I was a very young man."[42]

He campaigned effectively and energetically, making a thousand speeches in sixteen weeks. As in 1946, he enjoyed wide support from the California press, with the major papers favoring him by a six-to-one margin. Yet Representative John F. Kennedy (D-Mass.) told a colleague, "You have no idea what he's been through. Dick Nixon is the victim of the worst press that ever hit a politician in this country. What they did to him in the Helen Gahagan Douglas race was disgusting." Kennedy considered Nixon to be "an outstanding guy [who] has the opportunity to go all the way."[43] His victory by almost 700,000 votes, enhanced by the support of conservative Democrats, constituted the largest plurality of any senatorial candidate in 1950. When he was sworn in in December at the age of thirty-seven, after the incumbent resigned early, Nixon became the second youngest member of the Senate. To Senator Robert Taft (R-Ohio), the leader of the conservative Republicans, he was "a little man in a big hurry" with "a mean and vindictive streak."[44]

During his two years in the Senate, Nixon became one of the most popular Republican stump speakers, appearing at party fund-raisers three times a week in 1951. As a senator, he supported the Truman administration's containment policies in Europe; assailed its policies in Asia, especially China; spoke out often about the corruption in the White House; and adopted a conservative, free-market approach to economic and social policy. He voted with his party only 70 percent of the time. A panel of political scientists rated Nixon the seventy-first best senator in the 82d Congress.

Back and neck pains, caused by the tensions associated with the frenetic pace of life as a national political figure, led him in 1951 to seek relief from a New York internist specializing in psychosomatic medicine and to see him periodically over the next four years. That same year he met Charles

"Bebe" Rebozo, a Florida realtor, who soon became Nixon's closest confidant, one of the few people with whom he could truly relax.

By 1951, Nixon had emerged as a possible candidate for vice president in the upcoming election. He was acceptable to members of the eastern old guard such as Thomas E. Dewey, being an anticommunist internationalist, young and vigorous, and from an extremely important state. After Eisenhower emerged as the leading candidate for the presidency, Nixon played an influential role in the California delegation to the Republican convention. He worked behind the scenes against favorite-son candidate Earl Warren, as well as second-ballot threat Robert Taft, to help the general win a first-ballot victory. Eisenhower most likely met Nixon in 1949 when, as president of Columbia University, he had asked the second-term congressman for a briefing on the anticommunism issue. But he left the choice of vice president to the professionals in his entourage. After Nixon obtained the nomination, Eisenhower was astonished to discover that his running mate was only thirty-nine, which soon made him the second youngest vice president in history.

During the campaign against Democratic candidate Adlai Stevenson, Eisenhower remained above the partisan fray while his running mate did the rhetorical dirty work. For example, Nixon labeled Stevenson "Adlai the appeaser . . . who got a Ph.D. degree from [Dean] Acheson's College of Cowardly Containment."[45] Many years later, Nixon regretted "the intensity of the attacks."[46] During the 1968 campaign, a "new Nixon" generally took the high road, whereas *his* running mate, Spiro T. Agnew, was the master of alliterative invective.

Nixon's political career was almost destroyed during the campaign by sensational revelations about a secret political fund his supporters had put together. In the fall of 1950, the chair of his senatorial campaign committee, Dana C. Smith, had established a fund to help finance a potential 1956 Senate campaign. Because Nixon's senatorial salary and office allowances were insufficient to carry on national political activities, or even to operate effectively in such a large and complicated state as California, Smith and seventy-six other contributors, mostly from California, contributed about $16,000 a year to defray expenses for such items as Christmas cards and postage, which cost almost $5,000. Nixon himself lived modestly, never accepted fees for his speeches, and never used the money in the "slush fund" for personal expenses. Other politicians, including Adlai Stevenson, had established similar funds. Nixon did dissemble when he maintained that his fund was not secret and that he never gave favors to the donors.

Stories about the fund, spread by Nixon's Republican opponents in California, had been making the rounds even before the Republican convention. Those stories, however, were not widely publicized until 18 September, when the *New York Post* hit the stands with an article headlined "Secret Rich Man's Fund Keeps Nixon in Style Far beyond His Salary." The disclosure raised serious problems for Eisenhower, whose campaign formula of K-1, C-3 (Korea, communism, corruption, and controls) had made the perceived corruption in the Truman White House a central issue. Revelation of the slush fund deeply troubled Eisenhower, as it unleashed a "storm of criticism of hurricane proportions."[47] He insisted that "Nixon had to be clean as a hound's tooth."[48] Many in the Republican leadership, led by the influential *New York Herald Tribune,* immediately called for Nixon's resignation from the ticket. The pressure on Nixon was enormous. To make matters worse, Eisenhower kept him dangling by delaying a decision about his future for three days after the existence of the slush fund became public.

The Republicans faced a difficult problem. As a perplexed Eisenhower shrewdly commented, "Well if Nixon has to resign, we can't possibly win."[49] Thomas E. Dewey suggested to Nixon, with Eisenhower's approval, that he go on television to explain the fund, and if the public's response to the unprecedented presentation was 90 percent in his favor, he could stay on the ticket. Dewey also suggested that Nixon offer his resignation on the show. Nixon rejected the latter advice.

During the run-up to the speech, in a conversation with an undecided Eisenhower, an exasperated Nixon exploded, "There comes a time on matters like these when you've either got to shit or get off the pot." (A more decorous Nixon later claimed he said "fish or cut bait.")[50] Few people in recent years had spoken to the dignified general so intemperately; Eisenhower most likely never forgot the incident. More seriously, he was displeased when, during the televised performance on 23 September, Nixon asked all the candidates to make full financial disclosures. Eisenhower did not want to reveal the special deal Congress had arranged for him concerning royalties for his memoirs *Crusade in Europe.*

In the speech delivered on 23 September without notes and with Pat at his side, Nixon described his humble origins and meager resources, including his wife's "Republican cloth coat" (as opposed to the Democrats' mink coats that had figured in corruption charges). As for gifts from supporters, he refused to return a little dog named Checkers that his daughters loved. Appearing as a common, plainspoken man with no pretensions, he struck a chord with much of the population. The Republican National Committee (RNC) received an astonishing 160,000 telegrams and 250,000 letters running 350 to 1 in Nixon's favor, an outpouring that convinced all 107 members to urge his retention. After what seemed to Nixon to be interminable hemming and hawing, Eisenhower finally told him that he was his boy.

Most political commentators missed the fact that the performance they perceived as mawkish and maudlin played very well with the average American viewer. The dean of American columnists, Walter Lippmann, commented, "That must be the most demeaning experience my country has ever had to bear."[51]

Pat Nixon was humiliated by the Checkers ordeal. Never enthusiastic about her husband's political career, she "lost the zest" for campaigning and reported, "It kills me" to talk about the Checkers speech.[52] She soon extracted a written promise from her husband to leave politics after his first term as vice president. The enormous success of his televised speech taught Nixon about the potential power of the new medium and, in 1960, bolstered his confidence when he agreed to debate John F. Kennedy on television.

On the night of the inaugural, Hannah Nixon gave her son a note: "You have gone far and we are proud of you always—I know that you will keep your relationship with your maker as it should be for after all that, as you must know, is the most important thing in life."[53] Nixon carried the note around in his wallet for the rest of his life.

Although his office was in the traditional out-of-the-way vice-presidential quarters in the Senate, Nixon was one of the most visible and active vice presidents in history. He attended 171 cabinet meetings (and chaired about 20) and 217 National Security Council (NSC) meetings (and chaired 26). He was the first vice president to attend those important meetings routinely. Nixon was also involved in 173 sessions with legislative leaders, functioning as one of the administration's primary liaisons with Congress.

Like most vice presidents, he represented the president on foreign tours, making eight official trips to fifty-eight countries. In the fall of 1953, he traveled to fourteen Asian and Middle Eastern countries, including Vietnam, covering 45,500 miles in sixty-nine days. When he returned, he delivered a nationwide radio address in which he enunciated the domino theory: "If Indochina falls, Thailand is put in an almost impossible position. The same is true of Malaya with its rubber and tin. The same is true of Indonesia."[54] Vietnam became one foreign policy issue over which Nixon disagreed directly with his president, especially in 1954, when he advocated military intervention to save the French in their war with the Vietminh. On other foreign policy issues, he tended to be slightly more hawkish than the president, but this mattered little. In an authoritative study coauthored by Eisenhower aide Robert Bowie, Nixon does not appear as a significant participant in national security decisions.[55]

Nixon was the administration's chief campaigner and link to the Republican Party, although Eisenhower had to tone down his vice president's harsh rhetoric during the 1954 and 1958 congressional campaigns because he needed Democratic support on foreign policy matters. Nixon did help structure the political demise of his old friend Senator McCarthy, who had become an embarrassment to the administration. He felt that "McCarthy's intentions were right but his tactics were, frankly, so inept that he probably did our cause more harm than good."[56] Nixon learned about the uses of executive privilege when the administration refused to release documents to the senator during the army-McCarthy hearings in 1954. He also chaired the Committee on Government Contracts and the Cabinet Committee on Price Stability for Economic Growth. He was not a very efficient administrator, however, as he had difficulty organizing his staff.

The vice president earned respect for the dignity and intelligence he displayed during the president's three major debilitating illnesses—a heart attack in 1955, an operation for ileitis in 1957, and a stroke that same year. Secretary of State John Foster Dulles and presidential chief of staff Sherman Adams worried after the heart attack that Nixon and his right-wing friends might try to take over the administration. To make certain that the vice president did not overstep his bounds, Adams traveled to Ike's bedside in Denver to serve as liaison between the cabinet, chaired by the vice president, and the ailing president. Further, Eisenhower told Nixon that while he was ill, Dulles would be in charge of foreign policy. Eisenhower and Nixon signed an unprecedented document in 1958 outlining procedures to be used in the case of a future presidential illness. This agreement preceded ratification of the Twenty-fifth Amendment in 1967, which prescribed procedures to be followed in case of presidential disability.

Even though Nixon was an effective vice president, Eisenhower was not certain he wanted him to be his running mate again. In December 1955, the president advised Nixon to accept an important cabinet post to get "executive experience."[57] Eisenhower was serious about the benefits Nixon would gain by working in such a capacity and was grooming him for the presidency, but perhaps not as early as 1960. He considered his vice president to be too political and somewhat immature. "He just hasn't grown," commented the president, and was not yet "presidential timber"; he did not know "if Nixon would measure up."[58] Also, as the president and moderate Republican leaders of a growing "dump Nixon" movement knew, the controversial vice president could cost them votes. The Democrats had already begun to make Nixon an issue for the 1956 campaign. When contemplating potential running mates early in 1956, Ike gave A pluses to five Republicans and only an A to Nixon and another candidate. Although Nixon finally convinced Eisenhower in April to tell the press that he was an acceptable candidate, the president did little to stop other Republicans from scheming against his vice president, almost until convention time.

17

The Eisenhower-Nixon ticket was reelected, winning 57 percent of the popular vote. Nixon may have cost the Republicans votes in the South, since he was perceived to be a moderate or even a progressive on race. He reinforced this perception in 1957 when he encountered Dr. Martin Luther King, Jr., in Ghana and invited him back to the White House. King later thanked Nixon for his assistance in promoting passage of the 1957 Civil Rights Act.

During his second term as vice president, Nixon was involved in two major foreign policy confrontations. In May 1958, he traveled to South America to attend the inauguration of the president of Argentina and to make goodwill visits to seven other countries. The problems began at the University of San Marcos in Lima, Peru, where anti-American young people threw stones and even spit on Nixon and his entourage. Nixon admitted that he "felt the excitement of battle" at the university, where he kicked a protester, and someone in the crowd commented, *"el gringo tiene cojones"* ("the yankee has balls").[59] A much more serious and even life-threatening attack occurred in Caracas, Venezuela, where mobs beat his limousine with rocks, pipes, and clubs, injuring two occupants with spraying glass. Nixon was cool under pressure, ordering the Secret Service to hold its fire until the last possible moment, despite the dangerous assault. He also learned from the experience, as he told the cabinet on his return, about "the advent of the lower classes into the political scene and the ensuing requirement that American ambassadors . . . broaden their contacts beyond the traditional elite."[60]

Nixon again displayed his coolness under fire and the glare of television cameras at the first American Trade Exhibition in Moscow in July 1959 when he engaged in a "debate" with Soviet premier Nikita S. Khrushchev in front of a model American kitchen. Television viewers in the United States saw the vice president going toe-to-toe with the Soviet leader, a man whom Nixon considered "a bare-knuckled slugger who had gouged, kneed, and kicked" his way to power. Nixon claimed that he "knew the value of keeping cool in a crisis." For his part, Khrushchev considered Nixon "a man of reactionary views . . . a McCarthyite," as well as a "son of a bitch."[61] Krushchev claimed to have cast "the deciding ballot" in the 1960 election when he withheld the release of several downed American flyers until after Kennedy had been safely elected.[62] He later told Kennedy, "we voted for you."[63]

Nixon's drinking habits first became a possible political problem during the Russian trip. Milton Eisenhower, a member of the American mission sent by his brother to keep an eye on the vice president, reported that one night before a Moscow dinner a nervous Nixon drank "about six martinis" and became quite vulgar.[64]

That same year, Nixon met another anti-American leader who figured prominently in his future. When Cuba's new premier, Fidel Castro, came to the United States in April 1959, Eisenhower asked the vice president to size him up. In response, Nixon reported that the Cuban was "either incredibly naive about Communism or under Communist discipline—my guess is the former," and "his ideas about . . . how to run a government or an economy are less developed than those of almost any world figure I have met."[65]

By the time of his meeting with Castro and his rhetorical duel with Khrushchev, Nixon had emerged as the front-runner for the 1960 presidential nomination. He was vying to become the first sitting vice president to represent his party in a presidential campaign since Martin Van Buren. Still not certain that he was the best man, Eisenhower worried that "Nixon will never be President. People don't like him." He asked RNC chair Leonard Hall to try to talk him out of the run in a "very, very gentle" way.[66] Eisenhower later denied that he ever lacked confidence in Nixon, telling him in 1963, "Newspaper people are never going to cease their attempts to make it appear that you and I have been sworn enemies from the beginning of our relationship."[67]

Nixon was not pleased with the administration's economic policies during the recession years 1959–1960. The candidate preferred an expansionist economic program; Eisenhower was most concerned about inflation and its "inequitable and damaging effects."[68] One eyewitness recounts Nixon "literally shaking with tension" during a White House meeting when the president endorsed a tight economic program that might hurt the vice president in the upcoming campaign.[69] One of those in the minority in the administration who backed Nixon's approach was economist Arthur Burns, who later became President Nixon's chief domestic adviser. As he prepared to run for his second term in 1971, Nixon did not forget the lesson he had learned in 1959 about the relationship between economic stimuli and electoral success.

Nixon faced opposition to his nomination from a fast-growing conservative movement led by Arizona senator Barry Goldwater and from liberal Republicans led by New York governor Nelson Rockefeller. Concluding that he could win the nomination by accommodating the liberals, Nixon met Rockefeller before the convention on 22 July 1960 to fashion a moderate platform in what came to be called "The Compact of Fifth Avenue." The compact helped guarantee Nixon's first-ballot victory by a 1,321-to-10 vote at the convention in Chicago five days later. Embittered conservatives termed it the "Munich of the Republican Party." Eisenhower himself was not pleased with the compact's defense program and considered his vice president too "liberal" on social issues.[70]

Eisenhower also questioned Nixon's vice-presidential choice, former Massachusetts senator Henry Cabot Lodge, Jr., who turned out to be a weak and erratic campaigner. Lodge's off-the-cuff promise that a Negro would serve in the Nixon cabinet may have cost the party votes in the South.

During the campaign, Nixon tried to keep his distance from Eisenhower, both to establish his independence and to permit himself space to make oblique criticisms of unpopular administration policies. Eisenhower encouraged Nixon's independence but was not happy about those criticisms. On several occasions, Nixon ignored the president's tactical advice, for example, when Eisenhower warned him against "those benighted debates" with Democratic candidate Senator John F. Kennedy, and then when he offered to loan him his own television expert, actor and director Robert Montgomery, for the first debate.[71]

Ike certainly did not help Nixon during a 24 August 1960 press conference. When asked to cite a policy for which Nixon was responsible, the president responded, "If you give me a week, I might think of one. I don't remember." Eisenhower later explained that "he was being facetious, he didn't mean it the way it sounded." Regardless, that remark wounded Nixon.[72] During the last week of the campaign, when the still popular Eisenhower offered to go all out to help Nixon, who was then running neck and neck in the polls with Kennedy, Nixon rejected the offer. This was not another example of the candidate's resolve to appear independent. Instead, he was honoring Mamie Eisenhower's private request that her ailing husband not launch an enervating speaking tour.

Nixon thought that the media treated him unfairly during the campaign. Whether or not that charge was true, journalists covering the Kennedy camp felt that they were treated better by the Democratic candidate and his staff than they were by the Nixon team. J. Edgar Hoover, who hoped that Nixon would win, provided him with secret reports on Kennedy and his family. CIA officials may have balanced the FBI's intervention by providing Kennedy with unauthorized intelligence reports about Cuba and other classified foreign policy issues.

The 1960 campaign was the first campaign in history to feature televised debates. As an accomplished debater and creator of the Checkers triumph, Nixon thought that he would easily demonstrate his mastery over his less experienced opponent. But he was tired, in part because of his ill-considered promise to campaign in all fifty states, and "sick as a dog" when he showed up for the all-important first debate on 26 September 1960.[73] It was less what he said than the way he looked—"an awkward cadaver," according to one observer, and "as tense a man as I had ever seen,"[74] according to another—that convinced television viewers that the cooler and more natural Kennedy had "won" the first of four debates and proved that he was "presidential." As many as 100 million Americans watched at least one of the four debates.

The 1960 election turned out to be one of the closest races in history, with Kennedy winning the popular vote by a 49.7 to 49.5 percent margin and the electoral vote by a more comfortable 303 to 219. But if Nixon had taken Illinois and Texas, where he was convinced that ballot-box-stuffing Democrats had "stole[n] the election," he would have won the electoral vote 270 to 252.[75] Although Eisenhower may have been among those who urged him to demand a recount, Nixon decided that such an action would "tear the country to pieces."[76] The next time he ran for president, Nixon organized a group of 100,000 poll watchers, headed by a former FBI official, to protect him against fraud.

Kennedy won because there were more registered Democrats than Republicans and because the economy was in recession. Nixon felt that he lost because "I spent too much time . . . on substance and too little time on appearance."[77] Aside from the televised debates, the campaign was noted for a hawkish and even irresponsible Kennedy prodding Nixon to do more about communist Cuba (while most likely aware that the administration was planning a secret invasion); the Kennedy camp's intervention to protect Martin Luther King, Jr., who had been arrested just prior to the election; and the publication of stories about a $205,000 loan that Nixon's brother Donald had obtained from Howard Hughes and the possibility of influence peddling. This story appeared again and again during Nixon's subsequent political career and may have had something to do with the Watergate break-in.

Nixon and his family left Washington for California after the defeat, but he felt that "this was not the end . . . someday I would be back here."[78] He bought a house on North Bundy Drive, went to work for a Los Angeles law firm, and, along with an able staff, began writing his memoirs. President Kennedy, a Pulitzer Prize–winning author, had suggested the project to his defeated opponent. Nixon's best-selling *Six Crises* (Hiss, Checkers, Ike's heart attack, the Venezuela stoning, the Khrushchev debate, and the 1960 campaign) sold 300,000 copies, earned Nixon $250,000, and received generally favorable reviews.

Although Nixon "had no great desire to be governor of California," the party asked him to make a run against Democratic governor Edmund "Pat" Brown, who looked vulnerable in 1962.[79] For Nixon, a victory in California would offer him an important political base for the presidential election in 1964 or 1968. To secure the Republican nomination, he had to endure a tough primary contest against a right-wing Republican backed by the John

Birch Society. In the general campaign, he ran in a rather dispirited way, appearing to be more interested in national and international issues than California politics. He lost by 297,000 votes out of 6 million cast, a victim, he felt, of the Democrats' success in taking advantage of Kennedy's "victory" over the Russians in the Cuban missile crisis of October 1962. Nixon claimed that "if I had been elected Governor in '62 I would never have been elected President in '68. On the other hand, if I had not run in '62 I also might not have been elected President in '68 because the Party would never have forgiven me for not heeding its call when it was in need."[80]

Few thought that he would have another opportunity to achieve national office after his disastrous press conference on the morning after he lost the California election. Tired, angry at the press, and perhaps a bit hung over, he "just had to say what I felt and get it off my chest."[81] After rambling through a bitter critique of the media, he announced, "You won't have Nixon to kick around any more, because gentlemen, this is my last press conference."[82] In the days that followed, President Kennedy privately questioned Nixon's mental stability, ABC television ran a special called "The Political Obituary of Richard M. Nixon," and *Time* magazine concluded, "Barring a miracle, Richard Nixon can never hope to be elected to any political office again."[83]

It certainly looked that way when he burned his political bridges behind him and left California to move to New York City, where he joined the law firm Mudge, Stern, Baldwin, and Todd. There he first met bond lawyer John Mitchell, whose forcefulness impressed him, and Leonard Garment, a liberal Democratic attorney. Exploiting his extensive political connections, Nixon served as a rainmaker for the firm, attracting important clients such as Pepsi Cola. In 1966, he also did a professional job in a losing cause, arguing *Time, Inc. v. Hill*, a celebrated First Amendment case, before the Supreme Court.

In New York, Nixon broadened his cultural and intellectual tastes, noting, "This is where the action is—not with those peasants in California," and he kept his name in the news with articles in magazines and newspapers.[84] He quickly assumed a prominent role in national politics, which were thrown into confusion because of President Kennedy's assassination. In a curious coincidence, Nixon had been in Dallas attending a meeting of Pepsi Cola bottlers the day before the assassination. Moreover, Lee Harvey Oswald's wife claimed that her husband had targeted Nixon for assassination in April because of an anti-Castro speech he had delivered.

Although Nixon opted not to become an active candidate for the presidential nomination in 1964, he positioned himself as a compromise selection if the conservatives failed to nominate Barry Goldwater. Unlike other moderate Republicans, Nixon worked hard for Goldwater in the general campaign, making 150 appearances in 36 states on his behalf, even though he knew that Goldwater's chances of winning were slim.

Through 1965 and 1966, he continued his labors for the party as a fund-raiser, appearing before 600 groups in 40 states, deciding "that there was no other life for me but politics and public service."[85] As early as 1965, he began assembling a political staff with the hiring of Pat Buchanan, a pugnacious young conservative journalist from the *St. Louis Globe-Democrat*, as speechwriter. Nixon spoke out often on the Vietnam War, calling on President Johnson to adopt more hawkish military policies. In fact, Johnson helped put Nixon firmly on the political map again when he criticized him publicly as a "chronic campaigner" in 1966. Nixon took advantage of that opening to have the *New York Times* publish, in response, his own foreign policy program.

That chronic campaigner again worked hard for Republican congressional candidates in 1966, picking up political debts wherever he visited, especially in the emerging Republican South. On election night 1966—a happy one for Republicans, who gained forty-seven House seats, three Senate seats, and eight governorships—Smith College student Julie Nixon and her future husband, Amherst College student David Eisenhower, President Eisenhower's grandson, had their first date.

While his staff began to take on more paid and volunteer help in 1967, including Ray Price, Maurice Stans, Dwight Chapin, and Charles Colson, Nixon took a six-month hiatus from politics for foreign travel. After his return, he published a widely noted article in the October 1967 issue of *Foreign Affairs* titled "Asia after Vietnam," in which he suggested that Communist China would someday become part of the international community. Nixon had become something of a closet intellectual and philosopher, reading books by or about the politicians he most admired: Theodore Roosevelt, Woodrow Wilson, Charles de Gaulle, and Winston Churchill.

As the 1968 campaign season began, he appeared more and more to be the only candidate acceptable to all factions of the party. He also projected a good deal more gravitas than he had displayed in 1960. Nixon now described himself as "a pragmatist with positions grounded in pretty solid principles"; he was "a man for all factions."[86]

He faced competition for the nomination from the moderate Michigan governor George Romney, the front-runner for much of late 1966 and early 1967; California governor Ronald Reagan; and New York governor Nelson Rockefeller. Romney faded after he admitted on a Michigan television program in August 1967 that "when I came back from Vietnam, I just had the greatest brainwashing that anybody can get," a comment that led the witty Democratic candidate, Senator Eugene McCarthy of Minnesota, to say that "a light rinse would have been sufficient."[87]

Following impressive primary wins in early 1968, Nixon assumed the lead in the race, with Reagan and Rockefeller in an informal unholy alliance, waiting to pounce if he faltered. He was helped by an endorsement from Eisenhower. The key to Nixon's victory was his ability to secure the vote of southern delegates, most of whom favored the conservative Reagan. Nixon assured Senator Strom Thurmond of South Carolina that he would respect the views of southerners on the anti–states' rights federal courts, as well as support the antiballistic missile (ABM) project, and with the senator's assistance, the South held. When it appeared at the convention in Miami that a Nixon failure to win on the first ballot would open the way for Rockefeller and others, Nixon promised southern delegates that he would not support "some professional civil-rights group," that he would oppose busing to achieve desegregation, and that he would appoint "real men" to the courts, to the Justice Department, and as his vice president.[88] He also promised to help southern textile manufacturers facing stiff competition from the Japanese.

Nixon went over the top at the Miami Beach convention on the vote of the next to last state, tallying 692 votes to Rockefeller's 272 and Reagan's 182. Rockefeller later commented, "Ronnie didn't do as well as I thought. I was counting on him for a little more muscle."[89]

The first payoff to the South came when Nixon selected Spiro T. Agnew, the governor of Maryland, as his vice-presidential running mate. Nixon had earlier tentatively offered the nomination to Robert Finch, his friend from California, and to Michigan representative Gerald R. Ford, both of whom turned it down. Nixon had met Agnew only four months earlier; he and campaign manager John Mitchell had decided only two weeks before the convention to consider Agnew as a running mate. Formerly a Rockefeller supporter, Agnew had earned conservative plaudits for the way he had lectured black leaders after rioting tore Baltimore apart in the wake of the murder of Martin Luther King, Jr., in April. But he was, according to a Nixon aide, "absurdly unqualified" and caused a good deal of embarrassment on the campaign trail when he playfully called a journalist in his entourage a "fat Jap."[90] Republican doyenne Alice Roosevelt Longworth asked of Nixon, "Promise me Dick, that if you're elected, you'll *always* make Governor Agnew travel with you on your plane."[91] The Democrats ran commercials with thirty seconds of laughter as the screen displayed "Agnew for Vice-President"; the *Washington Post* considered Agnew "the most eccentric political appointment since the Roman Emperor Caligula named his horse a consul."[92]

In his acceptance speech at the convention, amid fresh memories of the nationwide riots following the King assassination that resulted in 46 deaths and 2,600 injuries, Nixon referred to the "unprecedented racial violence" in the country. Those remarks were punctuated by looting and sniping in Miami on the night before his nomination that had resulted in several deaths. But his speech was best remembered for his lyrical description of the United States as a land of opportunity, of a young boy from humble origins who "hears a train go by at night and . . . dreams of far away places where he'd like to go," an "impossible dream" that can come true.[93]

Nixon was fortunate to be running for president at a time when the Democratic Party was coming apart at the seams. In the fall of 1967, the relatively obscure Senator Eugene McCarthy agreed to be the antiwar forces' candidate in the primaries against Johnson. After the communists' Tet offensive in February revealed that there was no light at the end of the tunnel in Vietnam, and after the backbenching senator almost beat the powerful president in the New Hampshire primary in March, a more formidable challenger, Senator Robert F. Kennedy of New York, entered the campaign. On 31 March 1968, Johnson announced that he would not seek another term in order to concentrate on ending the war in Vietnam, a decision that led Vice President Hubert Humphrey to throw his hat into the ring as Johnson's heir apparent, the "official" candidate of the regular Democrats. Meanwhile, the insurgents, Kennedy and McCarthy, competed with each other in the handful of states that had primaries in 1968. After Kennedy was assassinated on the night he won the California primary in June, Humphrey emerged as the favorite for the nomination, despite the fact that he had not won a single primary.

Beholden to Johnson, Humphrey could not meet the antiwar Democrats halfway as he clung to a position of unwavering support for administration policy in Southeast Asia. At the Chicago convention in August, 10,000 antiwar demonstrators gathered on the streets and in the parks to protest the anointing of Humphrey ("Dump the Hump" was one of their slogans), an alleged "pro-war" candidate, while the allied McCarthy and Kennedy camps prepared to do battle inside the convention hall. The result was the most tumultuous convention in American history. Millions of Americans were horrified to watch on television as convention host Mayor Richard J. Daley's people roughed up journalists in the hall while, according to a commission report, a "police riot" took place outside the hall.

The riots at the convention cost the Democrats millions of votes. Conservative Democrats fled their party for the "law and order" promised by the Republicans, repelled by such lawlessness (and already deeply troubled by urban rebellions and disruptive antiwar demonstrations). Conversely, millions of liberal and left-leaning Democrats were alienated by the brutal tactics used to suppress dissent. Even though many liberals ultimately voted for Humphrey, their tepid support denied the Democratic nominee the free, youthful campaign volunteers on whom the party depended for electoral success.

Humphrey set out on what soon became a "transcontinental trail of gaffes."[94] One politico complained, "We had no money. We had no organization. We were fifteen points behind in the polls. We did have a media plan but we didn't have the money to go with it."[95] As the campaign developed, Humphrey began to contemplate an independent foreign policy. His advisers suspected that Secretary of Defense Clark Clifford was correct when he confided to a friend in September that "the President wants to see him [Humphrey] defeated."[96] Another Democratic warhorse, W. Averell Harriman, the chief negotiator at the Paris peace talks that had opened in the spring, was so distressed by the prospect of a Nixon victory that he often went beyond his instructions to try to obtain an agreement before election day to boost Humphrey's chances.

Nixon also profited from the rise of the independent candidacy of Alabama governor George C. Wallace, who took more votes from Humphrey in the North than he took from Nixon in the South. Wallace, a right-wing populist and segregationist, railed against the establishment, the "overeducated, ivory-tower folks with pointy heads" who wore "sissy britches." He promised, "If I ever get to be president and one of those demonstrators lay down in front of my car, it'll be the last car they ever lay down in front of."[97] His American Independent Party was on the ballot in all fifty states. By September, he could claim support from 21 percent of Americans polled. Although he had no realistic chance of winning, Wallace could have denied victory to the other two major candidates by taking enough electoral college votes to throw the election into the House, where, in exchange for his votes, he could have exacted promises to slow the pace of desegregation. This was not a far-fetched plan. A small shift of votes toward him in three southern states and toward Humphrey in two northern states would have sent the election into the House.

Knowing that he could not beat Wallace in the Deep South, where Goldwater had achieved success in 1964, Nixon concentrated on the border states as part of a larger "southern rim" strategy, appealing to voters opposed to "forced busing" and for the freedom-of-choice approach to school selection. Nixon's southern operatives also warned that a vote for Wallace was a vote for Humphrey. Wallace wounded himself when he chose as a running mate General Curtis LeMay, a loose cannon who threatened to unleash nuclear weapons in Vietnam. Democratic union leaders helped blunt the Wallace challenge through a vigorous drive to convince their membership that although the southerner's social policies may have been attractive, his economic and antiunion policies were not.

Nixon dealt in generalities on the campaign trail, suggesting that he would solve the problems of crime, inflation, and Vietnam and reduce the big government programs of the Democrats. He appealed to the "silent center," a phrase speechwriter William Safire had expropriated from Senator Paul Douglas (D-Ill.).

Nixon's campaign manager was his gruff and strong willed law partner John Mitchell, who coincidentally had been the commander of the naval squadron in which John F. Kennedy's *PT 109* had been a famous part. Mitchell boasted during the campaign, "I'm running the show. I bring more business into the firm than he does. When I tell Dick Nixon what to do, he listens. I'm in charge."[98] Whether the candidate listened to everything Mitchell said, Nixon considered him one of his most valuable advisers on all issues.

Nixon's chief of staff, H. R. "Bob" Haldeman, had come from an advertising background, as did many of the people he recruited, leading speechwriter Leonard Garment to observe that "the issues men are now superfluous."[99] Several of the advertising people, Dwight Chapin, Larry Higby, and Ronald Ziegler, would later join the White House staff. These merchandisers helped put together the most impressive media campaign in history to that point, emphasizing town meetings produced by commercial television experts that were carefully scripted to look like spontaneous events. One critical observer compared them to a sporting contest in an indoor stadium "where the wind would never blow. The temperature would never rise or fall, and the ball never bounce erratically on the artificial grass."[100] According to a CBS executive on the Nixon team, "without television, Nixon would not have a chance . . . of being elected because the press would not let him get through to the people."[101] At the same time, the candidate was shielded from journalists and their probing press conferences. As one reporter commented, "The press corps calls [Nixon] 'the cardboard man' because we can't see past the facade of the candidate. I've never met the real Richard Nixon."[102]

Congress, which had waived the equal-time provisions in 1960 in order to exclude lesser-party candidates from the televised debates, had reinstituted the provisions in 1964. Nixon thus refused to debate Humphrey, leading the frustrated Democratic candidate to assail "Richard the Chickenhearted." (In 1964, then Senator Humphrey had voted for equal time to protect his president from having to debate Goldwater.) Ahead in the polls, fearing a misstep, why should Nixon agree to a debate? In any event, the carefully managed campaign, in which the candidate appeared dignified and statesmanlike, worked. Walter Lippmann endorsed a "new Nixon, a maturer and mellower man who is no longer clawing his way to the top . . . who has outlived and outgrown the ruthless politics of his early days."[103]

The 1968 campaign took place while the war was raging in Vietnam. Throughout the summer and early fall, peace talks continued in Paris. Any major breakthrough would be a bonus for the Democrats. Nixon received secret reports on the progress of the talks from a friend of aide Bryce Harlow and from Harvard professor and Rockefeller adviser Henry Kissinger, who was in Paris conducting research for a *Foreign Affairs* article.

A hard-line critic of the administration in the past, Nixon prepared a major address on Vietnam that he intended to deliver on 30 March 1968, the night before Lyndon Johnson's surprise speech to the nation. In his speech, Nixon planned to place Vietnam in a global context and to promise a new military strategy. But he confided to an adviser on the eve of the speech, "I've come to the conclusion that there's no way to win the war. But we can't say that of course. In fact, we have to say the opposite just to keep some degree of bargaining leverage."[104] He had been asked earlier during the New Hampshire primary whether he had "a secret plan" to end the war. He responded, "Yes, I have a plan to end the war" and later promised that he would "end the war and win the peace in the Pacific," but he never said that he had a secret plan. In fact, he complained that he did not "like this 'secret plan' business" attributed to him.[105]

Briefed several times during the campaign by President Johnson, he promised not to talk about Vietnam in any detail while the peace talks were continuing. Expecting that Nixon's Vietnam policies would be closer to his own, Johnson was not very helpful to Humphrey. For example, he refrained from revealing that the CIA had discovered that the authoritarian Greek government had illegally contributed more than $500,000 to the Republicans. Late in the campaign, Secretary of State Dean Rusk observed that Nixon had "actually been more responsible on this [Vietnam] than our own candidate" because he had not criticized administration policy.[106] In any event, dovish Americans could vote either for Humphrey, who for most of the campaign vowed to continue Johnson's policies, or for Nixon, who had a plan to end the war that he could not reveal because of his patriotic unwillingness to undercut the president.

Behind in the polls, Humphrey decided to distance himself from the White House to a modest degree on the question of the cessation of bombing North Vietnam in a speech in Salt Lake City on 30 September. He complained privately, "I've had Lyndon Johnson around my neck just long enough."[107] The speech pulled antiwar Democrats back into the fold, and throughout the month of October, Humphrey began to catch up to Nixon in the polls to the point where the race was too close to call on 31 October.

During that month, Nixon discovered through both official and unofficial channels that a breakthrough on a U.S. bombing halt was near, in what could be a dramatic "October surprise." On 12 July, Nixon and Mitchell had met with Anna Chennault, cochair of the Women for Nixon Committee, who had close ties to the South Vietnamese government and to Bui Diem, the South Vietnamese ambassador (they had previously met in February). At this meeting, Nixon asked Chennault to relay messages from the Republicans to Saigon. She claims to have called Mitchell at least once a day throughout the campaign.

Facing the prospect of a Nixon presidency, Soviet leaders suddenly agreed to cooperate with the Johnson administration to pressure the North Vietnamese to be more conciliatory at the Paris peace talks. Although Politburo leaders had hedged their bets by authorizing back-channel contacts with Nixon aides, most still considered Nixon "too unpredictable and reactionary to be a reliable partner."[108] On 31 October, Johnson announced an agreement to halt the bombing. Two days later, the South Vietnamese rejected the deal. Mitchell had asked Chennault to encourage Saigon to reject it publicly. The South Vietnamese would have done so even without her prodding.

Despite Johnson's denials, Nixon and his principal advisers felt that they had been tricked and that the president was allowing electoral politics to affect a crucial national security decision. For his part, Johnson was furious that the Republicans had convinced the South Vietnamese "to drag their feet."[109] Humphrey exploded, the "sonofabitch China Lobby . . . could make Nixon president, and I'm not going to let that happen."[110] The administration had learned about Chennault's contacts through FBI bugging of both her home and the Vietnamese embassy in Washington. Johnson even warned Nixon about her potentially treasonous behavior. The Republican candidate denied all knowledge of Chennault's activities. The FBI had also bugged Spiro Agnew on the hustings in New Mexico, after picking up the information on Chennault's line that her contact was an official in that state. But Agnew was not involved. The FBI had erred—Chennault's contact was John Mitchell in New *Hampshire*.

On the dramatic weekend before the election, Johnson, and especially Humphrey, contemplated going public with the information that Republican operatives had sabotaged the peace. Johnson told aides that Nixon had committed "treason."[111] But to make that charge, he would have to reveal information about illegal or embarrassing wiretaps of an American citizen, an allied embassy, an allied government, and even vice-presidential candidate Agnew. The FBI investigation, moreover, had uncovered no direct links between Nixon and Chennault. Nonetheless, had Humphrey made an issue of Republican "treason," he might very well have won what turned out to be an extremely close election.

The Saigon announcement rejecting the agreement resulted in a loss of momentum for Humphrey, just as the well-financed Nixon campaign began a massive media blitz. On election day, Nixon won the presidency, taking 43.4 percent of the popular vote to Humphrey's 42.7 and Wallace's 13.5, of which 40 percent came from outside the South. Nixon captured the electoral vote by the more comfortable margin of 301 to 191 to 46. He carried the big electoral college states of California, Illinois, New Jersey, and Ohio, along with most of the border, plains, and Sun Belt states. Nixon picked up support from traditional ethnic Democratic voters while losing black voters. His plurality, or perhaps Nixon and Wallace's majority, reinforced the argument made by Kevin Phillips in *The Emerging Republican Majority*, which came out after the election and soon became a bible for the Nixon administration. Phillips pointed out that the Republicans were beginning to control the fast-growing states of the South and the West, while the Democrats were left with New England, the Pacific Northwest, and decaying urban areas.

The Republicans failed to win control of Congress, an ominous development that meant that Nixon became the first president since 1853 to assume office without his party's having a majority in at least one house of Congress. All the same, the election seemingly spelled the end of the New Deal—Nixon and Wallace appealed to a conservative alienated majority opposed to big government and the social and cultural liberalism of the Democrats, whom they deemed responsible for the chaos and disorder of the late 1960s.

Nixon's victory was less a vote for a program or for himself personally than a vote against big government, taxes, inflation, welfare, riots, liberals, and pornography and obscenity. Nixon recognized this in a private comment he made when filming a commercial: "It's all about law and order and the damn Negro–Puerto Rican groups out there."[112] Yet in the early morning after the election, recalling a sign on the campaign trail in Deshler, Ohio, that read plaintively, "Bring Us Together," Nixon promised that that would be "the one great objective of the administration at the outset: to bring the American people together. This will be an open administration open to new ideas . . . open to the critics."[113]

2

★ ★ ★ ★ ★

ORGANIZING THE WHITE HOUSE

To bring the United States together in 1969 would not have been easy for any president, let alone such a polarizing figure as Richard Nixon. His campaign for law and order and his appeal to voters based on the politics of resentment made such a task virtually impossible.

The year 1968, the year that census figures surpassed the 200 million mark, was the most turbulent year of the turbulent sixties, a "decade" that began with Kennedy's assassination in 1963 and ended with Nixon's resignation in 1974. The social and cultural revolutions taking place while Americans were engaged in an increasingly unpopular and seemingly endless war in Vietnam, across a backdrop of unprecedented urban riots and political assassinations, made Americans long for the "Happy Days" of the fifties. Walter Lippmann, who had seen his share of revolution and turbulence, thought that "The world has never been more disorderly within memory of living man."[1]

In the first place, after seeming to have solved the problem of racial segregation and discrimination with the passage of the Civil Rights Act of 1964 and the Voting Rights Act of 1965, the nation experienced an unprecedented series of urban riots or rebellions that swept across the desegregating South and the legally desegregated North. Los Angeles, Detroit, Newark, Chicago, Washington, and several hundred other cities were devastated by disturbances that caused hundreds of deaths, thousands of injuries, and billions of dollars in property damage. Moreover, the civil rights leaders of the fifties and early sixties, who promoted integration and relied on the ballot box and nonviolent civil disobedience to achieve their goals, had been challenged by those who advocated Black Power or Black Nationalism and who proclaimed that the time for turning the other cheek had come to an end.

At the same time, the war in Vietnam continued with no end in sight. When Nixon took office in January 1969, there were still 536,000 American troops in Southeast Asia. More than 30,000 military personnel had been killed in combat since 1961, with almost half of those deaths occurring in 1968 alone. The failure of Johnson's policies had led a majority of Americans to conclude that entry into the war in Vietnam had been a terrible mistake.

That mistake had unleashed the largest and most effective antiwar movement in the nation's history, a movement that flourished particularly on elite college campuses, which themselves were in an uproar over issues of curriculum, governance, and the universities' relationships to the federal government. By 1967, President Johnson could not travel in his country without facing picketers, foul-mouthed chanters, and even the threat of violence. Furthermore, many young people began to call for revolutionary change. Not since the 1930s had so many Americans adopted anticapitalist, anti-imperialist perspectives as they carried Cuban and Vietcong flags and chanted derisively, as American boys died in Vietnam, "Ho Ho Ho Chi Minh, the NLF [National Liberation Front] is gonna win."

Confounding the political problems on campuses and even in high schools was the so-called countercultural or hippie movement, in which young people abandoned middle-class values en masse as they "turned on, tuned in, and dropped out." In a few short years after the death of President Kennedy, many young Americans—and young people in Europe as well—let their hair grow long; traded in their high heels and skirts and their ties and button-down shirts for torn jeans, tie-dyed T-shirts, and dirty sneakers; talked openly about and even practiced "free love"; listened to music that was incomprehensible to their parents; smoked marijuana; and rejected authority.

Most young Americans were not foul-mouthed hippies, dope users, free-lovers, members of antiwar coalitions, or Marxists. But there were enough of these telegenic countercultural, antiestablishment types at Columbia, Harvard, and Berkeley to suggest that the next generation of the establishment might not be like the last. And if the campuses were the breeding grounds for rebellion, things were clearly getting worse, because the number of people between the ages of eighteen and twenty-one attending college had risen from 23 to 35 percent from 1960 to 1970, while the median age of Americans had dropped from 29.5 to 28.

The Supreme Court had seemingly contributed to the social revolution by expanding the bounds of free speech to permit words and behaviors previously considered "obscene" to be heard and seen in the media and in concerts, nightclubs, and public demonstrations. The "culture wars" that were to rage through the last quarter of the twentieth century had begun. Reflecting these wars were the contemporary Academy Award winners. *Midnight Cowboy*, an X-rated film dealing with drugs and homosexuality, was the 1969 winner, sandwiched between the wholesome musical *Oliver!* in 1968 and the patriotic biography *Patton* in 1970.

For many Americans, the new women's liberation movement, galvanized by the publication of Betty Friedan's *The Feminine Mystique* in 1963, the founding of the National Organization for Women (NOW) in 1966, and the widespread use of the birth-control pill during the same period, was as destabilizing and distasteful a threat as the hippie and radical movements. Some were troubled by the emotional issue of abortion rights, one of the fundamental demands of the women's movement. Others expressed concern about what became known as "traditional family values." They claimed that the women's movement was responsible for the decline in the birthrate from twenty-four per thousand in 1960 to seventeen per thousand in 1970, as well as a 50 percent increase in the number of divorces per thousand during the same period.

The lower birthrate and increased marital instability were most likely affected by the increasing number of women holding full-time jobs. By the time Nixon became president, almost 50 percent of American women held jobs, and many had begun to complain about the discriminatory practices of their employers. As for that supremely conventional Middle American in the White House, Nixon joked, "Let me make one thing perfectly clear, I wouldn't want to wake up next to a lady pipefitter."[2] Nixon's remark resonated in a mainstream America that was still shocked by the feminists' raucous protest in Atlantic City outside the auditorium that housed the 1968 Miss America contest.

Nixon represented those Americans—a majority of the population—threatened by these social and cultural revolutions, people who thought that society was too promiscuous and who resented the pernicious impact of eastern opinion makers, West Coast moviemakers, and liberals in general on the American value system. Many of these same citizens felt that the Great Society had gone too far, that government was sticking its nose into too much of their private business and giving away their tax money through welfare and other poverty programs to undeserving, lazy people. One of the most popular television shows during the Nixon years was *All in the Family*, whose main character, Archie Bunker, was a lower-middle-class family man outraged by the excesses of the sixties. Although the liberals who created the show made Bunker seem foolish, many who watched it identified with his hostility to people of color, feminists, homosexuals, and hippies.

Within the political system, the rapid growth of the South, Southwest, and West had significantly altered the balance of power, with the more conservative Sun Belt states challenging the eastern establishment, especially in the Republican Party, not only for political supremacy but also for control of the social and political agenda. Nixon's establishment of two official vacation homes, one in Florida at Key Biscayne and the other in California at San Clemente, and the relatively large number of his political appointees who came from Sun Belt states symbolized the new era.

The economy that Nixon inherited seemed to be booming. Since 1960, the gross national product (GNP) had increased 50 percent (controlled for inflation), while Americans living below the poverty line had declined from 40 million to 26 million during the same period. In 1968 alone, wages rose by 6.5 percent, and unemployment stood at 3.3 percent. The key economic problem was inflation, which had reached 4.7 percent when Nixon took office, the highest since the Korean War. This rise in inflation was in part a product of Lyndon Johnson's fiscally irresponsible decision to borrow to pay for guns (the Vietnam War) and butter (the Great Society) at the same time.

Harry S. Truman was the last president to face such massive societal dislocation upon taking office. Many observers, even Democrats, hoped that the experienced Nixon—more moderate on most issues than the majority of his party—might be the person to "bring us together." They thought that the man who won the election in November was a "new Nixon" who deserved the traditional "honeymoon" from criticism during his first months. Reflecting this attitude, Herbert Block (Herblock) of the *Washington Post,* whose cartoons of a sleazy, unshaven Nixon were so unflattering that Pat had banned the newspaper from their home, ran a cartoon of an attractive, clean-shaven president-elect on the day after election day featuring the sign: "This shop gives every new President of the United States a free shave. H. Block, proprietor."[3]

Reconstructing the history of the Nixon presidency should be relatively easy, considering the unprecedented amount of primary material available. Yet after reading the memoirs and historians' accounts of the administration, H. R. Haldeman, who had been privy to most of Nixon's activities until the spring of 1973, wrote, "I read it [the history] with the assumption that virtually all of it is wrong. It's only a matter of *how* wrong it is, because it's virtually impossible to re-create accurately an ongoing entity— what happened and why it happened, even with access to all the memos and all the tapes."[4] Most participants in historical events have made the same criticism of the way scholars and journalists have chronicled those events. The historian of the Nixon administration must pick and choose carefully among the millions of bits of conflicting and often derogatory information, all the time paying heed to John Mitchell's famous admonition, "instead of listening to what we say . . . watch what we do."[5]

The Nixon team experienced, in the words of Haldeman, an "ideal transition" period.[6] Johnson, whom Nixon had rarely criticized directly during the campaign, personally saw to it that the changeover in government would be a smooth one, although he refused Nixon's request for prior consultation and agreement on foreign policy initiatives. Nixon indicated to the South Vietnamese that now, in the aftermath of the election, he too supported the breakthrough in the peace talks that Johnson had achieved on 31 October. Mitchell even asked Chennault to urge her friends in Saigon to accept the president-elect's about-face.

When the Johnsons showed the Nixons around the White House on 11 November 1968, the former vice president and his wife saw the upstairs living quarters for the first time. Transition-team member Robert Finch reported that after a December visit during which a Johnson aide had demonstrated the president's taping system in the Cabinet Room, the Oval Office, and several other places, Nixon ordered, "Get rid of it. I don't want anything like it."[7] There would be no regular taping in the Nixon White House until 1971. One highlight of the interregnum was the 22 December marriage of Nixon's younger daughter, Julie, to David Eisenhower.

The characteristically thorough Nixon first read all the previous inaugural addresses before completing his own. One could hear echoes of Kennedy's famous 1960 inaugural in Nixon's—not surprising, considering the way he continually compared himself to his old and much envied rival. After being sworn in by Chief Justice Earl Warren, he explained to the nation:

> We are caught in war, wanting peace. We are torn by division, wanting unity. We see around us empty lives, wanting fulfillment. We see tasks that need doing, waiting for hands to do them. To a crisis of the spirit, we need an answer of the spirit. . . . I ask you to join in a high adventure—as rich as humanity itself, and exciting as the times we live in. . . . Where peace is unknown make it welcome; where peace is fragile, make it strong, where peace is temporary, make it permanent.

His new director of communications and old friend Herb Klein reported that "at times, President Kennedy obsessed [sic] the President-elect."[8]

Unlike Kennedy, and unlike all other incoming presidents in American history, Nixon's moment of triumph produced the first significant violence at an inaugural parade, another example of the breakdown of American society at the end of the sixties. On that cold and overcast day, in a counterinaugural, or InHoguration, several thousand demonstrators gathered from 13th to 15th Streets near the parade route, some carrying signs that read "Four More Years of Death" and "Number One War Criminal," others chanting the "Ho" mantra, while still others wore grotesque Nixon masks. A few in the crowd threw rocks and bottles that struck cars in the procession. For a while, Nixon and his wife stood up in their limousine. He commented that he "didn't even think about risking my life. I just did it to show those goddamned protestors that this president was not going to be pushed around."[9] Over the three-day inaugural period, beginning with a vice-presidential reception on 19 January, 119 protesters were arrested, 6 of whom were charged with flag desecration.

By the time of his inauguration, Nixon had selected department heads and most of the key White House staff through a process that took place at his transition headquarters in the Hotel Pierre in New York during November and December. To demonstrate that his would be an open and even bipartisan administration, his staff began the process by sending letters of inquiry to all 64,988 people listed in Who's Who in America. The president-elect made an effort to attract Democrats, blacks, and, to a lesser degree, women to his cabinet and staff. He offered the United Nations (UN) ambassadorship to Democrats Sargent Shriver and Hubert Humphrey, the undersecretary of state post to Johnson's secretary of the army Cyrus Vance, and secretary of defense to Senator Henry Jackson (D-Wash.) and former Texas governor John Connally. Nixon also inquired through his friend Reverend Billy Graham whether Connally would be interested in the Treasury Department, the post that the Texan accepted in 1970.

As for African Americans, Nixon offered the UN position to Republican senator Edward Brooke of Massachusetts and the Department of Housing and Urban Development (HUD) to Whitney Young, the head of the Urban League. Nixon did so despite having attracted only 12 percent of the black vote, in contrast to 32 percent in 1960. James Farmer, head of the Congress of Racial Equality (CORE), accepted an undersecretaryship at the Department of Health, Education, and Welfare (HEW), and Nixon appointed Walter Washington mayor of Washington, D.C. Ignoring the genuine difficulty Nixon faced in recruiting blacks for his administration, the head of the National Association for the Advancement of Colored People (NAACP) complained, "with few exceptions the policy of the White House has been to think white first, and merit second."[10]

The highest position that Nixon offered to a woman was director of the Civil Service, but Ersa H. Poston chose not to serve. Nixon appointed Virginia Knauer as consumer affairs adviser and, in his second term, Anne

Armstrong as a White House counselor. Despite Nixon's genuflections in the direction of diversity, his first cabinet was made up of white males, at least seven of whom were millionaires. Like Nixon himself, none of them had been born wealthy—they were self-made men.

Nixon admired the structure and order of the Eisenhower administration, in which the cabinet had played a central role, although he had found most of its meetings "unnecessary and boring."[11] Nonetheless, he originally planned to have his department heads, or "deputy presidents," run their programs with a good deal of independence while he concentrated on foreign policy, the area that most interested him and the one in which a president has the most flexibility.[12] During the campaign, he had told a reporter that "when a president takes all the real power himself, those around him become puppets."[13] As for the White House staff, Haldeman, the man who was to become Nixon's powerful chief of staff, said before the inauguration, "Our job is not to do the work of government, but to get the work out to where it belongs—out to the departments."[14] In keeping with this original intention to delegate authority, Nixon allowed department heads to appoint most of their subordinates without much oversight from the White House. He would rue that decision.

Nixon's secretary of state was William Rogers, an old friend from congressional days who had been Eisenhower's attorney general. Rogers was not the first choice. Nixon would have preferred veteran diplomat Robert Murphy or former Pennsylvania governor William Scranton. But whoever became secretary of state had to live with Nixon's intention to run diplomacy out of the White House through the National Security Council (NSC). Unexperienced in international affairs, Rogers possessed the skills to be a discreet negotiator and an adequate administrator. According to one of his aides, he was "impatient to the point of indifference with long-range geostrategic analysis," the sort of intellectual exercise Nixon enjoyed.[15] After an unhappy four years and six months of constant combat with national security adviser Henry Kissinger, Rogers resigned and was replaced by Kissinger.

For the Treasury Department, Nixon chose David Kennedy, a Chicago banker. Despite his position, Kennedy was not a major figure in the administration. Nixon would have preferred David Rockefeller, who rejected the offer. In December 1970, the president replaced Kennedy with John Connally. Unlike Kennedy, the strong-willed and self-assured Connally became one of the most important cabinet members, groomed by Nixon as either a vice-presidential candidate in 1972 or even a presidential candidate in 1976. George Shultz, another central figure in the administration, replaced Connally in 1972, and he, in turn, was replaced by William Simon in 1974.

To head Defense, Nixon selected Melvin Laird, a shrewd Wisconsin congressman who had originally advised the president to offer the job to Henry Jackson. When Jackson changed his mind, Nixon told Laird, "You son-of-a-bitch. You talked me into this. Now you've got to do it." Feeling guilty, Laird reluctantly accepted the post, admitting, "I got sandbagged into it."[16] Laird was skilled at defending his department against his old colleagues in Congress and against competing agencies within the administration, especially the NSC. He was also clever and powerful enough to ignore direct orders from the White House on occasion, relying on his friends in Congress for protection. According to Henry Kissinger, one of his rivals for influence and power, Laird was the "master of the inspired leak."[17]

Laird also proved adept at discovering White House policies that were supposed to be kept secret from him and others in the cabinet. John Ehrlichman, one of Nixon's chief aides, so distrusted Laird that he brought civilian rather than the traditional military telephone operators to Camp David because he feared that the secretary was picking up secrets from them. The fact that Laird had to spend a good deal of time on intelligence work within the U.S. government indicates how Nixon reneged on his original promise about the role of the cabinet in his administration. In a late 1970 evaluation of his cabinet, Nixon found Laird "sneaky but manageable."[18] By prearrangement, Laird left office in 1973 and was replaced by Elliot Richardson, who was replaced by James Schlesinger that same year. Laird returned to government service briefly in 1974 as a White House counselor.

The most powerful member of the cabinet was Attorney General John Mitchell, whom Nixon considered his closest adviser on a variety of issues, including foreign policy. Mitchell was not enthusiastic about taking over Justice, in good measure because of his wife, Martha, a heavy drinker and gossip who was in delicate mental health. By the end of 1970, Nixon had become somewhat dissatisfied with his friend's job performance because he was "a lousy spokesman" with "a good mind, able but not the compleat AG."[19] When Mitchell resigned to head the Nixon reelection drive in 1972, he was replaced by Richard Kleindienst, who had served as deputy attorney general. Kleindienst was one of those appointments from the Goldwater wing of the party, along with Dean Burch of the Federal Communications Commission (FCC) and William Rehnquist, head of the Office of Legal Counsel at Justice. The Arizona senator had been so helpful to Nixon during the campaign that the president told him, "Barry, if there is ever anything you want, just ask for it."[20] When Kleindienst resigned in 1973, his post was assumed by Elliot Richardson, the jack-of-all-trades for the administration, who was fired when he refused to fire Watergate special prosecutor Archibald Cox that year. Richardson was succeeded by William Saxbe.

For postmaster general, Nixon selected Alabama Republican Winton Blount. Blount served until 1971, when the Post Office Department lost its cabinet status and became the Postal Service.

Walter Hickel was Nixon's first secretary of the Interior Department. The appointment of the former Alaska governor, who had been campaign director of the western states, made environmentalists nervous because he had not been much of a friend in the past. He turned out to be not only an environmentalist but also the most rebellious member of the cabinet. Fired by an exasperated Nixon in 1970, he was replaced by Rogers Morton, a Republican congressman from Maryland.

Clifford Hardin of the University of Nebraska became secretary of agriculture. Early in 1972, he was succeeded by Earl Butz, who, according to one of Nixon's headhunters, was "as close to a John Connally of Agriculture as can be found."[21]

Maurice Stans, who had been budget director in the Eisenhower administration, became secretary of commerce. Stans, whom Nixon decided in 1970 "never will be great," resigned in 1972 to manage fund-raising for the 1972 campaign.[22] Peter G. Peterson, the assistant to the president for international economic affairs, replaced Stans. Peterson's successor was Harry Dent, originally Nixon's chief southern expert in the White House, who had begun working on the 1972 campaign early in the first administration.

George Shultz, an economist from the University of Chicago who headed Nixon's Labor Department, had to cut short his stay at the prestigious think tank the Center for Advanced Study in the Behavioral Sciences to move to Washington. His influence increased in 1970 after he left Labor to take over the Office of Management and Budget (OMB). James D. Hodgson replaced him, only to be succeeded by Peter Brennan, head of the New York construction workers, in 1973.

Only three Nixon intimates were in the cabinet: Mitchell, Rogers, and Robert Finch, a liberal California Republican who was his first secretary of HEW. Finch arrived at HEW brimming with confidence: "I was the fair-haired boy. I could have whatever I wanted. I was convinced . . . that the budget of HEW was going to get larger and larger. . . . I wanted to be where the action was."[23] Almost from the start, he came into conflict with the Justice Department and the White House over desegregation in the schools. Disillusioned and physically and emotionally crushed, he left HEW in 1970, kicked "upstairs" to serve briefly as a White House counselor. Elliot Richardson, who replaced him, lasted at HEW until 1973, when he was succeeded by Caspar Weinberger.

Two other liberal Republicans, Governor George Romney of Michigan and Governor John Volpe of Massachusetts, headed HUD and Transportation, respectively. Both were strong personalities who fought hard for departments that Nixon hoped to shrink, if not dismantle entirely. The president did not care for either man, especially since they made incessant demands to see him in person to lobby for their departments. Frustrated by his inability to gain an audience with the president, Volpe once went to a White House prayer service and, as Nixon shook his hand, took out a three-by-five card and began explaining his agenda. Romney, along with several other secretaries who found themselves ignored by the president, organized unofficial rump cabinet meetings in a "Cabinet cabal."[24]

Considering Romney and Volpe "seriously juvenile types," Nixon would have fired them early in his term, but he had a difficult time firing anybody, especially when etiquette demanded a face-to-face meeting.[25] They finally received their pink slips early in the second administration; the undersecretary of commerce, James Lynn, took over from Romney at HUD, and Claude Brinegar, an oil company executive, assumed Volpe's post at Transportation.

Several department heads, including Mitchell, Volpe, and Stans, took up residence at the new and fashionable Watergate apartment complex, where they joined Nixon aides Arthur Burns, Robert Dole, Pat Buchanan, protocol chief Emil Mosbacher, and Rose Mary Woods, as well as Anna Chennault.

During his more than five years in office, Nixon appointed thirty cabinet heads. That number broke the old record held by Ulysses S. Grant of twenty-six appointments in eight years. Of course, Grant worked with fewer departments than Nixon. In addition, prior to Nixon, the median length of tenure for cabinet officials had been forty months. For him, it was eighteen.

The original Nixon cabinet also broke the modern record for the fewest number of secretaries from the Ivy League, with Shultz, a Princeton man, the only one with that distinction. This was not just a coincidence. Nixon bore a special animus to the East Coast establishment, of which he was not a part. On one occasion in early 1970, he specifically told his aides not to hire anyone from the Ivy League but to concentrate on graduates from schools such as Southern California, California, UCLA, and Stanford and comparable universities in the Midwest and the South. The old last-string Whittier College football player particularly resented those who "were on teams together playing those frilly games—squash, crew."[26] But he could not resist the Ivy League for long. By 1973, he had hired cabinet secretaries Richardson, Kleindienst, Schlesinger, Lynn, and Weinberger, as well as Kissinger, OMB chief Roy Ash, personnel director

Frederick Malek, and special prosecutor Archibald Cox, all of whom had attended Harvard.

On 11 December 1968, Nixon broke with precedent, as was his wont, to present the entire cabinet and their families to the nation. Presidents usually announced secretarial appointments one or two at a time, often not until the administration was well under way in late January or early February. According to two respected conservative journalists, the cabinet as originally assembled that December was "perhaps the least distinguished in the postwar era," a product of being "selected without pattern or theme, first laboriously and finally in haste."[27] Other commentators were pleased with the cabinet's apparent ideological diversity, at least in terms of the political spectrum within the Republican Party. If anything, moderates generally headed the key departments.

Nixon made many selections on the basis of politics rather than competence, ideology, or loyalty. He did not even know three of his appointees: Shultz, Kennedy, and Hardin. The more he became acquainted with his cabinet, the less he liked the entire institution. At first, he met with the cabinet on a regular basis every other Friday for two hours. Soon bored by these meetings, preferring memos to discussions of weighty issues in person, and distressed with the lack of progress for his departmental programs, he ended up holding only a dozen cabinet meetings in 1969, most of which were perfunctory. In addition, the number of cabinet secretaries and cabinet-level officials who had to attend the meetings made them rather ungainly, compared with more intimate cabinet meetings in the twenties or even during Eisenhower's tenure.

By the middle of 1969, Nixon had begun to rethink his approach to the cabinet. Weighing heavily in that process was the slow pace of progress on his legislative program. Nixon confronted an iron triangle of bureaucrats, lobbyists, and members of Congress who together could alter or sabotage programs to streamline the departments or legislation emanating from them. Of most concern was the permanent bureaucracy, many of whom were liberals or Democrats. From the start of his administration, he set out to seed the bureaucracy with more Republicans. According to one survey, 40 percent of high-level career executives in 1969 were Democratic, 45 percent independent, and only 15 percent Republican. By 1976, the Democratic number had dropped to about 24 percent, while the number of independents had increased to 53 percent and Republicans to 24 percent.

His staff became more skillful at recruiting Republican loyalists when Fred Malek, who had impressed the White House with his hiring procedures as deputy undersecretary at HEW, replaced Harry Flemming as the chief White House appointments officer in 1970. He demonstrated his effectiveness by targeting sixty-two appointees for removal in November

1970, seventeen of whom came from HEW, and finding replacements for forty-two by March 1971. All the same, three months later, Nixon complained, "We've checked and found that 96 percent of the bureaucracy are against us; they're bastards who are here to screw us."[28]

No matter the political persuasion of the new department heads, most of them and their immediate aides became co-opted by the permanent bureaucracy, without which they could not run their fiefdoms. Powerful allies in Congress defended "their" officials against White House retribution. In addition, in an administration full of entrepreneurs vying for funds and programs, secretaries would naturally associate their progress with the progress of their departments. As Kissinger described the scene, "The administration turned into an array of baronies presided over by feudal lords protecting their turf as best they could against the inroads of a central authority that sallied forth periodically from its fortress manned by retainers zealous to assert their power."[29] For his part, Nixon complained that Washington "is a place where every morning 300,000 people drive to work, have a cup of coffee, then start writing memos to each other. No wonder the damn town won't work."[30]

Aside from the bureaucrats, well-heeled lobbyists, who worked for institutions dependent on the programs of one department or another, and powerful legislators on relevant committees, who developed their own cozy relationships with favorite departments, made it difficult for any president, particularly a Republican president, to change the way departments and agencies operated.

For these reasons, before the end of his first year in office, Nixon had shifted so much of the policy making and implementation to the White House staff that virtually a new cabinet developed, one that did not have to be approved by Congress or even appear before Congress to explain policy. There is some irony in this development, since Nixon had been one of those who opposed Eisenhower's 1959 proposal to create unofficial positions of vice presidents for domestic and foreign affairs in the White House to coordinate policy. But that is exactly what happened in his administration—first with Kissinger for foreign policy, and then with Ehrlichman for domestic policy—with Haldeman, another super vice president, supervising the entire operation.

As the White House weakened the power of the departments, Nixon's chief of staff became more important. Haldeman, whose father had been one of the contributors to the famous California "fund," had begun working for Nixon during the 1956 campaign. A successful advertising executive with the J. Walter Thompson agency and a member of Mensa (the society for people with high IQs), Haldeman explained that "every President needs a son of a bitch, and I'm Nixon's. I'm his buffer, I'm his bastard."[31] Something of a political eunuch who rarely pushed a program or idea of his own, he shielded Nixon from having to make small talk with people from the vice president to department heads, and he was the only White House aide authorized to wake up the president at night. He screened visitors and memos both to save the president's precious time and to avert "a real danger of some advocate of an idea rushing in to the President . . . and artfully managing to convince [him] in a burst of emotion or argument."[32] Haldeman also protected Nixon from himself, often ignoring irrational requests made by the volatile president in a fit of pique. Five months into his first term, Nixon, who understood this important activity, asked Haldeman to begin providing him with an action list, especially actions he had ordered that were not carried out because they were "unreasonable or unattainable."[33]

The first White House chief of staff since the Eisenhower years, Haldeman admitted, "I was tough because I had to be tough."[34] He was a demanding boss for White House staffers, who always seemed to be in crisis created in part by Haldeman's—and Nixon's—demands for things to be done at once. "The place had a structure," recalled one aide, "had a way of doing things and had a follow-up system that was beyond belief." One always felt a "sense of urgency"; the staff was "uptight as hell."[35]

Haldeman was responsible for changing the title of the president's key aides from the Johnson era's special assistant to the president to just assistant to the president, since he did not know what "special" meant. Haldeman, whom most considered humorless, once explained that he always initialed his documents with only an "H" because HRH (His Royal Highness) might have given people the wrong impression.

Reflecting on Haldeman's powerful role after he left the presidency, Nixon confided, "You know, if I had it to do over again, I would never let a guy position himself between me and the staff people the way I permitted Bob to do. . . . I allowed him to isolate me."[36] But Nixon needed someone like Haldeman, because he had limited administrative ability and did not have the temperament to make the tough personnel decisions. Moreover, Haldeman's rejection of the isolation charge is correct; through memos and carefully screened and timed meetings, he made certain that Nixon heard all sides of the issues. It was Nixon's idea, not Haldeman's, to secrete himself in an office in the Executive Office Building (EOB) adjacent to the White House, where he spent sizable portions of his workday considering policy options accompanied only by his ubiquitous yellow legal pads. "The fact is," noted Ehrlichman, "he was down under his desk saying 'I don't want to see those fellows,' and we were trying to pull him out."[37]

Haldeman's imperious manner rubbed many in the White House, in government, and especially in Congress the wrong way. He certainly did not get along with Rose Mary Woods, who soon found her access to the president diminished. Nixon himself may have had something to do with her "demotion," because he could not be bothered by the small matters she insisted on bringing to his attention.

John Ehrlichman came on board in 1969 as a White House counsel. He became assistant to the president for domestic affairs in November, and by July 1970, when Nixon appointed him executive director of the Domestic Affairs Council, he had emerged as the second most powerful White House operative in domestic politics. A Seattle land-use lawyer who had known fellow Christian Scientist Haldeman from campus politics days at UCLA (Haldeman had managed one of Jeanne Ehrlichman's campaigns), Ehrlichman began working for Nixon in 1960 as a spy in another Republican's camp. Close to being a "closet liberal," he was particularly responsible for Nixon's progressive policies on the environment and Native Americans.[38]

Like Haldeman, he was a no-nonsense, demanding boss who worked long hours at a frenetic pace. On one occasion, when he snuck away for a rare bit of recreation at The Greenbrier in nearby West Virginia, Ehrlichman instructed White House operators to put the president's calls through but not to tell Nixon that he "was out of town."[39] He almost did not accept Nixon's offer to join the administration after the 1968 election. Troubled by Nixon's drinking, he extracted a promise from the president-elect that he would do no heavy drinking while president.

Despite their friendship, Haldeman was Ehrlichman's superior. Like everyone else on staff except for Henry Kissinger and later Charles Colson, Ehrlichman had to go through the "doorkeeper" Haldeman to see the president. Nonetheless, Haldeman and Ehrlichman worked as a team, with their crew cuts, short tempers, and imperious demeanors. Journalists called them the "Germans" or the "Berlin Wall," and their staffs were the "Katzenjammer Kids." Sometimes Kissinger was included as part of the "Teutonic Trio" that shielded the president from his critics. Haldeman's family background was more Swiss than German, Ehrlichman's paternal grandfather was an Austrian Jew, and Kissinger was a German Jew. Haldeman's and Ehrlichman's "high performance standards," according to one of their aides, were "more intense than in any organization" he had ever seen and may have led to Watergate.[40] The White House ombudsman, journalist Clark Mollenhoff, quit his unique post after a year because of the "obsessive secrecy" and "atmosphere of totalitarianism" in the White House.[41] He was not replaced—his duties were assigned to young White House counsel John Dean.

The White House did not lighten up much after Haldeman resigned in April 1973. His replacement, General Alexander Haig, was, according to

Nixon, "the meanest, toughest, most ambitious son of a bitch I ever knew."[42] On one occasion, when a telephone operator connected a senator directly to Nixon without going through Haig, the chief of staff exploded, "I run this White House and don't you forget it! Don't *ever* let that happen again! *I* run this White House."[43]

At the start of the administration, however, before Nixon demanded more structure, a tighter ship, and a better legislative performance, White House operations were more freewheeling. This was due in good measure to Nixon's appointment of two domestic advisers, Arthur F. Burns and Daniel Patrick Moynihan, who seemed to have as much influence and relative power as Haldeman and Ehrlichman. Nixon gave a reluctant Burns, a distinguished economist who had been head of Eisenhower's Council of Economic Advisors (CEA), the title of first counselor to the president, a cabinet-ranking position. Burns had impressed Nixon when he, along with Professor Martin Anderson, who also joined the administration, directed the domestic task forces during the transition period.

The conservative Burns was balanced by Moynihan, a former Johnson aide and Harvard professor who had recently begun to criticize big-government approaches to social problems. Moynihan wondered, "How could I, a lifelong Democrat, direct domestic policy in a Republican administration? . . . But how could I refuse to try?" He contended that "we may have well been the most progressive administration on domestic issues that had ever been formed."[44] Though exaggerated, such an evaluation was not that far off the mark, especially for a Republican administration, with the economic team centrist to right of center and the human services team slightly left of center.

Initially, Nixon enjoyed the adversarial relationship that predictably developed between Burns and Moynihan, but he ultimately tired of their bickering and bureaucratic infighting. Moynihan had an advantage, since Nixon, while respecting Burns, dreaded having to meet with him because of his pedantic style. Haldeman finally had to limit Burns to one thirty-minute meeting a week with the president.

In contrast, Nixon enjoyed talking about philosophy to the witty and erudite Moynihan, whom a critic labeled "the consummate courtier."[45] It was Moynihan who first suggested that Nixon read Robert Blake's biography of Disraeli because, he contended, the president bore a resemblance to that great British conservative reformer. The president exclaimed on one occasion, "My God, four minutes with Pat is worth four hours of Arthur Burns."[46]

Moynihan and Burns clashed over the major domestic policies being fashioned in the White House during 1969; their conflict was one of the reasons why the administration's programs developed so slowly. After less than six months had gone by, Haldeman agreed with Moynihan that "the principal problem is, of course, Arthur Burns; but I don't think that's the only problem."[47] Nixon was more than happy to appoint Burns the chair of the Federal Reserve Board when William McChesney Martin announced his resignation in October 1969. Moynihan, whose own influence dramatically diminished when Ehrlichman took over the Domestic Council, resigned at the end of 1970, leaving Nixon without the intellectual sparring partner and irreverent Democratic Party gossiper he so enjoyed.

In November 1969, Nixon hired Charles Colson, a conservative Massachusetts lawyer who had worked on his campaign, to beef up public relations. Over the next year and a half, Colson's importance increased to a point where he boasted, "I was the only guy on the whole White House staff that could walk into the President's office without Haldeman's OK."[48] He often was the last aide Nixon saw each night. Unlike Ehrlichman and Haldeman, Colson was the one adviser who attempted to carry out just about every presidential request, no matter how irrational or unwise. He was a tough political operative who promised in 1972 that he "would walk over my grandmother if necessary" to get Nixon elected.[49] A self-described "generalist trouble shooter," he was White House liaison to organized constituency groups such as the Chamber of Commerce and military organizations, an expert on the media and broadcasting law, and a link to organized labor.[50] To colleague Jeb Stuart Magruder, he was an "evil genius."[51] Colson employed a staff of twenty-three for his projects.

The Nixon administration was the first to delegate full-time staffers to constituency groups from the business, military, and ethnic communities. For example, holding the portfolio for the Native American, Jewish, and artistic communities, among other portfolios, was Nixon's liberal law partner Leonard Garment. The president considered this innovation a necessity to put pressure on a Democratic Congress reluctant to accept his legislative program.

His key liaison to Congress was Bryce Harlow, an old Washington insider who had worked in the Eisenhower administration and as a lobbyist for Procter and Gamble. Legislators respected the experienced and personable Harlow. He came into conflict with other staffers, who often ignored him and marched up to Capitol Hill to ruffle congressional feathers in what he called "anarchy revisited."[52] After resigning in December 1970, he returned to the White House in 1973 to help out during the Watergate crisis.

Harlow's problems with the White House staff reflected the fact that only seven of the twenty-eight key aides in 1969 had previous government experience. Legislators preferred the older, more experienced, and more congenial Harlow, Burns, and Director of Communications Herb Klein to the younger, more insecure, and often pompous staffers. Many of those young men—and they were virtually all men—had come from advertising backgrounds and had worked on public relations for candidate Nixon. Although Johnson had brought public-opinion analysts to the White House and was obsessed with his image, Nixon was the first to develop a full-fledged public-relations unit. His flacks devoted enormous energies to public-relations projects, convinced from the start that the media did not report the administration's accomplishments fairly.

Because Nixon and Haldeman did not want Klein, who got along all too well with the media, to serve as press secretary, they invented a new post for him, director of communications. The press secretary, Ronald L. Ziegler (initially designated a "press assistant"), had been one of Haldeman's J. Walter Thompson advertising protégés. Haldeman's other protégés included Larry Higby, Kenneth Cole, and Bruce Kehrli, who worked on his staff, and appointments secretary Dwight Chapin. Derisive journalists called these and the other energetic, eager, straitlaced young men who constituted most of the senior staff and who cut their hair short and wore conservative white shirts the "Beaver Patrol."

The appointment of Ziegler, a twenty-nine-year-old political novice, to this heretofore important position was another indication of the administration's contempt for the press. Kept on a very short leash and often out of the information-policy loop, the obedient Ziegler was little more than "a ventriloquist's dummy," according to Magruder, who became head of public relations by the end of 1969.[53] Ziegler came to play a much more important role during the Watergate crisis, when he and Haig were virtually the only private confidants Nixon had.

A highly skilled speechwriting team worked with the public-relations people. Nixon employed speechwriters for every occasion—from the feisty conservative journalist Pat Buchanan, a master of alliteration, to the relatively liberal former public-relations man and future wordsmith William Safire. Somewhere in between were moderates David Gergen and Raymond Price. Filling out the team were Ken Kachigian, Lee Huebner, and, in 1974, a Jesuit priest who later became a television personality, Father John McLaughlin. Nixon prided himself on his own speechwriting abilities—few of the speeches prepared for him escaped his editorial supervision. Many of the speechwriters met with the media people twice a day, at 10 A.M. and at 5 P.M., to plan the day's public-relations activities. The times for these meetings coincided with press deadlines.

Harry Dent, the operative responsible for the southern strategy during the campaign and a former aide to Senator Thurmond, was the chief White House political strategist. In 1970, Murray Chotiner, Nixon's old political adviser, joined the growing political team, but in a sub-rosa capacity because of his seamy reputation. By that time, Colson had become more involved in direct political action for the president as well.

The White House Advance Office was another Nixon innovation. Mostly volunteers from businesses and law firms, as many as a thousand Republican Party members were on call to help the president and his entourage on trips around the country. In general, their companies paid their expenses, except during the 1972 campaign.

During Nixon's first two years, the White House senior staff increased from 39 in 1969 to 70 in 1970. The White House staff itself increased from 341 in 1969 to 528 by 1973. Although these increases seem dramatic, expansion was greater (proportionally) during periods in the Truman, Eisenhower, and Johnson administrations. The executive bureaucracy grew through reorganization from four agencies with 570 people in 1969 to twenty agencies employing more than 6,000 in 1972, the year that Nixon began talking about cutting back the growth of government in his as well as in every other bailiwick.

Nixon constantly reorganized the White House, hoping to address new problems or crises through changes in institutional arrangements. Few administrations in history match his for periodic wholesale reorganization. It was far easier to reorganize the White House, through initiatives that did not need the approval of Capitol Hill, than to pass legislation through the Democratic Congress or restructure departments and agencies.

Plans to reorganize the government had begun during the interregnum, with president of the Itek Corporation Frank Lindsay's task force on the organization of the executive branch. Lindsay's report led to the formation of the President's Advisory Council on Executive Reorganization, headed by Roy L. Ash, who ran Litton Industries. The Ash council became one of the most important of all the many presidential reorganization committees.

In 1970, Nixon had adopted the council's Reorganization Plan 2 as the basis for his first major executive branch reorganization. The reorganization followed a corporate model that arranged positions by functional and horizontal, not vertical, lines. The earlier Hoover commissions under Truman and Eisenhower had also suggested more of a functional structure. In addition, the council encouraged streamlining, for example, when it discovered that almost fifty officials theoretically reported directly to the president in 1969. Tidying up and simplifying structure pleased Nixon, who wanted to rearrange the government in ways "that would enhance his power without demanding his time."[54]

Ash himself, who became head of a beefed-up OMB in 1973, played an important role in domestic policy during the last year of the administration, when much of the White House was tied up with Watergate. In addition, through his work as a member of the Ash council, John Connally further recommended himself to Nixon as a forceful and bold leader.

During his first week in office, Nixon formed two new White House committees: the Urban Affairs Council (UAC) and the Cabinet Committee on Economic Policy (CCEP). The UAC, headed by Moynihan, attempted to bring together cabinet members with common interests in ten White House domestic affairs committees. The CCEP included the vice president; the secretaries of labor, agriculture, and treasury; the director of the Bureau of the Budget; the head of the CEA; and Arthur Burns. Nixon also introduced the Quadriad, a much smaller and far more important economic committee composed of the secretary of the treasury, the head of the CEA, the chair of the Federal Reserve, and the head of the Bureau of the Budget.

Disappointed with his cabinet, Nixon transformed the weak UAC into the Domestic Council in March 1970. Its members included the vice president; the secretaries of treasury, interior, agriculture, commerce, HEW, labor, HUD, and transportation; the attorney general; the director of the Office of Economic Opportunity (OEO); and the postmaster general, while he held cabinet rank. Ehrlichman, the executive director of the council, changed its name from the Domestic Policy Council, having concluded that "policy" narrowed its mandate. The full council met only twenty-two times in six and a half years; the real work went on within the White House in eight committees staffed mostly by White House aides, even though Nixon originally proposed the hiring of a professional staff. A disappointed Pat Buchanan considered the aides "ex-advancemen, managers, and technicians" who were "pragmatists," not true believers in conservatism.[55] Whatever they were, their powers were enhanced as they moved from coordinators and facilitators to real decision makers not subject to congressional oversight.

The council's committees—which dealt with drugs, crime, urban development, health, education, youth, civil rights, and the environment—had twenty to twenty-five working groups in existence at any one time. In some ways, the Domestic Council resembled the NSC, vesting control of domestic policy firmly in the White House. The departments were not totally left out of the operation, however; the White House staff recruited officials from relevant departments, identified as sympathetic to the administration, to participate in the working groups. Through this procedure, Nixon's aides could outflank department bureaucrats who were not always enthusiastic about White House proposals.

The second and even more important reform that Nixon announced in March 1970 transformed the Bureau of the Budget to the OMB. Instead of just clearing all budgets except those of the Central Intelligence Agency (CIA) and Defense before they were sent to Congress, the OMB would be concerned with policy and operations management. This was another way for the White House to exert more control over the departments. On paper, the OMB appeared to be an even more powerful institution than the Domestic Council, as could be seen when George Shultz left the Labor Department to become head of OMB. But as long as John Ehrlichman ran the Domestic Council, it maintained its preeminence. Following Ehrlichman's resignation in 1973, the head of OMB, Roy Ash, and the head of the Domestic Council, Ken Cole, clashed over policy and turf issues.

Despite numerous other attempts to reform, rationalize, and streamline, Nixon's White House never really ran smoothly. In August 1971, Colson complained about the "backbiting" in the staff. "There is an awful lot of grumbling. The Domestic Council people feel that we are running with a bedraggled, mammoth public relations apparatus. Everybody on the other side of the fence bitches at the Domestic Council. The Congressional Relations staff are convinced that no one around here understands politics. I have the Klein problem, as you know; Buchanan's morale is bad, highly critical of everyone . . . ; Safire has been grumbling; there's a real bitter feeling between Connally and Shultz. . . . This is not a really upbeat team kind of spirit."[56]

Colson was commenting only about the domestic operations of the White House. White House foreign operations presented an even more devastating picture of bitter rivalry, secret cabals, pernicious leaks to the media, and nasty ad hominem attacks. Of all Nixon's reorganizations, the most important though least heralded at the time involved the restructuring of the NSC and the consequent diminution of the State Department, the CIA, and the Defense Department. Under Kennedy and Johnson, the president's assistants for national security affairs, McGeorge Bundy and Walt Whitman Rostow, had gradually increased their role from coordinators, as the assistants had been under Truman and Eisenhower, to proactive participants in the policy-making process. But few within the Beltway were prepared for the way in which Henry Kissinger, Nixon's national security adviser, became not only the president's chief planner, coordinator, and operator of U.S. foreign policy but also the most popular, respected, and internationally famous of all the president's advisers.

A Jewish émigré from Nazi Germany, Kissinger became a prominent Harvard political scientist in the 1950s. Several of his books that dealt with nuclear weapons and international relations attracted the attention of experts and officials beyond the academy. In addition, Kissinger participated actively in the Council on Foreign Relations, where he met the elite of the American foreign policy establishment. Although serving as an occasional consultant to the Kennedy and Johnson administrations (including undertaking several informal diplomatic missions), he was best known in the 1960s as the chief foreign policy adviser for Nixon's Republican Party rival Nelson Rockefeller. Kissinger admitted to "hat[ing] Nixon for years," having concluded that he was "paranoic" and the "most dangerous of all the men running to have as president."[57] As late as 1969, Rockefeller retained Kissinger on his payroll, presenting him with a "retirement" bonus of $50,000.

Nixon had once met Kissinger at a party and had read some of his articles and books in which the professor argued for the tough, realistic foreign policy Nixon was planning to institute. Impressed that Kissinger was Rockefeller's intellectual, the president-elect was also grateful to him for providing valuable intelligence from the Johnson administration and the Humphrey camp while he was presumably supporting the election of the vice president. John Mitchell claimed that "Henry's information was basic. We were getting all of our information from him."[58]

Kissinger had no idea of his future role when he met Nixon at the Hotel Pierre on 25 November 1968. Although the president-elect decided on the spot to offer Kissinger the job of the president's adviser for national security affairs, Nixon had always had a difficult time hiring and firing people, perhaps because of his lifelong fear of rejection. It was not until their second meeting on 27 November that he told Kissinger about his appointment. When introducing his new NSC adviser to the press on 2 December, Nixon emphasized his intention to select a strong secretary of state and that Kissinger would be involved in long-range planning, not tactical activities. Kissinger then promised that he would not be appearing much in public. Nixon might not have known what was going to happen to the NSC when he announced the Kissinger appointment, but he did know that he was going to be his own secretary of state.

General Andrew Goodpaster, an influential Eisenhower staffer with expertise in national security matters, helped Kissinger's Harvard colleague, Morton Halperin, prepare the document restructuring the NSC, which Nixon approved before the year was out. Goodpaster and Halperin hoped to refine the Eisenhower administration's NSC decision-making procedures, which had often resulted in weak "bureaucratic compromise," to provide a mechanism to ensure that the president would be confronted with real policy alternatives.[59]

Nixon's most important NSC structural change abolished the Senior Interdepartmental Group that heretofore had been headed by the State Department. In addition, at the start, Kissinger planned to eliminate the CIA from playing a meaningful role in NSC deliberations, believing that the agency should not be involved in advocating policy. Secretary of Defense Laird fought successfully to ensure that the intelligence agency would retain its previous status.

Under the new procedures, State Department assistant secretaries chaired interdepartmental groups, but those groups were responsible to a review group chaired by Kissinger. An undersecretary's committee also reported directly to Kissinger. Working with Nixon, Kissinger would charge those groups, which included an NSC staffer, with preparing a national security study memorandum (NSSM), which would then be reviewed by Kissinger's group and, when acceptable, sent on to the NSC. On many occasions, since the NSC staff had already made up its mind about an NSSM, the full NSC meeting was "theatre," often resembling a Nixon cabinet meeting.[60] (Over time, as with the cabinet, the number of NSC meetings declined dramatically.) After NSC discussion, the NSSM went to the president with a cover memo from Kissinger—a memo that no one else ever saw—and out of this procedure came an official policy paper, a national security decision memorandum (NSDM). Nixon issued approximately 250 NSDMs during his tenure.

This elaborate NSC process did not come into play for such closely held policies as the overture to China, Vietnam peacemaking, and the economic decisions of the summer of 1971. If a policy needed bureaucratic support, it was likely to involve the NSC system. Kissinger also changed his formal title from the president's adviser for national security to the special assistant to the president for national security affairs in NSDM-2, signed by Nixon on 19 January 1969. Shortly thereafter he had his office moved from the White House basement to the first floor of the West Wing.

By removing the State Department from a major leadership role in the NSC, the president hoped to avoid the conflicts between State and Defense that had been endemic under the old system.[61] Nixon also found the State Department too stodgy, noting that if it "has had a new idea in the last twenty-five years, it is not known to me."[62] Above all, by centering foreign policy in the White House, Nixon would have an easier time maintaining secrecy. According to Al Haig, Kissinger's most trusted NSC aide, the foreign policy bureaucracy, penetrated by a "pervasive press corps," was "unable to maintain security" and thus "leaked like a sieve." Haig maintains that there might not have been the opening to China, arms-control agreements, and other Nixon foreign policy triumphs had the bureaucracy been involved in decision making.[63] The White House assumed control over the foreign policy process with the promulgation of NSDM-2, which, among other things, empowered Kissinger to request information from relevant agencies.

Over time, Kissinger also organized and chaired the Verification Panel, dealing with arms control; the Washington Special Action Group, in charge of crisis operations; the Vietnam Special Studies Group; the 40 Committee, which monitored White House–organized covert activities; and the Defense Program Review Committee. Not surprisingly, the busy NSC expanded rapidly, roughly doubling in size from twenty-eight staffers in 1969 to fifty-two in 1971, while its budget increased from $700,000 in 1968 to $2.2 million in 1971. Organized into regional and functional departments, it resembled a miniature State Department.

Of the twenty-eight original members of what Kissinger called "the most brilliant National Security staff in history," only seven remained by the summer of 1971.[64] Kissinger personally handpicked his staff from other departments and from the academy. Some staffers resigned over policy disputes, but most who left were frustrated with Kissinger's chaotic and tyrannical administrative style, his volcanic temper, and their frequent lack of access to the principals. It proved difficult for Kissinger to be at Nixon's beck and call, to serve as a diplomat, and to oversee his growing and ever more complex operation. Nevertheless, proud of the quality of Kissinger's staff, Nixon wanted to outfit the NSC with blue blazers with a special emblem.

Kissinger's NSC fought vigorously to protect its influence and power against rivals in the White House and the departments. A malicious gossip, Kissinger endeared himself to liberal newspeople and the so-called Georgetown set by leaking material favorable to himself. For example, he convinced much of Washington that he was a lone dove among hawks. One State Department press aide observed admiringly that Kissinger "turned the use of the press by a public official into an art form."[65]

Loyal to a fault, even obsequious in front of Nixon, Kissinger let assistants listen in on phone calls from what he called our "meatball president," as well as from the "fanatics" Haldeman and Ehrlichman. The tables were turned when he listened to wiretaps he had ordered for some of his assistants in 1969, causing him to exclaim, "It is clear that I don't have anybody in my office I can trust except Colonel Haig."[66] That last remark is ironic in light of the bitter rivalry that developed between Kissinger and his former protégé when Haig replaced Haldeman in 1973. But in 1969 and 1970, he desperately depended on the efficient Haig, who one critic saw as playing "Stalin to Henry's Lenin," to organize his chaotic office.[67]

Kissinger's biggest problem was his relationship with Secretary of State Rogers, who naturally became jealous as he began to lose turf to the ambitious and skilled bureaucratic infighter at the NSC. Nixon, who understood the conflict, sometimes had to serve as a mediator. He knew that Rogers felt that Kissinger was "Machiavellian, deceitful, egotistical, arrogant, and insulting" and that Kissinger considered Rogers "vain, emotional, unable to keep a secret, and hopelessly dominated by the State Department bureaucracy."[68]

In the end, Nixon's support generally went to Kissinger rather than to his old friend, because Kissinger was only following his instructions to direct foreign policy from the White House. Undersecretary of State for Political Affairs U. Alexis Johnson complained, "The President and Kissinger never lost an opportunity to humiliate and degrade Bill Rogers."[69] Nixon later admitted that his treatment of Rogers had been "terrible."[70] The president told his staff that he did not want foreign policy run "by the striped-pants faggots in Foggy Bottom."[71] When calling for the appointment of Adolph W. Schmidt as ambassador to Canada, he scribbled on a letter, "*Don't* send a career jerk to Canada."[72] Not to be outdone, Kissinger railed against the "moronic bastards" and "goddam anti-Semites" in the State Department.[73] Over at State, career diplomat Johnson was surprised at "how dense" many of the administration's ambassadorial appointments were.[74]

With the president's approval, Kissinger established back-channel meetings with the Soviet ambassador, instructed the Paris peace talk negotiators, drafted Nixon's instructions for Rogers, secretly approved many of Rogers's appointments, and generally kept the secretary uninformed about most of the White House's major foreign policy enterprises. Kissinger even used translators provided by foreign officials rather than State Department translators to keep Rogers in the dark about his activities. Kissinger admitted that by 1971, "To the credit of neither of us, my relations with Rogers had deteriorated to a point where they exacerbated our policy differences and endangered coherent policy."[75]

Although Kissinger's insults to the secretary of defense were not as egregious, he sometimes routed orders to the military without going through Laird's office. Laird struck back through an alliance with Noel Gayler, the head of the National Security Agency (NSA), who provided the Defense Department with many of Kissinger's back-channel messages.

The Joint Chiefs of Staff, also frozen out of decision making, maintained their own covert intelligence-gathering operation in the White House. In the fall of 1970, Navy Yeoman Charles Edward Radford, an aide to NSC liaison Rear Admiral Rembrandt C. Robinson, who in turn was a confidant of Chairman of the Joint Chiefs Admiral Thomas H. Moorer, began to photocopy classified White House documents on Moorer's orders. In over a year, Radford copied more than 5,000 documents. He boasted that he "took so darn much stuff I can't remember what it was."[76] Laird was cut out of this conspiratorial loop. The Chiefs contended that they needed the information to determine just what was going on in American foreign policy. Haig, claiming that the affair was "blown out of proportion," contends that departments always engage in internal espionage.[77]

When the White House investigated a leak that appeared in Jack Anderson's syndicated column during the Bangladesh crisis in December 1971, it uncovered the Radford-Moorer plot. Nixon later reported that this "potential time bomb" concerned him primarily because of the danger of leaks to the press, not necessarily because the Chiefs were purloining documents.[78] Radford and Moorer were not punished or exposed for their conspiracy, although Radford was transferred out of the White House. Nixon let Moorer know that he knew about the affair but was not going to make it public. Nixon thereby gained potential leverage over Moorer for the future. Moorer, however, still had one ace up his sleeve—the fact that the White House had been going behind the back of the secretary of defense to communicate directly with the Chiefs. This astonishing story did not become public until 1973 during the Watergate investigations.

Their practice of bypassing or circumventing officials in the foreign policy and defense bureaucracies denied Nixon and Kissinger valuable expertise and often led them to work at cross-purposes with their own agents. On occasion, the State Department's public positions on China, South Africa, Pakistan, Chile, Biafra, and Cyprus, for example, differed from those of the White House. More important, Nixon and Kissinger, with their relatively small staff, could not stay on top of all foreign policy issues. Could Nixon really digest the sixty-one NSSMs that he ordered during the first six months of 1969, one of which had a seventy-five-page summary alone? How could they juggle all the balls in September 1970 when confronting multiple crises in Jordan, Cuba, and Chile; a visit from Golda Meir; and Nixon's announcement of a new Vietnam peace plan? If one accepted the Nixon-Kissinger notion that there were only a handful of powers that really mattered in the international system, then perhaps the highly centralized system could work—at least most of the time.

Nixon bore a special animus toward the CIA, which he felt was "a refuge of Ivy League intellectuals opposed to him."[79] He still blamed the agency, particularly former director Allen Dulles, for not setting Kennedy straight when he had scored points in 1960 by decrying a missile gap. More generally, Nixon found the leaders of the CIA too liberal, too soft on the Soviet Union, and too much a part of the despised Georgetown set. He targeted the CIA director he had inherited, Richard Helms, for removal sometime in the future. For the short run, Nixon made certain that one of his loyalists, Lieutenant General Robert E. Cushman, was made deputy director, and he rarely if ever saw Helms alone. Helms frequently met with both Kissinger and Haig. When Nixon finally fired Helms early in 1973, he reaped some revenge on the agency when the new director, James Schlesinger, purged 7 percent of the staff in less than four months to become, as one CIA official commented, the "most unpopular director in the CIA's history."[80]

Surprisingly, Nixon encountered more problems with the FBI than with the CIA, despite the fact that he had enjoyed good relations with J. Edgar Hoover ever since the Hiss case. Lyndon Johnson told Nixon after the election, "If it hadn't been for Edgar Hoover, I couldn't have carried out my responsibilities as Commander in Chief. Period. Dick, you will come to depend on Edgar. . . . He's the only one you can put your complete trust in."[81]

Hoover demonstrated his trustworthiness when he sent Nixon thousands of files on his political enemies in 1969 and when he agreed to an administration request to wiretap journalists and NSC officials in the spring of 1969 after a story appeared in the *New York Times* about the secret bombing of Cambodia. In 1971, fearing that Hoover might misuse the illegal wiretaps for blackmail purposes, William Sullivan, third in command of the FBI and something of a White House mole within the bureau, turned the materials over to another Nixon loyalist in the Justice Department, Robert Mardian, who gave them to Ehrlichman.

The FBI had not always been so cooperative. When in 1969 Hoover refused to tap journalist Joseph Kraft's phone, Ehrlichman had to hire private investigators to do the work. Nixon was also disturbed about the Hoover-declared cold war that had existed between the FBI and CIA for years, which virtually precluded the agencies from cooperating. In addition, he was frustrated by what he considered the bureau's less than satisfactory efforts to curb domestic terrorism and monitor radical groups.

On 5 June 1970, Nixon arranged a meeting at the White House attended by Hoover, Helms, Gayler, Donald Bennett of the Defense Intelligence Agency, Haldeman, Ehrlichman, Finch, and a young White House lawyer, Tom Huston. At the meeting, according to one of the participants, "The President chewed our butts" and then appointed a special interagency committee on intelligence to be coordinated by Huston, with FBI liaison William Sullivan representing Hoover, the titular chair of the committee.[82] Huston, working closely with Sullivan, who was operating behind Hoover's back, came up with a secret plan to centralize intelligence in the White House, with the agencies receiving indirect presidential authorization to conduct illegal wiretaps, buggings, and break-ins. Nixon approved the Huston Plan on 23 July. Hoover, who hated Huston and considered him a "hippie intellectual," disassociated the FBI from those parts of the plan that he deemed illegal in footnoted reservations.[83] The FBI chief's unwillingness to accept the total plan caused Nixon to withdraw his approval several days later. Hoover fired Sullivan that fall.

Hoover opposed the plan not just because of personal animosity to Huston. He was reluctant to surrender so much of his agency's authority to the president, was worried that the media might discover the plan, and feared that the White House would involve the FBI in illegal activities. Since the mid-sixties, the agency, concerned about congressional investigations, had dropped its black-bag jobs and had become more circumspect in the employment of other extralegal or illegal procedures. Hoover told Attorney General John Mitchell directly that the FBI would agree to undertake illegal missions only on the written orders of the president. After listening to Hoover, Mitchell informed Nixon that the Huston Plan was too dangerous politically, especially if, as he suspected, Hoover leaked information about it to the media.

When the plan finally did become public knowledge in 1973, Nixon defended it as necessary to coordinate the war against violent radicals such as the Black Panthers. As for its possible illegality, he later asserted that when the president "approves an action because of national security, because of a threat to internal peace . . . the President's decision . . . is one that enables those who carry it out to carry it out without violating a law."[84] Huston himself claimed that he drafted his plan to enable the president to end the threat from radicals before other less scrupulous politicians demanded truly repressive activities or institutions. In reality, his prime motive, aside from hoping to become the Henry Kissinger for the intelligence services, was to invent a mechanism to circumvent the FBI.

But nothing was going to be accomplished on this front with Hoover at the FBI, contended Huston. "At some point Hoover has to be told who is president."[85] Nixon agreed, telling Ehrlichman in April 1971, "We've got to get him out of there."[86] Several months later, Mitchell asked Cartha DeLoach, the second in command at the FBI, "How can we get J. Edgar Hoover to leave office without him kicking over the traces."[87] Nixon and his aides finally decided to invite Hoover to a breakfast meeting at the White House on 20 September 1971 to discuss retirement. When Nixon mentioned retirement in general, Hoover replied coolly, "Why that's ridiculous. You're still a young man."[88] And that was the end of that, with Nixon telling his aides to "forget such a meeting ever took place."[89]

Hoover died on 2 May 1972, the same day that Nixon confidant Vernon Walters was sworn in as deputy director of the CIA. Nixon then appointed another loyalist, L. Patrick Gray, to be acting FBI director. Although it appeared in the spring of 1972 that Nixon finally had a handle on his intelligence agencies, even without the Huston Plan, the Gray appointment soon proved to be a drastic error. At the time, however, it represented the latest successful attempt to control the bureaucracy, a central theme in Nixon's approach to governing.

But that development was far in the future as the administration prepared to get down to business in January 1969. Nixon's prime order of business in 1969 and throughout his years in office would be foreign policy.

3

★ ★ ★ ★ ★

ENDING AMERICA'S
LONGEST WAR

Three years before he made his second run for the presidency, Nixon and Leonard Garment shared a room on a friend's estate. They talked through much of the night and, at one point, Nixon told his law partner that "his life had to be dedicated to great foreign policy purposes" because of his "pacifist mother's idealism" and the general "importance of foreign affairs."[1] Those who find much to admire in the Nixon presidency celebrate his foreign policy breakthroughs, which include opening relations with China, achieving détente with the Soviet Union, and ending the Vietnam War.

Nixon considered himself an expert in foreign affairs who would make his mark in history in that realm. A year before his election, he observed, "I've always thought this country could run itself domestically without a President. All you need is a competent Cabinet to run the country at home. You need a President for foreign policy; no Secretary of State is really important; the President makes foreign policy."[2] The stakes were much more serious in international affairs. He maintained that "the American economy is so strong it would take a genius to ruin it, whereas one small mistake in foreign policy could blow up the world."[3]

Two of Nixon's personal heroes, Theodore Roosevelt and Woodrow Wilson, were presidents who left their marks on the world through bold foreign policies. Both, he thought, were men of action and ideas who combined Old World realism and American idealism. He also admired the way Harry Truman had led the nation from dangerous isolationism to responsible internationalism during the early years of the cold war.

59

Nixon understood that a president enjoyed considerable freedom of action in international relations and that the chances of achieving successes there were far greater than in trying to resolve intractable domestic problems. Highlighting his preference for foreign affairs, Nixon broke existing presidential records by hosting 142 foreign leaders, many of whom he had encountered on unofficial fact-finding trips in the sixties. During his first two years in office alone, he met with forty-two heads of state on fifteen trips abroad.

When Nixon began to score successes in international affairs, many incredulous critics and inveterate Nixon haters, who underestimated the president's intelligence and sophistication, claimed that Henry Kissinger was the brilliant genius behind the throne running American foreign policy. One historian refers to the popular conception of "Nixinger" diplomacy, a suggestion of partnership that did not please Nixon, especially when Kissinger began to receive more favorable press than the president.[4] In reality, Kissinger, who in 1972 called himself the Lone Ranger of foreign affairs, was Tonto, a generally faithful assistant who knew what his boss wanted.[5] The following year, Kissinger explained, "Nixon doesn't really give me instructions. We simply meet at great length and work over what he likes to call 'the game plan.'"[6]

The relationship between the two was never one of equals, as Kissinger played the role of courtier at a very Byzantine court. Nixon reported that his volatile and sensitive adviser threatened to resign "maybe a half dozen times," a threat he made to Haig and Haldeman even more frequently.[7] Most of the time, Kissinger delivered such threats when he believed he was being undercut by the State Department. Complaining that both Kissinger and Secretary of State Rogers were "performing childishly," Nixon thought that his assistant for national security affairs needed a psychiatrist on at least one occasion.[8] On other occasions, Nixon came close to firing Kissinger for insubordination or disloyalty.

By the time he became president, Nixon had dropped a good deal of the ideological baggage of the early cold war years for a Realpolitik approach to foreign affairs in general and the communist bloc in particular. This approach permitted him to pursue systemic "stability over reform," an anathema to conservative supporters, who, in 1953, had hoped that Eisenhower and Nixon would "roll back" the Iron Curtain.[9] Kissinger, borrowing from Goethe, explained, "If I had to choose between justice and disorder, on the one hand, and injustice and order, on the other, I would always choose the latter."[10] Longtime Soviet foreign minister Andrei Gromyko considered the new Nixon "a pragmatist uninterested in the theoretical aspects of an issue."[11]

Nonetheless, Nixon understood that his old reputation as a hard-line ideologue could help him in several ways. First, he could more easily make deals with the Russians and even the Chinese because few Americans could question his anticommunist credentials. "Only Nixon Could Have" was one of the themes of his foreign policy breakthroughs.[12] In addition, Haldeman claims that Nixon intended to capitalize on his cold-warrior reputation by having aides tell foreign leaders that their boss was a "madman" who might act unreasonably if they were not more conciliatory—"I call it the Madman Theory, Bob. I want the North Vietnamese to believe that I've reached the point where I might do *anything* to stop the war."[13] Although Nixon himself did not remember the now legendary conversation with Haldeman, Kissinger reported that Nixon instructed him to tell foreign leaders, as a tactical ploy, "I'm trying to do this but I'm not sure I can get the old man to do it."[14] More to the point, Kissinger instructed Leonard Garment, before his visit to the Soviet Union in July 1969, to tell the Russians that his boss was "crazy," unpredictable, and brutal.[15] Nixon certainly was not crazy in 1969, but he did believe that "unpredictability" was a great asset for a diplomat, much as it was for a poker player.[16]

By 1969, Nixon had recognized the emergence of a new multipolar world order, marked by the American acceptance of nuclear parity with the Soviet Union and the rise of competing power centers in Europe, China, and Japan. In part, this was another example of the relative decline of the United States since the early cold war years. Not only had the nation lost its nuclear monopoly and invulnerability, but its geopolitical position, economic dominance, ability to project its military power, and, especially important for Nixon, national will had all weakened. Polls revealed the growing primacy of domestic over foreign issues and the concomitant public demand for less defense spending.

Aside from these problems, Congress was attempting to restore constitutional balance. As early as March 1969, the Senate Foreign Relations Committee approved a National Commitments Resolution that would have inhibited the president from freely sending American troops abroad in the absence of a declaration of war.

It was at this juncture that Nixon arrived on the scene to fashion an approach to diplomacy that would not only decrease congressional oversight but also decrease the control exercised by the public. He wanted to demonstrate that the president of the democratic United States could plan and execute foreign policy as covertly and, from his perspective, as effectively as historic leaders such as Metternich and Bismarck and contemporary leaders such as Leonid Brezhnev, Mao Zedong, and even Charles de Gaulle. In addition, through covert diplomacy, Nixon and Kissinger could pull off the daring big plays in international politics of which they were inordinately fond.

Above all, Nixon did not want it to appear that a shortsighted, unsophisticated, and narrow Congress, operating alone or in tandem with an irrational and uninformed mob in the streets, could dictate policy to the White House. He knew that many in Congress and among the public would have been disturbed to discover that he was prepared to jettison morality and idealism when dealing not only with right-wing dictators but with left-wing dictators as well. This need to play his diplomatic cards very close to his vest underlay Nixon's obsessive concerns about the media and leaks.

After only four months in office, the administration counted nineteen secret NSC decisions that had been reported in the *New York Times*. The CIA contended that in 1969, forty-five stories appeared in the media that threatened national security. But no matter what he tried, including legal and illegal wiretaps, surveillance, and lie-detector tests (sometimes conducted by intelligence agencies and sometimes by private White House investigators), Nixon could not plug all the leaks. As Robert Reich, President Bill Clinton's secretary of labor, later pointed out, "Every memorandum will leak. Every memorandum marked 'confidential' will leak faster."[17]

Nixon never jettisoned conventional morality and idealism in his public rhetoric on foreign policy. Neither Machiavelli nor Metternich could be found in his unique "State of the World" reports. For four years, Nixon presented to Congress a comprehensive inventory of accomplishments and goals for "U.S. Foreign Policy for the 1970's," patterned after the Department of Defense's annual posture statement and meant to parallel the State of the Union Address. "Peace" was the central theme in these reports, beginning with the first in February 1970, "A New Strategy for Peace," followed by "Building for Peace" in February 1971, "The Emerging Structure of Peace" in February 1972, and "Shaping a Durable Peace" in May 1973. Nixon and Kissinger thought that these reports, which often went through as many as twelve drafts, were important guides for the bureaucracy, the general public, and friends and foes alike. Although running more than 100 pages and full of boilerplate rhetoric, they contained new announcements and subtle hints of things to come, such as the 1971 report in which Nixon referred to the People's Republic of China instead of "Red China." Overall, especially after the first one, Nixon and Kissinger were disappointed in the limited attention paid to the reports by both the media and the public. Kissinger decided not to issue a world report for 1974, even though one was in the works.

Nixon used his first report to explain what has come to be called the Nixon Doctrine, a program that defined much of his new approach to foreign affairs. He had described this approach informally on 25 July 1969 in Guam, during a background meeting with reporters. There were even hints of it in his 1967 *Foreign Affairs* article, which many observers began to re-examine in 1969.[18] All the same, the new doctrine came as a surprise to the State Department and even to Kissinger, who had not expected Nixon to make it public in Guam.

As Nixon explained more formally on 18 February 1970, "America cannot—and will not—conceive *all* the plans, design *all* the programs, execute *all* the decisions, and undertake *all* the defense of the free nations of the world. We will help where it makes a real difference and is in our interests. . . . our interests must shape our commitments, rather than the other way around." He told a journalist that the doctrine was an "effort to withstand the present wave of new isolationism . . . with a revised policy of involvement."[19] This was quite a departure from John F. Kennedy's inaugural nine years earlier, when the president had promised to "pay any price, bear any burden, meet any hardship, support any friend, oppose any foe to assure the survival and success of liberty."

Recognizing the limits of American power as well as the limits of its national security interests, and reflecting the popular weariness with the long and inconclusive war in Vietnam, Nixon implied that the United States would no longer provide troops to any country in the Third World defending its system against communism. Although some countries and areas of the globe were more vital than others, Nixon never presented a priority list or an explicit set of circumstances under which the United States might intervene. He planned to rely on friends in different regions, such as the shah of Iran in the Middle East, who, armed with modern American weapons, could keep the peace in their areas. Not surprisingly, over the next few years, the Nixon Doctrine led to a dramatic increase in American arms transfers, continuing a project begun in the Kennedy administration, in part to improve the balance-of-payments problem. The decrease in global commitments envisioned in the Nixon Doctrine meant that the American military would have to prepare to fight only one and a half wars at the same time, rather than the previous goal of readiness for two and a half wars.

Nixon also introduced the idea of "linkage" politics, a term invented by Kissinger, for structuring relations with the communist powers. The United States would cooperate with its major antagonists on bilateral economic and strategic relations as long as they used their influence in other areas of the globe to maintain the status quo. Nixon wrote to Rogers, Laird, and Helms on 2 February 1969, "The great issues are fundamentally interrelated. . . . Crisis or confrontation in one place and real cooperation in another cannot be sustained simultaneously."[20] He and Kissinger tried to employ a form of "behavior modification" whereby Soviet cooperation in one region of the world would be rewarded with American cooperation in another region.[21]

Such a policy, which, at bottom, represented U.S. cold war orthodoxy, suggested that most anti-American activities in the world could somehow be controlled by the Soviet Union and its friends. The Nixon administration would interpret revolutions and other negative developments in the Third World as emanating from Moscow. Nixon assured his aides in early March 1970 that "I do care [about the Third World] but what happens in those parts of the world is not, in the final analysis going to have a significant effect on the success of our foreign policy in the foreseeable future."[22]

The State Department did not always see things Nixon's way; in turn, he believed that parochial and unimaginative desk officers failed to understand the relationship between their regions and larger cold war issues. On 23 January 1969, Kissinger sent out an NSSM asking the State, Defense, and Treasury Departments and the CIA to respond within a month to a long series of questions that would constitute an "inventory" of the international situation at that moment.[23]

State Department officials were not sold on the linkage concept. As one noted after examining a preliminary draft of State's European inventory, "NSC staff members may feel that the paper does not deal directly enough with the formulation used by the President linking missile talks with progress in political settlements, such as the Middle East."[24]

The State Department's skepticism about the concept was not unique. Soviet leaders never accepted it either, even though Nixon and Kissinger assumed that they understood the importance of cooperating with the United States around the globe, from the Middle East to Vietnam. One high-ranking Soviet diplomat reported that his bosses were "incensed at the linkage concept."[25] They did not have absolute control over their allies in the Third World, especially in Southeast Asia. This proved to be a crucial matter, since Nixon considered the negotiation of a speedy and honorable end to the Vietnam War his first order of business, and here he thought that linkage politics would be decisive. That is, if the Soviet Union wanted progress in other areas of mutual interest, it would use its influence to prod the North Vietnamese to be more forthcoming at the bargaining table.

Henry Kissinger, once a supporter of U.S. involvement in Southeast Asia, later called the war in Vietnam a "nightmare" and "a Greek tragedy. We should have never been there at all."[26] But the United States was there on 20 January 1969, with 530,000 troops in the field and no immediate end to the war in sight. The previous year had been the bloodiest for Americans, who suffered 14,600 battle deaths. Nixon knew that it was essential to end the war that had cost the nation so much in human and financial treasure and had led to unprecedented domestic turbulence and the alienation of a good part of the next generation. He had to end the war as quickly as possible so that he could launch dramatic diplomatic initiatives that, if successful, might avert future Vietnams.

But Nixon was "convinced that how we end this war will determine the future of the U.S. in the world."[27] He had to obtain what he would characterize as "peace with honor"; he could not just "cut and run," leaving the 17 million people of South Vietnam to be taken over by the communist North Vietnamese. Much like his predecessors, beginning with Truman, Nixon saw U.S. credibility at stake in Southeast Asia. Washington had to hold the line to demonstrate its willingness to pay a steep price to defend its interests. All the architects of postwar American policy, including Nixon, were influenced by the experience of the thirties, when, they believed, the lack of will of the democratic states encouraged aggressors to launch World War II.

Nixon and Kissinger were also certain that how the United States ended the war in Vietnam would influence upcoming negotiations with the Russians and Chinese. Relations with the communists could not be stabilized unless the United States left Vietnam with dignity.

Nixon had always been hawkish on Vietnam, from his advocacy of U.S. intervention to assist the French in 1954 to his criticism of Lyndon Johnson's graduated escalatory policies in 1965 and 1966. By 1967, and certainly 1968, however, he came to understand that the war was unwinnable in a conventional sense. During the summer of 1968, he promised an end to the war if elected, although he never said directly that he had a "secret plan" to accomplish that goal. In fact, when he and his colleagues began to organize the transition at the Hotel Pierre in December, it became clear that he had no plan, not even a general strategy, to end the war. Melvin Laird later insisted, "I don't care what anybody else told you. He had no plan." Laird boasted, somewhat inaccurately, "I developed the plan."[28]

During those discussions in New York before the inauguration, Nixon and his advisers quickly rejected escalation, including invading North Vietnam, blockading its ports, using tactical nuclear weapons, or bombing its dike system. In effect, the president accepted the general strategy of the lame-duck Johnson administration—the United States would not send any more troops to Vietnam, would continue to observe the bombing pause, would trust that the Paris peace talks and Soviet assistance could produce an acceptable arrangement, and would hope that the South Vietnamese could make the needed economic and military progress to confront the North with a formidable opponent. The last bit of strategy and the one that set the nation on a new path, "Vietnamization," was based on a program developed in Johnson's Pentagon by Assistant Secretary of Defense for International Security Affairs Paul Warnke that had, in effect, begun to be implemented in 1968. Vietnamization marked a return to the early sixties, when the Kennedy administration hoped that a massive buildup of Saigon's economic and military infrastructure would enable the South Vietnamese to defend themselves against the National Liberation Front (NLF).

In the definitive history of the administration's Vietnam policy, historian Jeffrey Kimball concludes that Nixon had no new Vietnam policy when he took office and never really developed one, as he and Kissinger constructed ad hoc and often contradictory strategies in reaction to military and political events. The closest Nixon came to establishing anything resembling a consistent approach to Vietnam was his so-called madman strategy.[29]

Whatever it was, Nixon and Kissinger held their Vietnam policy close to their vests in January 1969, as they would throughout the first term. Although demanding a thorough review of the situation in Southeast Asia in NSSM-1, they had decided on their course of action before the agencies submitted their final reports. It was just as well, for the CIA and the Defense Department not only disagreed with each other but were both critical of White House policies. The CIA reported that bombing North Vietnam and Laos had not been successful and that the domino theory did not apply to that theater. The Defense Department had little confidence in Vietnamization, and throughout the first two years of that program, the military command in Vietnam consistently opposed Nixon's troop withdrawals, arguing that Washington overestimated the quality of the South Vietnamese army.

The limited patience of the American people affected all Nixon's Vietnam strategies from 1969 through 1973. By the spring of 1968, a majority of Americans thought that getting involved in Vietnam had been a mistake. They did not call for an immediate withdrawal—only a small minority of Americans ever favored that option—but they desired an end to the war and the unprecedented societal dislocation that had come with it. The administration had to demonstrate a slow but steady commitment to bringing all the boys home. As Secretary Rogers wrote to W. Averell Harriman, who was finishing up his work at the Paris peace talks, "it was essential to reduce American casualties and get some of our troops home in order to retain the support of the American people."[30]

The administration's hands were tied. It could escalate only covertly, since almost all Americans demanded that the war wind down on Nixon's watch. During the campaign, Americans had expressed greater confidence in Nixon's ability to end the war than in Humphrey's by a two-to-one margin. When Nixon took office, 40 percent of the population considered the war to be the nation's most serious problem. In addition, many Democrats in Congress, who had previously supported Johnson's policies, no longer confronted a Democratic president armed with the powers of patronage. They could begin coming out of their dovish closets, posing a variety of threats to Nixon's policies on Capitol Hill.

Nixon also had to worry about the antiwar movement and antiwar sentiment among Americans in general, which had contributed to Johnson's decision on 31 March 1968 not to seek the presidency again. For example, the administration was rocked in June 1969 when the popular, mainstream *Life* magazine printed pictures of the 242 young Americans who had died in Vietnam during the previous week. As a State Department official later recalled, "The fact of the matter is that we were continually trying to calm down the opposition—in Congress, the press, and the demonstrations, the academic circles—by making unilateral concessions" in the peace talks.[31]

Like all presidents, Nixon began to think about his second term almost as soon as he took office. Daniel Patrick Moynihan wrote to him on 5 January 1969 that his would be a one-term presidency unless the war in Vietnam soon ended. Nixon had to be concerned about the political implications of the way the war ended. Although a speedy peace agreement would please almost all Americans, what would happen if the South Vietnamese government fell to communism before the 1972 election? Could even such a reputed hard-line anticommunist as Nixon survive the Democratic catcalls, "Who lost Vietnam?" Although no hard evidence suggests that the president thought about his reelection prospects as he fashioned his Vietnam policy—few presidents have ever admitted that domestic politics affected their foreign policies—he undoubtedly had his eye on a second term throughout his first term.

Despite the potential political problem posed by "losing" Vietnam, Nixon was optimistic about obtaining an honorable peace in a short time. The previous summer, he had told dovish Michigan congressman Donald Riegle, then a Republican, that "if we're elected we'll end this war in six months."[32] Kissinger later used that same six-month time frame. Even considering his constraints, as well as the previous administration's failure to extricate itself from Vietnam, Nixon confidently believed that he could end the war on favorable terms through Vietnamization and by employing Moscow to convince Hanoi to be more flexible in negotiations. Haldeman affirms that Nixon "had fully expected that an acceptable, if not totally satisfactory, solution would be achieved through negotiation within the first six months."[33] As he told his aide, "I'm not going to end up like LBJ, holed up in the White House afraid to show my face on the street. I'm going to stop that war. Fast."[34]

Nixon overestimated Moscow's influence with Hanoi. He failed to understand that the Soviet Union had limited control over anti-Western Marxist regimes and revolutions around the world, few of which were more independent than the venerable Vietnamese nationalist movement led by Ho Chi Minh. In many ways, the Soviet Union's inability to coerce North Vietnam to accept its "advice" mirrored the United States' inability to coerce its own "puppet" in Saigon.

From 1965 through November 1968, one of the sticking points to opening negotiations was the North Vietnamese precondition that the United States stop bombing them. Once the United States conceded this point, the two key issues that would be negotiated from 1969 through 1973 involved the withdrawal of "foreign" forces from South Vietnam and the nature of the postwar regime in Saigon. The U.S. position, which the Nixon administration inherited and initially supported, was that the North Vietnamese army was a foreign force that had to withdraw from South Vietnam when the Americans withdrew. The North Vietnamese, in turn, insisted on U.S. withdrawal from South Vietnam, refusing even to acknowledge that they had a military presence in the South. They also demanded a coalition government in Saigon to replace the pro-Western regime of President Nguyen van Thieu. Once the United States committed itself to no further escalation, and once the Nixon administration began its phased withdrawal, the North Vietnamese had little incentive to make a speedy peace, since there would come a day when the last American combat soldier would leave Vietnam. In addition, they felt that they had been burned twice in previous negotiations (in 1946 with the French and in 1954 at the Geneva Conference) when they had accepted compromise agreements that their enemies violated. Kissinger, who did the most important negotiating with the North Vietnamese, was frustrated by their "maddening dictatorial style" and the way "Vietnamese history and Communist ideology combined to produce almost morbid suspicion and ferocious self-righteousness."[35] The communists, in turn, were frustrated by his condescending attitude and carrot-and-stick approach.

Quickly discovering what he was up against, Nixon hoped to obtain his peace with honor by employing covert escalations and diplomatic pressure. He also had to demonstrate to Hanoi that, unlike Johnson, protesters in the streets and dissenters in Congress would not influence his policies.

The prisoner of war (POW) issue was the new element introduced by the Nixon administration during the peace negotiations. No peace would be made until the communists accounted for all American POWs and promised to return them once the war was over. The National League of Families of American Prisoners and Missing in Southeast Asia, founded by relatives and supporters of American prisoners and those still listed as missing in action (MIA), pressured the administration to do something about this cause. By the fall of 1969, Nixon opportunistically adopted the cause as his own, declaring a National Day of Prayer for the POWs on 9 November and meeting with organization leaders in December.

One of the leaders of the POW drive was then little-known millionaire H. Ross Perot. Perot and his organization, United We Stand, worked closely with the White House on several activities, including a television program about the issue and Perot's dramatic albeit abortive flights to Southeast Asia to bring gifts and mail to the POWs in Hanoi. In general, however, the administration found Perot a troublesome ally. He never contributed the millions for television time that he promised, his "monumental ego" led to incessant demands to see Nixon in person, and his "*total* lack of sophistication" appalled Haldeman.[36] Nonetheless, Perot's activities, among others, kept the POW-MIA issue on the front pages. As negotiations moved beyond 1969, the lack of progress on that emotional issue helped Nixon explain why it was taking so long to end the war.

Nixon finally obtained peace with the communists on 27 January 1973. But South Vietnam fell to communism in 1975. During Nixon's four years, the United States lost more than 18,000 of its more than 58,000 battle deaths during the entire war. Most of these deaths occurred in 1969. As U.S. casualties declined from that year to 1973, the pressures to end the war eased. All the same, considering Nixon's earlier conviction that he had to end the war with dispatch to reestablish domestic tranquility and to free himself internationally, his ability to maintain support for his policies over four years and win reelection by a landslide in 1972 was a more remarkable feat than ending the war itself.

Although most Americans were unhappy about the war, they were even more unhappy with what they perceived to be an unruly and revolutionary antiwar movement. Considering the movement "a brotherhood of the misguided, the mistaken, the well-meaning, and the malevolent," Nixon used the public anger at the "hippies" in the streets to buy support for his policies.[37] The president believed that "many leaders of the antiwar movement were hard-core militants of the New Left who hated the United States," and many of their followers opposed the war not out of "moral conviction" but "to keep from getting their asses shot off."[38] He was especially upset about the antiwar movement's "encouragement to the enemy" that "prolonged the war."[39]

Hanoi did count on the American public, influenced by antiwar critics, to tire of the war just as the French public had. One prominent Vietnamese diplomat later explained that his government believed that the antiwar movement was more important under Nixon's than Johnson's presidency because it helped constrain Nixon from reescalating the war.[40]

Like his predecessor, Nixon ordered the CIA and FBI to identify the alleged foreign connections of the antiwar movement's leaders, and like Johnson, he was incredulous when they could not do so. The intelligence services' apparent failure in this realm was one reason Nixon contemplated establishing the secret White House intelligence organization envisioned in the Huston Plan.

But Nixon did not need the foreign connection to rally most Americans to his side. Disorder on the campuses and in the streets continued into 1969. Most Americans easily conflated the increasingly violent revolutionary splinter groups with the mainstream antiwar movement, thus playing into the president's hands. Between 1 January 1969 and 15 April 1970, authorities recorded over 8,000 bombings or threats of bombings, and during the academic year 1969–70, 7,200 young people were arrested for violent acts on college campuses, a number almost double that of 1968–69. Many Americans who saw disheveled and foul-mouthed protesters carrying Vietcong flags on the nightly news concluded that if those are the sort of people who oppose Nixon, then we must be on his side.

Seven times from 1969 through 1971, the president preempted prime-time television programs to ask the nation to support his foreign policies as part of the offensive against his critics. That offensive also led to an intensification of the intelligence agencies' surveillance and harassment of antiwar opponents, activities that came back to haunt him during the Watergate investigations.

But the movement was quiescent when Nixon took office in 1969. Like the rest of the nation, it was giving the new president time to enact his "plan." Although Nixon and Kissinger knew that victory in Vietnam was no longer possible, they still thought that tough military action might convince the North Vietnamese to make concessions at the peace table. The president encouraged the U.S. commander in Vietnam, General Creighton Abrams, to maintain the pressure on the communists while his diplomats saw what they could extract from them.

For their part, the North Vietnamese and the NLF were still recovering from the battering they took during the Tet offensive of the previous year. Consequently, in 1969, they retreated from the massive, conventional attacks of that offensive and returned to small-unit guerrilla warfare. Their leaders instructed cadres to concentrate their fire on U.S. troops to keep American body counts high, thus increasing the pressure on Nixon. This strategy succeeded. During Nixon's first six months in office, Americans suffered approximately 8,000 battle deaths, making it the second most lethal six-month period of the war. Especially disconcerting to the administration was a three-week offensive launched on 22 February in response in part to U.S. offensive activities. Washington asserted that the communists' offensive, which resulted in 1,100 American battle deaths, violated the November 1968 bombing agreement because it also targeted civilians.

Barely a month into his term, Nixon decided to show the North Vietnamese that they could not push him around. First, he took advantage of a loophole in the 1968 agreement that permitted the United States to launch "protective reaction" strikes against antiaircraft sites in the North whenever their radar locked on to American reconnaissance flights. Under the guise of protective reaction, the administration ordered thousands of "legal" bombing raids against the North. It also stepped up covert cross-border raids into Laos and continued the bombing of that country begun under the Johnson administration. By the fall of 1969, American military activities in Laos had produced 600,000 refugees out of a population of 3 million. Nixon's decision in February 1970 to increase the brutal B-52 bombing runs in Laos made matters even worse. To its misfortune, Laos was home to hundreds of miles of the Ho Chi Minh Trail system through which North Vietnam supplied its cadres in the South.

Eastern Cambodia was an even more important part of that supply system. Although the American military had earlier recommended bombing the trails in neutral Cambodia, Johnson had rejected that option, despite the fact that Special Forces units had performed small-scale ground operations in the area. To Nixon, Cambodia seemed the perfect place to weaken the communists and to demonstrate to them that he could secretly escalate without suffering domestic political damage. Secretary of State Rogers and Secretary of Defense Laird worried about the possible repercussions if Americans learned about the proposed Cambodian bombing, but Nixon and Kissinger were not dissuaded by their arguments. Throughout 1969 and 1970, Rogers and Laird generally opposed the president's escalations.

Nixon obtained the informal approval of Cambodian leader Prince Norodom Sihanouk, who opposed North Vietnamese use of his country to infiltrate materiel and soldiers into South Vietnam. He was also disturbed by Hanoi's support for a small communist insurgency, the Khmer Rouge. Sihanouk warned the Americans, however, that if they made the bombing public, he would disavow it.

Accordingly, the president developed a system to keep Americans, including some of the brass in Vietnam, in the dark about the bombing. He accomplished this by ordering the tampering with the computerized navigational systems on the B-52s and by maintaining two sets of flight plans—one that reported that the bombers in question had hit targets in South Vietnam, and the other, sent to the NSC, that revealed the true targets. Even the secretary of the air force was not immediately informed about Operation Menu, which began on 18 March 1969 and continued through April 1970 with Operations Breakfast, Lunch, Dinner, Supper, and Snack. Over the fourteen months of its existence, Menu operations involved 3,875 sorties dropping 108,823 tons of bombs. In a vague way, Nixon shared the secret of Menu with several key hawkish congressional leaders.

The bombing of Cambodia made it more difficult for the North Vietnamese to deliver materiel to the South. But it produced two far more important consequences. For one thing, it pushed the North Vietnamese further inland, along with their Khmer Rouge allies, thereby increasing popular support for indigenous anti-Western forces who profited politically from the civilian casualties and the destablization of normal life caused by the bombing.

Even more important, on 9 May 1969, *New York Times* reporter William Beecher revealed the bombing. Although his story attracted little public interest, it did attract the interest of the White House. Fearing that someone from the NSC (which included Democrats and liberals) was the source of the leak, Kissinger asked the FBI to identify the culprit. In response, the bureau wiretapped eleven officials and four journalists. One of the officials, Morton Halperin, later sued the president for the violation of his rights. He won his case, and for the first time in history, a president was forced to pay damages ($5) for acts committed while in office. Kissinger's and Nixon's Cambodian wiretaps, which failed to turn up the leaker, became part of the bill of particulars in the Watergate investigations.

Although Americans did not know or care about the bombings, despite the brief flurry of attention in the White House created by the Beecher story, Moscow certainly did. In the spring, Kissinger privately warned Soviet ambassador Dobrynin on several occasions that unless the North Vietnamese were more forthcoming at the peace talks, the United States would escalate further.

On 14 May 1969, the president told the nation about a new eight-point peace plan that featured an American withdrawal six months after the North Vietnamese had left South Vietnam. Having "ruled out attempting to impose a purely military solution" as well as a "one-sided withdrawal," he called for mutual withdrawals of Americans and their allies and North Vietnamese from South Vietnam and free elections in the South under international supervision. He also called for support from "the American people united behind a generous and reasonable peace offer."

Despite Hanoi's rejection of the U.S. terms, Nixon began the process of Vietnamization on Midway Island on 8 June when he met with an unhappy President Nguyen van Thieu. Announcing the imminent withdrawal of 25,000 U.S. troops, Nixon promised more withdrawals, depending on the progress of Vietnamization, movement at the peace table, and enemy activity. From this point on, Nixon periodically addressed the nation to announce the latest withdrawal of American troops. He had no options. An aide recalled, "We were under immense domestic pressure to give an appearance of a kind of steady diminution of the American role."[41]

When the North Vietnamese did not respond positively to his initiative, Nixon sent a private letter to Ho Chi Minh on 15 July calling for action on his proposals. If the North Vietnamese leader was not willing to compromise, he could face "measures of great consequence and force," later referred to by Kissinger as a "savage, punishing blow."[42] The letter may have induced the North Vietnamese to request secret peace talks, which the United States had sought. Kissinger first met with Xuan Thuy on 4 August, at which point he informed the North Vietnamese diplomat that if his government did not respond positively to Nixon's 15 July message by 1 November, the United States would adopt new military measures.

As part of Nixon's new "go-for-broke" strategy, NSC staffers began working on Duck Hook, feasibility studies of escalatory measures, including the use of tactical nuclear weapons, blockading the ports of Hanoi and Haiphong, and bombing the North's flood-control system. Kissinger could not believe "that a fourth-rate power like North Vietnam doesn't have a breaking point."[43] To demonstrate their determination, Nixon and Kissinger apparently placed the Strategic Air Command on a seventeen-day special alert in October, an alert easily identified by Soviet intelligence. The letter to Ho, the ultimatum delivered by Kissinger, the planning in the White House basement, and the alert were all kept secret from the American people. Americans did know about Nixon's trip to Vietnam late in July, when, accompanied by his wife, he became the first president to visit a war zone since 1943, aside from Johnson's brief touchdowns at Cam Ranh Bay Naval Base in 1966 and 1967.

While Nixon was developing his new, more assertive strategies, the somnolent antiwar movement began to move into action once again. By the summer of 1969, many doves had become convinced that Nixon was not doing all that he could to bring the war to a speedy end. Antiwar moderates who formed the Vietnam Moratorium Committee (VMC) at the end of June devised a new tactic for their sometimes unpopular movement. This time, they would not call for the traditional mass march in one or two cities on a weekend. Instead, on Wednesday, 15 October (two weeks before Nixon's ultimatum, of which they were unaware), citizens around the country would take time off from work or school to attend rallies, ceremonies in cemeteries, and other symbolic activities to signal their dissatisfaction with the pace of troop withdrawals from Vietnam. Should the war continue, the VMC intended to organize further moratoriums, adding a day each month to the protests.

The battle lines were drawn. Nixon told his cabinet in September that he would not be the "first American President to lose a war," because the "first defeat in history would destroy the confidence of the American people in themselves."[44] As the moratorium gained momentum, especially among middle-class adults, Nixon went on the offensive. On 16 September, he announced a troop withdrawal of 35,000. Four days later, he announced the reassignment of General Lewis Hershey, the outspoken chief of the Selective Service System. In addition, at a press conference on 26 September, referring to the upcoming protest, he declared, "under no circumstances will I be affected whatever by it." Finally, two days before the moratorium, Nixon replied publicly to a letter from a student, explaining that "to allow government policy to be made in the streets would destroy the democratic procedure. It would give the decision not to the majority . . . but to those with the loudest voices."

Despite the administration's counteroffensive, the moratorium turned out to be the most successful antiwar demonstration in history, involving over 2 million people in over 200 cities. It was decorous enough that people such as W. Averell Harriman and Defense Secretary Laird's college-student son participated. The media emphasized the peaceful and middle-class nature of the telegenic rallies and prayer vigils. Yet the majority of Americans still supported the president. In one poll taken on 16 October, more than 68 percent of the respondents approved of the way Nixon was handling the war. All the same, the moratorium had shaken the administration. The 1 November deadline came and went without movement from Hanoi or retaliation from Washington. Years later, Nixon blamed the moratorium, complaining that it had "undercut the credibility of the ultimatum" and, by encouraging the North Vietnamese that they could count on support in the American population, had "destroyed whatever small possibility may still have existed to end the war."[45] He decided not to retaliate because Duck Hook planners had concluded that their contemplated escalations would not work. In addition, the death of Ho Chi Minh on 2 September may have made it difficult for the new regime in Hanoi to take any bold negotiating initiative.

Concerned about the renewed strength of the antiwar movement and its apparent effect on Hanoi, Nixon developed a strategy to mobilize the majority of Americans who did not take part in or sympathize with the moratorium. He needed them for the long haul but, more immediately, to dampen enthusiasm for the second moratorium scheduled for 13–14 November. The key component would be his 3 November "Silent Majority" speech, which he began working on almost immediately after the first moratorium. Nixon considered this speech, which he wrote himself, the most important of his career. He worked through twelve drafts, sometimes spending entire days on them, until he was satisfied. He received advice, especially on the way to rally support, from former secretary of state Dean Acheson, a Democrat.

In his televised address, seen by as many as 80 million Americans, Nixon outlined his Vietnamization program; revealed his secret letter to Ho, but not the ultimatum; and explained why the United States could not cut and run. He then appealed to "the great silent majority" to support him and warned, "North Vietnam cannot humiliate the United States. Only Americans can do that." He had thrown down the gauntlet to the antiwar movement.

A major part of this new offensive involved neutralizing the media, which he felt favored the doves. At the least, he hoped that the networks would not devote as much attention to the next moratorium as they had to the first. In the days that followed, his spokespersons assailed the generally balanced roundtable network analyses of the speech for being unfair to the president. Vice President Agnew struck a raw nerve when he delivered an address on 13 November in which he attacked a small, powerful, almost conspiratorial group of liberal television executives and their counterparts on the major newspapers and newsmagazines, all centered in New York City or Washington, for not representing the opinions of the rest of the country. Agnew delivered his speech the day after investigative journalist Seymour Hersh published a sensational story in the *New York Times* about unspeakable atrocities committed by U.S. troops at My Lai in South Vietnam.

The appeal to a silent majority and the companion assault on the eastern liberal media resonated with many Americans who despised the counterculture and the radicals and worried about the political and social changes they had experienced over the past few years. The president who promised to bring the nation together relied on a polarizing strategy to regain the upper hand in the battle for the hearts and minds of the American people.

Nixon's and Agnew's offensive did the trick. The momentum toward the doves slowed. The media did not devote commensurate time and space to moratorium activities on 13–14 November, which included 40,000 peaceful protesters participating in a March Against Death past the White House and a mass rally of more than 250,000 in Washington on 15 November sponsored by the Mobilization. Moreover, the media concentrated on protesters at the fringe of the main events who broke windows and provoked riots that resulted in 338 arrests and 606 injuries. As Nixon gloated in late November, "We've got those liberal bastards on the run now . . . and we're going to keep them on the run."[46]

On 15 December, Nixon again addressed the nation on Vietnam, announcing the withdrawal of another 50,000 troops by the following April, based on the improved political and military situation, but he had to report no progress in the peace negotiations. He was pleased with the "demonstration of support by the American people" that "has dashed those hopes" of the North Vietnamese that "division in the United States would eventually bring them the victory they cannot win over our fighting men in Vietnam."

The president's cautious optimism made sense. American battle deaths had declined dramatically during the second half of 1969. Moreover, the millions of dollars of aid for Vietnamization had led to the increased viability of the South Vietnamese regime. In September 1969, Saigon seemed to control more than 50 percent of the countryside, in striking contrast to 20 percent only the year before.

This relative success was related in part to a change in U.S. tactics from large-unit to small-unit engagements. In addition, in 1968, the CIA, in conjunction with the military command, had launched the Phoenix Program, a covert project meant to disrupt the NLF's infrastructure. Under this program, small teams of Navy SEALs, South Vietnamese commandos, and specially trained local militias kidnapped, imprisoned, tortured, assassinated, and converted tens of thousands of suspected Vietcong (VC). The head of the program, William Colby, claimed that Phoenix operations led to the capture of 29,000 communist leaders, of whom 18,000 accepted amnesty. More than 20,000 communists were also killed, "mostly in combat situations."[47] The program copied the VC tactic of infiltrating villages and one way or another "neutralizing" local leaders. Captured VC personnel attested to the success of the Phoenix Program. Nixon was enthusiastic, declaring, "We've got to have more of this. Assassinations. Killings. That's what they're [the enemy] doing."[48] But when the press finally uncovered information about the program, many Americans were so outraged that their side was using the same tactics as the VC that Nixon had to cancel Phoenix operations in 1972.

Whereas the military situation appeared to improve in 1969, the state of the American military did not. Once the United States announced its plans to leave the fighting to the South Vietnamese, it became difficult to motivate American soldiers. To make matters worse, an increasingly large percentage of the combat forces in Vietnam were draftees who were not as supportive of the U.S. war effort as were volunteers and professional military people. Furthermore, some of the young men who came to Vietnam in the late sixties brought with them the same attitudes toward authority and drug use that prevailed in the youth culture of the day. By 1969, 30 percent of those arriving in Vietnam had used marijuana at least once; by the time they returned home, that figure rose to at least 45 percent. Two years later, the number of GIs who experimented with marijuana reached 69 percent, while 38 percent admitted to having tried opium and 34 percent heroin. By the last year of the war, more Americans were evacuated from Vietnam because of drug usage than because of wounds. However, there was little if any drug use on the front lines.

Desertion rates rose, battlefield and shipboard mutinies occurred, racial tensions mirrored those stateside, and the number of reported incidents of "fragging," the attempted murder of officers by enlisted men, increased in the army from 96 in 1969 to 209 in 1970. Symptomatic of the morale problem was the bloody battle of "Hamburger Hill" (Ap Bia Mountain), which took place over ten days in May 1969. After making twelve assaults on the small mountain and losing fifty-six men, the army finally won the heights and then almost immediately abandoned them. After the battle, rumors circulated that servicemen had offered a bounty of $10,000 for the assassination of the commanding general. The sorry experiences with draftees in Vietnam reinforced Nixon's determination to establish an all-volunteer army.

After more than a year in office, Nixon still appeared to be a long way from bringing the war to a peaceful and honorable conclusion. The situation seemed to improve somewhat on 18 March 1970, when pro-Western General Lon Nol, backed by the Cambodian National Assembly, led a coup that overthrew Prince Sihanouk's neutralist regime. Although American intelligence agents knew about the coup in advance and informed the plotters that they would assist them once they deposed the erratic Sihanouk, this was not a CIA operation.

When Lon Nol demanded that the North Vietnamese leave his country and then closed the port of Sihanoukville through which much of their war materiel flowed, Washington was pleased. From the earliest days of the war, the Pentagon had wanted to deny Cambodian border areas to the enemy. But Lon Nol was a weak leader of a weak country who needed assistance to defend himself against both the 40,000 North Vietnamese troops and the lesser numbers of Khmer Rouge rebels who, by the middle of April, controlled one-third of Cambodia.

To assist its new ally, the United States began sending military and economic aid to Phnom Penh. Through 1975, the amount of such aid totaled $2.3 billion. The more immediate problem was how to help Lon Nol's forces against the better-armed and better-trained North Vietnamese with whom they had become involved in combat.

Despite Cambodia's shift from neutrality to the U.S. camp, April 1970 was not a good month for Richard Nixon. The secret Paris peace talks between Kissinger and Le Duc Tho had broken off, new Soviet military advisers appeared in Egypt in the midst of the undeclared War of Attrition with Israel along the Suez Canal, talks with Moscow about a summit were on hold, the *Apollo 13* moon shot was aborted, and advisers informed the president that he could not attend daughter Julie's graduation from Smith College and son-in-law David's from Amherst College that spring because of inevitable student hostility. Anticipating problems the previous fall, he had asked Haldeman "to plan some sort of trip out of the country at the time of Julie's graduation."[49] Above all, on 8 April, the Senate rejected his Supreme Court nomination of G. Harrold Carswell, after having rejected Clement F. Haynsworth in November. On 13 April, Nixon told Kissinger, "Those senators think they can push Nixon around on Haynsworth and Carswell. Well I'll show them who's tough."[50]

It is too simple to say that Nixon decided to send American and South Vietnamese troops into Cambodia on 30 April because of his domestic travails. Such an invasion had long been on the Pentagon drawing boards. He felt that he owed the North Vietnamese a response after they had called his bluff the previous November. Nonetheless, Nixon's anger and frustration influenced his decision making in April. After a 27 April meeting, Haldeman noted, "K. [Kissinger] takes whole deal as test of P's [Nixon's] authority and I think would go ahead even if plan is wrong just to prove P can't be challenged."[51] Further, Ehrlichman told Kissinger that the president "needs a bold stroke," since he was not doing so well "on [the] domestic side."[52]

That bold stroke, characteristic of Nixinger diplomacy, took even high-level administration officials by surprise. On 20 April, the president had presented to the nation an upbeat Vietnam progress report in which he announced the withdrawal of an additional 150,000 troops. Yet on 22 April, he hurriedly, almost feverishly, began planning to invade Cambodia, making the final decision to go on 28 April. At first, he and his advisers talked about an invasion by South Vietnamese troops alone, but General Abrams insisted that Saigon was not prepared for such an operation.

Nixon informed only a few people about his decision to approve a joint United States–South Vietnamese invasion of Cambodia. Lon Nol himself did not find out about it until the last minute. Nixon did consult Chairman of the Joint Chiefs Moorer but kept Secretary of Defense Laird and Secretary of State Rogers in the dark until virtually the eleventh hour. The president knew that Laird and Rogers would oppose it, and he was right. After hearing about the plan, the usually dignified Rogers groaned, "This will make the students puke."[53] At Langley, CIA analysts considered the invasion impractical, but CIA director Richard Helms did not offer their arguments to Nixon because he did not want to anger him.

Tension was high in the White House during late April. Nervous about the momentous nature of his decision, Nixon drew inspiration from watching the patriotic Hollywood blockbuster *Patton* over and over. On 23 April, he called Kissinger ten times and, demonstrating his agitation, would "bark an order and immediately hang up the phone."[54] The next night, perhaps a little high from drinking with Bebe Rebozo at Camp David, a slurring Nixon warned Kissinger on the phone, "If this doesn't work, it'll be your ass Henry. Ain't that right, Bebe?"[55]

On the evening of 30 April, Nixon went before the nation to announce his surprising escalation. He referred to the invasion as an "incursion" needed to defend Cambodia against North Vietnamese aggression and also to capture the enemy's Central Office for South Vietnam (COSVN). He concluded, "If when the chips are down the world's most powerful nation acts like a pitiful helpless giant, the forces of totalitarianism and anarchy will threaten free nations and free institutions throughout the world."

Almost immediately, the antiwar opposition exploded. Students poured out of college dormitories to launch the most widespread series of campus protests in American history. By the time the crisis ended in mid-May, 89 percent of all private universities and 76 percent of all public universities had experienced demonstrations. At least 448 colleges experienced strikes or closures, with some even shutting down for the academic year because it was no longer possible to conduct classes. Nixon did not aid his cause when on 1 May, while walking through the Pentagon, he criticized the "bums . . . blowing up the campuses."[56] He was referring to a few specific cases of recent violence, including the firebombing of the Center for Advanced Study in the Behavioral Sciences in Stanford, California, the previous week, but many students thought he was labeling all youthful dissenters bums.

Because of the Cambodian incursion, Roger Morris, Anthony Lake, and William Watts resigned from the NSC, and 250 foreign service officers sent a protest note to Secretary Rogers. Learning of this protest on 1 May, Nixon called the undersecretary of state in a rage: "This is the president. I want you to make sure all those sons of bitches are fired first thing in the morning."[57] The president's orders were ignored.

Secretary of the Interior Walter Hickel, not one of Nixon's favorites, publicly expressed his criticism of an administration that lacked "appropriate concern for . . . our young people," as did Commissioner of Education James Allen.[58] Nixon removed Allen from office twenty days after his offensive remarks. He waited until November before firing his "adversary" Hickel, who not only became popular because of his protest but also was a champion of the environmentalists.[59]

Having expected some reaction over what many would deem a widening of the war, Nixon was confident that he could weather this storm—

but not after 4 May. On that day, four young people were killed and fourteen wounded at Kent State University after poorly trained and jittery National Guardsmen fired into crowds of students; some were demonstrating against the war, but others were merely going to class. Although the Kent State campus had experienced violence in the previous days, including the burning of a Reserve Officers' Training Corps (ROTC) building, and although a handful of stones may have been thrown at the guardsmen on the fateful day, to some Americans, especially college students, it appeared that the government had deliberately murdered dissenters. On 15 May, two students were killed and eleven wounded under similar circumstances at the predominantly black Jackson State University in Mississippi.

In the ensuing days, a shaken Nixon and his staff met with college presidents, academics, and governors in an attempt to calm what one aide called the "absolute public hysteria."[60] Although the VMC itself had disbanded earlier that month, antiwar leaders hastily put together a Washington protest for the weekend of 9–10 May that drew 100,000 activists. In the most bizarre incident of that weekend, after making more than fifty telephone calls from 10:35 P.M. to 3:50 A.M. (Kissinger eight times, Haldeman seven times), an anxious and depressed Nixon left the White House without telling anyone, accompanied only by his valet, to visit the area around the Lincoln Memorial where young demonstrators were encamped. With the Secret Service quickly following after him, the president tried to explain to sleepy and incredulous students that he understood their concerns. Although many of his conversations dealt with serious subjects, albeit not much on Vietnam, he also talked about the students' football teams and foreign travel, and that sort of frivolous banter is what appeared in newspaper accounts of the strange visitation.

Julie Nixon, who would soon be subjected to "Fuck Julie" chants at her Smith College graduation, reported that the White House that weekend was like "a tomb."[61] Charles Colson compared the "besieged" White House to a presidential palace in a Central American country during a coup; a battalion of the 82nd Airborne, hidden in the EOB, prepared to deploy to protect a White House surrounded by district transit buses.[62] The demonstration was peaceful, however.

Nixon took solace in the fact that more than a majority of those polled supported his Vietnam policies during the period of the Cambodian invasion, but he did not command a majority of the elite media or those on Capitol Hill. In a dramatic challenge to presidential authority in wartime, the Senate passed the Cooper-Church Amendment to cut off all funds for the Cambodian operation after 30 June. The vote was fifty-eight to thirty-seven, with sixteen Republicans joining the majority. In a symbolic action that June, the Senate also repealed the 1964 Gulf of Tonkin Resolution.

Although the House rejected the Cooper-Church Amendment, Nixon announced that he was going to withdraw the troops by 30 June anyway, claiming that they did not need any more time to accomplish their task of clearing out a twenty-one-mile-deep area. After Kissinger's assistant Alexander Haig informed Lon Nol of the pullout, the Cambodian leader began to cry.

When the president went before the American people on 30 June, he claimed a great victory. The allied forces had captured as much as 40 percent of all enemy arms in Cambodia, including 22,892 individual weapons, 15 million rounds of ammunition, 14 million pounds of rice, 143,000 rockets and mortars, and almost 200,000 antiaircraft rounds. Nixon did not talk about COSVN, the presumed reason for invading Cambodia. COSVN was a mobile field headquarters that was easily moved out of harm's way once the North Vietnamese learned of the invasion. The invasion did damage the communists' ability to conduct military operations in South Vietnam and disrupted their supply lines. Nixon later claimed that he was able to be more flexible on peace terms and also to announce the withdrawal of another 40,000 troops in November because of the blow he had dealt the enemy in May. Left unsaid was the fact that the invasion forced the communists further inland, where they began to pose more of a threat to the survival of the pro-Western regime in Phnom Penh.

The administration's support for Cambodian participation in the war, which included increased bombing further inland from the Vietnamese border, had the unintended consequence of increasing the popularity and effectiveness of the once marginal communist Khmer Rouge rebels. When the United States pulled out of Southeast Asia in 1975, the Khmer Rouge took over their country and proceeded to institute one of the most brutal revolutionary systems in history. During the three years they controlled Cambodia, they killed or permitted to die from starvation or disease as much as 20 percent of the population. Nixon's Cambodian policy of 1969 and 1970 was partly responsible for the rise to power of the murderous Khmer Rouge. Naturally, no one in the United States or the rest of the world in the spring of 1970 could have imagined such an outcome of the Cambodian invasion.

By the end of May, Nixon had ridden out the Cambodian storm. Through a variety of public-relations ventures, including an appearance with Reverend Billy Graham, he appealed once again to the Silent Majority that did indeed support him. That support was evidenced in the violent and unprovoked attack by several hundred construction workers in Lower Manhattan on antiwar protesters on 8 May. Only ten days earlier, Vice President

Agnew had compared protesters to the Ku Klux Klan and Nazis and had asked Americans to "act accordingly" against them.[63] After the bloody attack, 100,000 "hard hats" held a peaceful pro-Nixon demonstration in New York on 20 May. Encouraged by Colson and against the advice of Ehrlichman and Shultz, Nixon invited hard-hat leaders, including Peter Brennan, to the White House. After the 1972 election, he selected Brennan to be secretary of labor.

Kent State was a distant memory for many by 4 July when Nixon sponsored an Honor America Day in Washington. Bob Hope, the Mormon Tabernacle Choir, and Red Skelton entertained an audience of 500,000. By that time, 58 percent of Americans blamed the students for what had happened at Kent State. That view was reinforced on 28 August when radicals bombed a military research center at the University of Wisconsin, killing one graduate student.

Nixon's recovery of popular support, however, did not mean that he had a free hand to escalate again. The North Vietnamese, who watched patiently as more and more American combat troops went home, refused to budge in negotiations. They were heartened when the Senate mustered thirty-nine votes in early September for the McGovern-Hatfield Resolution, which demanded the recall of all American troops from Vietnam by 31 December 1971. Unprepared to accept anything but their maximum terms at this point, the North Vietnamese believed that if they continued to delay, despite the heavy punishment from "protective reaction" bombings, a time would come when the American public would demand that the last American combat soldier leave Vietnam. In the fall of 1970, they began to plan for their next major offensive to be launched in the spring of 1972, when the South Vietnamese might have to go it alone against them.

Nonetheless, on 7 October, Nixon announced a "new initiative for peace," with the centerpiece being a cease-fire in place. He did not mention a mutual troop withdrawal in that address. However, at a press conference the next day, he returned to mutual withdrawal as a major element in U.S. peace proposals, thus undercutting the apparent 7 October breakthrough. Critics suggested that Nixon had presented the "new initiative," which turned out to be not all that new, as a cynical appeal to those concerned about the war who would soon cast their ballots in the congressional elections. In much the same way, the announced withdrawal of 40,000 additional troops on 12 October was geared to those elections. As he told Americans while on the campaign trail on 17 October, "I can say confidently that the war in Vietnam is coming to an end, and we are going to win a just peace in Vietnam."

While offering words of encouragement, Nixon was secretly planning another surprise—an attempt to free about fifty POWs who were being held in a camp at Son Tay, twenty-three miles northwest of Hanoi. The daring raid would unnerve the North Vietnamese and rescue eyewitnesses to the tortures suffered by those under communist "care." Hanoi tortured most POWs as a matter of routine. But this planned raid would be a tricky operation. Worrying about its failure, the president reportedly remarked, "Christ, they surrounded the White House, remember? This time they will probably knock down the gates and I'll have a thousand incoherent hippies urinating on the Oval Office rug."[64]

After practicing the mission more than 170 times, the American raiders pulled off a brilliant technical feat by landing their six helicopters at Son Tay undetected, despite sophisticated air defenses, and they suffered only two minor injuries while mauling enemy troops, including Chinese forces. By the time the raid was launched, however, the POWs at Son Tay had been moved to another camp. Although last-minute intelligence reports suggested that the prisoners might have been moved, according to one official, the White House "didn't want to know" about them.[65] Even though the raid failed, most Americans supported Nixon's effort. At least he was doing something to help the POWs. The raid convinced the North Vietnamese to move almost all their prisoners to the "Hanoi Hilton," an impregnable camp in their capital. There would be no more Son Tays.

Despite the troop withdrawals and continued opposition to further escalation, Nixon had to maintain pressure on the North Vietnamese both to help the South Vietnamese and to demonstrate to Hanoi that the United States could still punish it. For those reasons, the administration began planning Lam Son 719, an incursion into Laos similar to the previous spring's incursion into Cambodia, in another attempt to disrupt the Ho Chi Minh Trail supply system. Domestic considerations made it impossible for the president to employ American troops this time; Lam Son 719 would be an all–South Vietnamese operation. The operation, according to Kissinger, which was "conceived in doubt" and "assailed by skepticism," "proceeded in confusion."[66]

The invasion, which began on 8 February 1971, was a disaster. The North Vietnamese knew that the South Vietnamese were coming and were well dug in, and the South Vietnamese withdrew before achieving their goals. President Thieu had committed only 17,000 soldiers to the incursion—far fewer than the number recommended by the American high command—fearing that he could lose his crack troops in the campaign into which Nixon had dragooned him. Kissinger railed against the Saigon leadership: "Those sons of bitches. It's their country and we can't save it for them if they don't want to."[67]

The South Vietnamese lost 8,000 men and the North Vietnamese 12,000; the communists downed between 100 and 200 helicopters and damaged

600. Fifty-five Americans, performing support roles, died in the operation. Nixon had told congressional leaders two days into the incursion that Lam Son 719 would prove that Vietnamization was working. Instead, Americans saw shocking films on the nightly newscasts of South Vietnamese clinging to helicopters taking them out of Laos. An embarrassed Nixon ordered Haldeman, "Have Agnew blast T.V. for the distorted coverage."[68] He told a press conference on 17 February that everything "has gone according to plan" and that General Abrams had assured him that the South Vietnamese "are fighting . . . in a superior way." On 4 March, at another press conference, he announced that the South Vietnamese army had "come of age" and reported that Abrams had concluded that "the South Vietnamese by themselves can hack it."

Privately, Nixon, Kissinger, and Abrams knew that the incursion demonstrated that the South Vietnamese were not ready to go it alone. Moreover, it showed the North Vietnamese that the United States was hesitant to commit its own troops to such operations. They were further encouraged when the "success" of Vietnamization permitted Nixon to announce on 7 April the withdrawal of another 100,000 personnel, bringing total withdrawals to 365,000.

Spring 1971 was not a good period for President Nixon. Washington was rocked by "The Selling of the Pentagon," a CBS documentary revealing that the Department of Defense spent $190 million annually on public relations. In addition, Lieutenant William Calley went on trial for ordering the My Lai massacre, the antiwar movement mounted one of its largest demonstrations, and the *New York Times* and *Washington Post* published sections of the Defense Department's classified history of the war, the *Pentagon Papers*.

On 16 March 1968, Lieutenant Calley had led his platoon into My Lai, a South Vietnamese village from which suspected enemy fire had recently come and around which mines had killed American soldiers. Calley's men murdered almost everyone in the village, as many as 500 men, women, and children, in the worst single atrocity committed by Americans during the war. Although the higher-ranking brass were aware of the incident, they covered it up until March 1969, when a veteran wrote letters to public officials about the affair. On 12 November 1969, two months after the army had quietly brough charges against Calley, his immediate superior Captain Ernest L. Medina, and twenty-six other officers, investigative journalist Seymour Hersh published a story on the massacre that brought it to the world's attention. On 29 March 1971, Calley alone was found guilty of murdering South Vietnamese civilians and, two days later, was sentenced to life imprisonment. In his defense, he claimed, "They were all enemy. They were all to be destroyed," and contended that he was only following orders.[69]

A majority of Americans polled sympathized with Calley, who appeared to be a scapegoat. Many conservatives accepted his argument about the nature of the enemy in a guerrilla war, and liberals were angered by the military's failure to prosecute Calley's immediate superiors, as well as those in the Defense Department who had covered up the story for over a year. The Pentagon demoted only one officer and censured another for their roles in the cover-up.

Responding to the widespread support for the lieutenant and angered by the assault against the military, Nixon initially was inclined to simply pardon Calley. For the short run, he took the less controversial action of having Calley released from the stockade and placed under house arrest on the base while promising on 29 April to "review the case . . . in my capacity as the final reviewing officer." No one doubted where the president's sympathy lay. In August, the military commandant at Fort Benning reduced Calley's term to twenty years; in April 1974, the secretary of the army reduced it to ten years. Following the overturning of Calley's conviction by a U.S. district court in Georgia, President Gerald Ford released him in November 1975.

The antiwar demonstrations scheduled for late April and early May posed a much greater threat for the administration. From 19 through 22 April, several thousand members of the Vietnam Veterans Against the War (VVAW) encamped in Washington to protest the continuation of the war. Although the administration obtained legal sanction to evict them from the Mall, Nixon decided at the last moment that television shots of police forcibly removing men in uniform, some of whom were in wheelchairs, would create sympathy for the protesters. As Pat Buchanan advised, they should choose their enemies carefully and wait for the "crazies" who would soon be arriving in Washington for a mass demonstration.[70]

The VVAW received a good deal of favorable publicity, despite the administration's use of the leaders of the American Legion and the Veterans of Foreign Wars to attack them. Most memorable was the congressional testimony of Lieutenant John Kerry, a young naval officer who had been wounded in Vietnam, and especially the final action at the Capitol on 22 April, covered in depth by the media, when VVAW members threw their medals over a fence after making impassioned statements about their opposition to the war.

Two days later, the National Peace Action Coalition drew as many as 300,000 people to Washington and 150,000 to San Francisco in the last great mass demonstration against the war. Senator Vance Hartke and former

Alaska senator Ernest Gruening were among those who addressed the multitude in Washington that weekend. The administration was convinced that the media inflated the numbers at such events, even though their reports were often based on official park police tallies. Nixon secretly sent U-2 planes over some demonstrations to take allegedly more accurate aerial counts that were invariably lower than those of the police.

As many as 30,000 protesters, members of the radical People's Coalition (the May Day Tribe), remained in Washington for a week of civil disobedience the likes of which the capital had never seen. Claiming that peaceful protesting and petitioning were not working, the May Day Tribe promised to close down Washington by committing acts of civil disobedience on the bridges and streets of the district that would make it impossible for civil servants to get to work. Charged with defending the White House and the capital in general, Nixon's counsel John Dean prepared an emergency declaration to be employed if matters got out of hand.

Because of careful preparation and excellent intelligence (including Assistant Attorney General William Rehnquist's advice about the constitutionality of their proposed actions), the administration was able to keep the capital open during the week of 3 May. It accomplished this by arresting several thousand people in dragnet sweeps, described by one aide as a "military operation," and then detaining those arrested in ways that violated their constitutional rights.[71] In a bit of highjinks, Charles Colson sent a crate of oranges to the detainees in Democratic presidential candidate Edmund Muskie's name. Nixon laughed when he heard about it: "he's . . . gonna get caught at some of these things. . . . But he's . . . got a lot done that he hasn't been caught at."[72] Colson also promised to send teamster "thugs" to assist the police. Nixon liked the idea: "They've got guys who'll go in and knock their heads off." Haldeman chimed in, "They're gonna beat the shit out of some of these people."[73]

At a press conference on 1 June, Nixon defended the police, who "showed a good deal more concern for their [protesters] rights than they showed for the rights of the people of Washington." But Nixon and his aides knew at the time that the attorney general's effective battle plan to crush the demonstration had violated basic constitutional rights. The courts ruled in 1975 that most of the arrests had been illegal and awarded monetary damages to 1,200 of the detainees.

The spring 1971 demonstrations were the last major mass demonstrations of the period. Although Nixon still confronted resolutions from a dovish Senate, most Americans were pleased that more and more of their boys were coming home from Vietnam and that the war did indeed appear to be winding down. By the end of 1971, only 156,000 U.S. troops remained in Vietnam, and during the previous six months, only 276 personnel had lost their lives.

More mass demonstrations would not pressure Nixon to move any more quickly toward his peace with honor. Moreover, the pending end of the Selective Service System eliminated one prime motivation for young people to actively oppose the war. To be sure, antiwar activists continued to hold marches, rallies, and petition drives, but these were generally small affairs that the media did not cover. Nixon still periodically confronted protesters, as at a White House dinner on 28 January 1972 when a performer with the all-American Ray Coniff singers held up a banner in the middle of a performance that read "Stop the Killing."

While dealing with these difficult problems during the spring of 1971, Nixon made the most important concession to date in the peace talks. On 31 May, the United States, albeit in a vague manner, informed the North Vietnamese that its demand for a mutual withdrawal was no longer a sine qua non. That is, although all U.S. troops would leave South Vietnam, the North Vietnamese would not necessarily have to leave. With this concession, the key stumbling block to settlement became the nature of the post-war regime in the South.

Until the fall of 1972, the North Vietnamese held firm to their demand that Thieu would have to resign or otherwise be rendered politically ineffective before they would accept a peace agreement. They even allegedly suggested to Kissinger that he have the CIA assassinate Thieu. Refusing to alter his position significantly despite U.S. concessions, North Vietnamese negotiator Le Duc Tho told Kissinger in September 1971, "I really don't know why I am negotiating with you. I have just spent several hours with [South Dakota] Senator [George] McGovern and your opposition will force you to give me what I want."[74] Between April and July 1971 alone, Congress had voted seventeen times on measures to restrict Nixon's actions in Southeast Asia. These activities contributed to Kissinger's pessimism in the fall of 1971. Hanoi, he wrote to Nixon, had "every incentive to wait for the interreacting [sic] combination of unrest in South Vietnam and an American domestic squeeze to topple [Thieu's government] . . . and pave the way for their eventual control."[75]

To please the United States, Thieu submitted to the holding of an election that he won handily on 3 October 1971. Even so, the administration had been unable to encourage a serious opponent to run against him in what turned out to be another stacked South Vietnamese election. The CIA even offered the popular general Duong Van Minh a sizable bribe to ensure that he would remain in the race to preserve the illusion of a democratic choice. Nixon admitted the problem at a 16 September press conference: "We would have preferred to have a contested election in South Vietnam. We, however, cannot get people to run when they do not want to run." Despite this disappointment on the political front, the generally low level of enemy activity permitted the president to announce a further troop withdrawal of 45,000 on 12 November. This proved to be the lull before the storm as the North Vietnamese continued their buildup in a prelude to a full-scale offensive in four months.

With the U.S. presidential election less than one year away, Nixon worried about the ramifications of the failure of his diplomatic efforts to end the war. Hoping to shore up public support for his policies, he launched a propaganda blitz in January 1972. First, in a televised interview on 2 January, he emphasized the "very cruel action" of North Vietnamese in rejecting administration queries about POWs. Then, on 13 January, he announced the withdrawal of an additional 70,000 troops, which would bring troop levels down to 69,000 by 1 May. Finally, and most important, he told the nation on television on 25 January about his offer to withdraw all U.S. troops within six months of an agreement, and then, in a bombshell, announced that since August 1969, Kissinger had engaged in secret negotiations on twelve different occasions with North Vietnamese diplomats. Nixon then outlined U.S. positions in those meetings that went beyond those presented at the public talks in Paris and portrayed the North Vietnamese propaganda war against the U.S. diplomatic posture as disingenuous. "Nothing is served by silence when it enables the other side to imply possible solutions publicly that it has already flatly rejected privately," he argued. His decision to reveal the secret talks, which played on Kissinger's widespread popularity, was intended to demonstrate the administration's flexibility during the negotiations.

Haldeman followed up Nixon's Vietnam blitz when he said on the *Today* television program on 2 February that critics in the Senate "are consciously aiding and abetting the enemy." He admitted later that his controversial comment had been made "on the direct and explicit orders of the President."[76]

While Nixon was attempting to win the hearts and minds of the American people, the North Vietnamese were preparing their largest offensive since Tet. Although American intelligence analysts expected the offensive, they were taken aback by its scale and by the fact that it was a conventional and not a guerrilla operation. In an attempt to occupy large areas of South Vietnam, bloody Saigon's army, and weaken President Thieu, thereby paving the way for a coalition government in the South, fourteen divisions and twenty-six independent regiments of North Vietnamese regulars, employing two hundred Soviet T-54 tanks and a host of modern weapons they had just received from Moscow, took part in the offensive that began on 30 March. Virtually all North Vietnamese regulars participated in a three pronged attack that resulted in the communist capture of Quang Tri on 1 May, despite Nixon's contention that South Vietnam had created "a formidable fighting force."[77] With almost all U.S. combat troops out of the fray, the North Vietnamese rather easily cut through the well-equipped but poorly trained and poorly motivated South Vietnamese.

The United States saved the South Vietnamese from defeat with the massive use of tactical airpower in the South and B-52 bombing of Hanoi and Haiphong in the North. On 16 April, American planes hit four Soviet merchant ships anchored in Haiphong harbor, an action that could have jeopardized the long-awaited Soviet-American summit in Moscow scheduled for May. The next month, in the midst of the offensive, Nixon announced the withdrawal of another 20,000 troops.

When on 2 May General Abrams reported that the South Vietnamese were still in desperate shape, and Kissinger reported an especially bitter session in Paris with Le Duc Tho on the same day, Nixon made another daring decision. He would mine, from the air, the harbors of Hanoi and Haiphong, severely limiting the North's ability to obtain supplies. The Pentagon had recommended such mining as early as October 1966. The president also announced the resumption of large-scale bombing attacks on the North with over 40,000 sorties from May through October. An angry Nixon warned, "The bastards have never been bombed like they're going to be bombed this time."[78] Whatever his intentions, he soon became "thoroughly disgusted" with the air force's "pusillanimous" performance in the North, which was not as devastating as he had hoped.[79]

Most of Nixon's advisers feared that the mining decision, announced on 8 May, would force the Russians to cancel the summit. Nixon wrote to Kissinger the next day that North Vietnam "has gone over the brink *and so have we. We have the power to destroy his war making capacity. The only question is whether we have the will to use that power. What distinguishes me from Johnson is that I have the will in spades."*[80]

With Kissinger ambivalent about the move, only Haig, Connally, and Agnew initially supported the mining decision. Nixon was not happy about possibly having to forgo the summit, but he wanted to punish the Soviet-backed North Vietnamese. He had concluded that although the Russians would protest vigorously in public, the odds were fifty-fifty that they would not cancel the summit; they needed it more than the United States, especially since Nixon had concluded a very successful summit with their archenemies, the Chinese, in February. The president was correct, although it was a near thing in Moscow, with several important members of the Politburo calling for cancellation of the summit, an action that might have hurt Nixon in the presidential election.

Nixon was buoyed by public-opinion polls that showed that at least 60 percent of the population supported the minings and by his reception of 22,000 favorable telegrams at the White House. Many of those had been generated by Republican operatives. His operatives also fixed a *Washington Star* and a local television poll by "stuffing" the ballot boxes. These operations were unnecessary, because a majority of Americans supported Nixon's actions, especially since he had made good on his promise to bring their boys home. The last ground combat forces, the Third Battalion of the 21st Infantry, left Vietnam on 23 August 1972.

By August, Hanoi acknowledged that its offensive had failed and American retaliatory blows had taken their toll. Both the Russians and Chinese, intent on improving their relations with the United States, had been pressuring the North Vietnamese to bring the war to an end by offering compromises. Finally, North Vietnamese officials read the U.S. presidential polls, and with Nixon's reelection appearing to be a certainty, they concluded that he would be less likely to make peace on terms favorable to them after the election than before. Toward the end of August, they began to back away from their long-held position that Thieu would have to leave office before they would agree to peace.

Kissinger and Le Duc Tho achieved a breakthrough on 8 October, with the North Vietnamese agreeing that Thieu could remain in office until a multiparty committee arranged elections in South Vietnam. At this point, Kissinger was far more anxious to achieve a settlement than Nixon, who expressed concern about a peace that left Saigon in a weak position. "It cannot be a shotgun marriage," he instructed Kissinger.[81] But the national security adviser worried that Nixon might initiate a dangerous reescalation in January and feared what the Democratic Congress might do that month as well.

The South Vietnamese had never been involved in Kissinger's negotiations. Kissinger and Nixon knew that Thieu would oppose any settlement that left North Vietnamese troops in South Vietnam. Nonetheless, after the 17 October negotiating session, Kissinger left Paris for Saigon to obtain the South Vietnamese leader's approval of the settlement. He then planned to move on to Hanoi for a joint announcement of the peace on 26 October, with the cease-fire set for 30 October. As Kissinger should have expected, a bitter Thieu rejected the terms, which his intelligence operatives had already obtained for him. Incensed over what appeared to be a sellout, he "wanted to punch Kissinger in the mouth."[82] Kissinger told Nixon that the South Vietnamese leader's "demands verge on insanity."[83]

Suspecting that something had gone wrong in Saigon, the North Vietnamese jumped the gun on 25 October, publicly announcing that a peace
agreement had been reached. Kissinger agreed the next day that "peace is
at hand" and thus completely undercut dovish Democratic presidential
candidate George McGovern.[84] Nixon, who knew that peace was not at
hand and that he had not approved his adviser's proclamation, complained,
"I suppose now everybody's going to say that Kissinger won the election."[85]

The president was displeased with what he correctly perceived to be
Kissinger's insubordination on previous occasions when he had ignored
instructions from Washington. In turn, Kissinger was displeased when he
correctly perceived that his aide Alexander Haig was undercutting him
with the president. The national security adviser did not know that Nixon
had ordered Charles Colson to monitor Kissinger's phone calls in December to document his leaks to the press. But he did know that his relations
with the president were strained. When he discovered that *Time* magazine
was going to name both him and Nixon "Men of the Year," he begged the
editor to rescind the honor.

On 20 November, Kissinger met with Le Duc Tho to deal with the alleged "technicalities" in the draft treaty that were holding up progress. They
involved sixty-nine changes in the document, including the withdrawal of
some North Vietnamese troops from the South and the prohibition of troop
movements across the Demilitarized Zone. The next day, North Vietnam
countered with changes of its own, and the negotiations bogged down over
the next few weeks. The American public was never told that the major
sticking points stemmed from *South* Vietnamese objections to the terms.
On 12 December, Le Duc Tho announced his intention to return home.
Convinced that the North Vietnamese were stalling, an exasperated
Kissinger formally broke off the talks, calling them privately "just a bunch
of shits. Tawdry, filthy shits."[86]

Nixon then decided to bomb the North Vietnamese back to the peace
table, ordering a massive B-52 attack on Hanoi and Haiphong (Operation Linebacker 2) from 18 through 30 December. Aware that the real
problem was the South Vietnamese, Nixon hoped that the bombing would
demonstrate his willingness to go to almost any length to defend their
interests. He backed up the bombing of the North with Operation Enhance
Plus, the dispatch of $2 billion worth of military and other supplies to
South Vietnam.

For twelve days, the B-52s rained down 36,000 tons of bombs on North
Vietnam, more tonnage than had been dropped on the North during the
1969–1971 period. Although the communists claimed that "only" 2,200
civilians were killed during the Christmas bombing, damage to Hanoi and

Haiphong was considerable. The United States paid heavily for this "success." The North Vietnamese shot down at least fifteen B-52s—up to that point in the war, they had been able to bring down only one—with six alone hit on 20 December. And they disabled several more of those $8 million planes. During this campaign, more than 120 Americans lost their lives, and the North Vietnamese ended up with 31 additional POWs. The early B-52 losses concerned the administration, but as the bombing continued, more and more of the once formidable North Vietnamese missile sites were destroyed, so that by 26 December, American pilots could bomb North Vietnam in relative security.

Congress was not in session when the bombing began, and most college students were home for vacation. Even without an uproar on the campuses or Capitol Hill, the bombing aroused passions around the world. The Dow-Jones average of leading industrial stocks listed on the New York Stock Exchange fell further than it had fallen in a year and a half, a majority of the American public told pollsters that they disapproved of the bombing, and foreign leaders spoke out, with Swedish premier Olaf Palme comparing the United States with Nazi Germany. Nixon rode out this storm, which abated when the North Vietnamese blinked first and on 28 December asked to reopen peace talks on essentially the terms laid out by Nixon, in exchange for cessation of the bombing. Two days later, Nixon declared an end to Linebacker 2. Kissinger met Le Duc Tho on 8 January in Paris while Nixon let Thieu know that this time he would have to accept the deal. Nixon assured Thieu on several occasions in January that if the North Vietnamese violated the agreement, the United States "will respond with full force."[87] His promises to South Vietnam appeared in informal letters that did not bind either Congress or his successor. In Saigon, Haig was finally able to convince a still unhappy Thieu of the futility of continued resistance.

The agreement reached on 13 January resembled the one arranged in October, with twenty or so minor changes. On 23 January, Kissinger and Le Duc Tho initialed the treaty, which was to go into effect on 27 January. (That fall they were awarded the Nobel Prize for peace for their efforts.) The military sections of the Agreement on Ending the War and Restoring Peace in Vietnam called for an immediate cease-fire. In addition, the United States agreed to terminate all offensive operations against North Vietnam, to remove the mines from North Vietnamese harbors, to withdraw all troops from South Vietnam, and to dismantle all bases in sixty days. Hanoi agreed to return all POWs within sixty days. Neither side would send more troops to South Vietnam, and an international commission would be established to enforce the cease-fire. In a side agreement, the North Vietnamese agreed to use their good offices with the Communist Pathet Lao to halt the civil war in Laos, something that was accomplished in February. They claimed, accurately, that they did not have the same influence with the Khmer Rouge in Cambodia.

The political section of the agreement established that both Saigon and the Provisional Revolutionary Government (Vietcong) had political status and that their delegates, along with neutralists, would constitute a Council of National Reconciliation and Concord that would arrange for elections in South Vietnam. To further sweeten the deal for the North Vietnamese, Nixon promised reconstruction aid if they lived up to the agreement—and if Congress approved it. He fixed the figure at $3.25 billion in February.

As one of Kissinger's aides accurately remarked, "We bombed the North Vietnamese into accepting our concessions."[88] Although Nixon at the time claimed that the January draft was "substantially" better than the October draft, he later admitted that he wished Thieu had accepted the first draft.[89] The president told the nation on 23 January, "The important thing was not to talk about peace—but to get peace—and to get the right kind of peace. This we have done." Kissinger was not all that confident that the peace, which left North Vietnamese troops in South Vietnam, would hold. He told Ehrlichman, "If they're lucky, they [the South Vietnamese] can hold out for a year and a half."[90]

Nixon entitled one chapter in his No More Vietnams "How We Won the War." Throughout all his writings and discussions of the way the war ended, Nixon insisted that the 27 January agreement was a solid peace that could have preserved an independent South Vietnam indefinitely. When the North Vietnamese violated the agreement, he would have retaliated against them. But his presidency soon became enmeshed in the Watergate scandal, and as a result, it was impossible for him to exercise his authority as commander in chief. He claimed that he was prepared to renew bombing of North Vietnam just when White House counsel John Dean began talking to prosecutors about Watergate in the spring of 1973. Further, because of Watergate, he and his successor were not able to deliver adequate supplies and economic aid to South Vietnam in 1974 and 1975. In the chapter of No More Vietnams titled "How We Lost the Peace," Nixon complained that "Congress proceeded to snatch defeat from the jaws of victory."[91]

Nixon's defense of his peace agreement overlooks the likelihood that by 1973, even a strong president would not have been able to convince a Democratic Congress and the public to accept a reescalation in Southeast Asia. Moreover, when Nixon agreed that the 140,000 North Vietnamese troops in South Vietnam did not have to withdraw after the war ended, he effectively sealed the fate of the Saigon regime. And, of course, Vietnamization was never a complete success; Thieu's regime, though backed by a massive, well-armed military, had not developed the mature political and economic infrastructure needed to withstand the internal and external pressures it soon confronted.

Could the peace Nixon achieved in 1973 have been obtained in 1969? During the four years that his administration prosecuted the war in Vietnam, the United States lost over 18,000 troops, the South Vietnamese at least 107,000, and the communists perhaps as many as half a million. Had Nixon surrendered the principle of mutual withdrawal in 1969 instead of in 1972, the North Vietnamese might have compromised on political issues, and the war could have been brought to a much speedier end, with the concomitant saving of hundreds of thousands of Asian and American lives.

A final issue involves the POWs. The North Vietnamese returned 587 POWs to the United States in March 1973, but the families of POWs and MIAs and their millions of supporters suspected that many hundreds of others had been held back in North Vietnam, perhaps out of sheer cruelty, perhaps for use as bargaining chips later. In their haste to withdraw from the war, Kissinger and Nixon had not pushed the North Vietnamese aggressively for an accounting of MIAs. Although no convincing evidence has emerged that suggests that the North Vietnamese held back POWs, Kissinger did little to obtain perhaps as many as sixty prisoners held in Laos. Many of them had been involved in embarrassing activities in the covert war in that country. At the time, however, most Americans were happy when Nixon celebrated the bravery of the returned POWs at a White House gala on 24 May.

The last legacy of this controversial war for Nixon revolved around the question of whether to pardon or grant amnesty to draft resisters at home and abroad. He wrote on a memo that outlined Truman's generous policy after World War II, "Never."[92] In March 1973, Americans agreed with him by a three-to-one margin in their opposition to amnesty.

During the first three weeks after the signing of the peace, observers recorded 3,000 truce violations committed by both sides. In the months that followed, South Vietnam went on the offensive, capturing more territory, while Thieu refused to take seriously the parts of the treaty dealing with new elections in the South. Most of the military glory belonged to Thieu in 1973, as a rebuilding North Vietnam had been forced on the defensive. The United States contributed to the violations by sending an additional $800 million in military aid and maintaining 8,000 "civilian" advisers in the South who were really military personnel.

From March through May, the United States dropped 95,000 tons of bombs on Cambodia, three times the amount in all of 1972, in an attempt to aid Lon Nol in his civil war against the Khmer Rouge. Demonstrating its opposition to continuing military activities in Southeast Asia, Congress, over Nixon's veto, prohibited the bombing of Cambodia after 15 August 1973.

The withdrawal of the United States from South Vietnam spelled economic disaster for the Thieu regime. An already difficult situation worsened when, as in most Third World countries, rapid oil price increases in the fall of 1973 rocked Saigon's shaky economy. By the end of 1973, unemployment reached 30 percent, and inflation was running at 65 percent. Congress continued to supply South Vietnam with economic aid, but never at the level Nixon called for. Compounding South Vietnam's problems, Thieu's 1973 offensive used up a good deal of weapons and ammunition that were not replaced in 1974 and 1975. During 1974 and the first five months of 1975, the South Vietnamese became increasingly weaker and the North Vietnamese increasingly stronger, until the latter launched a major offensive in the spring of 1975 that resulted in the fall of South Vietnam to North Vietnam and its NLF ally.

Nixon took pride in obtaining the peace with honor he had promised Americans in 1969. But at what cost and with what ultimate outcome? Could he have achieved a comparable settlement in 1969, and if so, what would that settlement have meant for the thousands of Americans and millions of citizens of Vietnam, Cambodia, and Laos who died while he was slowly withdrawing from Southeast Asia? Nixon contended that an early U.S. withdrawal from Vietnam on unfavorable terms would have made it impossible for him to create the opening to China and achieve détente with the Soviet Union. An examination of his diplomacy with those two communist powers does not support that contention.

4

★ ★ ★ ★ ★

THE GREAT GAME

When Richard Nixon proclaimed in his first inaugural address that "after a period of confrontation, we are entering an era of negotiations," the quintessential cold warrior signaled dramatic departures in U.S. foreign policy. However one may evaluate the long-term significance of those departures, Nixon undeniably reoriented American foreign policy at least as dramatically as had one of his role models, Harry Truman, who led his country from isolationism to internationalism in the years after World War II. Nixon intended to lead the United States away from the brink toward an era of peaceful coexistence with the communist world. His proudest foreign policy achievements were interrelated—the establishment of détente with the Soviet Union and the opening of relations with China.

The idea of détente did not begin with Nixon. There had been earlier thaws in the cold war, notably in 1955, 1959, and the 1963–1964 period. More recently, the Johnson administration had made serious efforts to normalize Soviet-American relations. At the Glassboro summit in 1967 and in other meetings with Soviets, American leaders, especially Secretary of Defense Robert S. McNamara, pushed for Strategic Arms Limitation Talks (SALT) on two new weapons systems—antiballistic missiles (ABMs) and multiple independently targetable reentry vehicles (MIRVs)—whose development promised to usher in a dangerous new round in the nuclear arms race. The Johnson administration planned to begin preliminary arms talks with the Soviet Union on 30 September 1968. However, after the Soviets and their allies invaded Czechoslovakia on 20 August to restore the pro-Soviet regime, Washington put off the talks. Following Nixon's election,

Johnson wanted to convene a summit conference during the interregnum. Nixon vetoed the initiative, warning the outgoing president that the new administration would not be bound by any deal Johnson and the Russians arranged.

Central to the development of the Johnson administration's arms-control policy was the adoption of the doctrine of mutually assured destruction (MAD). MAD was premised on the idea that both the Soviet Union and the United States had reached a point where they possessed so many offensive nuclear weapons that any exchange would lead to the destruction of both countries, no matter who struck first, because of their impregnable second-strike capabilities. Nixon implicitly accepted MAD when he announced at a 27 January 1969 press conference that his goal was "sufficiency not superiority" in nuclear weapons.

As he began his presidency, Nixon viewed the Soviet Union as becoming a "normal" great power, more interested in preserving international stability and devoting resources to its infrastructure than in sponsoring revolutions or engaging in diplomatic or military contests with the West. The president had a variety of reasons for promoting the concept of détente. For one thing, he feared that the Soviets had not accepted MAD. They had been outspending the United States on missile development during the sixties and, after reaching parity, may have been seeking superiority. Nixon wanted to slow the arms race, concerned about its great cost and destabilizing effects. The United States' commanding economic position of the fifties had declined in recent years, in part because its main commercial rivals in Europe and Japan did not have to devote so large a percentage of their economies to defense.

The Vietnam War had been a heavy drain on the U.S. economy. As discussed in the preceding chapter, Nixon felt that a more friendly Soviet Union might pressure its ally to accept a compromise peace. But the CIA warned Nixon from the start that Moscow had even less control over North Vietnam than the United States had over South Vietnam. Thus, when Nixon informed the Soviets that the development of détente depended on what happened in Vietnam, he held up real movement for much of 1969. Not until June did Nixon signal his willingness to discuss arms control without Soviet assistance in Vietnam.

A normalization of U.S.-Soviet relations might also produce an economic bonanza for American exporters. Although not a major reason for Nixon's policy originally, it soon became one of the rationales employed by the administration to convince American capitalists of the benefits of a thaw in the cold war. Holding out a carrot to both the Soviet Union and the American business community, Nixon successfully lobbied Congress to enact in December the Export Administration Act of 1969, which permitted him to begin liberalizing trade with Warsaw Pact countries, particularly in Eastern Europe, where the Western allies had already established an economic foothold. This act did not, however, grant the Soviet Union the much-coveted most favored nation (MFN) status.

More generally, Nixon believed that a policy of détente would lead to the creation of mechanisms that would improve crisis management around the world. Neither country had any interest in becoming involved in another Cuban missile crisis.

The president and his national security adviser were also nervous about the development of *Ostpolitik,* German foreign minister Willy Brandt's policy of forging Europe's own détente with Moscow. An increasingly self-sufficient and independent Western Europe desired to normalize relations with the Eastern bloc in what some in Washington feared might lead to appeasement. Kissinger, Brandt recalled, told him in no uncertain terms that Washington would take the lead in establishing détente with the Soviet Union. The German leader, who considered Kissinger "too old fashioned for my taste," resented that the American "saw Europeans as pawns in the great game of the superpowers."[1]

The Western European nations were troubled by the MAD doctrine. American acceptance of MAD and Nixon's correlate of "sufficiency" meant that Washington might not use its nuclear weaponry to defend its allies against the much larger ground forces of the Warsaw Pact. Characteristically, in its major negotiations with the Soviet Union involving Europe—including détente, SALT, and ABMs—the administration rarely consulted with its NATO allies, another reason why *Ostpolitik* seemed attractive to France and Germany.

In a related matter, since 1966, Senate Majority Leader Mike Mansfield (D-Mont.) had introduced resolutions calling for the reduction of American force levels in Europe. Rather than being compelled to make such a unilateral concession to Moscow, NATO leaders had hoped to launch talks with the communists on mutual and balanced force reductions (MBFR) in Europe.

According to Ambassador Dobrynin, Soviet leader Leonid Brezhnev was "largely incapable of conceptual thinking in foreign policy."[2] But even without having developed a sophisticated *Weltpolitik,* Brezhnev had his own reasons for moving toward normalization of relations with the West. He too worried about the burdens that high defense spending imposed on his nation's economy. Soviet subsidies to Cuba alone cost more than $1 million a day. In addition, its "metal-eaters alliance," the parallel to the U.S. military-industrial complex, was not certain that it could compete with the West in the development of the next generation of high-tech weaponry.

Moreover, Brezhnev, who in 1968 had sent Warsaw Pact troops into Czechoslovakia to keep that satellite in line, had an interest in reducing tensions between Eastern and Western Europe, and especially in solving the Berlin problem. The Soviets were as attracted to *Ostpolitik* as the Americans were repelled by it because it might weaken NATO. At the same time, Nixon understood that all was not well in the Eastern bloc, as he demonstrated in early August 1969 when he became the first president to visit Romania, one of the most independent of the Soviet Union's allies. Tensions in the bloc increased in December 1970 when food riots in Poland led Moscow to force the Poles to replace Wladyslaw Gomulka with Edward Gierek and then to convince East German leader Walter Ulbricht, an opponent of *Ostpolitik,* to surrender his office to Erich Honecker.

The Soviet Union also was interested in liberalizing trade with the United States and its allies. One way to catch up with the capitalist world economically was to purchase Western technology. Liberalized trade with the United States could lead to grain purchases that would relieve the pressure on the Soviets' troubled agricultural sector. The chemical, automobile, paper and pulp manufacturing, and machine-tool sectors of their economy also needed help. The Soviets' problems were further compounded by the rising public demand for consumer goods, a demand that Brezhnev recognized in March 1971 at the 24th Party Congress, when, for the first time in Soviet history, consumer-goods production took priority in a Five-Year Plan.

Finally, China had replaced the United States as the Soviet Union's most threatening enemy. Trouble had been brewing between the two centers of communist power since the formal Sino-Soviet split in 1961. In 1969, between January and April, the Soviet Union claimed that the Chinese invaded their border regions on at least ninety occasions, leading to skirmishes that resulted in scores of casualties. One Soviet diplomat described his "almost frantic" colleagues who felt an "electric shock" from the Chinese attack on Damansky Island in March, fearing a full-scale invasion.[3] A few in the leadership, including the powerful chief of staff, Marshal Andrei Grechko, advocated a preemptive attack on Chinese nuclear missile bases (something the Kennedy and Johnson administrations had also considered). Ironically, during this era in Soviet-American relations, decision making in Brezhnev's Politburo was more open and freewheeling than in Nixon's White House, where the president rarely heard much forceful dissent.

Nixon made it clear to Moscow that the United States would strongly disapprove of a Soviet attack against China, even implying that his country would assist China in a crisis. Already developing a triangulation policy to deal with China and the Soviet Union, Nixon told his cabinet on 14

August 1969 that the United States could not permit the Soviets to upset the balance of power by attacking Chinese nuclear facilities. Nixon's warnings had little influence on Moscow's decision not to attack China. One prominent Russian historian now reports that the Soviet threats were only part of a "propaganda campaign" to frighten Beijing.[4]

Among Brezhnev's more intangible reasons for normalizing relations with the United States was the prospect that détente would represent an acknowledgment of the Soviet Union's coequal status in the world. Having been considered a pariah for much of its half century of existence, the communist state would finally attain the respect it deserved.

Moscow clearly had as many good reasons to pursue détente as did Washington. The process was launched in February 1969 when Kissinger and Dobrynin established a special relationship ("the channel"), whereby the two men would meet without secretaries or interpreters, often without telling the State Department, to negotiate major issues in Soviet-American relations. During difficult periods, especially after 1970, the two men often met daily. In 1972 alone, they had more than 130 conversations in Washington, the same year that a direct "hot line" between the White House and the Soviet embassy was installed.

From the start, Dobrynin explained to Nixon and Kissinger the Soviets' rejection of linkage, which they considered a form of bribery. To Moscow, all questions "had to stand on their own feet and be settled accordingly."[5] Although Nixon and Kissinger relented in the summer of 1969 by agreeing to talk about SALT in the absence of a Vietnam breakthrough, as late as 20 October, the two were still haranguing Dobrynin about Moscow's lack of assistance with the North Vietnamese. That same day, the Russians opened negotiations with the Chinese to cool off the border strife. The next day, Willy Brandt paid an important visit to Moscow to talk about his own version of détente.

Despite Washington's concern about linkage, both sides agreed to begin SALT negotiations in Helsinki on 17 November and arranged seven more meetings held alternately in the Finnish capital and Vienna. That same month, Nixon finally signed the Nuclear Non-Proliferation Treaty that had been negotiated by the Johnson administration.

His negotiators came to Helsinki armed with the threat that the United States was poised to develop an ABM system. When Nixon took office, the Johnson administration had been committed to the construction of the Sentinel System, a small ABM system that might protect the United States from Chinese attack. Few scientists were sold on the efficacy of that or any other ABM system that would easily be overwhelmed by the fast-developing MIRV missile programs. In March 1969, Nixon announced his support for an enhanced ABM program, the Safeguard System, which envisaged as many as twelve sites, four of which would protect Minuteman missile bases. At the time, the Soviets had deployed sixty-four interceptor missiles in their Galosh System around Moscow in their relatively small-scale ABM program. Nixon also announced in June his decision to begin testing MIRVs.

Although the president could not publicly reveal his strategy, he was unenthusiastic about developing ABM systems, given their cost and dubious effectiveness against the latest generation of missiles. But he wanted to be able to use Safeguard as a bargaining chip in SALT. His problem was the Senate, which quickly introduced an amendment to prohibit spending on the ABM system. In a few weeks, peace-movement activists rallied around the nation against an American ABM.

To meet their challenge, Nixon rallied Democratic hawks to his side, with former secretary of state Dean Acheson and defense analyst Paul Nitze, among others, forming the Committee to Maintain a Prudent Defense Policy. Nixon certainly needed all the help he could get in the Senate, where only a fifty-fifty vote on 6 August defeated the anti-ABM amendment. The ABM struggle involved a good deal of hardball politics; the president declared, "This is war."[6] He instructed Attorney General Mitchell that if Republican senators Marlow Cook and John Sherman Cooper from Kentucky "kick us in the teeth" on the ABM, he should give the vacancy on the Sixth Circuit Court of Appeals to Tennessee, where Senator Howard Baker was supporting the ABM.[7]

The administration viewed the vote as "the first battle of '72, vs. Teddy Kennedy, and we *must* win."[8] Nixon was very pleased with the outcome, which he ordered trumpeted throughout the nation with the public-relations line: "But over it all is the massive effort that was made by RN on this project. Never in history has a President, individually and collectively, talked to more Senators on an issue than in this case."[9] Considering the fact that both sides ultimately renounced building more ABMs, a decision that helped clear the way for the SALT I agreement, Nixon appeared to have the better of the argument against those who opposed the ABM program. Of course, they—and the Russians—did not know that he was not really interested in ABMs.

Nixon had an easier time ignoring the Senate's nonbinding resolution of April 1970, which passed by a seventy-two–to–six vote, calling for both countries to defer deploying MIRVs until after the completion of SALT. With the United States far ahead in MIRVs, Nixon deployed them in June as a response to the Soviet Union's greater number of non-MIRVed missiles. Although recognizing that MIRVs represented a dangerous escalation in the arms race, he needed them to weaken support for ABMs, and he also thought that it would be politically impossible to convince the Pentagon to forgo both ABMs and MIRVs. Nixon and Kissinger later commented that the failure to obtain an agreement to ban MIRVs was a costly blunder that led to a dramatic escalation in the arms race. They may have been too hard on themselves, since verification of any MIRV ban depended on on-site inspections, something the Soviets would not have permitted in 1972.

Through the first part of 1969, Nixon delayed major movement in Soviet-American relations until he recognized the failure of linkage to produce peace in Vietnam. With the Chinese border quieter and Brandt's *Ostpolitik* beginning to look promising, the Soviets were the ones to move slowly through the second part of the year. After it became apparent that Nixon wanted to hold his first summit in 1970, before the congressional elections, the Soviets, suspecting his political motives, balked, contending that much groundwork had to be laid before a meaningful meeting could be arranged. They suggested that the summer of 1971 was the earliest possible date for such a meeting, hoping for a Berlin settlement by that time.

Nixon did not forget how the Soviets had rejected his call for an early summit when *he* later chose the strategy of delay, as he prepared to shock the Soviets and the rest of the world with the July 1971 announcement of a Sino-American summit in 1972. A Soviet diplomat later reported that Foreign Minister Andrei Gromyko "went about for weeks with a black expression" after learning of the China breakthrough.[10] By announcing the astounding Chinese summit before making final arrangements for the Soviet summit, Nixon repaid the Russians in spectacular fashion for their previous foot-dragging.

As the president worked out his strategy during the first part of 1969—a strategy based in good measure on demonstrating to Moscow that, unlike the previous administration, he would not be constrained by doves in Congress and among the public—a crisis with communist North Korea tested his mettle. On 15 April, the North Koreans shot down an unarmed American EC-121 over international waters, killing all thirty-one crewmen. The reconnaissance plane had been on an intelligence mission related to the Sino-Soviet border conflict. The previous year, after North Korea had seized the *Pueblo,* Nixon had been among those criticizing Johnson for not taking stronger action against the communists.

Kissinger was especially exercised by the EC-121 shoot-down, which he interpreted as a test for the new administration. He urged retaliatory bombing raids and even considered the use of nuclear weapons. Nixon, Agnew, and Mitchell supported his recommendation to take strong action, while Rogers, Laird, Helms, and the Joint Chiefs weighed in against it. They feared sparking a full-scale war on the Korean peninsula over what might have been a North Korean error. They also pointed that the air force on Guam lacked fighter escorts for the B-52s to be used in any attack. Nixon finally decided on using strong rhetoric, sending a twenty-three-vessel task force to the area, and continuing the secret bombing of Cambodia. He vowed, "They got away with it this time, but they'll never get away with it again," and later contended that the EC-121 crisis was the "most serious misjudgment of my Presidency, including Watergate."[11] For his part, Kissinger later commented that in a crisis, "boldness is the safest course," and he worried that U.S. inaction had made the North Vietnamese draw the wrong lessons from the affair.[12]

Both Nixon and Kissinger were also distressed about the way the seemingly ponderous NSC system had worked in this crisis. Ironically, it had worked exactly as originally designed. In the future, they would try to keep Rogers and Laird from butting into their business. Nixon was even more distressed when he discovered that Laird, on his own, had ordered the grounding of all reconnaissance flights in the region for three weeks. But he refused to confront his defense secretary over the matter.

Nixon and Kissinger did not employ linkage politics during the crisis, except insofar as they linked it to Vietnam. They understood that the Soviet Union could do little to control its renegade ally in Pyongyang. Soviet-American relations were affected somewhat when Nixon revealed an intelligence secret, blurting out at a press conference on 18 April, "We, incidentally, know what the Russian radar showed" during the incident. Such are the dangers of holding on-the-record, live press conferences in a democracy.

The administration fared better in its next small crisis with the Soviet Union and one of its allies. On 16 September 1970, a U-2 flight over Cuba revealed the construction of what looked like a submarine base at Cienfuegos. The Soviet Union was surreptitiously building a base that violated the American understanding of the 1962 settlement of the Cuban missile crisis. Once again the communists were apparently testing the administration. Haig, prone to overreaction, considered the action in Cuba "a reckless Soviet adventure."[13]

In this case, even though newspapers published stories about the affair, Nixon used quiet diplomacy to convince the Russians, without embarrassing them in public, to agree to dismantle the base. For its part, Moscow had been worried about the fact that the CIA, on Nixon's orders, had recently intensified anti-Castro activities. In August, even before the discovery of the submarine base, a Russian diplomat had inquired about the standing of John F. Kennedy's 1962 pledge not to invade Cuba. Because it had been a conditional pledge based on on-site inspections in Cuba that

Castro did not permit, it was theoretically no longer valid. In the secret negotiations involving the dismantling of the submarine base that fall, Nixon implicitly pledged that the United States would not invade Cuba when he approved an agreement drawn up by Gromyko.

Despite the resolution of the crisis, its occurrence revealed to the administration that the Soviets' approach to détente differed from its own. Moscow wanted to improve relations with the United States and Western Europe and especially desired an arms-control agreement, but this did not mean that it would alter its policies in the Third World. This was again demonstrated in 1970 when the Soviets sent generous shipments of military matériel and offered training to their faction in the Angolan war for independence from U.S. ally Portugal. A fair-minded observer might wonder what in the name of détente was a U.S. submarine doing wiretapping an undersea Soviet military telecommunications cable in the Far East late in 1971.

Soviet and American interests in détente did coincide in certain regions, the most important of which was Europe. Moscow wanted to relax tensions in general and obtain formal Western recognition of the permanency of its system, especially the legitimacy of the East German regime. If achieving that goal could weaken U.S. ties with Europe, so much the better. From the Soviet perspective, resolving the German question had a higher priority than convening a summit to sign a SALT treaty. On 10 August 1971, Brezhnev finally invited Nixon to come to Moscow, but only after it appeared that a Berlin settlement was nigh.

On 12 August 1970, Willy Brandt had traveled to the Soviet Union to initial the Treaty of Moscow, a nonaggression pact that implicitly accepted the boundary settlements that followed World War II. Four months later, Brandt normalized relations with Poland and thus recognized the Oder-Niesse boundary line. These treaties helped clear the way for a settlement of the Berlin issue, which was then under discussion among the Soviet Union, England, France, and the United States.

Three of the architects of containment, John J. McCloy, Lucius Clay, and Dean Acheson, were so concerned that Brandt was about to break away from NATO that they warned President Nixon in person about the dangerous German activities. The president, who did not care for the independent Brandt, was not as worried about a German defection. In fact, he thought that the Russians might be worried that Brandt's opening to East Germany could lead to unification on the West's terms.

On 3 September 1971, the problem was settled with the Quadripartite Agreement on Berlin, which established the legal basis for civilian access from West Germany to Berlin, as well as Four-Power rights in both Berlin sectors. The West Germans could no longer hold elections in the Reichstag

Building or try to annex West Berlin (but they could maintain an official presence in the city), and the West accepted East Germany as being in de facto control of East Berlin. The treaty worked well, in that the city was no longer a flash point in the cold war from 1971 until the fall of the wall in 1989. Kissinger had assumed a leading role in these negotiations through back-channel discussions with Ambassador Dobrynin. Bypassing the State Department, as usual, he set up direct links between his office and U.S. ambassador to Germany Kenneth Rush (one of Nixon's old law professors) and Brandt's national security aide. Nixon was pleased with the settlement. He had noted in March, "progress on Berlin can be the breakthrough to progress on normalization on East-West relations generally."[14]

Such progress came to a halt during the India-Pakistan war of 1971, which Kissinger aptly described as "perhaps the most complex issue of Nixon's first term."[15] He ended up in Nixon's doghouse for a few weeks after he told the press that the president might cancel the summit the following year because of Moscow's behavior during the war.

The 1947 territorial settlement that split the subcontinent into two countries, India and Pakistan, had really created three countries, since East and West Pakistan were separated by 1,000 miles of Indian territory. West Pakistan was the dominant and, to those in East Pakistan, oppressive partner in the union. Run by a military dictatorship, Pakistan was a U.S. ally, in part because neutral and relatively democratic India was an outspoken opponent of Western imperialism. During the Nixon administration, Pakistan also served as an intermediary between the United States and China. The Chinese, who had fought a border war with pro-Soviet India in 1962, were allies of Pakistan.

The people of East Pakistan, the poorer and less developed part of the nation, demonstrated their hostility to West Pakistan in a December 1970 election when 97 percent of the voters expressed support for the party that promised to work for autonomy within a reformed Pakistan. After the government of West Pakistan arrested the leader of the East Pakistan autonomy movement in March 1971, a bloody civil war began that ended in December with the independence of East Pakistan (Bangladesh).

Observers the world over sympathized with the brutally suppressed people of Bangladesh. Over 10 million refugees fled to India, and as many as 50,000 East Pakistani women were raped by West Pakistani soldiers. From Nixon's amoral perspective, the United States' international position was at stake in this civil conflict. The administration continued to supply Pakistan with American-made arms and sought to ensure that its ally was not attacked by the more powerful India. During the summer of 1971, the

Indians, who had fought two previous wars with Pakistan, had threatened to intervene, if only to stop the flow of refugees.

Nixon disliked India's prime minister Indira Gandhi, having concluded that she had not treated him with proper respect during a trip to the subcontinent before he became president. To make matters worse, he believed that the independent and proud Indian leader had insulted him again when she visited the United States on the eve of the crisis on 4 November 1971. This came on top of the signing of the Indian-Soviet friendship treaty, negotiated in 1969 but announced on 8 August 1971, as a partial response to Nixon's announcement of Chinese-American rapprochement the previous month.

For men who were proud of their hard-boiled, realistic approach to international politics, Nixon and Kissinger often permitted personal feelings about foreign leaders to color their national security decisions. Thus, whereas Nixon especially disliked Gandhi, he felt warmly toward Pakistan's leader Yahya Khan, who served as the key intermediary in his secret Chinese diplomacy.

On 21 November the Indian military moved into East Pakistan, and by 1 December it had liberated the territory from West Pakistan. On 2 December, Yahya Khan, fearing a general Indian-Pakistani war, invoked a secret 1962 U.S. commitment to aid Pakistan against Indian aggression. Without waiting for a response from Washington, he foolishly launched an air attack on Indian forces in Kashmir and the Punjab. Whatever its formal commitment, the United States could not permit Pakistan to be swallowed up by India, and, as an NSC aide put it, it had to do something "demonstrating to China we were a reliable country to deal with."[16]

On the day the war started, Kissinger complained, "I'm getting hell every half hour from the President that we are not being tough enough on India."[17] Although Nixon believed that Gandhi was preparing to destroy her mortal enemy, she later claimed, "We had no intention of doing anything with West Pakistan."[18] The CIA had concluded that India was going to move; the State Department was not so certain.

Officially, American policy in the India-Pakistan war was neutrality. Most Americans, who did not understand the international complexities on the subcontinent, supported India against the brutal rapists of West Pakistan. Thus, Nixon had to keep secret from his constituents the fact that the United States was "tilting" toward Pakistan during the first week of December. When word of the tilting leaked in Jack Anderson's syndicated newspaper column, operatives in the Nixon White House began talking about ways of silencing the muckraker forever in what later came to be a shocking footnote in the Watergate scandals. On 12 December, using the hot line for the first time in his presidency, Nixon asked the Soviets to curb their Indian allies or face cancellation of the upcoming summit. He also told them about the secret U.S. commitment to aid Pakistan. Complaining that they did not have that sort of influence with New Delhi, the Soviets pointed out that, in any event, Gandhi, who was merely acting defensively, had no intention of invading West Pakistan. Kissinger and Nixon were among the few who later concluded that U.S. pressure on Moscow helped keep the Indians within their borders.

In addition, without telling Secretary of State Rogers and Secretary of Defense Laird, or even telling the commanders what they were supposed to do when they got there, Nixon ordered naval Task Group 74 to the Bay of Bengal to threaten the Indians. The task force began moving into position on 10 December, one day after the Indians and Pakistanis concluded a tentative agreement to settle the war. Explaining his actions to the American people on 9 February 1972, Nixon asserted, "It was not in my view in the first place that the war was the solution to a humanitarian problem. The complete disintegration by force of a member state was intolerable and could not be acquiesced in by the United Nations." But the United States had operated in secret, and certainly not on behalf of the United Nations. Nixon believed that his constituents would not understand or approve of the anti-Indian measures he had taken during the war to support his complicated triangular diplomacy with the Soviet Union and China.

Although linkage politics had not worked, Nixon and Kissinger were pleased with their boldness. They claimed that they had saved Pakistan, had impressed the Chinese, and had not destroyed détente. It now seems that the crisis in Soviet-American relations they created was a tempest in a teapot, and their macho posturing little affected Indira Gandhi, who never intended to launch a full-scale war against Pakistan.

While U.S.-Soviet relations blew hot and cold from the fall of 1969 through the end of 1971, Russian and American negotiators patiently worked in Helsinki and Vienna on a SALT agreement, the main reason for a 1972 summit conference. As the time for the summit approached—a summit that was part of Nixon's intricate triangulation policy—the Americans settled for a less-than-perfect agreement. Defense Secretary Laird admitted that "short-term expedience dominated the final stages of the SALT I agreement in 1972, when the urge to get an agreement at any cost became the chief end."[19] The head of the U.S. SALT negotiating team, Gerard Smith of the Arms Control and Disarmament Agency (ACDA), worried about how "lust for a summit affected the SALT negotiations."[20]

Nonetheless, looking back in 1975, Kissinger boasted that "without a question" SALT had been his crowning achievement.[21] His pride had more to do with the success of the Moscow summit than with SALT's contribution to arms control. From his perspective—and on SALT, he played a far more important role than Nixon, who did not care to involve himself in the complicated details of throw weights and deterrence strategies—the key was to achieve a major agreement with the Russians and to start a process. SALT I, which may not have been perfect, was to be followed by SALT II through SALT V or VI. But there are those, especially from Smith's negotiating team, who thought that the chances for real disarmament in SALT I itself had been sacrificed for the political symbolism of signing any deal in Moscow in May 1972.

Kissinger distrusted Smith and ACDA because he feared that they were doves and were overly enthusiastic about disarmament. He dealt with that problem by running parallel back-channel negotiations with Dobrynin. Yet even Kissinger had to admit that he was not an expert on all the details of the arms race. And because he handled the negotiations by himself, he made major blunders that might have been avoided had he been able to employ the considerable expertise of U.S. arms-control experts.

His lack of understanding on some issues led him to blunder on the arrangements for submarine-launched ballistic missiles (SLBMs) and on the freeze on the size of silos for ground missiles. Because of his lack of contact with the Joint Chiefs, he did not know or had forgotten that the United States did not plan to build or deploy more SLBMs. At the last moment, he was able to include submarines in the deal, albeit not in a manner advantageous to the United States. As a domestic quid pro quo, the navy and its supporters on Capitol Hill were permitted to go ahead with the costly Trident submarine program. When Gerard Smith tried to explain to Nixon several of the technical problems with the agreement, the president dismissed his arguments with "Bullshit."[22]

Although the Soviets in Helsinki and Vienna knew about Kissinger's back-channel negotiations, which often undercut Smith because they prematurely revealed U.S. fallback positions, Smith and his own team did not learn about them until May 1971. Thus, for example, when Kissinger gave up trying to achieve a comprehensive disarmament agreement on 20 May 1970, the Soviets knew it, but the ACDA delegation continued to negotiate as if such an agreement were possible. Further, the Pentagon was often kept in the dark about the negotiations, one of the reasons the brass felt compelled to spy on Kissinger's NSC in the Radford affair.

When the SALT process began in 1969, the United States had the advantage over the Soviet Union in two of the three elements of the triad that constituted its nuclear defense. Washington had 250 more long-range bombers than Moscow and a lead in nuclear submarines of 41 to 30, while the Soviet Union had 1,060 intercontinental ballistic missiles (ICBMs) to the United States' 1,054 and had a clear lead in throw weight. The Soviets were also ahead in civilian defense with their ABM system deployed around Moscow. The United States was several years ahead of the Soviet Union in the development of MIRVs, however, and was certainly ahead in the technology that would guarantee that a missile would come close to its target.

Kissinger admitted that SALT "wasn't the best deal but it was better certainly than nothing."[23] For one thing, the treaty on ABMs that limited each nation to two systems to protect cities, not missiles, was certainly an accomplishment. The Senate agreed, approving the ABM treaty by a vote of eighty-eight to two. The 1974 SALT II agreement cut back the 1972 arrangement to one ABM installation each, and in 1975, the United States unilaterally gave up its right to build even one of the costly and ineffective systems.

The interim agreement on SALT was another matter. Although not a formal treaty, it had to be submitted to Congress under the terms of the 1961 act that had established ACDA. SALT I was a five-year agreement that set upper limits for offensive missiles at 1,600 for the Soviet Union and 1,054 for the United States. It also limited submarine building and the upgrading of existing missile systems. It did not deal with MIRVs. Congress was not as pleased with the missile agreement as the Senate had been with the ABM treaty. It approved SALT by joint resolution on 30 September 1972, but only after Senator Henry Jackson (D-Wash.), a leading opponent of détente, had included a statement that Congress supported arms control as long as the number of weapons in future agreements would be symmetrical. Doves who thought that the agreement did not go far enough and hawks who felt that the Soviets had gained the most united in opposition. Nixon understood this, instructing Haig, "we must stay right on the tightrope—hold the hawks by continuing adequate defense—Hold doves by pointing out that *without* SALT the arms budget would be *much larger* because of an all out race—*and* no hope for permanent offensive limit talks."[24] The hawks received new arms systems and the doves the promise that the SALT process would continue. But even as the two sides gathered to begin the long process of negotiating a SALT II agreement, the arms race continued apace, with SALT I mandating only limits to growth, not cutbacks.

Already thinking about running for the Democratic presidential nomination in 1976, Senator Jackson exacted his revenge by leading a congressional putsch against ACDA and those responsible for SALT I. In 1973, the agency's budget was cut by one-third, an action that led to the loss of almost 20 percent of its employees. Of the seventeen top officials in 1972, only three remained by 1974, a result, in part, of Nixon's attempt to assuage

Jackson. Among those to go was Gerard Smith, who resigned and was replaced by Fred Iklé, a SALT skeptic.

Jackson's anger against ACDA was misplaced; the final agreement was virtually a 100 percent Kissinger product. Some of the weaknesses in the treaty had to do with the fact that it was not formally completed until the summit itself. Nixon had instructed Kissinger in March that "no final agreements be entered into until we arrive in Moscow," because he wanted the achievements at the summit to have "real news value."[25] Thus, Kissinger had to hurriedly tie up loose ends in one room as Nixon and Brezhnev were discussing generalities down the hall.

Because of the recent mining of Hanoi and Haiphong harbors, Nixon received a subdued public welcome when he arrived in Moscow on 22 May, the first sitting president to visit the Soviet Union. Not everyone in the Soviet capital was pleased to see him. One diplomat complained, "You people have even distorted history to please that son of a bitch," while another high-ranking official avowed, "I don't trust Nixon or his little professor."[26]

Nixon, who compared the burly and practical Brezhnev to "an American labor leader," had to sit still for three hours while the Soviets made their obligatory spirited attacks against U.S. aggression in Vietnam.[27] After the summit, Brezhnev concluded, "You can do business with Nixon."[28] The two leaders got along quite well, and that relationship carried over to the next two summits.

Aside from SALT, the centerpiece of the summit, the Soviets and Americans concluded agreements on scientific and technological cooperation, including a joint space mission. These agreements were part of a process that began in February 1971 with an agreement to ban nuclear weapons from the seabed, followed by an "accidental measures" agreement and a modification of the hot-line arrangement to include satellite communications in September, and a biological weapons convention in April 1972. All in all, from 1971 through 1973, the Soviet Union and the United States completed more than twenty treaties or agreements that improved mutual relations and relaxed tensions.

At the summit itself, the Soviets were pleased with the "Basic Principles of Relations between the Soviet Union and the United States of America," which accorded them equal superpower status with the Americans and proclaimed that "there is no alternative to conducting their mutual relations on the basis of peaceful coexistence." Both parties promised to refrain from trying "to obtain unilateral advantage at the expense of the other."

Nixon also approved the calling of a Conference on Security and Cooperation in Europe (CSCE), something the Soviet Union and some Western European nations dearly wanted. Brezhnev hoped that the CSCE talks, which came to a successful conclusion with the Act of Helsinki in August 1975, would lead to closer relations between Eastern and Western Europe and to a recognition of the permanency of the 1945 boundaries. In a sort of quid pro quo, Nixon obtained Soviet agreement to enter into MBFR talks, which appealed to American supporters of the Mansfield Amendment.

Finally, Nixon and Brezhnev agreed to a wide range of cooperative economic activities that were formally consummated during the fall of 1972. Secretary of Commerce Maurice Stans spent ten days in the Soviet Union the previous November to discuss trade, credits, and the Soviets' lend-lease debt from World War II. Wined and dined in Moscow, Stans returned to the United States enthused about the prospects for mutually beneficial Soviet-American trade. For the Soviets, the prospect of economic cooperation was a more important achievement than SALT. Trade liberalization with the United States would soon pay huge short-term dividends for the Kremlin.

One final summit highlight involved Nixon's televised address to the Soviet people on 28 May. In a well-crafted speech, he talked about both countries' concern for peace and international stability and how "the people of our two countries are very much alike." He filled his talk with aphorisms and proverbs—"When a man walks with a giant tread, he must be careful where he sets his feet"—and announced to China and others that "it has not been our aim to divide up the world into spheres of influence."

On the way home, Nixon paid a brief visit to Poland, where he was greeted warmly. He enjoyed proclaiming his many presidential "firsts," among them traveling to countries where no other president had dared to go. He told the Polish people on 31 May that "for the first time in the long and friendly history between our two countries, a President of the United States stands on Polish soil" and then went on to talk about Polish Americans' contributions to his nation. Aside from the importance of the visit diplomatically, he was aware of its impact among Polish American voters, many of whom were in the process of moving from the Democratic to the Republican column.

When he arrived home on 1 June, Nixon went straight to Capitol Hill to deliver a rare address to a joint session of Congress. With some hyperbole, he boasted, "Last Friday in Moscow we witnessed the beginning of the end of that era which began in 1945. We took the first step toward a new era of mutually agreed restraint and arms limitation." Although he oversold the "disarmament" in SALT, Nixon's preening was justified. Whether or not the arms-control agreement favored the Soviets, the Moscow summit symbolized a dramatic lessening of tension in the cold war and the promise that the United States and the Soviet Union had begun to learn to manage their potentially lethal competition. And it was that

112

tough old anticommunist, not a liberal peacenik, who had accomplished the feat.

While some on the Republican Right, most notably William F. Buckley and his *National Review*, felt that the prospect of détente disillusioned dissidents in the Soviet bloc, most Americans were pleased with Nixon's achievements. Anticommunist capitalists, especially, looked forward to opening trade with the Soviet Union. Between 1971 and 1974, Washington and Moscow signed more than ten economic agreements, including those related to shipping, taxes, and grain purchases. The most important was the 18 October 1972 trade agreement in which the United States gave the Soviets MFN status (pending congressional approval) and promised credits from the Export-Import Bank. As part of the deal, both nations established commercial offices in each other's capitals and reached a maritime agreement; the Russians also promised to pay their World War II lend-lease debt of $772 million over the next thirty years.

Under the terms of the agreement, U.S. companies TRW, Continental Can, Monsanto, General Electric, Brown and Root, Control Data, and others signed commercial contracts with the Soviets. In 1971, the United States exported $162 million worth of goods to the Soviet Union; in 1972, $542 million; in 1973, $1,190 million; and in 1974, $612 million. During the same period, Soviet exports to the United States rose from $57 million in 1971 to a rather modest $296 million in 1972 and $220 million in 1973. On the surface, the United States did well in opening up the Soviet Union to its products, while maintaining a splendid balance-of-payments advantage. However, most of the bulge in U.S. exports came from the agricultural sector, where the Marxists, according to Kissinger, "outwitted" the capitalists in what came to be called the "Great Grain Robbery."[29]

In November 1971, a year before completion of the trade agreement, the Soviets bought 3 million tons of feed grain from the United States. Concerned about the food riots in Poland in 1970, they had promised to provide their people with more meat for their daily diets. Not surprisingly, Americans thought that most of the post-summit grain purchases would involve feed grain, not wheat. When Secretary of Agriculture Earl Butz went to the Soviet Union in April 1972, he was convinced that the Russians intended to buy feed grain, even though he saw evidence of massive wheat crop failures to come.

To facilitate the grain trade, Nixon had announced in June 1971 that he would suspend the Kennedy-era rule that at least 50 percent of the grain exported to communist countries had to be carried in U.S. vessels. Working through his friend Jay Lovestone of the American Federation of Labor (AFL) and Teddy Gleason of the maritime union, Charles Colson was able to convince the seafarers to go along with revocation of the 50 percent rule for the 1971 purchase by promising them more U.S. subsidies to merchant marine shipbuilding programs and a bilateral shipping agreement with the Soviet Union.

Then the Russians began to move. There were worldwide crop failures in 1972, with only the United States having significant reserves. At the time the Soviets began buying wheat in the United States, the Agriculture Department, with an eye toward the 1972 election, ordered farmers to cut their acreage in an attempt to raise prices. Using the $750 million in credits the United States had offered them in the trade deal, as well as hundreds of millions of their own reserves, the Soviets made the largest single grain purchase in U.S. history up to that point, which came to more than one-quarter of all wheat production. After buying the grain at the artificially low subsidized American price, they cornered the world grain market. During one year, from the summer of 1972 to the summer of 1973, the price of grain tripled, from $1.61 a bushel, the price the Soviets had paid for the wheat, to $5 a bushel, a startling increase that fueled inflation in the United States and around the world. In just one month, from December 1972 to January 1973, the consumer price index rose by 2.3 percent, much of it accounted for by wheat price hikes.

Those hikes were a product not only of clever Soviet manipulations but also of global agricultural and economic developments that included a drought in Africa, the failure of the rice crop in Korea, and the 1971 devaluation of the dollar. The Department of Agriculture's mismanagement of the problem did not help matters. Had the department not waited until January 1973 to ease acreage restrictions, and had it not maintained an unnecessary wheat export subsidy during the period, the crisis might not have been so severe.

The Nixon administration, according to Senator Jackson, had created "one of the most notorious foulups in American history."[30] Ignoring the devastating impact of the Soviet deal on the price of grain and on inflation levels, the White House responded that the arrangement improved the lot of farmers, created jobs in the agricultural and shipping industries, reduced federal expenses for storing surplus wheat, improved the balanced of payments, and significantly contributed to détente—the key issue for Nixon and Kissinger, who never quite understood the mess they had made. The administration neglected to point out that U.S. grain companies profited as well, with their after-tax earnings leaping from $19.4 million in 1971–72 to $150 million in 1972–73.

And therein lay another tale. During the 1972 campaign, Democratic candidate George McGovern, from the farm state of South Dakota, charged that speculators and exporters had had inside information that enabled them to purchase huge stocks of wheat before the price rose. Clarence

Palmby, the assistant secretary of agriculture who was involved in the initial negotiations with the Soviets, including Butz's trip to Moscow in April 1972, resigned to take a position with the Continental Grain Company, which bought 150 million bushels of wheat three days before the Soviet deal was announced. Despite appearances, the Justice Department decided that Palmby was not guilty of conflict of interest.

The widespread perception that the Russians had tricked the United States into the grain deal contributed to the growth of antidétente sentiments. The issue of Jewish emigration from behind the Iron Curtain was even more important to the eventual disposition of the president's request to Congress to grant the Soviet Union MFN status. Dobrynin referred to it as "a sore spot in our relations."[31]

The problem began after the 1967 Arab-Israeli War, which sparked widespread anti-Semitic attacks in the Eastern bloc, which in turn led to requests from hundreds of thousands of Jewish citizens to emigrate. The right to emigrate freely from communist states did not exist. Moreover, had thousands of Soviet Jews been permitted to go to Israel, Moscow's Arab allies would have been furious. As early as 1970, Jewish American groups began daily picketing of the Soviet embassy in Washington over this issue, with extremists occasionally attacking Soviet diplomats.

Nixon was proud that his quiet diplomacy had increased the number of Soviet Jews permitted to emigrate from 400 in 1968 to 35,000 in 1973. He understood that the Soviets would never permit Jews to leave if it appeared that they were being pressured by the United States. But the Kremlin committed a major public-relations blunder on 3 August 1972 when it announced that emigrants would have to pay an exit tax to compensate for the costs of the free education they had received. Apparently, hardliners in the Politburo had pushed the measure through while Brezhnev and Gromyko were on holiday. Although Brezhnev rescinded the tax on 30 March 1973, the damage had been done.

On 4 October 1972, Senator Jackson, with seventy-two cosponsors, added an amendment to the trade bill that made MFN status contingent on the Soviet Union permitting free emigration of its citizens. The following April, Charles Vanik (D-Ohio) introduced the amendment in the House. On 12 December 1973, the Trade Reform Act, including the Vanik Amendment, passed the House by a 272-to-140 margin.

The Soviets would never accept such interference in their domestic politics. Kissinger complained, "How would it be if Brezhnev comes to the United States with a position about the Negroes in Mississippi?"[32] The national security adviser had conveniently forgotten that the "old" Nixon in 1964 had wanted to make President Kennedy's earlier wheat deal with Moscow conditional on liberalization. But the architect of détente was correct in his approach if the end goal was to permit Jews to emigrate from the Soviet Union. Once Jackson and his supporters began to pressure Moscow, the number of Jews permitted to leave declined from 33,500 in 1973 to 20,000 in 1974 to 13,000 in 1976. On 14 January 1975, after the Trade Reform Act of 1974, with the Jackson-Vanik Amendment, finally made it through Congress, the Soviet Union canceled the 1972 trade agreement.

Despite the conflict over Jewish emigration, Brezhnev and Nixon met in the United States for the second of their summits in the summer of 1973. The Soviet leader spent two days at Camp David from 16 June to 18 June, and then ended up at the summer White House in San Clemente from 22 June to 24 June. One American diplomat, commenting on Nixon's hosting of Brezhnev, which included a cruise on the presidential yacht, a ride on *Air Force One* to California, and a trip to Hollywood, noted caustically, "No friendly chief of state ever received such lavish hospitality."[33]

The formal accomplishments of this summit were not as significant as those of the previous year. Nixon and Brezhnev signed a prevention of nuclear war agreement that extended earlier agreements from crisis management to crisis prevention through early consultation, but the Soviets could not convince the Americans to agree to no first use of nuclear weapons. The two leaders did not achieve any breakthroughs on the SALT II talks that had begun in Geneva the previous November.

Brezhnev, who insisted on staying with Nixon in his rather modest home in San Clemente, spent two nights sleeping in Tricia Nixon's bedroom. Aside from warning Nixon about the Arabs' growing impatience with Israel and suggesting an informal "condominium" among "we Europeans" to protect the world against the Chinese, the cozy sessions included a tipsy Soviet leader playing host in Tricia's room to several Aeroflot "hostesses," and Russian security guards in the hallway witnessing an episode of sleepwalking by Pat Nixon.[34] In one ominous note, the Senate Select Committee on Watergate delayed John Dean's testimony until the summit was over so as not to embarrass the president. The Soviets, who did not understand Watergate, attributed it to American enemies of détente.

They were correct in part, recognizing that the Watergate crisis had weakened the president's ability to defend his détente policy against liberals who were concerned about humanitarian issues and against conservatives who felt that the administration had given away too much. Even within Nixon's own administration, most of the Joint Chiefs of Staff and new Secretary of Defense James Schlesinger opposed détente in general and the way SALT II was developing in particular. In June 1974, Paul Nitze resigned from the Salt II delegation because he feared that "Nixon was too preoccupied with surviving and that in his effort to get an arms control agreement, he might collapse under Soviet pressure."[35] By playing their cards so close to the vest during the negotiating stage and then by overselling the benefits of détente, Nixon and Kissinger weakened public support for their program.

On top of these problems, in January 1974, Schlesinger introduced a new flexible nuclear targeting doctrine in NSDM-242, "Policy for Planning the Employment of Nuclear Weapons." The doctrine looked provocative to the Soviet Union, especially since it involved developing counterforce capabilities against the Soviets' hardened targets. It was with this background that Nixon, facing possible impeachment in the House over the Watergate scandals, arrived in Moscow on 27 June 1974 for his third and final summit with Brezhnev. The Russian crowds that greeted him at this seven-day summit were far more friendly than comparable American crowds during that Watergate summer. Nixon spent time on the Black Sea but declined to appear in the famous resort town of Yalta, a name that meant "sellout" to Republicans. To save him embarrassment, the Soviets called their meeting place Oreanda, a Yalta suburb where they housed the American delegation.

At the summit, Nixon and Brezhnev initialed a draft on a threshold test-ban treaty. Brezhnev preferred a comprehensive test ban, but in any event, the treaty was never submitted to the Senate. In addition, the two leaders agreed to set up consulates in Kiev and New York City, to limit ABMs to one site apiece, to cooperate on energy and environmental problems, and to complete SALT II by 1979. They made no progress on SALT II itself. Nixon was embarrassed by Admiral Elmo Zumwalt, his chief of naval operations, who retired while the president was in Russia and then appeared on *Meet the Press* to denounce SALT.

By the time Nixon left the White House, the days of his détente seemed numbered. In 1976, facing spirited Republican opposition from the Right, the Ford administration retreated to a less cooperative strategy with the Soviet Union. Democrats, led by their presidential candidate Jimmy Carter, assailed the Republicans from the Left for ignoring morality in their cold-blooded diplomacy.

But the economic, cultural, and political treaties of Nixon's détente remained in force, helping to create more openness in the Soviet Union and the Eastern bloc and a bit more freedom for personal travel, communication, and interchange with the West. Despite the confrontational early years of the Reagan administration, the mid-1980s saw a renewed détente and Mikhail Gorbachev's policies of perestroika and glasnost, which might not have been promulgated had it not been for the Nixon administration's making the Soviet Union a more "normal" member of the international system. Although Nixon oversold détente and failed to achieve agreement on rules of engagement on the periphery, in the long run, his Soviet diplomacy was a success.

Détente with the Soviet Union might not have been possible had it not been for Nixon's even more audacious policy of opening relations with "Red China." In 1988, Nixon took justifiable pride in his China policy: "If it had not been for the China initiative, which only I could do at that point, we would be in a terrible situation today with China aligned with the Soviet Union and with the Soviet Union's power."[36]

Only someone like Nixon could do it, because years of Red-baiting by him and his allies made it virtually impossible for more liberal Democrats to go to China, at least in 1972. Nixon noted in July 1971 how "ironic" it was that he, the old anticommunist, was the one going to China.[37]

By the mid-1960s, Johnson's policies toward China began changing imperceptibly. For one thing, he began to see opportunity for the United States in the Sino-Soviet split, which he finally believed was real in 1965. Moreover, around the same time, he came to the conclusion that Ho Chi Minh was not the spearhead of Chinese aggression. Thus it was that the U.S. ban on travel to China was eased a bit in 1966, and State Department personnel were instructed to establish "informal social contacts with the Chinese Communists."[38] But that was the same year that China began its xenophobic Great Proletarian Revolution. Even if the Democrats had had the courage to go further than they did, China was not receptive to such overtures at the time. In November 1968, in response to a September post-Prague State Department initiative, the Chinese asked to resume ambassadorial talks in Warsaw, but Beijing canceled them the following February because of Nixon's somewhat hostile statements about China in January or because of internal conflict in Beijing.

Nixon had advised President-elect Kennedy not to try to recognize China. However, by 1966, he told a friend about the need to "bring China into the world," and in his important 1967 *Foreign Affairs* article, he repeated that sentiment, albeit with an implicit timetable that took its development well into the future.[39] After the ambassadorial talks were canceled, Nixon began hinting to the Chinese that he would like to engage in serious negotiations. He was completely in charge of the China policy—Kissinger was not very supportive when Nixon told him on 1 February 1969 to "put out the line" that he was interested in a rapprochement and to request the Departments of State and Defense and the CIA to examine, in NSSM-14, the possibilities of a breakthrough.[40] At roughly the same time in Beijing, Foreign Minister Zhou Enlai called for new studies on relations with the United States.

That same month, Nixon told French president de Gaulle to tell the Chinese that he was interested in a change of policy. The president knew that most Democrats would support his démarche, particularly after Senator Edward M. Kennedy (D-Mass.) called in March for admitting China to the United Nations and removing all trade and travel restrictions. On 21 July 1969, Nixon eased travel and trade restrictions with China, an act followed three days later by the Chinese release of several American yachtsmen who had been captured on 16 July. During his August visit to Romania, Nixon asked President Nicolae Ceauşescu, who enjoyed good relations with the Chinese, to inform them about the new U.S. approach. In November, he removed the Seventh Fleet from permanent patrol of the Taiwan Straits and the following month announced that he was going to withdraw all nuclear weapons from Okinawa.

Behind these signals was Nixon's declaration at an NSC meeting on 14 August 1969 that the Soviet Union was more aggressive than China. During the two previous years, China had begun to acknowledge that the Soviet Union was more of an enemy than the United States. This seemed even more apparent to the Chinese with the outbreak of border conflict with the Soviets in the spring of 1969. The Soviet Union's UN ambassador's comments in March 1969 may have reached Beijing: "Now those squint-eyed bastards will get a lesson they'll never forget. Who do they think they are? We'll kill those yellow sons of bitches."[41] The Chinese were also impressed with the announcement of the Nixon Doctrine in July and his intention to withdraw U.S. troops from Vietnam.

After the Soviets proclaimed the Brezhnev Doctrine to justify their invasion of Czechoslovakia in 1968, Beijing became alarmed. Foreign Minister Zhou Enlai led the pro-Western forces against Marshal Lin Biao, who favored closer ties with the Soviet Union. Their struggle did not end until the latter died in a mysterious plane crash in September 1971. From 1969 through 1971, the Chinese alternated their approach toward the United States, sometimes accepting Nixon's overtures but at other times hoping to strike a deal with their old ally the Soviet Union. Both Chinese factions worried about the prospect of a Soviet-American rapprochement and the warm relations between India and the Soviet Union.

The Chinese had other reasons to move closer to the Americans. Like the Soviets, they were interested in achieving the status that rapprochement with the United States might bring and looked forward to gaining access to Western technology. Both the Chinese and the Americans also realized that better relations meant reductions in defense burdens as the

Chinese confronted the Soviets, who doubled their divisions along their mutual border from twenty-one in 1969 to forty-five by 1973.

Nixon's policy of triangulation might have failed had it driven the Chinese into Soviet arms. But Nixon guessed correctly that Sino-Russian relations were so strained that it was unlikely that Beijing and Moscow would get together in the near term. As things turned out, both communist powers worried so much about their main enemy moving closer to the United States that they engaged in a sort of détente competition that played into Nixon's hands. Yet a 2 February 1971 NSSM claimed, "We reap benefits from Sino-Soviet hostility, but our policies are not directed specifically at exacerbating or, for that matter, lessening Sino-Soviet tensions."[42] The Soviets or Chinese would not have accepted that analysis, especially since in October of that year Kissinger wrote to Nixon, "we want our China policy to show Moscow . . . that it is to their advantage to make agreements with us, that they must take account of possible US-PRC [China] co-operation. . . . The beneficial impact on the USSR is perhaps the single biggest plus that we get from the China initiative."[43]

The on-again-off-again Warsaw talks began on 20 January 1970, less than two weeks after a State Department spokesperson for the first time publicly referred to the "People's Republic of China" instead of "Red China." At Warsaw, the Americans proposed a high-level visit to China. If things went well, the United States might begin thinning out its forces on Taiwan. Although the Chinese accepted the idea of a high-level visit in principle, they presented strict preconditions and appeared through most of 1970 to have second thoughts about the entire idea. This was a period when the arguments of the anti-American Lin Biao faction, reinforced by the U.S. invasion of Cambodia, were in ascendancy. Nonetheless, the president continued his flirtation in his 1970 State of the Union Address when he proclaimed, "The Chinese are a great and vital people who should not remain isolated from the international community." And at a state dinner in late October, he referred for the first time in public to the People's Republic of China. Several weeks earlier, Mao Zedong tried to send his own signal to Nixon when he invited American author Edgar Snow to stand next to him on the reviewing platform during an independence day ceremony. He told Snow that Nixon would be welcome in China in 1972, which the crafty Mao noted was an election year. American officials paid little attention to the left-leaning Snow. Nonetheless, in March and April 1971, Nixon further relaxed travel and trade restrictions. The Chinese responded in April when their table-tennis team, which was in Japan for a tournament, invited a touring American team to play in China, with Zhou himself receiving the Americans. Here, Beijing misinterpreted a friendly personal interaction between one nineteen-year-old American player and a Chinese player as an official gesture from Washington. But it certainly worked out for the best.

After these positive developments, a key breakthrough came later in April when the Chinese finally conveyed directly to the administration that they were prepared to receive a high-level American envoy to discuss a broader range of issues than just Taiwan. Henry Kissinger was that envoy. On a trip to Pakistan, he developed "stomach flu" for forty-eight hours and disappeared from 9 to 11 July. His visit to China, code-named "Polo" after Marco Polo, was so secret that Nixon did not tell Secretary of State Rogers about it. Not surprisingly, Beijing was temporarily confused when Rogers made a strong anti-Chinese statement only days after it had agreed to receive an envoy.

Kissinger got along famously in Beijing with the sophisticated Zhou. Nixon also admired the Chinese foreign minister, so much so that he told Kissinger on his return from China to tell the press "how RN . . . ironically in many ways has similar characteristics and background to Chou."[44]

At their epochal meeting, Kissinger and Zhou agreed that Nixon would come to China in 1972 before he went to Moscow. As a sign of good faith, the American gave Zhou photographs and other intelligence materials relating to Soviet positions along the border and offered to brief him on Soviet-American negotiations. In addition, he was able to obtain Zhou's promise that, as Nixon had earlier demanded, "no Democrat is to go to China before the President."[45]

The 1972 election was never far from Nixon's thoughts. Democrats suggested that his trip to China was planned for February to shift the media spotlight from the New Hampshire primary. At a press conference on 2 January 1972, Nixon, protesting too much, remarked, "but I can assure you it [the summit] wasn't delayed because I was thinking, 'Well, if I could just have it before the New Hampshire primary, in the year 1972, what a coup.'"

Nixon certainly engineered a coup when he astounded the world by announcing on 15 July 1971 not only that Kissinger had gone to Beijing but also that a summit conference would be held in 1972. Among those most astounded was close ally Japan, which had always tried to concert its China policy with Washington. The Nixon announcement hit Japan with "typhonic force," according to the American ambassador.[46] Because of a slipup, the message about Nixon's trip, which was to be delivered to the Japanese prime minister three hours before the president went on the air, never arrived. At the time, the United States and Japan were at loggerheads over textile exports. Nixon did try to make amends by flying to Anchorage on 26 September to meet the Japanese emperor during a refueling stop.

Kissinger returned to China in October for a public six-day visit. While he was away, the United Nations admitted the People's Republic of China and expelled Taiwan, ending a twenty-two-year struggle about which was the "real" China. The previous November, counting the ever-increasing votes in the United Nations supporting China's entry and in light of the opening to Beijing, Nixon asked the NSC to prepare a study on revamping U.S. policy on the Chinese admission issue. Up to that point, the United States had almost single-handedly led the fight against seating "Red China." Although Nixon accepted the fact that China would enter the UN during next fall's session, he hoped that Taiwan would be given a seat as well. The administration's path to acceptance of China was smoothed when in May 1971, for the first time, a majority of Americans told pollsters that they thought Beijing should be in the United Nations.

When the General Assembly voted to seat China and expel Taiwan on 25 October 1971, Nixon quickly responded by sending Governor Ronald Reagan to Taiwan to reassure the Nationalist Chinese about the American commitment to their defense. The failure of the United States' two-China policy in the UN was hard enough to take. What made matters worse was the wild jubilation, including dancing in the aisles, that greeted the American defeat. Nixon was upset at the "shocking demonstration of undisguised glee," and an angry Senate Minority Leader Hugh Scott (R-Pa.) promised, "I think we are going to wipe off some of the smiles from the faces we saw on television during the United Nations voting."[47] He and his colleagues then temporarily held back a $141 million payment to the world body.

No amount of dancing in the UN aisles could deter Nixon from his dramatic visit to China, which captivated the world from 21 to 27 February 1972. The visit was almost ruined when a member of the advance party, while smoking marijuana and drinking vodka, started a relatively serious fire in the hotel housing the Americans. But few at the time knew of the incident.

In 1954, rumor had it that Zhou Enlai had been insulted when Secretary of State John Foster Dulles refused to shake his hand at the Geneva Conference. When he landed in China with his entourage of 391 people, 90 of whom were from the media, Nixon extended his hand first to the foreign minister and later took note of the symbolism: "When our hands met, one era ended and another begun."[48] Many years later, the president claimed that he was unaware of the 1954 incident when he extended his hand, but the Chinese certainly were not.

Few Americans knew that Nixon had traveled to China without a guarantee that he would see the ailing Mao Zedong. The leader of the most powerful nation in the world was, in effect, a supplicant seeking favors from the Chinese, dependent on their goodwill to meet the legendary Mao. Fortunately, after his first lunch in China, Nixon was told that Mao would see him in one hour. He brought along Kissinger and Winston Lord, Kissinger's China expert on the NSC, but not Secretary of State Rogers, who literally had to beg Nixon just to be taken along to China. Nixon did not even use a State Department interpreter but relied on Mao's, because he did not want the department to know what transpired at the meeting. To spare Rogers even more humiliation, Nixon had Lord cropped from official photos of the meeting.

Spinning off one subtle Chinese allegory after another, Mao impressed Nixon with his wit, intelligence, and sheer presence. He was also pleased that Mao had read his 1967 *Foreign Affairs* article and beamed when the Chinese leader told him that *Six Crises* was "not a bad book."[49] So impressed with Mao was Nixon that during much of the meeting he appeared to be flattering the Chinese leader, as when he quoted him, "I know that you are one who sees when an opportunity comes, and then knows that you must seize the hour and seize the day."[50]

Although some diplomatic negotiation did take place, much of the China visit, seen night after night on television in the United States during prime time, involved the American entourage on tour or at banquets where a Chinese army band played "O Susannah" and "America the Beautiful." By the end of the visit, 98 percent of Americans knew that Nixon had been in China. At one memorable photo opportunity at the Great Wall, journalists poked fun at the president by quoting him as saying, "This is a great wall." They left out the rest of the sentence—"and it had to be built by a great people."[51] Most Americans were fascinated by the glimpses of a once-forbidden, exotic country and by the obviously polite and friendly reception the Chinese gave the Nixons.

As for the direct diplomatic accomplishments of the visit, American and Chinese diplomats worked feverishly behind the scenes to produce the difficult Shanghai Communiqué. They had no problem agreeing that they would not "seek hegemony in the Asia Pacific region and each is opposed to efforts by any other country or group of countries to establish such hegemony." That was a message for Moscow.

It was not so easy to find acceptable language to deal with U.S. relations with Taiwan. In the final communiqué, each side explained its policy. The Chinese declared that Taiwan was part of China and that the United States should withdraw its troops from the island. The United States agreed "that Taiwan was part of China," a concession that was not so startling, since the government on Taiwan had always maintained that position. The United States then affirmed "the ultimate objective of the withdrawal of all U.S. forces and military installations from Taiwan" when Taipei and Beijing resolved their problems peacefully and "as the tension in the area diminishes." Nixon allegedly told the Chinese verbally that after he was reelected he would recognize Beijing and break relations with Taiwan.

When on 26 February the State Department's China expert, Marshall Green, saw the draft of the communiqué (about which he and his colleagues had been left in the dark), he complained to Kissinger that the United States appeared to have sold out Taiwan, because there was no reference to the U.S.-Taiwan defense treaty. Rogers complained directly to Nixon, accurately pointing out the problems the communiqué would pose with conservatives back home. The president and Kissinger were furious at what they considered to be a trivial correction. Nixon was so upset that he talked about firing Rogers, who had also harangued him several times about being shunted aside during the trip. Kissinger finally recognized the problem. Unwilling to renegotiate the communiqué, he referred to the U.S. treaty commitment to Taiwan at a news conference on the last day of the visit. That night, Nixon toasted his hosts, "This was the week that changed the world."

Although the *Philadelphia Inquirer* headlined its story on the Shanghai Communiqué, "They Got Taiwan, We Got Eggroll," almost all Americans—Republicans and Democrats alike—were pleased with the colorful visit.[52] Liberal Democratic senator George McGovern and conservative Republican senator Barry Goldwater both approved of the trip. Public-opinion polls revealed that whereas only 23 percent of Americans had felt favorably toward China in 1972, that number rose to 49 percent by 1973. But it plummeted to only 20 percent in 1976, as many Americans began to find fault with the policy of détente.

A few on the extreme Left were horrified that Mao Zedong would sit down with Richard Nixon. They reacted by writing off the Chinese as true Stalinists and turned to the last real communists, the Albanians, for their models. More serious for Nixon were the reactions from a minority on the Right who worried about Taiwan. In describing one of Nixon's toasts to his Chinese hosts, William F. Buckley commented, "You almost expected him to lurch into a toast to Alger Hiss."[53] Even before he went to China, Nixon had assured actor John Wayne that "we have no intention of abandoning Taiwan."[54] Nixon also had to face skepticism from Vice President Agnew, whom he ordered to "stay off this topic."[55]

American businesspeople looked forward to penetrating the huge Chinese market, something they had hoped for ever since the *Empress of China* made the first voyage to Asia from the United States in 1784. They were not aware of a 24 March report in which China experts had warned, "Prospects for rapid growth in US-PRC trade are poor. The PRC is almost certain to subordinate economic to political considerations." Moreover, Beijing, they contended, would demand MFN status but would not easily obtain it.[56] In May 1973, China and the United States set up liaison offices in Washington and Beijing to help facilitate trade.

U.S. China trade, which amounted to $5 million in 1971, grew to $930 million in 1974, four-fifths of which was exports, mostly agricultural, from the United States to China. Although the growth was not only dramatic but also favorable to the United States in terms of balance of payments, it was still a relatively small amount of trade, considering the size of the markets. More dramatic was the flow of American officials, cultural groups such as the Philadelphia Symphony, and thousands of American tourists to China. From 1972 to 1977, at least eighty members of Congress also took China junkets. Not many Chinese came to the United States during that period.

At the February 1973 meeting at which Kissinger and the Chinese formally agreed to liaison offices, Mao, referring to the Soviet Union, told the American that "we can work together to commonly deal with a bastard."[57] During that same year, Brezhnev made similar comments about the Chinese when he visited Nixon in San Clemente. Nixon's policy of triangulation had worked brilliantly. Whatever one may think of the Soviet grain deal, the less than perfect SALT treaty, the failure of the Chinese market to develop for American exporters, and the overselling and then demise of détente during the late seventies and early eighties, Nixon's openings to China and Russia marked the beginning of the end of the cold war. Taking political gambles, he was able to convince the vast majority of his constituents that the United States had to normalize relations with China and the Soviet Union. In old-fashioned, Great Power diplomacy with his two communist rivals, Nixon and his foreign policy team displayed skill and acumen. Their foreign policy record with the rest of the world was not as successful—or as admirable.

5

★ ★ ★ ★ ★

BEYOND THE GRAND DESIGN

For Nixon, Kissinger, and their supporters, the ending of the Vietnam War, the construction of détente with the Soviet Union, and the opening of relations with China were monumental accomplishments that reflected the administration's brilliant handling of foreign affairs. However, there is more to the story of U.S. foreign relations during Nixon's presidency. In much of the rest of the world, he achieved a decidedly mixed record that included blundering before and after the October 1973 war in the Middle East and the associated oil crisis; the successful attempt to destabilize Chile because its democratically elected president, Salvador Allende, was a Marxist and a cold war neutral; and the straining of relations with Japan, European allies, and Canada.

These less than stellar performances were affected by the fact that Nixon did not pay much attention to other areas of the globe until they were in crisis. Adhering rigidly to linkage politics, both he and Kissinger considered almost all anti-U.S. activity in the Third World to be fomented by the Soviet Union and China. Moreover, foreign policy was run directly from the Oval Office and the NSC by a relative handful of people who simply did not have enough time and resources to devote to the innumerable problems that confronted the world's greatest power.

The Middle East was one exception to that rule, at least in 1969 and 1970. Yet even there, the meddling White House kept the State Department on a very short leash. As a result of Nixon's and Kissinger's very full plates in

1969, as well as Arab leaders' suspicions of the Jewish national security adviser and the president's need to give his secretary of state something to do, William Rogers was assigned the Middle East.

In 1967, Israel won the Six Days War and thereby changed the map of the region by taking the Golan Heights from Syria, the West Bank and East Jerusalem from Jordan, and the Sinai Peninsula and the Gaza Strip from Egypt. As in the two previous Arab-Israeli wars (1948–1949, 1956), the 1967 war ended with an armistice but no peace treaty. Israel announced its willingness to return much of the conquered territory in exchange for recognition and a peace treaty from its Arab neighbors, while the Arabs demanded the return of all the territory before they would talk about peace. So matters stood when Nixon took office.

In December 1968, the president-elect had dispatched former Pennsylvania governor William Scranton to the Middle East to inform the parties that the new administration would be evenhanded. The Israelis worried about this apparent change in policy from the common-law ally status they had enjoyed during the Kennedy-Johnson administration, and the Arabs hoped for more understanding from the new foreign policy team in the White House. As they would throughout the world, Nixon and Kissinger viewed the Arab-Israeli crisis through the prism of Soviet-American relations. They were especially concerned that Egyptian leader Gamal Abdel Nasser had convinced the Kremlin to take a more active role in the region.

On 1 February 1969, the NSC established general goals for the Middle East that included land for peace, an American-Soviet agreement on a comprehensive peace, and an evenhanded approach. The administration was overly optimistic about its ability to obtain both Soviet cooperation in the region and Israel's agreement to surrender most of its conquered territory.

These general guidelines were tested in March, when Egyptian and Israeli troops began skirmishing along the Suez Canal. In April, Nasser formally abrogated the 1967 cease-fire, and the so-called War of Attrition of 1969–1970 began. It became much more serious for the United States when, after deep Israeli air raids, the Kremlin gave Nasser SAM-3 antiaircraft missiles manned by Russian crews; 150 pilots to train Egyptians to fly MIG-21 fighters, or perhaps to fly the planes themselves; and 10,000 military technicians. This was the first time since World War II that the Soviet Union had employed so many military personnel so far outside its borders.

After a long series of meetings with Arabs, Israelis, Russians, and others, Secretary of State Rogers unveiled a peace plan on 9 December 1969, a ten-point proposal including withdrawal from occupied territories, peace and mutual recognition, border adjustments, and settlement of the refugee problem. The Israelis correctly perceived the plan as less favorable to their

.interests than previous American initiatives, particularly considering the amount of territory the secretary of state proposed they return to the Arabs. Israeli foreign minister Abba Eban, a moderate on peace with Arabs, hyperbolically called the plan "one of the major errors of international diplomacy in the postwar era."[1] Nixon knew that the Rogers Plan would not be accepted by the Israelis but hoped that the Arabs would recognize it as a signal that Washington was going to be an honest broker.

Kissinger also considered the plan a nonstarter, but it would buy time. He thought that the longer the stalemate continued, the weaker the Soviet Union would appear to the Arabs, since Moscow would prove incapable of helping them achieve their goals. They would then turn to the United States as the only power capable of mediating a just peace. In addition, as long as the Suez Canal remained closed (a by-product of the 1967 war), the Soviet Union found it difficult to send military supplies to North Vietnam by sea. Kissinger was also somewhat jealous of Rogers's new celebrity. For whatever combination of reasons, on Nixon's authority, he ordered Leonard Garment, the president's liaison with the Jewish community, to deliver a message to Israeli prime minister Golda Meir as she began a nationwide speaking tour: "Tell her wherever she goes, in all her speeches and press conferences, we want her to slam the hell out of Rogers and his plan."[2]

Nasser, who was interested in considering aspects of the Rogers Plan, was exasperated by the mixed signals he received from the United States. His diplomats were confused when the State Department offered positions that conflicted with those of the White House and the NSC. What were they to make of the department's Middle East expert, Joseph Sisco, telling Nasser in April 1970 that the Rogers Plan was "ninety-five percent in your favour" when it was clear that Nixon and Kissinger were undercutting it?[3] Of course, the Americans never trusted Nasser and were pleased when he died in 1971 and was replaced by Anwar Sadat.

When Soviet-manned MIG-23s intercepted Israeli fighters for the first time near Cairo in March 1970, the War of Attrition became more serious. On 30 June in Moscow, Soviet leaders urged a visiting Nasser, now well-defended against further Israeli attacks, to end the increasingly dangerous war for which Egypt was paying dearly in men and materiel. The United States nonetheless considered the Soviets to be an unhelpful, destabilizing factor in the region.

After the failure of his first plan, Rogers floated a less ambitious one aimed merely at achieving a cease-fire. The United States pressured Israel to accept it by sweetening the deal with a new arms package and by obtaining the Egyptians' promise to freeze their defensive buildup on the canal. Egypt and Israel accepted the cease-fire on 8 August, but the deal almost came undone when Nasser, with Moscow's connivance, cheated by moving new missile batteries up to the canal. Washington informed Nasser that his deceit meant $7 million more in arms for Israel.

Fortunately for the United States and Israel, the cease-fire held, because just as the guns along the canal went silent, a new regional crisis, even more dangerous than the War of Attrition, developed in Jordan. The pro-Western but anti-Israeli King Hussein had been confronted by increasingly bolder, well-armed Palestinian guerrilla groups who wanted to destroy his regime. On 9 June, he escaped an assassination attempt directed by the Popular Front for the Liberation of Palestine (PFLP), and on 1 September, a squad from the Palestine Liberation Organization (PLO) tried to assassinate him. On 1, 6, and 7 September, Palestinian commandos hijacked three commercial airliners and landed them in the Jordanian desert. Ten days later, a full-scale civil war, called "Black September" by the Palestinians, broke out between them and King Hussein's forces. Jordan faced the most serious crisis in its history.

Nixon once again feared dangerous escalation in the region: "It was like a ghastly game of dominoes, with a nuclear war waiting at the end."[4] He warned the Soviets not to permit their Syrian ally to intervene in the civil war. Two days after receiving Moscow's assurance that it had no intention of intervening, a large Syrian tank force, manned by Palestinians but led by Syrian officers directed by Soviet advisers just across the border, moved a kilometer into Jordan. Nixon, who was convinced that "they're testing us," immediately went into action.[5] With six weeks to go before the congressional elections, the president thought that the Soviets and their allies in the Middle East had recklessly thrown down a challenge to him. Demonstrating to Moscow that the Nixon Doctrine did not mean that the United States could not act decisively, he obtained Hussein's lukewarm permission for the Israeli Air Force to help out along the Syrian border. Hussein adamantly refused to permit Israeli ground troops to assist him. Nonetheless, Israel did mobilize its forces in the Golan Heights.

As it turned out, the Jordanian air force and ground troops performed brilliantly against the tanks, destroying 130 Soviet T-54s. Alexander Haig is one of the few participants who claims that the Israeli air force did intervene in a decisive way but that it was kept secret to spare Hussein embarrassment.[6] The United States also deployed a naval task force in the eastern Mediterranean during the crisis and placed 20,000 airborne troops on alert. There is evidence that Nixon may have called for the bombing of fedayeen guerrilla bases in Jordan but that Defense Secretary Laird, citing weather conditions, never carried out the order.

The badly beaten Syrians retreated on 23 September. Hussein's well-trained ground forces quickly gained the upper hand over the Palestinian guerrilla groups and ejected them from his country. The real and threat-ened U.S. and Israeli interventions gave the Soviets and Syrians pause.

The behavior of Soviet ally Syria during the crisis hardened Nixon's and Kissinger's views about the unreliability of the Soviet Union as a partner in arranging an Arab-Israeli peace. Over the next three years, they remem-bered Black September as they tried not only to resolve the conflict but also to minimize Soviet influence in the region. As in other regions, they exag-gerated the ability of the Soviet Union to control its allies. After all, the Americans could not compel Israel, heavily dependent on Washington for arms, to do their bidding. Nevertheless, Black September irritated them, because it occurred at almost the same time that the Soviets started to build a submarine base in Cuba.

By the end of 1970, with the crisis in Jordan resolved and the cease-fire holding along the Suez, U.S. activity in the region declined. In part, this was because Kissinger finally assumed control over U.S. policy in the Middle East, the only major area that had been out of the NSC's direct reach. Convinced that the time was not ripe for a comprehensive peace, he was in no hurry to pursue more Rogers-style plans, at least as long as the Soviet Union continued to play an important role in the Arab world. The United States did rhetorically support the failed attempt by UN envoy Gunnar Jarring to mediate a settlement through indirect talks.

Anwar Sadat, the new Egyptian leader, told the Americans in February 1971 that he was prepared to open the Suez Canal if Israel left the east bank, and that he would exchange land for peace. But Sadat conditioned the exchange on Israeli withdrawal from all the land it had conquered in 1967, including East Jerusalem. He announced to anyone who would listen that 1971 was the year of decision for Egypt; he was ready to deal with the Israelis, but only if they moved toward his position.

In a successful attempt to woo Sadat in 1971, the United States revealed to him that the CIA had uncovered evidence that a pro-Soviet faction in Cairo, led by Ali Sabry and encouraged by the Kremlin, was planning his overthrow. Sadat's own intelligence confirmed the CIA report. After arresting the plotters, he bided his time before taking action against their apparent sponsors.

On 8 July 1972, Sadat asked 15,000 Soviet military advisers and other personnel to leave his country in reaction to Brezhnev's lack of support for the Arab position at the Moscow summit, as well as his involvement in the aborted Sabry coup. Sadat had concluded that the United States would not press Israel to come to the peace table until he expelled the Soviets. At this point, Nixon and Kissinger may have missed the boat. During the rest of

1972 and into 1973, Sadat told the Soviets and Americans that unless there was some movement from the Israeli side, he would take unilateral action. The Soviets believed that he was serious, warning Sadat on at least four occasions not to attack Israel and informing Nixon and Kissinger that the Egyptian leader apparently meant business. There was a bit of the boy who cried wolf in this situation, since the more Sadat talked of war without doing anything, the more observers concluded that he was bluffing. But he was not bluffing; as he lamented, "The Americans have left us no other way out" but war.[7]

The Americans and Israelis discounted Sadat's threats, having underestimated his and Syria's abilities to mount an attack against Israel's supposedly impregnable positions, especially now that the Soviets had been thrown out of Egypt. All the same, Nixon planned to begin pushing the Israelis a bit in the spring of 1973, but the onset of the Watergate crisis made it impossible for him to challenge the Jewish state's powerful supporters on Capitol Hill.

The sixteen-day Yom Kippur or Ramadan War, which began on 6 October 1973 with a joint Egyptian and Syrian attack on Israeli-occupied territory, led to the second most serious Soviet-American crisis of the cold war era. While the war was going on, the administration was being rocked by domestic crises involving Nixon's firing of the special Watergate prosecutor and by a nasty scandal that led to the resignation of Vice President Agnew. On occasion during the turbulent few weeks, Kissinger and his aides directed American foreign policy without much involvement from a depressed and preoccupied president. During the sixteen-day period, Nixon did not attend any of the formal White House meetings devoted to the war.

Although American and Israeli intelligence operatives certainly noticed that the Egyptians and Syrians were mobilizing their forces on 4–5 October in preparation for war, their leaders thought the Arabs were bluffing. Nixon later admitted that he and the CIA officials had been surprised by the attack. Kissinger told Abba Eban on 4 October, "In any case, nothing dramatic is going to happen in October."[8]

When at the eleventh hour Washington finally realized that war was likely, Kissinger warned Prime Minister Golda Meir that the United States would not support the sort of preemptive strike that had earned Israel international condemnation in 1967. Israel, however, was in no position to preempt, even if it wanted to.

Egypt had informed the Soviets about the attack two or three days before it occurred, but despite détente, Moscow did not tell Washington. Regardless, the Soviets had serious reservations about the consequences of the Arabs' resort to arms.

Woefully unprepared and supremely overconfident, with enough military supplies for only three or four days, Israel took terrible losses at the start of the war. The Egyptians crossed the canal and easily penetrated the not-so-impregnable Bar-Lev line, and Syrian forces advanced in the Golan Heights. Israel could throw only 400 troops and 30 tanks into the breach to meet Egypt's massive assault on its positions in the Sinai. During the first twenty-four hours of battle, Israel suffered 1,000 battle deaths. In less than a week, the Israeli Defense Force (IDF) lost 500 tanks, one-third of its inventory.

After the first few days, Nixon and Kissinger began to view the Israeli setbacks as not necessarily inimical to their Middle East designs. Confident that the IDF could successfully counterattack, they reasoned that should the Arabs sustain their gains or at least not lose the war, they would be more willing to come to the peace table, prepared to negotiate from a position of strength. The trick was to ensure that Israel would not be defeated during the first week and that the Arabs would not be too badly beaten up during the final phase of the war. The Israelis might also be more willing to deal if they finally realized that the allegedly backward Arab nations could use modern weaponry to launch a successful offensive.

Nixon and Kissinger were correct. Despite the fact that Israel won the war, the early Egyptian gains permitted Sadat to proclaim a great victory (a victory still celebrated in Egypt), making it easier for him to begin talking seriously about peace with Israel. Yet that outcome was anything but clear when Kissinger and Nixon took their high-stakes gamble and adopted policies that initially worked to Egypt's benefit.

By the end of the war's fourth day, Israel began to run out of supplies. Two days earlier, Israeli ambassador Simcha Dinitz had asked Kissinger for an emergency resupply airlift. Washington did not move with dispatch to meet his request. At one point, the Israelis became so exasperated by the delay that they placed their nuclear missiles on alert in such a fashion that the United States would notice them.

On the one hand, the Americans did not want Israel to lose the war or launch a nuclear attack. Further, they had to demonstrate their willingness to stand by their ally in the same way that the Soviets, who began to airlift supplies to Syria and Egypt on 10 October, stood by theirs. On the other hand, Kissinger hoped that the Egyptians would consolidate their gains before the Israelis went on the offensive. The Arab threat to cut off oil from any nation that assisted Israel further complicated matters.

At the start, the United States tried unsuccessfully to resupply Israel without using American planes, either by using El Al planes or by hiring charter fleets. European allies, fearful of the Arab oil threat, would not permit the United States to use its own bases on the continent to refuel any cargo planes flying from the United States to Israel. At the same time, NATO allies Turkey and Greece permitted the Russians to overfly their countries on their way to the Middle East. Under pressure from the Arabs, Exxon even instructed Esso of Germany to stop delivering oil to American bases. Washington finally strong-armed NATO ally Portugal into permitting U.S. planes to refuel in the Azores on the way to the Middle East.

These problems took time to work out. Nonetheless, most observers believe that the United States purposefully delayed delivering the goods to Israel until 13 October, five days after Dinitz's first request and four days after the U.S. decision to rearm Israel. Kissinger blamed the Defense Department for dragging its feet after Nixon approved the resupplying of Israel. His supporters point the finger at Deputy Secretary of Defense William Clements, a Texas oil man chummy with the Arabs. Others in the military worried about giving away valuable arms to Israel, as well as the inherent risks of flying into a war zone.

Secretary of Defense Schlesinger, who denied that his people had caused the delay, informed Ambassador Dinitz that it was Kissinger's idea not only to delay but also to blame the Pentagon. According to Schlesinger, Kissinger told him that Nixon wanted him to take his time making arrangements for the airlift; blaming the Pentagon was a convenient White House "cover story."[9] Admiral Zumwalt, no friend of the Nixon administration, reported later that Schlesinger had told the Defense Department to be "overtly niggardly and covertly forthcoming" with Israel.[10] Kissinger and Nixon used the delay to obtain an Israeli promise to tell Jewish American groups not to support the Jackson-Vanik Amendment and also to convince Jerusalem to ask for a cease-fire. Sadat unwisely refused to accept the Israeli request on 12 October.

Leonard Garment also believes that Kissinger was the main footdragger who convinced a preoccupied Nixon that he was being sabotaged by the Pentagon. Once he heard about it, the president ordered Kissinger to "get your ass out of here and tell these people to move."[11] An Israeli reporter claims that Nixon later said, "Henry, do you remember that on the fourth day you came and suggested that I send five planes?—and I said if it's all right to send them five, let's send them fifty."[12] The U.S. airlift finally involved more than fifty planes. Beginning on 13 October, Washington sent almost 1,000 tons of supplies to Israel every hour; the Americans sent more in one day than the Soviets sent in four days. And that did not include the delivery of forty phantom jets. Further, on 19 October, Nixon asked Congress for an emergency appropriation of $2.2 billion for Israel. The next day, King Faisal of Saudi Arabia announced that the Arab nations would embargo oil to the United States.

Golda Meir later commented that there was not much of a delay in the resupply effort—President Nixon never broke a single promise. Abba Eban as well had no hard feelings about the delay, which he attributed to the difficulty of making complicated and delicate logistical arrangements in a short time. Whoever was responsible, the Pentagon did not move quickly, given the emergency.

The American airlift permitted the Israelis to launch a powerful offensive to regain the Golan Heights, with the road to Damascus open, and to cross the Suez Canal in the south into Egyptian territory, encircling Cairo's Third Army. Israel's columns were sixty miles from Cairo, but Egyptians still controlled the Israeli side of the canal in the north. The Israeli moves compelled the Egyptians and Syrians to request Soviet assistance to end the war before they were defeated. Brezhnev summoned Kissinger to Moscow, where they hammered out a cease-fire agreement on 21 October, much to the consternation of the Israelis, who were in the process of completing their encirclement of the Third Army. To compensate the Israelis, Kissinger hinted that Washington would not object if they continued their offensive for a few days, telling them, "Two or three days? That's all. Well, in Vietnam the cease fire didn't go into effect at the exact time that was agreed on."[13]

The Israelis ignored the cease-fire scheduled to begin on 22 October and continued their movements in Egypt. In support of the furious Egyptians, Brezhnev fired off a stern note to Kissinger. His corresponding directly with Kissinger reflected Moscow's knowledge that Nixon was too preoccupied with Watergate to be involved in detail with the war. Sadat asked both the United States and the Soviet Union to send troops to supervise the cease-fire, which the UN had adopted on 22 October as Resolution 338.

Kissinger later explained that he was "determined to resist by force if necessary the introduction of Soviet troops into the Middle East regardless of the pretext under which they arrived."[14] On 24 October, Brezhnev accepted Sadat's invitation to intervene and warned the Americans, "I will say it straight that if you find it impossible to act jointly with us in this matter, we should be faced with the necessity urgently to consider the question of taking appropriate steps unilaterally."[15] Upon hearing about Brezhnev's ominous message, Nixon told Haig, "This is the most serious thing since the Cuban Missile Crisis. Words won't do the job. We've got to act."[16] Tensions were heightened when American intelligence reported the movement of Soviet planes to Cairo on the same day, as well as troop maneuvers in Transcaucasia.

The Soviets later claimed that they had no intention of intervening unilaterally. They were merely trying to pressure the United States to pressure Israel into accepting a cease-fire at once. In fact, Dobrynin suggests that the ominous phrase in Brezhnev's 24 October message had not been approved by the full Politburo but had been carelessly added by someone at the last moment.

The United States thought that the Russian leader was dead serious, however. Acting for Nixon, Kissinger ordered a worldwide U.S. military alert, moving the armed forces to a Defcon (Defensive Condition) III status, a notch more serious than the normal Defcon IV but not as serious as Defcon II. It was the sort of change in the U.S. order of battle that Soviet intelligence was bound to pick up. In a short time, not only the Soviets but the entire world had picked it up. Schlesinger explained to Kissinger, "There's no way that you can keep this secret when you put two million people around the world on alert."[17] With an enhanced American naval force facing an enhanced Soviet force in the Mediterranean, and with the Soviets apparently on the move, Kissinger believed that the world was on the brink of nuclear war; and thus, he claimed, he orchestrated the "deliberate overreaction."[18] He feared that the Soviets might miscalculate and think that they could insert themselves in the Middle East while Nixon was paralyzed by Watergate.

That night the decisions were made by Kissinger, Schlesinger, Admiral Moorer of the Joint Chiefs, William Colby of the CIA, and Haig, now Nixon's chief of staff. Nixon had gone to bed perhaps a bit tipsy, but certainly reeling from the Watergate "Saturday Night Massacre." He was not directly involved in the crisis decision making, although Haig, ever his defender, claimed that the president had instructed him, "You know what I want Al; you handle the meeting."[19] It was not unusual, Haig maintained, for Nixon to absent himself from such meetings, and since Haig frequently left the room to inform the president about what was going on, Nixon was never really "decoupled" from the action.[20] Other participants and their aides report that the president was almost completely out of the loop on that dangerous night.

The Soviets made no move to intervene unilaterally, something that Kissinger and others attribute to the Americans' firm stand and the worldwide alert. Moscow was, however, angered by what it considered an unnecessary escalation. Dobrynin reported that Nixon told him on 30 October that he might have "lost his cool" during the crisis, and Kissinger admitted in November that "we could see now we had made a rash move damaging American-Soviet relations."[21] Such after-the-fact comments may have been intended to reestablish détente, which had unraveled during the crisis. As Dobrynin admitted, "détente had its limits."[22] Nixon similarly characterized the Soviet Union's unhelpful behavior during the war as displaying not the failure of détente but its "limitations."[23] Actually, with the exception of the Soviets' failure to warn the

Americans about Egypt's attack and their perceived threat on 24 October, most of the time Moscow and Washington worked together to try to contain the war.

Kissinger's alert impressed the Israelis enough that they agreed to adhere to the cease-fire and permit the Egyptian Third Army to maintain links with Cairo. It also demonstrated to the Arabs that only the United States had the ability and will to influence both sides in the Middle East conflict. They could not expect more than rhetoric and arms from Moscow.

The Egyptians and Israelis began their first face-to-face talks at Kilometer 101 in Egypt on 30 October to arrange terms for an armistice. The talks went so well that Kissinger had to intervene to slow down the Israelis because he had convened a conference in Geneva for 21 December to be attended by the United States, Egypt, Israel, Jordan, and the Soviet Union. The Geneva conference produced an almost redundant Egyptian-Israeli Disengagement Committee, which, with the secretary of state's assistance, reached an armistice agreement on 18 January.

During the process, Kissinger established a warm relationship with Anwar Sadat. At their first meeting on 7 November, Sadat agreed to reopen diplomatic relations with the United States, which had been broken since 1967. At a later meeting he told Kissinger, "You are not only my friend, you are my brother," and then kissed him.[24] The pro-Western Sadat had accepted the fact that the United States was being relatively evenhanded in its attempts to bring about a Middle East settlement. Kissinger achieved this position through duplicitous diplomacy, telling each side what it wanted to hear. As one Israeli critic commented, "The record of the discussions reveals a pattern of deception and broken promises that would have made even Kissinger's heroes, Metternich and Castlereagh, blush."[25]

When Kissinger first visited Cairo and Jerusalem after the war, Joseph Sisco commented, "Welcome aboard the Egyptian-Israeli shuttle!"[26] Thus was born "shuttle diplomacy." During 1973 and 1974, Kissinger made eleven visits to the Middle East, with the Syrian shuttle alone covering more than 24,000 miles in thirty-four days. Convinced that there was little chance to achieve a comprehensive agreement between the Arabs and Israelis, he worked on a "step-by-step" process that would at least disengage the combatants. Brokering an agreement between Israel and hard-line Syrian leader Hafez al-Assad proved more difficult for Kissinger than the Egyptian-Israeli deal. But he was finally successful on 29 May 1974. Nixon visited Syria two weeks later to reopen diplomatic relations and, as usual, to claim another "first" in presidential visits, along with his visits to Israel and Egypt, where he received warm and enthusiastic receptions. But the by-then fast-failing Nixon received little credit for opening relations with Syria or for any of the apparent successes in U.S.–Middle East relations. It all appeared to be Kissinger's doing. For his feat, the editors of *Newsweek* put him on the cover dressed in a Superman costume as "Super K." Because of his shuttle diplomacy, the Arabs, pressured by Sadat, lifted their oil embargo in March.

The potent oil weapon wielded by the Arabs helped explain why virtually no European leader offered a word of support for Israel, even though it had been attacked by Egypt and Syria. Seventy-seven percent of all non-communist oil reserves were in the Middle East.

The West's oil problems began in September 1969 when the nationalist Muammar Qaddifi overthrew the pro-Western king of oil-rich Libya. Although the Organization of Petroleum Exporting Countries (OPEC) had been founded in 1960, the Western oil companies generally controlled the price. In January 1970, Qaddifi pressured independent oil companies in Libya to accept a price increase, and when the State Department did not support them, a precedent was established. In quick order, the companies, fearing a possible loss of their concessions, accepted price rises demanded by the Gulf states. After the West meekly accepted a general price increase in February 1971, OPEC members assumed total control from the companies over pricing and production levels. The United States did not protest the 1971 price rises, believing that higher-priced oil would be an incentive to new, more expensive exploration at home.

OPEC's supremacy over the oil companies meant that its Arab members could use the oil weapon in a crisis. By 1970, the United States no longer had an oil surplus—one that could have been used to help Europeans, dependent on Arab oil, in the case of a shortfall. In 1973, Americans consumed 17 million barrels a day while producing only 10.8 million barrels. Twenty-three percent of U.S. imported oil came from the Middle East.

Well before the war, the Saudi Arabian minister of petroleum had warned the United States that the Arabs would embargo oil to any nation that helped Israel in the next war. Despite this warning, from 1970 to 1973, the Nixon administration did little to expand domestic production or to begin moving beyond rhetoric to adopt conservation measures.

U.S. policy toward Iran, the second largest oil exporter in the Middle East, further complicated matters. During Nixon's 1967 visit to Iran, the shah had told him that he needed more American arms for defense. This may have been one of the seeds of the Nixon Doctrine, enunciated two years later. With the British announcing in 1968 their intention to withdraw from their posts east of Suez, Iran and Saudi Arabia became the twin pillars in the region on which Washington would depend to keep the peace. A covert ally of Israel, Iran, although nominally an Islamic state, was not on good terms with most of the Arab world.

On 30–31 May 1972, Nixon and Kissinger stopped in Iran on their way home from the Moscow summit. The Americans told an eager shah that he could purchase almost anything he wanted from their arsenal, including advanced F-14 and F-15 fighter planes. The Defense and State Departments did not support the massive arms sales. Defense contended that the weapons were too advanced and complicated for Iran, and State complained that the shah was spending far too much on defense, considering his domestic political situation. The NSC did not accept their advice. From 1972 through 1977, the United States and Iran participated in the largest arms transfer in history, valued at $16.2 billion. By 1977, Iran was spending 40 percent of its budget on defense and was the largest buyer of U.S. arms. Armin Meyer, who had been a U.S. ambassador to Iran, reported that the shah became a "nightmare" only "when the Nixon-Kissinger people came in with all that military equipment," at which point "he went way off into outer space, and, in effect, became a megalomaniac."[27] The shah's reckless spending, especially after oil prices dipped in the mid-seventies, prepared the way for the revolution that led to his downfall in 1979.

The shah used revenues from oil sales to pay for the arms. During 1973, OPEC raised the price of oil fourfold. One of the hawks among oil producers, Iran demanded higher and higher prices. Although there is no direct evidence that Washington encouraged the shah to boost oil prices in order to buy arms, one high-level U.S. diplomat suggests that Nixon and Kissinger "tacitly accepted" his position in OPEC.[28] There is certainly no evidence that they protested the price hikes, which so dramatically affected the economies of all the nations in the world, including the oil-exporting Soviet Union, which reaped a bonanza.

At the 1972 Teheran meeting, the shah also asked for and received aid on another front. Iran and Iraq had broken relations the previous December, and in April, Iraq signed a friendship and aid treaty with Moscow. In an attempt to harass the Iraqis, the shah asked the United States to aid Kurdish separatists in their age-old conflict with Baghdad. Despite State Department and CIA misgivings, the United States sent $16 million to the Iraqi Kurds from 1972 through 1975. This covert activity paid off; the militant Iraqis were so tied down in their own country that they could not participate in the October 1973 war, let alone skirmish with Iran. In 1975, after Iran and Iraq reopened relations, the United States unceremoniously cut off aid to the Kurds, who were left virtually defenseless against the

Iraqis. When asked about the way the United States had ditched the Kurds, Kissinger coolly replied, "covert action should not be confused with missionary work."[29]

That was certainly the case in Chile, where Nixon and Kissinger helped to destabilize the country from 1970 to 1973 in a successful effort to depose Dr. Salvador Allende, the democratically elected Marxist president. He was replaced by a brutal authoritarian regime that ruled Chile for almost two decades.

Allende had failed to win three previous elections, in which the CIA had assisted centrist candidates against Allende and rightist candidates. For example, in 1964, the agency provided $3 million to help elect Eduardo Frei. As the 1970 election approached, the Nixon administration was slow to grasp the possibility that Allende might win a plurality of the votes in a three-way contest. Kissinger was not very interested in Latin America: "What happens in the South is of no importance."[30] During the run-up to the election, ITT and Pepsi-Cola (the latter headed by Nixon friend Donald Kendall), with major interests in Chile, provided sizable contributions to the pro-Western candidate. The CIA chipped in with $1 million. The 40 Committee (named after NSDM-40), which was the group that handled Chilean affairs from the White House, began its limited "spoiling operations" on 25 March 1970.[31]

Allende won the election in September, polling 36.3 percent of the vote to his chief opponent's 34.9 percent. Because no candidate won a majority, the Chilean Congress had to select a president. At this point, the Nixon administration flew into action to keep Allende from winning in the Congress. Nixon later claimed that he had been told by an Italian businessman, "If Allende should win, and with Castro in Cuba, you will have in Latin America a red sandwich. And eventually it will all be red."[32] Considering the map of Latin America, that was an unusual construction. Kissinger also asserted, "I don't see why we have to let a country go Marxist just because its people are irresponsible."[33]

Allende had announced his intention to lead Chile to socialism peacefully. One State Department expert concluded in August that his election "would bring to power political forces with the ultimate goal of establishing an authoritarian Marxist state." Yet in that same NSSM on Chile, the authors concluded, "We identify no vital U.S. national interests within Chile . . . no vital strategic interest which would be threatened even by the establishment of an enlarged Soviet presence in Chile." The analysts did express concern about the psychological and political fallout throughout the world were Chile to go communist.[34]

Reporting on a meeting with Nixon on 16 September 1970, a CIA official wrote that the president had said, "An Allende regime in Chile was not acceptable to the United States. The President asked the Agency to prevent Allende from coming to power or to unseat him. The President authorized ten million dollars for this purpose."[35] In an early version of what became known as the Reagan Doctrine, Nixon argued that if the Cubans could help Allende with $350,000, why could not the United States help its friends in Chile?

The White House established Track I and Track II approaches to deny Allende his victory in the Chilean Congress. The first approach involved a complicated political scheme, called by the CIA the "Rube Goldberg gambit," which would have ended up with Frei as president again.[36] As part of Track I, the nonviolent track, Nixon ordered the CIA to "make the economy scream."[37] Track II involved American encouragement of a military coup d'état or even the assassination of Allende, with the CIA instructing its station chief in Santiago on 16 October 1970, "It is firm and continuing policy that Allende be overthrown by a coup."[38] Democratic Chile had experienced its last military intervention in an election in 1932. Track II was so secret that even the 40 Committee did not know about it, nor did the American ambassador.

Both tracks failed; the Chilean Congress chose Allende to be president on 24 October 1970. He had not been in office six days before Nixon signed off on NSDM-93, authorizing the United States to make economic warfare on Chile and to expend millions to assist Allende's opponents. The warfare included cutting off U.S. aid. During the 1960s, Washington had sent Chile about $70 million a year. From 1970 to 1973, the country received a little more than $3 million, although unofficial American sources provided a modest amount of loans and other assistance. More important than the aid, Chile lost its ability to use U.S. credits to purchase the 200,000 tons of American wheat it had been used to buying annually. Chile was one of those countries most hurt by the tripling of wheat prices in 1972–1973. In addition, the CIA subsidized opposition newspapers and engaged in a campaign of misinformation to encourage Chilean military leaders to oppose Allende. The United States also used its influence to convince directors of the World Bank to deny Chile loans. Not without reason, the bank contended that the denial of loans was proper, since it was supposed to support capitalist not socialist projects.

The United States contributed to the conditions that led to Allende's being overthrown by the military in an 11 September 1973 coup directed by General Augusto Pinochet. Allende died during the attack on the presidential palace. The administration did not participate directly in the coup. Allende had encountered enough problems on his road to socialism even without U.S. destablization. Although able to count on the loyalties of a slight majority of Chilean citizens by 1973, he faced strong opposition from the Left, which opposed his slow, parliamentary drift toward socialism, and from the Right, which overthrew him. He had to deal with strikes, economic dislocation, and several abortive coups during his tumultuous three years in power. Whether the coup would have succeeded without U.S. destabilization activities is difficult to say. Whatever the answer, since 1973, leftist critics around the world have been convinced that the CIA directly overthrew Allende, all evidence to the contrary notwithstanding. For some observers, Nixon's alleged involvement in the coup was the most heinous example of American imperialism during his presidency.

Allende enjoyed a celebrated friendship with Fidel Castro, who spent a month touring Chile, and although he nationalized some businesses, even the CIA admitted that through 1973, Chile was still an operating democracy. The same could not be said for the Pinochet regime, which, in the wake of the coup, executed as many as 10,000 leftists and incarcerated tens of thousands more as it established an oppressive police state.

CIA director Richard Helms was another casualty of the affair. After Jack Anderson revealed in a column on 21 March 1972 that the CIA and ITT were working on schemes to topple Allende, Helms was forced to testify before Congress. On 7 February 1973, he lied to the Senate Foreign Relations Committee when he asserted that the United States was not involved in Chilean plots. Because of his testimony, a court fined him $2,000 in 1977 and gave him a two-year suspended sentence for lying to Congress.

Critics of Nixon's foreign policy in the Third World would have had even more ammunition had they known about his policies in sub-Saharan Africa. To start with, the administration had little respect for Africans. On one occasion early in his tenure, the president "pointed out that there has never in history been an adequate black nation, and they are the only race of which this is true.[39] On another occasion he said, "Henry, let's leave the niggers to Bill [Rogers] and we'll take care of the rest of the world." In February 1970, he asked Kissinger about an upcoming presidential address to Congress: "Is there something in it for the jigs?"[40] Haig sometimes made allusions to Tarzan when Africa came up for discussion at NSC meetings, and even Kissinger, trying to be one of the boys, cracked racist jokes.

Administration policy for Africa was affected by that racism. NSSM-39, completed on 10 April 1969, was the revealing blueprint for Nixon's policy. Throughout, the authors displayed little sympathy for Africans themselves and, at least for the time being, accepted white minority regimes on the belief that communists were behind most of the nationalist movements. They advocated maintaining "public opposition" to colonial regimes but "relax[ing] political and economic restrictions on the white states. . . . The Whites are here to stay and the only way that constructive change can come about is through them." For example, Rhodesia could "hold out indefinitely with South African help," as could Portugal in Angola and Mozambique.[41]

To look at the policy in a more favorable light, the White House, which saw Africa as "important but not vital," believed that the white regimes should reform and ultimately leave Africa. The best way to accomplish that goal would be to work with them in a constructive way, keeping a low profile, rather than supporting embargoes and other offensive and isolating actions.[42] Thus, from 1969 to 1973, U.S. trade with South Africa grew by 73 percent, the arms embargo on civil airplanes was relaxed, the CIA reduced covert aid to a rebel group in Angola, and Americans were permitted to purchase chrome from the white minority regime in Rhodesia. Further, the United States exercised its veto rights in the UN Security Council for the first time on 17 March 1970 to quash a sanctions resolution against Rhodesia.

The administration confronted two serious crises in independent Africa as well. In 1967, the region of Biafra broke away from Nigeria, the most important African state. A bloody civil war ensued, with the Ibos of Biafra opposing a regime that had discriminated against them. The State Department, following the approach of most African states that feared comparable minority revolts in their own countries, supported Nigeria against Biafra. Its experts also felt that since the Biafran rebellion would be a losing cause, the United States should not irritate oil-rich Nigeria by backing the rebels.

Both Nixon and Kissinger toyed with the idea of changing U.S. policy because of their knee-jerk animosity toward the State Department and because support for the Ibos, who were mostly Catholic, might have contributed to Nixon's growing popularity among Catholic Americans. Biafra's cause was also a popular one in the United States. In the end, the White House deferred to the State Department, even to the point of not prodding the department to expedite the shipment of food to starving Biafrans once the war was over. As Nixon acknowledged, "They're going to let them starve, aren't they Henry?"[43]

Nixon, Kissinger, and the State Department also ignored the slaughter in Burundi's civil war from 1972 to 1974. In 1972, the Tutsi minority began murdering about 1,000 members of the Hutu majority each day. By 1973, at least 250,000 people had died in the conflict, with 100,000 forced into exile. U.S. importers continued to buy Burundi's main cash crop, coffee, although Washington did suspend its modest $100,000-a-year aid program.

Since the feeble Organization of African Unity did not try to end the slaughter in Burundi, the United States had little reason to take an interest, especially since neither the Hutus nor the Tutsis were backed by international communism. In Africa, as in the Third World in general, the Nixon administration was uninterested in local disputes or crises unless they could be directly linked to superpower politics.

Although succeeding in bringing about détente or rapprochement with its communist enemies, the administration did not fare as well with its allies, especially Japan. Nixon resolved the difficult Okinawa problem, but issues relating to Japanese competition in textiles severely strained relations. In 1971, the twin shocks (shokku) caused by the opening to China and the sudden ending of the Bretton Woods agreement brought Japanese-American relations to their lowest point since World War II.

During the last months of the war, the United States had invaded the Japanese Ryukyu Islands, the most important of which was Okinawa, site of an especially bloody battle. From the late forties through the sixties, Okinawa was a major U.S. military and naval base in which Washington had invested more than $800 million. Tokyo wanted its possession returned, most Okinawans wanted to be returned to Japan, and many Japanese and Okinawans opposed the use of bases on the island to support U.S. activities in Vietnam and to store nuclear weapons. Okinawans and Japanese staged periodic protests against the bases. When Japan reaffirmed its 1960 security agreement with the United States in 1970, the opposition, although in the minority, staged boisterous demonstrations. To make it easier for Tokyo to maintain the agreement, Washington scaled down the number of troops in Japan from 40,000 in 1969 to 27,000 in 1972, and the number of bases from 150 to 116.

The United States had no intention of keeping Okinawa permanently, but the circumstances under which it would return the island to Japan became the sticking point in negotiations during the sixties. Nixon, who had been to Japan six times before he became president, understood the politics of the country and had met most of its leaders. When he became president, he was well aware of the importance of the issue to the Japanese.

It was also an important issue to the Senate, which in 1966 passed the so-called Byrd Resolution, calling for that body's advice and consent for any deal involving the return of Okinawa to Japan. On 21 November 1969, Nixon and Prime Minister Eisaku Sato announced a tentative agreement on Okinawa. But problems remained, including, as U.S. ambassador to Japan Armin Meyer noted, how to deal with Tokyo's "nuclear allergy."[44] Although Nixon made a point of not appearing to blackmail the Japanese, he delayed final arrangements on Okinawa until the two countries began moving toward a settlement of the much more problematic textile issue. As he warned Tokyo, "the dangers of a trade war" might make it difficult for him to convince the Senate to approve the return of Okinawa.[45] One Japanese critic later noted, "So we sold our threads to buy a string of islands."[46]

Washington and Tokyo signed the Okinawa treaty on 17 June 1971, the Senate approved it by a vote of eighty-four to six in November, and the transfer took place on 14 May 1972. Under its terms, the United States maintained bases on Okinawa, with Japan agreeing that the bases could be used to support combat activities in the Pacific. Nixon promised to withdraw nuclear weapons from the islands—a major concession to Sato to make it easier for him to make concessions on a textile agreement. When Nixon could not obtain Japan's approval of language permitting the United States to bring the weapons back in an emergency, he accepted face-saving language that allowed Washington to "raise the question" but acknowledged "the particular sentiment of the Japanese people against nuclear weapons."[47] In his "State of the World" message on 10 February 1970, Nixon proclaimed that his willingness to return Okinawa was "among the most important decisions I have taken as President."

He found it far more difficult to prod Tokyo to open its market to American goods and to limit textile exports. As late as 1958, the United States had maintained a rough balance in its textile imports and exports. By 1969, this balance had become a serious trade deficit that had reached $1.3 billion, in part because the Japanese bought only $10 million worth of American textiles while selling Americans more than $500 million worth. That same year, 2.5 million Americans worked in textile plants, many of which were in the South. As part of his southern strategy, Nixon had promised South Carolina senator Strom Thurmond that he would compel Japan to accept voluntary restraints on textile exports. Two-thirds of the industrial workers in Thurmond's South Carolina were employed in textiles. Nixon's commitment to Thurmond produced considerable political support in the South, as well as large campaign contributions from textile manufacturers in 1968.

Hanging over Japan's head was the threat that the Democratic majority in Congress would establish formal quotas, an action opposed by the president, who feared an all-out trade war with Japan. Nixon was philosophically a free trader. The problem soon reached crisis proportions; in 1970 alone, 11,000 U.S. textile workers lost their jobs, continuing an ominous trend, and between 1968 and 1970, 400 U.S. textile plants closed.

Negotiations between the United States and Japan over textiles took more than two years. On several occasions, it appeared that the Americans had obtained Japanese approval for voluntary restraints, only to have them renege on the agreements or have the Diet, responding to Japan's own powerful textile interests, reject them. A leading Japanese newspaper gloated after one of the breakdowns in the talks that it "turned out to be the first instance in which Japan rejected a U.S. demand, and could be considered the first example of 'independent foreign policy' in the postwar Japanese history of economic diplomacy."[48] Nixon was personally angered by "the Jap betrayal" in March 1971, when it appeared that Congressman Wilbur Mills (D-Ark.), the chair of the House Ways and Means Committee, had negotiated his own textile deal with Japanese businesspeople.[49]

After several false starts, former treasury secretary David Kennedy worked out an agreement on voluntary restraints on 15 October 1971. Kennedy succeeded because he gave the Japanese a firm deadline for settlement of what the American ambassador to Japan labeled his most "vexatious issue."[50] Ambassador Meyer also negotiated agreements to decrease the number of Japanese import quotas from 120 categories in 1969 to 33 in 1972 and to liberalize opportunities for American investors to operate in Japanese markets. This relative success came too late to affect the announcement in 1971 that the United States had experienced its first trade deficit in the twentieth century. An angry Nixon confided in November, after signing the textile agreement, that if he were a Democrat "I would give us hell" on trade policy; he complained that for "twenty-five years the United States has not bargained hard for a better position in world trade, the goddam State Department hasn't done its job."[51] Yet Nixon's economic diplomacy pleased the U.S. textile industry. On 6 April 1972, textile executive Roger Milliken delivered $363,000 in cash to Nixon's campaign finance chief just before new campaign-funding disclosure rules went into effect.

Although the United States successfully restrained Japanese textile exports, its overall textile trade balance remained negative because other Asian nations made up for the Japanese shortfall. By 1973, Japanese textile producers began demanding that other Asian nations also accept voluntary restraints.

The difficulties with Japan over textiles gave the secretive Nixon another reason to keep information about the imminent opening to China from the Japanese. On 5 May 1971, the authors of NSSM-124 warned that if the United States failed to consult on China policy, the humiliated Japanese government might fall. Undeterred, Nixon explained that he wanted to "stick it to Japan."[52] One week before the announcement, Defense Secretary Laird told Sato in Tokyo that the administration contemplated no change in its China policy.

The Japanese leader publicly welcomed Nixon's China announcement but was humiliated. As he told a visiting Australian politician, "I have done everything" the Americans "have asked," but "they have let me down."[53] Sato was not to blame—forces beyond his control had made it difficult to obtain the textile agreement. To make matters worse, on 15 August 1971, the anniversary of V-J Day, Nixon shocked both Japan and his European allies with the announcement of the New Economic Policy (NEP), which amounted to a revolution in the international financial world as dramatic as the opening to China in the diplomatic world.

Nixon's tough line toward the Japanese was a product of American domestic politics, where he faced increasing demands for the establishment of formal import quotas not just on textiles but also on steel and other products in which the United States was losing its competitive edge. As early as February 1970, the AFL-CIO, traditionally a supporter of free trade, began to move toward protectionism. Between 1969 and 1971, protectionists in Congress introduced more than 200 bills calling for import restrictions.

Never swerving from a belief in free trade, Nixon promised to do something about quotas. His main agent in the international trade field during the first years of the administration, Secretary of Commerce Stans, was himself a moderate protectionist. Kissinger did not involve himself much in trade policy. Although he understood intellectually the relationship between foreign trade and foreign politics, he admitted that "economics bored him" and that of international trade issues "my ignorance . . . was encyclopedic."[54] His international trade expert on the NSC, C. Fred Bergsten, who knew his business, sometimes worked at cross-purposes with the experts at Commerce, along with his counterparts in the State Department.

In May 1970, Nixon called for a White House review of international trade policies by the Commission on International Trade and Investment Policy. In its July 1971 report, the commission supported freer trade, calling especially for an American offensive against other nations' nontariff barriers. The president had also established the White House Committee on International Economic Policy (CIEP) in January 1971, headed by Peter G. Peterson, who held the title of assistant to the president for international economic affairs. After Peterson became secretary of commerce in 1972, Peter M. Flanigan took over at CIEP. In addition, in September 1971, Nixon enhanced the powers of the head of the Office of the Special Representative for Trade Negotiations, William D. Eberle. In December 1972, the president established a cabinet-level Council on Economic Policy, headed by the influential George Shultz. In a short time, the CIEP came under the control of Shultz's council.

Shultz and his council were instrumental in fashioning the administration's trade bill. A mixture of free trade and protectionist proposals, the trade bill introduced in April 1973 called for increased "fast-track" authority for the president to negotiate changes in tariffs and nontariff barriers, relief for American industries suffering from unfair foreign competition, and preferences for developing countries. Nixon's trade bill eventually passed Congress during the Ford administration in December 1974, despite opposition from union leadership, which considered the bill not protectionist enough. By the time Nixon left office, U.S. international trade balances had improved markedly, in part due to the 1971 devaluation of the dollar, as well as agreements his administration had worked out with several important trading partners. In September 1973, the United States enjoyed a trade surplus of $873 million, the largest surplus in one month since 1965.

Trade was also a central issue in the administration's relationship with its Western allies. It may seem strange to end a chapter on a president's foreign policy with his NATO allies, a subject that should come first in any *tour d'horizon*, but U.S. relations with them took second or even third place to relations with its enemies.

Things had not begun that way. Early in his administration, Nixon made a trip to Europe. While visiting Belgium, England, Germany, Italy, and France from 23 February to 1 March 1969, the new president hoped to reinvigorate NATO, which was muddling through a transitional period related to controversies over strategic doctrine.

Nixon impressed most of the European leaders he met. He proved to be a good listener and looked and sounded wise and rational. In a personal sense, the most important country on his tour was France, where the imperious Charles de Gaulle, who admired Nixon, gave him the singular honor of not only greeting the president at Orly airport but doing so in English. Nixon had always been impressed with de Gaulle, so much so that he was prepared to put up with his independence within the alliance. As with the other leaders, Nixon promised the French president that he would consult frequently with his European partners concerning major policies. He told a NATO council meeting in Brussels on 24 February, "The United States is determined to listen with a new attentiveness to its NATO partners—not only because they have a right to be heard, but because we want their ideas." Over the next few years, he ignored European advice as he crafted his major foreign policies.

Nixon lost confidence in his allies when de Gaulle resigned in April 1969 and the independent architect of *Ostpolitik*, Willy Brandt, took over in Germany in October. But the resignation of de Gaulle helped clear the way for the process that led to Britain's membership in the Common Market in 1973, long a U.S. goal. Great Britain's move closer to the Continent did, however, weaken Washington's "special relationship" with London. Nixon's failure to consult with Prime Minister Edward Heath over such issues as international monetary policy and China contributed to that development. Moreover, the British were initially displeased with Nixon's choice for ambassador to the Court of St. James, Walter Annenberg. An important contributor to the Republican Party, the millionaire publisher of the *Daily Racing Form* and *TV Guide* posed quite a contrast to the widely admired diplomat David Bruce, whom he replaced. But Nixon knew what he was doing; he despised the "unbroken line of the Eastern Establishment's stuffed shirts" who had been sent to England in the past.[55]

With his Vietnam, China, and Soviet policies in place, Nixon again turned to a neglected Europe on 15 February 1973 when he patronizingly proclaimed the "Year of Europe." This was mostly a public-relations announcement, as he and Kissinger had developed no new initiatives. Realizing that the United States had little to offer and being suspicious of Kissinger, President Georges Pompidou of France, Prime Minister Heath of England, and Prime Minister Brandt of Germany all reacted tepidly to Nixon's proclamation. By the time the administration gave any real thought to the "Year of Europe," Nixon was so paralyzed by Watergate that he could devote virtually no time to the subject.

He did succeed in relieving congressional pressure to cut U.S. NATO expenses by announcing on 16 May 1974 a favorable new offset agreement with Germany that covered Bonn's payments for U.S. troops in its country through 1975. That same month, the United States and the European Community signed a tariff agreement to reduce European tariffs on specific American exports worth $1 billion a year.

On the edges of Europe, the administration displayed its Realpolitik approach to international affairs. In 1970, Nixon became the first president since Eisenhower to visit fascist Spain. He also called on Tito in Yugoslavia, and in Greece, he quietly supported the dictatorship of the anticommunist colonels when he lifted the U.S. arms embargo on 12 September 1970. Circumstantial evidence suggests that this policy toward Athens was in part a payoff to one of the Republican Party's major fund-raisers, Greek American Thomas A. Pappas.

Finally, closer to home, Nixon developed a strong hostility to Canadian prime minister Pierre Elliott Trudeau, who had also been elected in 1968. The two did not hit it off, beginning with Trudeau's visit to the White House on 24 March 1969. Much of the tension between them was stylistic; the younger, wealthier Trudeau, who dressed in the latest trendy fashions and dated vocalist Barbra Streisand, offended Nixon's sensibilities. On at least one occasion, the president referred to him as an "asshole."[56] The feeling was mutual.

But Nixon also had reasons of state to oppose the nationalistic and independent Canadian, who electrified his country with several dramatic departures in foreign policy. Aside from continuing the policy of permitting American draft resisters and even deserters to seek admission to Canada as immigrants, he unilaterally reduced the size of Canada's NATO military contingent in Europe and announced its "Third Option" policy toward U.S. relations, which recommended more economic and political independence. One example was the establishment of a Foreign Investment Review Agency in November 1973 to discourage foreign—mostly American—investment in Canada. The Third Option became mandatory after Nixon failed to continue the tradition of treating Canada differently from all other states ("exemptionalism") by not exempting Ottawa from the temporary 10 percent tariff surcharge in his August 1971 NEP.

On the surface, the Third Option, which privately worried American diplomats, seemed in keeping with what Nixon told the Canadian House of Commons on 4 April 1972: "Our policy toward Canada reflects the new approach we are taking in our foreign relations, an approach which has been called the Nixon Doctrine. That doctrine rests on the premise that mature partners have autonomous and independent policies."

Eleven days later, Trudeau and Nixon agreed on a useful environmental treaty, the Great Lakes Water Quality Agreement. The treaty launched the comeback of the Great Lakes, particularly Lake Erie, which was, for all intents and purposes, dead. Nixon, however, soon impounded funds for municipal sewage treatment, which temporarily weakened the U.S.-Canadian agreement. Moreover, environmentalists in Canada, as well as the government, were distressed when Washington supported the attempt by the super oil tanker *Manhattan* to develop a route directly from the Alaskan oil fields through a northwest passage to the U.S. East Coast, and when the United States decided to build a trans-Alaskan–oil pipeline system instead of using the Canadian Mackenzie Valley Project.

Such problems were of little concern to Nixon and Kissinger. Their main interests were ending the Vietnam War and manipulating Great Power relations. For leaders who took pride in their mastery of foreign affairs, they certainly did not have much to boast about beyond self-proclaimed successes with Hanoi, Moscow, and Beijing. In their relations with nations in the Middle East, Europe, and Latin America and even with Canada, they compiled an unimpressive record. Partly, this was a result of the overcentralization of foreign policy in the White House; the inevitable consequence was that they could not be attentive to all the nations of the world. Even when they did pay attention to what they perceived to be minor players in the "Great Game," they generally adopted arrogant policies that did not make friends and influence people around the world and were not in the best national security interests of the United States. Theirs was a diplomacy of Realpolitik, which they played with only moderate skill, ignoring idealistic or moral factors and exacerbating regional crises. Richard Nixon and his many supporters both during and particularly after his presidency clearly oversold the wisdom and effectiveness of his foreign policy.

6

★ ★ ★ ★ ★

LAW AND ORDER

In her iconoclastic *Nixon Reconsidered*, Joan Hoff, one of the few professional historians to have interviewed Richard Nixon, contends that he deserves far more praise for his surprisingly progressive domestic policy than for his often unsuccessful or immoral foreign policies. Beginning from the premise that the buck stops on the president's desk and that he receives or takes credit for the quantity and quality of legislation enacted while he is in office, Hoff has a point.

Among the Nixon administration's domestic accomplishments, while working with a Democratic Congress, are the extension of the Voting Rights Act, postal reorganization, the end of Selective Service, the Clean Air Act, the Water Pollution Control Act, the establishment of the Environmental Protection Agency (EPA), the Consumer Product Safety Act and the establishment of an Office of Consumer Affairs in the White House, expansion of the national park system, the Occupational Safety and Health Administration Act (OSHA), the Rail Passenger Service Act that established Amtrak, the eighteen-year-old vote, the State and Local Fiscal Assistance Act (revenue sharing), the beginning of the federal "war" against cancer, and dramatic increases in federal support for the arts. The list could go on, to a point where it becomes clear that welfare-state programs and government regulatory bodies, against which Nixon railed during the 1968 campaign, actually flourished on his watch.

The amount of money spent on domestic programs further indicates Nixon's apparent progressivism. In terms of the change in domestic spending as a share of gross domestic product during each administration in the

153

twentieth century, Nixon leads all presidents. More specifically, in his FY 1974 budget, Nixon allocated 60 percent more for social spending than Johnson had allocated in FY 1968. Daniel Patrick Moynihan, a Democrat and one of Nixon's key domestic advisers in 1969–1970, labels the Nixon administration "the most progressive" administration of the postwar era.[1] Influenced by Moynihan, Nixon himself remarked, "You know very well that it is the Tory men with liberal policies who have enlarged democracy."[2]

The avatar of conservatism in the Nixon White House, speechwriter Pat Buchanan, certainly was disappointed with his president's performance. In a January 1971 memo he proclaimed, "The President is no longer a credible custodian of the conservative political tradition of the GOP."[3] Buchanan was upset that Nixon, who in 1968 had earmarked for dismantling "wasteful social programs," later supported the same programs as "spending for human resources."[4] Buchanan was convinced that Nixon was not a conservative but, at best, "a fellow traveler of the right."[5]

Despite the legendary anticommunism and pitbull anti-Democratic rhetoric of his early political career, Nixon had never been as conservative as those in the Goldwater-Reagan faction of the party. Conservative Republicans were not entirely comfortable with him as the 1968 election approached. Nixon was not as outspoken on emerging social issues, such as abortion and morality, as the hard Republican Right, and on most economic and political issues, he was to the left of his successor, Gerald Ford.

Speechwriter William Safire thought that although Nixon's "heart was on the right, his head was, with FDR, slightly left of center."[6] Another aide thought that Nixon "was a liberal on domestic affairs, even though he tried to make us forget that."[7] Nixon's discomfort with being associated with liberal policies may partly explain why he set out with such a vengeance to undo in his second term much of what he and Congress had done during his first term. By the fall of 1972, he was sounding like a conservative Republican again, complaining about departments that were "too fat, too bloated," a government that was "too big" and "too expensive," and promising that he would fight programs that just "threw money at problems."[8]

Yet Nixon once explained, "There is only one thing as bad as a far left liberal and that's a damn right wing conservative."[9] He told a friendly biographer in 1968 that he was a liberal on race, a conservative on economic issues, but otherwise a centrist or a "pragmatist"—"I'm a non-extremist."[10] On another occasion, however, he insisted that he was not a "mushy moderate." Nixon certainly held strong and consistently negative views about the Washington establishment, welfare programs, permissiveness, and the Kennedys.[11]

In a series of useful interviews with Nixon administration aides that A. James Reichley conducted for *Conservatives in an Age of Change*, almost all agreed that the president was at bottom a pragmatist who had few fixed ideological positions. He was "at once liberal and conservative, generous and begrudging, cynical and idealistic, choleric and calm, resentful and forgiving," according to Nixon biographer Tom Wicker, who related Nixon's pragmatic centrism to "psychic bipolarity" stemming from the dramatic personality and philosophical differences between his mother and father.[12] But then the same could have been said for Lyndon Johnson's parents.

Nixon had to be pragmatic if he wanted to get anything done, because he had to deal with a Democratic Congress during his entire term in office. Much more concerned with foreign than domestic policy, he had to cooperate with the Democrats if he wanted their support for his more controversial foreign policies. As had President Eisenhower in the fifties, Nixon faced more opposition from Republicans than from Democrats against "liberal" foreign policies, such as détente with the Soviet Union and the opening to China. Nixon took the offensive against the Democratic Congress in 1973, but only after he had accomplished his major foreign policy goals.

In addition, he launched his presidency as the least popular of all presidents from Truman through Carter. Jimmy Carter was the second lowest in initial approval ratings, with 66 percent in 1977; Nixon trailed him at 59 percent in 1969.

Further, he confronted a huge government bureaucracy dominated by Democrats that, as one Nixon aide complained, "was absolutely opposed to our programs" and would not provide "any straight answers," especially HEW and HUD.[13] Beginning in his second term, Nixon began to appoint White House aides to undersecretary positions in the departments. Fred Malek, Nixon's executive "headhunter," admitted that it was difficult to attract Republicans from the private sector to government service because they often had to take pay cuts, whereas Democrats generally improved their financial condition when they came to Washington.

But Nixon's most serious problem in putting together a domestic program was simply that he did not have one when he took office and was slow in organizing the White House's legislative functions. Moreover, most of his closest aides, who had been proficient in running a campaign, took months to learn how the government operated. To make matters worse, the White House, according to Jeb Stuart Magruder, "existed in a state of permanent crisis," as new councils and panels were invented in a frenetic attempt to get a handle on running the country.[14] Typical was Nixon's announcement in July 1969 of a new National Goals Research Staff, headed by Leonard Garment, which faded from view in a few weeks.

The two previous Democratic administrations had been better prepared to present their legislative programs. Kennedy introduced 76 percent of his 1961 programs during his first three months in office; Johnson introduced 94 percent of his 1965 programs during a comparable period. Nixon forwarded to Congress only 12 percent of his 1969 programs—six relatively minor proposals—during his first three months in office. This problem resulted in part from the conflict between Nixon's two chief domestic advisers, the conservative Burns and the liberal Moynihan. Overall, of the 171 legislative requests Nixon sent to Congress that year, only 35 were enacted into law, with, according to Nixon, only two important ones, draft reform and the tax bill, passing in 1969. The administration's slow start also was a by-product of the president's concentration on planning for and then taking his European tour early in the year.

Aside from promising to support law and order and to cut back on wasteful programs, Nixon's 1968 campaign was awash in generalities. This was not just a case of failing to raise difficult issues because he feared alienating his diverse constituencies. Nixon was genuinely uninterested in most domestic politics by the time he arrived at the White House; his experiences in 1969 reinforced his notion that the less he involved himself with domestic politics the better. In an 8 March 1970 memo to his closest aides, he complained that "our greatest weakness was in spreading my time too thin—not emphasizing priorities." He then explained that the only issues he wanted to be involved in were economic matters (but "I do not want to be bothered with international monetary matters"), crime, and school integration. He did not want to deal with family assistance, revenue sharing, job training, "New Federalism," health, housing, labor, or agriculture. About the areas he slighted, he stated, "our team is adequate to carry out policies. . . . I am only interested when we make a major breakthrough or have a major failure. Otherwise don't bother me."[15]

By allowing senior White House aides free rein on most domestic matters, and with John Ehrlichman overseeing the entire operation by the end of 1969, Nixon guaranteed a more liberal profile on such issues as the environment, the arts, health care, and civil rights than might have been the case had he been more involved. There were limits, however, as Ehrlichman discovered in the fall of 1970, when Nixon briefly froze him out of the Oval Office because his recent initiatives had been too liberal.

Another aide claimed that the administration proposed many new and interesting programs, but they were "undermined by the executive branch . . . destroyed by staff conflict. . . . some turned out to be too ambitious; others were technically impossible," and Congress was uncooperative.[16] For many, the main problem was the president, who, according to one political scientist, was a "Gaullist" who "tried to run a foreign policy without the Senate, an expenditure policy without the House, a national campaign without his Party, a government against the bureaucracy—and . . .

was against big business on whom the arm was put times too numerous to mention."[17] Nixon's frustrations in developing a successful legislative program led him to adopt an approach in 1971 that one of his assistants later labeled the "administrative presidency."[18] Exasperated by his inability to cut social programs, he tried to centralize domestic politics in the White House the same way that he and Kissinger had centralized foreign policy. But he was not as successful in this fundamental restructuring of the executive branch as he had been with the NSC, because the Watergate crisis erupted just as he was preparing to establish the administrative presidency.

Whatever legislative program the administration finally developed, the chief problem it faced in 1969 was the perception that the United States was coming apart at the seams. The nation was awash in unprecedented political and racial violence and a perceived rise in criminality that made many Americans insecure, even in middle-class neighborhoods and homes.

In 1969, there were 602 bombings or bombing attempts; in 1970, there were 1,577. Of the cataloged bombings that took place from January 1969 through April 1970 and caused forty-one deaths, 56 percent were the result of campus disorders, 19 percent from black extremists, 14 percent from white extremists, and 8 percent from criminal attacks. During that same period, there were over 37,000 bombing threats. In the spring of 1969 alone, over 300 colleges experienced demonstrations. Twenty percent of those demonstrations involved the bombing or trashing of buildings. In the fall of 1970, Boston University had to evacuate buildings on 80 occasions because of bomb threats, and 175 threats were made at Rutgers University that year. White House staffers and the Secret Service soon learned to wear their oldest suits in public venues because of the likelihood that they would be targets for eggs and other refuse. On 15 May 1969, Berkeley, California, experienced a violent clash between protesters and police over the disposition of "People's Park," which led to one dead and thirty wounded. Governor Reagan warned, "If it takes a bloodbath, let's get it over with. No more appeasement."[19]

Television cameras captured many of the most sensational occurrences of violence on the campuses and in the streets. The images of rioting and mayhem that Americans saw on the evening newscasts were frightening indeed. A turning point for many was the April 1969 protest by gun-toting African American students at Cornell University who demanded the establishment of a black studies program. This event, which came at a time of increased celebrity for the Black Panthers, who also made no secret of their gun toting, led many Americans to support extreme measures to return their nation to normalcy. One FBI report emphasized the danger posed by thousands of well-trained, radical, black Vietnam veterans who could become urban guerrillas.

During the 1968 campaign, Nixon had repeatedly promised to do something about lawlessness and to get tough with political extremists, criminals, and black and other ethnic militants. Early in his presidency, on 24 February 1969, he wrote to the president of Notre Dame University about the "small irresponsible minority" of students with "an impatience with democratic processes, an intolerance of legitimately constituted authority, and a complete disregard for the rights of others." Less publicly, he ordered the intensification of the activities of the CIA, FBI, NSA, and military intelligence services to monitor and harass campus radicals. Although many of these activities were directed more at suppressing antiwar and other political dissent than at curbing terrorism, the FBI's Cointelpro, the CIA's Operation Chaos, and the NSA's Operation Minaret (all of which had been established under previous administrations) led to more than a hundred grand jury investigations in eighty-four cities. The FBI alone employed 2,000 agents and 1,000 paid informants to keep tabs on the New Left.

The administration also prosecuted vigorously the colorful and controversial Chicago Eight, a group of eight radicals indicted in 1968 for traveling across state lines to foment riots. When the U.S. Court of Appeals reversed their 1970 convictions because of the trial judge's errors, the Justice Department decided not to retry the case, fearing that it might have to reveal wiretaps and other forms of illegal surveillance.

No amount of surveillance and wiretaps could have prepared the administration for the violence and disruption that followed the U.S. invasion of Cambodia and the killings at Kent State and Jackson State Universities in May 1970. To deal with the crisis, aside from trying to centralize intelligence in the White House through the abortive Huston Plan, Nixon asked William Scranton to head the President's Commission on Campus Unrest, instructing him not to "let higher education off with a pat on the ass."[20] The commission report, issued on 26 September 1970, generally blamed student radicals and government authorities equally for the disorder. Although the "actions of some students were violent and criminal," the commission concluded that "the indiscriminate firing of rifles into a crowd of students and the deaths that followed were unnecessary, unwarranted, and inexcusable."[21] Nixon rejected the findings of the Scranton commission, which he privately labeled "crap."[22]

For whatever reasons—increased legal, extralegal, and illegal surveillance; the end of the draft; the exhaustion of radical cadres—incidents of New Left and campus violence decreased dramatically after 1970. It was just in time for the Nixon administration. When the *New York Times* ran a story in January 1971 on the army's Continental U.S. Intelligence program (Conus Intel) and the so-called Citizens Commission to Investigate the FBI broke into the agency's Media, Pennsylvania, office on 8 March 1971 and stole 1,000 classified documents dealing with Cointelpro and other FBI operations, the government's covert antiradical programs suffered a body blow. Using the pilfered Media documents, the *New York Times* ran twenty-four articles over a ten-week period on the FBI's illegal activities. Within 120 days of the still-unsolved burglary, J. Edgar Hoover closed 100 of 538 resident agencies. More important, on 28 April 1971, he canceled Cointelpro, under which agents had been chasing and harassing communists and radicals since 1956. By that time, the worst of the bombings and campus disorders were over.

The administration had less success curbing nonpolitical crime. When Nixon ran on a "law and order" platform, he knew that there was little the federal government could do to affect local law enforcement. This was the first time that crime had been a central issue in a presidential campaign. After taking office, he maintained a high rhetorical profile on fighting crime. Two days into his administration, after reading crime reports in the local papers, he told Mitchell and Ehrlichman, "Let's get going with an announcement in 48 hours of *some* action. It is of the highest priority to do something meaningful on D.C. crime now."[23] A few weeks after Mitchell promised in a news conference that his department was going to be tough on crime, and after Nixon ordered lights to be turned on all over the White House grounds as a demonstration of crime prevention, someone burglarized Rose Mary Woods's apartment at the Watergate.

In April 1969, the administration sent four anticrime bills to Congress. Of the four, the Racketeer Influenced and Corrupt Organizations Act (RICO), which Congress passed in 1970, was the most important in the long run. At the time, however, attention focused on a possible prototype for national legislation, the District of Columbia Crime Control Bill, which included toughened bail and "no-knock" search provisions that Senator Sam Ervin (D-N.C.) thought "smells of a police state."[24] In diluted form, the legislation cleared Congress in July 1970.

Yet, after a year in office, the administration was dissatisfied with its anticrime campaign. The main problem, as Haldeman saw it, was not just "doing the right thing, but then maybe even more importantly, making sure that they have the appearance of doing the right thing." The administration had to do even more in portraying Mitchell as "a tough S.O.B. of a crime fighter."[25] However, three months later, with the 1970 election approaching, Haldeman noted a presidential instruction at a meeting: "Mitchell—

No prosecutions whatever re Mafia or any Italians until Nov."[26] Nixon also opposed a mild gun-control measure.

As with campus violence, there was a statistical decline in crime in 1972, most dramatically in Washington and New York City. That decline might have been related to administration rhetoric, tougher judges, and more vigorous police activity, but the figures rose again in 1973. A good portion of the crime was drug related, and there, particularly in the attempt to interdict the importation of drugs into the United States, the federal government had the central role. The administration was the first during the postwar era to make drug control a major issue.

During the 1960s, the number of heroin addicts increased from 50,000 to more than 500,000. In 1969, the administration launched Operation Intercept, more of a public-relations plan than a real program, which, in any event, received only lukewarm support from the bureaucracy. Egil "Bud" Krogh, an Ehrlichman assistant who was in charge of antidrug and anticrime policies, reported to his bosses about the tensions between the Justice Department's Bureau of Narcotics and Dangerous Drugs (BNDD) and the Treasury Department's Bureau of Customs. Those tensions included officers from the "competing" agencies occasionally drawing guns on one another.

To handle such problems, the administration restructured the way the government enforced its drug laws. In 1971, it established the Cabinet Committee for International Narcotics Control and the Special Action Office for Drug Abuse Prevention; in 1972, it created the Office for Drug Abuse Law Enforcement, which in 1973 joined with the BNDD and the Office of Narcotics Intelligence from Justice to become the Drug Enforcement Agency (DEA).

Although Krogh concludes that "nothing really was accomplished" during the war on drugs, by 1973, drug arrests doubled nationwide, and cocaine seizures increased sixfold.[27] The jurisdictional conflict between Justice and Treasury's Bureau of Customs continued despite the 1972 reorganization, causing chief of staff Alexander Haig to complain in July 1974 that "while this interagency bickering goes on, President Nixon's drug enforcement program is rapidly deteriorating. For the first time in two years, the heroin availability in our cities is *increasing*."[28]

The administration supported a methadone project in June 1971, which, by 1973, funded 450 programs that distributed 7.5 million doses annually. Although Nixon and Mitchell were skeptical about switching addicts from heroin to methadone dependency, Krogh told them, "Some very direct results could be presented to the President in time for the 1972 election."[29] Such positive results in the drug war apparently did not translate into political gains for the administration. Nixon was distressed early in 1973 when the polls showed that the "majority of people give us very negative ratings on the handling of crime and the handling of drugs. This is a case where we are probably doing a good job but where we are talking a very poor game." He demanded that Ehrlichman draft tougher language for an upcoming State of the Union message on his opposition to the legalization of marijuana and his support for mandatory jail terms for drug crimes and for the death penalty, even if the "legal eagles" in Justice disagreed.[30]

"Law and order," the central theme in the 1968 election, referred to far more than New Left militants, drug dealers, and muggers. When Nixon (and George Wallace) talked about law and order, they were also referring to the unprecedented series of racial disorders and urban rebellions that took place in the United States from Watts in Los Angeles in 1965 to the widespread violence in many cities following the assassination of Dr. Martin Luther King, Jr., in April 1968. During the campaign, Nixon also spoke out against HEW's desegregation plans and "forced busing," and he supported plans that permitted students to attend neighborhood schools or any school of their choosing in a district (the freedom-of-choice concept).

Nixon appealed to many Americans who were disturbed by the rise of Black Power and who perceived the War on Poverty and welfare programs to be expensive failures meant to benefit only blacks. In addition, to buttress his concern about "crime in the streets" and the alleged breakdown in family values, Nixon could point to the 130 percent increase in arrests of blacks for homicide between 1960 and 1970 and the rise in illegitimacy among blacks during the same period from 21.6 to 34.9 percent. The relative increase in illegitmacy was even greater among whites, rising from 2.3 to 5.7 percent.

Through much of his political career, Nixon had been somewhat progressive on racial issues. As late as 1972, he still maintained, with some exaggeration, "My feelings on race are, as you know, if anything, ultraliberal."[31] He was a life member of the NAACP and, as vice president, had invited King to the White House, where he "enjoyed" talking to him about voting rights and other civil rights issues.[32] He had also opposed the poll tax and supported antilynching laws.

In contrast, while president, he referred to African Americans in private as being "just down out of the trees" and "genetically inferior."[33] He did not appoint any blacks to his cabinet, was not vigilant in ordering the Justice Department to enforce the Voting Rights Act, and refused to meet with the Congressional Black Caucus, some of whom responded by boycotting his 1971 State of the Union Address. Finally, he supported the FBI's "war" against the Black Panthers and encouraged the IRS to audit the Urban League, the Ford Foundation, and Representative Charles Diggs (D-Mich.), among others in the forefront of civil rights activities.

Yet Pat Buchanan reports, "Though Mr. Nixon's government shorted the civil rights movement on rhetoric, it was not short on delivery." It raised the civil rights enforcement budget by 800 percent, doubled federal aid to black colleges, and increased the number of blacks in high federal positions by 37 percent.[34] As John Mitchell told a delegation of blacks in July 1969, "You would be better advised to watch what we do, rather than what we say."[35] Even more dramatic, during Nixon's tenure, segregation in southern public schools virtually came to an end as a result of Justice Department enforcement of court rulings. When he took office, 68 percent of black children in the South went to all-black schools, whereas 40 percent of black children nationally went to such schools. By 1974, those figures had fallen to 8 and 12 percent, respectively. Moreover, whereas Johnson had allocated $75 million for civil rights enforcement during his last year in office, Nixon allocated $602 million in 1973. It was true, however, that by the time Nixon left office, 53 percent of black children still attended black-majority schools in the South, and, more ominously, the number of blacks attending 95 percent black schools in the North had risen to 50 percent.

As in other areas of the Nixon administration, its approach to civil rights was schizophrenic. The president believed in ending legal desegregation but opposed forced integration. Ever since 1964 and the passage of the Civil Rights Act, the South had been a major element in the Republican coalition. In 1958, there were 2 Republican senators, 8 representatives, 100 state legislators, and no governors in the South. Ten years later, these numbers had increased to 6 senators, 29 representatives, 4 governors, and almost 300 legislators. Nixon received the votes of 228 of 292 southern delegates at the 1968 Republican convention and carried five of the ten southern states during the general election, with Wallace taking the other five. The Democrats were shut out in their once solid South in 1968, even though Nixon received less than 10 percent of the black vote.

There was even more to the story. The South was part of the southern rim of the United States, which had grown dramatically in power and population in the years since World War II. Prospering from agribusiness, defense contracts, real estate, oil, and leisure industries, the generally conservative Sun Belt had become a key to victory for presidential candidates. In addition to conservatives from the rim, Nixon could count more and more on blue-collar, northern, former Democrats who disagreed with the desegregation and welfare programs advanced by their party. They were part of an emerging Republican coalition about which Kevin Phillips had

written. As Nixon told Haldeman early in 1970, "go for Poles, Italians, Irish
... don't go for Jews & Blacks."[36]

Consequently, Nixon took a "low profile" on desegregation—"our people
have got to quit bragging about school desegregation. We do what the law
requires—nothing more."[37] Or as William Safire put it, "make-it-happen,
but don't make it seem like Appomatox."[38] Quietly supporting the laws of
the land prohibiting de jure segregation in the South did not preclude Nixon
from making political hay by vociferously opposing busing to end de facto
segregation in the North. The administration, according to its chief southern strategist, Harry Dent, could pull off the "miracle of this age" by achieving "total desegregation" in the South in such a way that the courts and
the Democrats received the blame.[39]

But that was not going to be easy. A handful of progressives on racial
issues in HEW embarrassed the administration in 1969 and early 1970 by
not being sensitive enough to the feelings of southerners. They included
Nixon's friend Secretary Finch; his undersecretary John G. Veneman; assistant secretary James Farmer; the head of HEW's civil rights division, Leon
Panetta; and Commissioner of Education James E. Allen. Robert Mardian,
the top lawyer at HEW; L. Patrick Gray, also working in that department at
the time; Harry Dent in the White House; Rogers Morton at the RNC; and
John Mitchell at Justice served to counterbalance the alleged radicals at HEW.

The administration's ability to make desegregation more palatable to
the South was diminished by the Supreme Court's 1968 decision in *Green
v. School Board of New Kent County*. There, the Court declared that freedom-
of-choice plans for ending de jure desegregation were unconstitutional if
they did not lead to integrated schools and implied that de facto desegregation was as unconstitutional as de jure segregation. The White House
found itself under the gun on 29 January 1969, the date of a Johnson administration HEW desegregation deadline for five southern school districts.
Abiding by the plan, Finch cut off federal funds to the noncomplying districts, but he offered them a chance to regain funding if they came up with
suitable desegregation plans in sixty days. Two of the districts were in
Strom Thurmond's South Carolina.

Even more important, the Johnson administration had established a
September 1969 deadline for the desegregation of all school districts. At
his 6 February press conference, Nixon announced, "As far as school
segregation is concerned, I support the law of the land." Howard "Bo"
Calloway, a Georgia Republican, responded, "The law . . . the law, listen
here. Nixon promised the South he would change the law, change the
Supreme Court, and change this whole integration business. The time has
come for Nixon to bite the bullet, with real changes and none of this com-
municating bullshit."[40]

To meet such criticism, Mitchell and Finch came up with a plan approved by Nixon on 3 July 1969. Instead of relying on HEW threats to cut off federal funding to segregated school districts in noncompliance, the Justice Department would pursue them through the courts. By using the courts, the administration could desegregate the southern schools but saddle the judiciary with the blame.

The new strategy came too late for thirty-three school districts in Mississippi whose HEW desegregation plans were supposed to go into operation in August. When the influential Mississippi senator John Stennis threatened the administration with withdrawal of his support for the ABM unless something was done to stay the desegregation process in his home state, Finch went to court to delay the implementation of the plans until December. This delaying strategy led sixty-five of the seventy-four line lawyers in the Justice Department's Civil Rights Division to protest to Mitchell. When they received no response from the attorney general, they went public with their complaint. Their action reinforced Nixon's concerns about disloyalty and sabotage among liberal civil servants.

Late in October, and after passage of the ABM legislation, the Supreme Court, in a unanimous decision in *Alexander v. Holmes County Board of Education*, ordered the Mississippi districts to integrate, leading Nixon to comment that "we disagree with segregation, not [that] Southerners are morally wrong."[41] The decision proved important for several reasons. First, for the first time since 1954, the NAACP had gone to court against the federal government. Justice Hugo Black had invited its lawyers to present the case to the full Court. Second, reemphasizing a point in the *Green* case, the Court called for virtually immediate school desegregation. Last, and most important for the administration, it permitted the president to point to the courts as the culprits.

In February 1970, Nixon established the Cabinet Committee on Education, headed by Vice President Agnew but run by George Shultz. Endorsed by the president, the committee's report issued on 24 March 1970 supported school desegregation but encouraged the resolution of problems at the local level, opposed school desegregation efforts that were related to de facto segregation in housing patterns, and asked for $1.5 billion from Congress to help districts desegregate. Congress provided only $75 million in start-up funds. Nixon followed up with the organization of nonpartisan, biracial state advisory commissions to help smooth the way toward integration. The commissions, which brought southern white and black leaders together, sometimes for the first time, fit well with Nixon's attempt not to coerce the South.

Southern segregationists suffered another blow in July 1970 when Randolph Thrower, the commissioner of the IRS, revoked the tax exemption for private white academies. Bryce Harlow and Leonard Garment, among others, had argued in the White House that it would be unfair to desegregate public schools and then make it easy for the children of rich southerners to escape from going to them. Senator Thurmond, who considered the ruling a "breach of faith," complained bitterly to Nixon, who promised that better days were coming for the South.[42]

Although the South lost its bid to halt desegregation, in several other ways the administration demonstrated that it would not actively pursue civil rights issues. In January 1970, someone leaked to the press a memo in which Moynihan, concerned about the rise of extremism on the race issue, advised Nixon that the "time may have come when the issue of race could benefit from a period of 'benign neglect.'"[43] The next month, Nixon fired Panetta from his HEW post, and Finch soon moved over from HEW to the White House to become a counselor. In addition, the Democratic head of the Equal Employment Opportunity Commission (EEOC), Clifford Alexander, and Father Theodore Hesburgh, the head of the Civil Rights Commission, left their positions because of disagreements over administration policies. Nixon also interpreted Title VI of the 1964 Civil Rights Act in such a way that the Pentagon could award contracts to southern textile firms that discriminated against blacks. Further, to address concerns about federal support for the construction of new public housing in neighborhoods whose citizens opposed such projects, on 11 June 1971, Nixon announced that the administration would not "attempt to impose federally assisted housing upon any community." Finally, Nixon's attempts to alter the Voting Rights Act of 1965 and to put an anti–civil rights southerner on the Supreme Court, and his opposition to forced busing to achieve desegregation, signaled to southerners—as well as northerners—that the civil rights revolution was coming to an end.

Two sections of the Voting Rights Act of 1965, one dealing with literacy tests and another requiring the states to submit changes in voting laws to the Justice Department, were due to expire in August 1970. Between 1965 and 1969, 800,000 new black voters had registered to vote in the seven southern states where the act applied. Many white southerners were upset about the development and the way their states had been singled out for federal monitoring. On 15 January 1969, outgoing attorney general Ramsey Clark proposed that the House of Representatives approve a five-year extension of the act. The Supreme Court took care of the literacy-test issue provisionally in June 1969 when, in *Gaston County v. United States*, it ruled that North Carolina could not employ a racially neutral literacy test.

John Mitchell made it clear that he was not pleased with the Voting Rights Act because it singled out southern states for attention. Over the next few years, the administration sought to nationalize the bill to remove the stigma from the South. It succeeded in 1972 when the extension of the bill, although still concentrating on the original seven southern states, included a provision for federal supervision of all districts in the country where less than 50 percent of the minority population was registered. The act also suspended literacy tests until 1975. Nixon almost vetoed the bill when the Senate tacked on a provision to permit eighteen-year-olds to vote. The president, who originally feared that young people would be mostly Democrats, felt better when he saw polling data that revealed that they were not knee-jerk liberals.

Nixon offered the South more than symbolism with his attempt to appoint justices to the Supreme Court who would undo the alleged damage done to that region by the activist and liberal Warren Court. Nixon promised as much again and again during his 1968 campaign. In June 1968, his old rival Chief Justice Earl Warren announced his retirement, in the hope that Johnson and not Nixon would name his replacement. Johnson nominated his longtime friend Justice Abe Fortas to replace Warren and Judge Homer Thornberry to take Fortas's seat. Republicans, who did not want the lame-duck Johnson to name the new chief, attacked Fortas for accepting money for lectures and also for being a secret presidential adviser while on the Court. Led by Strom Thurmond, they filibustered his nomination to death, an action that Democrats would not forget.

Warren could not retract his resignation and had to stand by while a man he despised and who had openly criticized his Court appointed his successor. The next year, Nixon became upset when Warren, in retirement, made what he thought were unjustified political criticisms. The head of the Justice Department's Office of Legal Counsel, William Rehnquist, advised Egil Krogh that Warren was misbehaving. Krogh then ordered an assistant to leak information to a friendly columnist on how the former chief justice had been violating "canons of judicial ethics."[44]

On 21 May 1969, Nixon nominated his own chief justice, Warren Burger, the chief judge of the Federal Court of Appeals in Washington. Nixon had first met Burger in 1948 at the Republican Convention, where he had been floor manager for Harold Stassen. Nixon had considered President Eisenhower's recommendation, Herbert Brownell, for the position, but he was too liberal for the South. He also approached Thomas E. Dewey and considered elevating Justice Potter Stewart. Burger, who campaigned for the job, had been a conservative assistant attorney general and was the sort of strict constructionist Nixon had promised to put on the Court to make inroads against the five-person liberal majority he had inherited. The Senate approved Burger by a vote of seventy-four to three after a brief eighteen-day confirmation process.

Although he turned out to be an effective administrator who was interested in modernizing the federal court system, Burger was not an especially distinguished jurist. According to one justice who reflected a good deal of Court sentiment, he was "abrasive to his colleagues" and was "without substance or integrity," a "product of Nixon's tasteless White House."[45] Moreover, he became Nixon's secret confidant, behaving in the same sort of impolitic manner that had earned Abe Fortas widespread criticism. Nixon often consulted with Burger about civil rights and other issues pending before Congress and the courts, and the chief justice often offered Nixon suggestions for court appointments. Most of the time, he dealt with the president in an obsequious manner unbecoming his station. After Nixon announced his October 1971 Court appointments, Burger sent a note to Rose Mary Woods: "Just tell him he handled this thing superbly tonight. I was particularly delighted that he treated the ABA [American Bar Association] properly by absolutely ignoring them."[46]

Even before Nixon appointed Burger, Attorney General Mitchell, J. Edgar Hoover, and Republicans in Congress had intensified their pressure on Fortas to resign from the Court. *Life* magazine received assistance from the Justice Department for its 4 May 1969 exposé describing how Fortas had accepted money for legal advice from a foundation whose head had been convicted of violating federal security laws. Pressured by the Justice Department, Warren had to ask for Fortas's resignation. On 14 May 1969, Fortas announced his retirement, the first time a justice had been forced off the Court for misconduct.

Fortas had held the so-called Jewish seat. His predecessors included Louis Brandeis, Benjamin Cardozo, Felix Frankfurter, and Arthur Goldberg. Nixon felt pressure to appoint a conservative Jew to the seat but, discovering that they were few and far between, told his aides that there would be no religious test for Fortas's seat. Instead, on 18 August 1969, he selected Clement F. Haynsworth, Jr., from Greenville, South Carolina, a judge on the Fourth Circuit Court of Appeals. Burger, who called Nixon about Haynsworth a number of times, was a "staunch supporter," as was Attorney General Mitchell, who had recommended him. Nixon had not consulted with either the ABA or key Republicans before he made the nomination.[47]

Haynsworth, a respectable nomination in terms of his judicial reputation, was conservative on civil rights and labor issues. Massachusetts Republican senator Edward Brooke, an African American, contended that Haynsworth's "treatment of civil rights issues is not in keeping with the historic movement toward equal justice for every American," and New Jersey Republican senator Clifford Case thought the nominee had "a degree of insensitivity to human rights."[48] As promised, Nixon had appointed a southerner who would go slow on civil rights.

Senators who opposed Haynsworth on ideological grounds, as well as those Democrats who were furious about the Fortas affair, could point to two cases of apparent conflict of interest when Haynsworth, who had not broken any laws, should have recused himself. Nixon, who had been warned early on about this problem, insisted on sticking with his man. But in the post-Fortas climate, a nominee had to be ethically clean. According to Senator Gale McGhee (D-Wyo.), "Had there been no Fortas affair . . . a man of Justice Haynsworth's attainments . . . undoubtedly would have been confirmed."[49]

The Senate Judiciary Committee approved the nomination by a ten-to-seven vote, but by the time it reached the floor, Haynsworth did not have a majority. Rather than withdraw the nomination, Nixon characteristically got his back up: "If we cave on this one, they will think that if you kick Nixon you can get somewhere . . . I didn't get where I am today by running away from fights."[50] As the situation appeared bleak, the administration pulled out all the stops. For example, Ohio Republican senator William Saxbe was a target of the "Fat Cat" program, with at least nine of his campaign contributors calling him to vote for Haynsworth. Saxbe considered this crude pressure from the White House to be orchestrated by "a bunch of amateurs."[51] In another example of how seriously the White House took the issue, it sped up the signing of an executive order banning Honduras meat products because of the aid it received on the nomination from the cattlemen's lobby.

Despite these efforts, the Senate rejected Haynsworth by a vote of fifty-five to forty-five, with seventeen Republicans, including the minority and assistant minority leaders, joining thirty-eight Democrats to defeat the nomination. From 1789 to 1900, twenty of eighty-five Supreme Court nominations had gone down to defeat, but Haynsworth's was the first since 1930. Nixon thought that it might be a good idea for Haynsworth to resign from the Fourth Circuit Court as a "martyr," because "we may gain enormously from this incident."[52] The Senate later "apologized" to Haynsworth by naming, by unanimous vote, a federal building in Greenville after him.[53] Nixon would exact revenge not only by nominating another southern judge but also by urging Gerald Ford, with help again from J. Edgar Hoover, to "get" liberal justice William O. Douglas for his alleged improprieties.[54]

After Haynsworth's defeat, Nixon told Harry Dent, "I want you to go out this time and find a good federal judge further south and further to the right." G. Harrold Carswell, the undistinguished jurist Dent and Mitchell found, "made Haynsworth look like Learned Hand," according to Senator Birch Bayh (D-Ind.).[55] William Safire considered the nomination of Carswell on 19 January 1970 "one of the most ill-advised public acts of the early Nixon Presidency."[56]

Only five months before, the Senate had easily confirmed Carswell to the Fifth Circuit Court of Appeals in Florida. Burger rated him first among three judges he had recommended for that position in April. But it was more difficult for Carswell to make it to the highest court in the land, especially after the media discovered that he had said in 1948, "I believe that segregation of the races is proper and the only practical and correct way of life in our states," and that he "believed in the principles of white supremacy."[57] Justice Hugo Black had overcome his earlier membership in the Ku Klux Klan, but there was little in Carswell's record to indicate that he had become a devotee of civil rights since 1948, despite his protestations to the contrary during the confirmation hearings. When he first learned about Carswell's segregationist comments, Nixon, who had been ill served by his advisers, wrote, "My God!"[58]

In a sad commentary on the sort of jurists easily accepted by the Senate for the lower courts, Carswell turned out to be a weak appointment whose reversal rate of 40 percent was twice that of the average federal judge. Such a record led the dean of the Yale Law School to testify to the Senate Judiciary Committee that Carswell "presents more slender credentials than any nominee put forth in this century."[59] Two hundred former Supreme Court clerks, including former secretary of state Dean Acheson, also publicly opposed Carswell, as did nine of the fifteen professors at the University of Florida Law School. Nixon's congressional aide, Bryce Harlow, commented, "They think he's a boob, a dummy. And what counter is there to that. He is.[60] His defenders made things worse. Senator Roman Hruska (R-Neb.) asserted, "even if he were mediocre, there are a lot of mediocre judges and people and lawyers. They are entitled to a little representation, aren't they, and a little chance. We can't have all Brandeises and Frankfurters and Cardozos and stuff like that there."[61] Senator Russell Long (D-La.) echoed Hruska when he suggested approving "a B student or a student who was able to think straight, compared to one of those A students who are capable of the kind of thinking that winds up getting us a one-hundred percent increase in crime."[62]

Despite this sort of bizarre support, the Senate Judiciary Committee recommended Carswell by a thirteen-to-four vote on 16 February. Nonetheless, vote counters at the White House soon recognized that the nomination would be in trouble when it reached the floor. Several Republicans asked Nixon to withdraw the nomination to avoid another embarrassment. Characteristically, he refused to give up. Colson suggested that he go to the public by releasing a tough letter to Senator Saxbe on 1 April. In it, Nixon questioned whether his responsibility "to appoint members of the Court

... can be frustrated by those who wish to substitute their own philosophy or their own subjective judgement for that of the one person entrusted by the Constitution with the power of appointment."

This assault against their prerogatives angered wavering senators. They resisted powerful pressure from the White House involving future judicial appointments, campaign financing, and other pork to be given or withheld depending on their votes on Carswell. Nixon even considered making public the fact that Senator Bayh had failed the bar exam in 1960. The White House's strong-arming backfired in some cases, where it appears that senators on the fence voted not to confirm because of their disgust with the crude tactics. When Mitchell became ill during this period, Nixon rejected the idea that Assistant Attorney General Rehnquist take his place leading the charge for Carswell's confirmation because he was "not a nutcutter."[63] In the end, the administration came up short as Carswell's nomination went down to defeat by a vote of fifty-one to forty-five on 8 April 1970.

A furious Nixon ordered that northern Republican senators Mathias, Case, Goodell, Percy, and Schweiker immediately be taken off the White House guest list. The day after the vote, he issued a statement in which he "reluctantly concluded—with the Senate as presently constituted—I cannot successfully nominate to the Supreme Court any Federal appellate judge from the South who believes as I do in the strict construction of the Constitution." He continued by labeling Haynsworth and Carswell "distinguished jurists" who "had the misfortune of being born in the South." There were two winners in this affair—the American people, who were not saddled with a "mediocre" justice, and Nixon, who proved to southerners that he was a loyal friend who did everything in his power to combat the prejudice against their section.

Four days later, Gerald Ford held a press conference at which he announced that he was opening an investigation that could lead to the impeachment of Justice William O. Douglas. With material leaked from the Justice Department and the FBI, Ford accused Douglas of being a radical who published unseemly material in the leftist and sometimes pornographic *Evergreen Review* and, like Fortas, accepted honoraria while on the Court from a foundation that had received some of its money from Las Vegas gambling interests. Genuinely upset about Douglas's rakish lifestyle, Ford had been working privately on the case before the administration asked him to take the lead. He had complained earlier, "If the Senate votes against a nominee [Haynsworth] for lack of sensitivity, it should apply the same standards to sitting justices."[64] Douglas blamed the president for the Ford investigation, claiming that "Nixon has sicked his gorillas on me" and that "Ford and his associates were planning a Roman holiday in the summer of 1970, with my impeachment as the main event" as retribution for the Carswell fiasco.[65]

In a tricky parliamentary maneuver, the Democrats called for the House Judiciary Committee, and not a special select committee, to hold hearings on the impeachment of Douglas. The Judiciary Committee found no grounds for impeachment; Ford later admitted that the assault on Douglas "was a mistake."[66] As early as 1 May, the administration also knew that it had made a mistake when Mitchell attacked the "irresponsible and malicious criticism of the Supreme Court."[67]

On 14 April 1970, Nixon announced that his third nomination for the Fortas seat would be Harry Blackmun, a northerner from Minnesota who came with recommendations from his former colleague, Warren Burger. President Eisenhower had appointed him to the Eighth Circuit, where he had compiled a solid record. In less than a month, the Senate confirmed him by a unanimous vote. At first, Blackmun followed Burger's lead so closely, voting forty-eight out of fifty times with the chief justice, that he was called "Hip-pocket Harry," a member of the "Minnesota Twins." But he soon moved to the left of Burger on many issues, as demonstrated by the fact that he wrote the January 1973 opinion supporting the legalization of abortion in *Roe v. Wade*. His wife and three daughters, whom Nixon had earlier feared might be "hippie types," were strongly supportive of the decision.[68]

Nixon had another chance to redirect the Court in 1971 when Justices Hugo Black and John Marshall Harlan announced their retirements on 17 and 23 September, respectively. Pat Buchanan recommended Representative Richard Poff of Virginia, an opponent of civil rights with a limited legal background. Mitchell proposed Herschel Friday, another lawyer with an anti–civil rights background, who also received support from Burger. Nixon toyed with the idea of appointing Vice President Agnew, Senator Howard Baker (R-Tenn.), or Senator Robert Byrd (D-W.V.). Pat Nixon wanted her husband to appoint the first woman to the Supreme Court, and for a while, the administration considered Los Angeles judge Mildred Lillie. Had the ABA approved of Lillie, Nixon probably would have nominated her. Burger did not think that the remaining pool of female justices was very large.

The names of potential nominees that were leaked to the media "lacked stature," according to the ABA, which called for more distinguished options. Angry at the ABA's meddling, Nixon scribbled a note to Ehrlichman, "Never again do they get a shot at *any* Judges after this performance (including District Court)."[69] Even though Burger had recommended several of the nominees, he told Mitchell "that he will resign if the P doesn't appoint distinguished judges to the Court, and he doesn't feel the current list meets that qualification." Nixon responded that he would not "cater to Burger's demands."[70]

Within the White House, John Dean and David Young worked on the nominations, with Ehrlichman's favorites, Lewis F. Powell, Jr., and William Rehnquist, finally getting the nod. Powell, who was Burger's first choice, had refused Nixon's offer of a nomination in 1970. A southerner from Virginia, he had maintained a low profile on civil rights issues while belonging to segregated clubs and working in an all-white law firm. The former president of the ABA, president of the American Trial Lawyers Association, and member of Lyndon Johnson's National Crime Commission was approved by a vote of eighty-nine to one on 6 December 1971.

Nixon's other appointee, Rehnquist, whom he had labeled a "clown" on one occasion because of the undignified way he dressed, was the intellectually impressive chief of the Office of Legal Council in the Justice Department.[71] From the Goldwater faction of the party, the forty-seven-year-old Rehnquist was a conservative law-and-order man who had opposed the 1964 Civil Rights Act and earlier had supported restrictive housing covenants and approved of the Supreme Court's 1896 *Plessy v. Ferguson* decision upholding government-mandated school segregation. Rehnquist, who was to become chief justice in 1986, gained Senate approval by a vote of sixty-eight to twenty-six on 10 December 1971.

With the appointment of Powell and Rehnquist, Nixon had made four appointments to the Supreme Court. Even though Powell and Blackmun turned out to be more centrist, even liberal, on many issues than Nixon had expected, the Supreme Court did move toward the Right because of his appointments. That did not necessarily mean that he could count on the Court during his second term. On issues relating to obscenity, abortion, the impoundment of funds, the death penalty, and especially Watergate, Nixon found limited support from the justices.

He did better on the federal courts. During his first two years, he appointed 115 federal judges. By the time he left office, he had appointed 230 (12 more than had Roosevelt). For these appointments, he had worked out an agreement with Senator James Eastland (D-Miss.), head of the Senate Judiciary Committee, whereby he would submit his nominations to the Standing Committee on the Judiciary of the ABA. The ABA considered all his nominees qualified. Nixon also worked closely with J. Edgar Hoover to identify candidates who would be tough on criminals. He appointed only six African Americans to federal court slots; Johnson had appointed seventeen.

Although unable to appoint southern Supreme Court justices to please the likes of Strom Thurmond, as the 1972 election approached, Nixon became an outspoken champion of the South and of people in other regions who opposed the latest Court remedy for segregation: busing. On 20 April 1971, in a complicated decision in *Swann v. Mecklenburg Board of Education*, the Supreme Court upheld unanimously a federal court plan for integrating a

North Carolina school district that included busing students from neighborhoods to balance the racial composition in district schools. The Supreme Court did not endorse busing in all cases but let stand a federal court ruling to employ that measure in this case involving 10,000 students.

During the same month, a federal district court ordered cross-district busing in Detroit that involved up to 300,000 students in fifty-three school districts. In March 1973, in *Keyes v. School District No. 1*, the Court again approved a busing scheme, this time for Denver. By then, it had become a highly emotional national issue, with polls showing that the public rejected busing to achieve racial balance by as much as eight to one. Not many parents in the North or the South wanted their children bused away from neighborhood schools. Michigan representative Don Riegle viewed the busing ruling as a "long-awaited day of reckoning" for the North; his own Michigan Republicans were "delighted by the dilemma the state's Democrats now face."[72]

On 24 May 1971, Nixon agreed with aide Edward L. Morgan that "if we can keep liberal writers convinced that we are doing what the Court requires, and our conservative Southern friends convinced that we are not doing any more than the Court requires, I think we can walk this tight rope until November, 1972."[73] However, the busing issue soon made it impossible for the administration to do what the Court required. In a memo early in 1972, Nixon spelled out his position, which he claimed was not "primarily motivated by political considerations." He was "convinced that while legal segregation is totally wrong . . . forced integration of housing or education is just as wrong," and he came "down hard and unequivocally against busing for the purpose of racial balance." He worried that "Burger and Blackmun, already having been exposed to the Washington elite, and Powell and Rehnquist, both smarting under the attacks of liberals . . . will come down on the side of an ultra-liberal decision on both forced integrated housing and in the school cases." Consequently, he was going to support an anti-busing constitutional amendment.[74]

On 16 March 1972, just after George Wallace won the Florida Democratic primary, the president explained his anti-busing policy to the nation, calling for legislation to impose a moratorium on all new busing rulings and to appropriate $2.5 billion to aid the poorest school districts in the nation. During the moratorium, Congress would draw up uniform national standards for desegregation, with busing to be used as a last resort. "Busing," he contended, "is a bad means to a good end."

When Congress did not accept his proposal, Nixon threatened on 23 June that "we will have no choice but to seek a constitutional amendment which will put the goals of better education for all our children above the objective of massive busing for some children." The previous year, he had commented privately on the amendment approach, "I know it's not a good idea, but it'll make those bastards [in the Democratic Party] take a stand and it's a political plus for us."[75]

Nixon's strong opposition to busing enhanced his position among the Silent Majority. The issue remained alive through the first year of his second term, without any constitutional amendment or moratorium being passed. The Supreme Court relieved the pressure on 25 July 1974 in the *Milliken v. Bradley* case when, by a five-to-four vote, the majority ruled that segregated practices in one school district did not justify a desegregation plan that involved other districts that had no record of de jure segregation. This opinion, which invalidated cross-district busing, represented the first occasion since 1954 that the Court did not approve a remedy advocated by the NAACP. Having moved toward the Right with Nixon's appointees, the Court appeared to be responding to the widespread, often violent reactions (including the burning of school buses) of white citizens toward court-ordered cross-district busing, especially in the North.

Although the Nixon administration did not promote new civil rights initiatives, it did establish several programs to assist minorities in the economic arena. In 1968, Nixon had called for "black capital ownership." Whereas minorities constituted 20 percent of the population, they owned only 4 percent of all the businesses in the United States, and those businesses produced less than 1 percent of all sales and assets. To improve this situation, Nixon established by executive order on 5 March 1969 the Office of Minority Business Enterprise (OMBE) within the Commerce Department. He told Commerce Secretary Stans, "Politically, I don't think there are many votes in it for us, but we'll do it because it is right."[76] Under the already existing Small Business Administration (SBA), Stans also set up an agency to obtain loans for minority enterprise small business investment companies (MESBICs), which in turn established fifty programs by 1972.

The OMBE, with a staff of ten and no budget of its own, had to scrounge for funds from other agencies. Congress did appropriate $40 million for the agency in 1971 and $60 million in 1972. In 1969, the government made grants, loans, and guarantees to minority businesses valued at $200 million. By 1972, that figure had increased to $243 million. Moreover, the value of government "set-aside" contracts for minority businesses rose from $8 million in 1969 to $243 million in 1972.

Modestly successful, the programs helped establish forty-five of the largest Hispanic American businesses between 1969 and 1976 and 30 percent of the largest black businesses between 1969 and 1971. In addition, private industry set up the National Minority Purchasing Council, which led to $50 million in new business to minority enterprises in 1969 and $12 billion by 1972. The number of businesses owned by blacks grew from 163,000 when Nixon took office to 195,000 in 1972, and their receipts rose from $10.6 billion to $16.6 billion. Some of that gain could be attributed to inflation. By 1972, only twenty-six black-owned companies had sales of more than $5 million, and the income of the top 100 black businesses *combined* would have earned a ranking of 284 on the famed *Fortune* 500 list. During the period, the rate of expansion of government loans to nonminority businesses grew more rapidly than the rate for minority businesses.

The programs were plagued by scandals, with whites sometimes establishing black-owned fronts for their companies in order to receive grants from the OMBE and the SBA. As one staffer noted, "Several highly placed officials from the Republican administration and their buddies have manipulated the program to their own enrichment." The head of the SBA did not think that there was anything wrong with whites having "joint ownership" with blacks who would qualify for minority loans.[77]

Far more controversial was the administration's Philadelphia Plan to foster minority employment in businesses with federal government contracts. It had its origins in 1966 in the Labor Department's Office of Federal Contract Compliance, which recommended that people working on federal contracts should reflect the local area's demographics. Two years later, after several experimental programs had been initiated, the comptroller general ruled that such a policy not only violated open bidding procedures but also represented reverse discrimination.

Nonetheless, Richard Nixon, who had told the EEOC that there would be "no quotas" while he was president, approved a program that came very close to being a quota system that went beyond affirmative action.[78] Secretary of Labor George Shultz, aided by Assistant Secretary of Labor Arthur A. Fletcher, a black Republican, resurrected the Democratic program that soon become known as the Philadelphia Plan, named after the city in which it was first mandated. Under the plan, employers that applied for federally funded work had to present "goals and timetables" for the employment of minority workers (blacks, Asians, Indians, and Spanish-surnamed Americans) and offer them training programs. Employers had to file an affirmative action program within 120 working days of signing a government contract. Further, the unions had to open their membership to more minority workers.

In February 1970, the administration applied the concept to all federal contracts worth $50,000 or more and, in December 1971, extended it to women. In May 1974, an administration executive order declared that the goal for contractors' affirmative action plans was "the prompt and full utilization of minorities and women at all levels in all segments of its work force."[79]

Originally, Shultz directed the plan at the construction industry. By helping to increase the pool of construction workers, the administration hoped to lower the inflationary spiral in the home-building industry, a key sector in the economy. When Nixon took office, of the 1.3 million construction workers in the United States, only 100,000 were black, and 80 percent of them were in the lowest-paid classification. Of 130,000 building-worker apprentices, only 5,000 were black.

Although Shultz and Nixon had no ulterior motive in developing the plan, the president soon recognized that it would create problems for the Democrats with two of their core constituencies: blacks, who wanted even more sweeping affirmative action programs, and union leaders, who were guilty of discriminatory practices. Most of the construction-union leadership opposed the Philadelphia Plan. That leadership, however, did not blame the Republicans, who appeared to be more moderate on the issue than the Democrats. The institution of affirmative action programs, which originated in the Johnson administration but was quietly supported by the Nixon administration, helped contribute to massive blue-collar defections from the Democrats in 1972.

But those defections to the presumably more anti–civil rights Nixon does not gainsay the argument that overall, his administration made significant progress in desegregation and affirmative action. Despite his rhetoric and unsavory role in exacerbating racial polarization over busing, Nixon could have boasted, had he wanted to, about his progressive civil rights policy. Aside from the administration's desegregation policies, his EEOC staff increased from 359 to 1,640 between 1969 and 1972, and the 1973 budget for civil rights enforcement was eight times that in the last year of the Johnson administration. And in another type of civil rights action, under Nixon, the District of Columbia, with its black majority, received home rule, along with other people of color in Guam, American Samoa, and the Virgin Islands.

Nixon encouraged the FBI to prosecute vigorously its war against the Black Panthers. Nixon's head of the Civil Rights Division called them "nothing but hoodlums and [said] we've got to get them," and the attorney general authorized the use of electronic surveillance during investigations. In a series of federal and local raids that began in 1968, the Panthers were destroyed, with 1,000 members ending up in prison. Further, FBI director Hoover, who once asserted, "There will be no negro special agent as long as I am Director of the FBI," continued his vicious campaign against the King organization and Reverend Ralph David Abernathy, and even defended as justified the killings at Jackson State University in 1970.[80]

Richard Nixon became president at a point when the modern women's movement had become one of the major political, social, and cultural movements of the era. In 1970, as a reflection of changing times even in mainstream America, the *Mary Tyler Moore Show*, which centered around an unmarried professional woman, was a top-rated television show. Two years later, *MS* magazine's first issue sold 250,000 copies in eight days. Throughout the land, women, mostly white and middle class, had begun to call more forcefully and in greater numbers for an end to gender discrimination in all areas of American life, especially in the workplace, where the number of women working outside the home had reached 40 percent. Women constituted 80 percent of all teachers but only 10 percent of principals, 40 percent of all university students but only 10 percent of the faculty. Whereas women in the 1950s had earned sixty-four cents for every dollar earned by men, that figure declined to fifty-eight cents during the next decade. No women attended the national service academies, and although composing one-third of the federal workforce, women held only 2 percent of the top jobs. They faced discrimination in professional schools, a situation that resulted in women constituting only 7 percent of all physicians and 3 percent of all lawyers.

Nixon understood that middle-class women had grown restive—his own wife prodded him on women's issues—but he had a conventional approach to gender relations. Those around him were not sensitive to women's issues either, with Arthur Burns observing, "I'm not aware of any discrimination against the better half of mankind."[81] Although Nixon's first gesture in gender relations was to invite cabinet secretaries' wives to a cabinet meeting, 3.5 percent of all his appointments were women, a figure that improved on Kennedy's and Johnson's records. On 21 April 1971, in a published memo, he instructed all executive departments to "develop and put into action a plan for attracting more qualified women to top appointive positions," even though he doubted "if jobs in Government for women make many votes from women."[82]

Although no cabinet members were women, Nixon did appoint Ann Armstrong counselor in February 1973 and Dixie Lee Ray to be head of the Atomic Energy Commission. He was responding in part to being labeled by Representative Bella Abzug (D-N.Y.) "the nation's chief resident male chauvinist" at a National Women's Political Caucus meeting. Participants hissed Nixon's polite written message of welcome, an act that caused him to ask rhetorically, "is it wise to throw pearls before swine?"[83]

Nixon had earlier flirted with the idea of a female Supreme Court justice and once mused about New York Republican lawyer Rita Hauser's being a good candidate. But when she said that the Constitution did not bar same-sex marriages, Nixon commented, "There goes a Supreme Court Justice! I can't go *that* far. . . . Negroes [and whites], okay. But *that's* too far!"[84]

He established a woman's task force in September 1969 that became the President's Task Force on Woman's Rights and Responsibilities in October. On 15 December 1969, the thirteen-member task force under Virginia R. Allen called for the establishment of a permanent office on women, support for the Equal Rights Amendment (ERA), and more effective anti-discrimination measures.

Nixon did not establish a permanent office on women, but he did support the ERA, as had every president since 1940, as well as more federal legislation to protect women's rights. The ERA guaranteed Americans equal rights regardless of their gender. Bryce Harlow considered the amendment "insane" but understood why Nixon had to support it; the "reason—its political."[85] Nixon was "stuck with the Equal Rights Amendment. . . . We are for it—I want some action taken to indicate maximum support—and get the publicity."[86] Despite the fact that Office of Legal Counsel chief William Rehnquist had testified against the ERA as being too ambiguous and unnecessary, the Senate approved it by an 84-to-8 vote and the House by a 354-to-23 vote in 1972. By the end of the year, twenty-three states had approved the amendment, but it fell short of the requisite three-quarters of the states needed for ratification.

The president signed the Equal Employment Opportunity Act on 25 March 1972, which strengthened the EEOC's enforcement power under Title VII of the Civil Rights Act of 1964. He had earlier ordered an EEOC review of discriminatory hiring policies in higher education against women. By August 1972, armed with its new powers, the EEOC filed over 350 gender discrimination suits. In 1971, the president also broadened the powers of the U.S. Civil Rights Commission to include gender discrimination and approved an act that prohibited such discrimination in educational institutions receiving federal funds. All these measures contributed to the gains women began to make in achieving equal rights and in ending gender discrimination.

Nixon, however, opposed unrestricted abortions, a central issue for many in the women's movement. He labeled the practice "an unacceptable form of population control" and restricted its use in military hospitals in April 1971, and he was not at all pleased by the Supreme Court's 1973 *Roe v. Wade* decision.[87] No doubt Nixon truly opposed abortion, but he also realized its importance to Catholic voters

The president approved a 1971 measure to make child care tax deductible, but on 10 December of that same year, he vetoed the Child Development Act, which would have provided free child care for the poor, because it was too costly and committed "the vast moral authority of the National Government to . . . communal approaches to child rearing." The Child Development Act could have been the foot in the door for the wholesale adoption of a system of national child care that would have made it easier for women to compete in the workplace.

Although many young women, especially those supporting the women's movement, may not have been pleased with the Nixon administration's approach to their issues, young men were elated by one of his reforms that applied directly to them: the ending of the draft. A longtime defender of the draft, in 1956, Nixon pronounced it "indispensable to national security."[88] However, influenced by Martin Anderson, who had been influenced by economist Milton Friedman, Nixon came to the conclusion by late 1967 that an all-volunteer force (AVF) would be the best solution to the problem of the increasingly unpopular Selective Service System (SSS). He also realized that a president interested in an aggressive foreign policy would have more freedom of action with an AVF than one dependent on draftees whose parents worried about their boys being sent abroad. He understood as well the relationship between the antiwar movement and the draft and that because of exemptions, the *Selective* Service System had always been unfair.

Nixon announced his intention to create an AVF as a campaign pledge in October 1968, and in March 1969, he appointed a fifteen-person commission headed by former defense secretary Thomas Gates and composed of five people favoring SSS, five favoring AVF, and five who were neutral. In the interim, on 19 May, he asked Congress to establish a draft lottery system, based on the random ordering of birthdates, which permitted young men to estimate the likelihood of their being drafted. The new system, which Congress approved in November 1969, went into effect with the draft call for January 1970.

On 20 February 1970, the Gates commission unanimously recommended the establishment of an AVF. With draftees constituting 60 percent of all enlisted men in 1969, the Department of Defense (DOD) was not pleased. Despite its problems with morale, mutinies, and discipline in Vietnam, DOD wanted to maintain the draft system because it needed warm

179

bodies for Vietnam. Until the details of an AVF could be worked out, including a public-relations program to sell it to Americans, Nixon extended the draft in 1969 and again in 1971. He did try to make it fairer by eliminating or phasing out several exemptions. In addition, the replacement of the controversial General Lewis Hershey, who had been in charge of the SSS since its inception, with Curtis Tarr, who took over in April 1970, brought needed reform and modernization to the agency.

In January 1972, the DOD issued no draft calls. That June, the president reported that no more draftees would be sent to Vietnam, and on 28 August, he announced that the SSS would be replaced by an AVF in July 1973. "Ending all dependence on the draft," he assured the nation, "will be consistent with maintaining the force level and degree of readiness to meet our vital long-term national security needs." Two weeks earlier, Nixon had told Haldeman that making the "announcement in the campaign could have a very significant effect."[89]

The Nixon administration also appeared to be progressive when it came to Native American rights, especially considering the major crises it confronted involving Indian activists. From 1969 to 1974, Native American activists illegally occupied forty-five different installations.

Although Nixon left much of the day-to-day handling of Indian policy to Ehrlichman and Garment, who, along with White House aide Bradley H. Patterson, Jr., were sensitive to Native Americans, he told Ehrlichman, "the sole reason for helping them is Presidential responsibility. There are very few votes involved and I doubt if many of them will move in our direction. . . . But . . . a grave injustice has been worked against them . . . and the nation at large will appreciate our having a more active program of concern for their plight."[90]

The Native American issue came to the forefront on 9 September 1969 when fourteen young Indians occupied the empty Alcatraz prison in San Francisco Bay as a symbolic act to "reclaim" their land. Although the government shut off all electricity and water to the trespassers, they received food and generators from supporters on the outside and maintained their occupation until it fell apart the following June, in "squalor and degradation."[91]

The law-and-order Nixon administration took no action to forcefully eject the Native Americans, who had made a variety of demands, many of which revolved around the fact that their group was the poorest and most unhealthy of all ethnic groups in the United States. In 1970, Indian unemployment ranged from 40 to 80 percent, and 80 percent of all Indians earned incomes below the poverty level. They suffered a tuberculosis rate eight times higher than the average and a suicide rate twice as high.

The administration adopted a similar nonviolent response to the more serious occupation of the Bureau of Indian Affairs (BIA) in Washington in November 1972. Over 300 activists, some of whom were armed with Molotov cocktails, took part in this destructive and costly protest against the BIA, which was misdirected, considering the BIA's policy of tribal self-determination, including control over bloc grants and tribal schools. In addition, the administration had recently increased the agency's budget by 214 percent. The executive director of the National Congress of American Indians asserted that Nixon was "the first U.S. President since George Washington to pledge that the government will honor the obligations of Indian tribes."[92]

Not surprisingly, a small minority of mostly young radical Native Americans who demanded more change more rapidly led the violent protests. Many of them found their voice in the American Indian Movement (AIM), which directed its energies not only against the government but also against what it considered traditional and autocratic tribal leaders. On 27 February 1973, 200 AIM members seized buildings and took hostages on the Pine Ridge Sioux Reservation at Wounded Knee, South Dakota, after looting and burning the trading post, destroying seven homes, and damaging churches—and after two Indians had been killed. They then began an occupation that lasted for more than seventy days at the site of the last major American massacre of Indians, the 1890 "Battle" of Wounded Knee.

AIM demanded tribal government reforms and claimed that Washington had violated an 1868 treaty with the Sioux. On the latter issue, the Supreme Court ruled in 1980 that the Treaty of Fort Laramie had indeed been violated and that the Sioux deserved compensation. With the FBI and the BIA police besieging Wounded Knee, the Indians and the government began a long negotiating process that led to a peaceful end to the standoff on 9 May, four days before the army, working with Nixon's chief of staff General Haig, planned to attack the occupiers in a "calculated preemption" of civilian law enforcement.[93] The administration prosecuted 150 persons for a variety of crimes related to the occupation, but it also initiated reforms at the BIA, in part in response to AIM's demands.

The administration also produced the important Alaskan National Claims Settlement Act in April 1971, which resolved a dispute over the ownership of oil lands in Alaska and cleared the way for the building of the Alaskan oil pipeline. Indians, Eskimos, and Aleuts gave up their rights to the land and received in exchange $1 billion and title to 44 million other acres they could sell and develop through their own private corporations. Native Americans held title to only 56 million acres in the rest of the United

States. The OMB opposed the settlement as too generous; it was more generous than anything the Johnson administration had offered the Alaskan Indians. But the "liberals" in the White House, Garment and Patterson, supported by Ehrlichman, prevailed.

Ehrlichman, assisted by White House fellow and Indian expert Bobbie Greene Kilberg, also was instrumental in the Blue Lake settlement. Convinced that the lands around Blue Lake in New Mexico, which had been part of the national forest system since 1906, constituted sacred land for the Taos Pueblo Indians, Ehrlichman returned it to them in December 1970, despite opposition from powerful congressional and business interests.

Not all minorities did as well as Native Americans under the Nixon administration. As more of the infamous tapes were released, even Nixon supporters became disturbed by the president's anti-Semitism. Although he insisted to Garment that "I never in my whole life used the term 'Jewboy,'" there are many references in his conversations that suggest that he was prejudiced against Jews.[94] This seems rather surprising, considering that many of his closest advisers—Kissinger, Burns, Safire, Stein, and Garment—were Jewish. It is even more surprising considering that Nixon's heroes included Disraeli and Justices Brandeis and Frankfurter, and his favorite fiction writer was Herman Wouk.

Yet he could say things like, "I think you will find that chain stores that control these prices [meat] are primarily dominated by Jewish interests. These boys, of course, have every right to make all the money they want, but they have a notorious reputation in the trade for conspiracy."[95] When he became suspicious that a "Jewish cabal" in the Bureau of Labor Statistics was providing incorrect information to embarrass him, he ordered Fred Malek to conduct a private investigation of the ethnic backgrounds of key bureau officials.[96] He also worried about the pernicious influence of Jews in the IRS and the Commerce Department.

Some of his ideas about Jews came from his friends, including the notoriously anti-Semitic Elmer Bobst, who filled his letters to Nixon with information about the worldwide Jewish conspiracy. But a lot of it had to do with the fact that at least at the start, Jews were disproportionately found among Nixon-hating liberal Democrats. According to Colson, the president was against those sorts of Jews "because the Jews were against him."[97] Nixon once asked Haldeman, "Aren't all the Chicago Seven Jews? [Rennie] Davis is a Jew you know." After Haldeman told him that he was in error, Nixon responded, "Hoffman, Hoffman's a Jew." Haldeman agreed, "Abbie Hoffman is a Jew and that's so."[98]

In examining which ethnic groups to cultivate and to spend time with, Nixon told Ehrlichman in the fall of 1970, "There is no justification whatever from a political standpoint for me to meet with Jewish groups . . . [who are] basically liberal Democratic in their orientation and will not support us."[99] Nixon even worried about the loyalties of his Jewish aides. He complained about leaks in 1973, singling out those by "our Jewish friends, even on the White House staff."[100] Nixon defender Garment concludes that if one was to rate Nixon's anti-Semitism on the basis of a 100 score (with 100 being the most anti-Semitic), his ranking would be between 15 and 20. Most observers would raise his score somewhat. Yet many Jewish Americans had to be pleased with administration policies in the Middle East, especially during and after the October 1973 war.

Whatever his personal feelings about blacks, women, and Jews, Nixon compiled a surprisingly progressive record on issues relating to minorities and civil rights. Despite his 1968 rhetoric, his party's increasingly conservative social agenda, and the way he played the race card for political reasons, his administration quietly completed the task ordered by the Supreme Court in 1954 to end school segregation. Moreover, his promotion of black capitalism and the Philadelphia Plan, approval of measures to end gender discrimination, and sympathy for Native Americans appear to be genuine responses to resolve America's social problems during the seventies. No doubt he was propelled in those directions by a liberal Democratic Congress, and his motives were not always the purest. Yet while he was president, the United States made significant strides toward achieving equal rights for minorities and women.

7

★ ★ ★ ★ ★

DISRAELI REDUX

Richard Nixon ran for president in 1968 against the Great Society, Lyndon Johnson's expansion of the New Deal and the Fair Deal. Like most Republicans since the thirties, he promised a smaller and less intrusive government. His rhetorical assault against the growth of the Washington bureaucracy, particularly in the area of welfare and poverty programs, resonated with many Americans, who expected that if elected he would begin to dismantle the welfare state.

Whether or not Nixon believed his rhetoric, Democratic control of Congress made it impossible to do away with the Great Society, even though his administration succeeded in scaling back some programs. Nonetheless, conservative Republicans, always suspicious of Nixon's conservative credentials, were disappointed that the president in action was not as conservative as his campaign had promised. They were horrified when Nixon proposed a guaranteed annual wage for poor people disguised as welfare reform and a variety of other social and environmental policies that placed him where they feared he had been all the time, within the confines of middle-of-the-road Eisenhower, even Rockefeller, Republicanism. Herbert Stein, one of his own conservative economic advisers, complained, "Probably more new regulation was imposed on the economy . . . than in any other presidency since the New Deal."[1]

If there was one thing Nixon promised to do on the domestic front, it was to clean up the "welfare mess."[2] Despite the relatively healthy economy, more and more Americans had become dependent on welfare, particularly Aid to Dependent Children (ADC), the federal program introduced with the Social Security Act of 1935. Nixon believed that such programs "encouraged a feeling of dependence and discouraged the kind of self-reliance that is needed to get people on their feet."[3] Here he was joined by the vast majority of Americans, 84 percent of whom told pollsters that "there are too many people receiving welfare money who should be working" and that "many people getting welfare are not honest about their need."[4]

In 1960, 3 million Americans received ADC. That number rose to 4.3 million in 1965 and 8.4 million in 1970; by 1972, one in nine children overall and one in three black children were on welfare. New Frontier and Great Society programs had helped decrease poverty from 1959 to 1968 by 36 percent, but the number of Americans on welfare during that period rose by 41 percent, and the number of illegitimate births during the same period rose by 42 percent.

Since the federal government paid for only part of the ADC program, there were huge inequities. For example, New York gave a family on ADC $197 a month, whereas Mississippi gave that same family $33. In addition, the growth of ADC and other welfare programs had led to the growth of huge bureaucracies, which in turn produced more cases of fraud and corruption. Finally, the programs made it easier for one-parent families to receive welfare, discouraged recipients from taking low-paying entry-level jobs, discriminated against the working poor, and may have encouraged illegitimacy.

In 1967, Wilbur Mills successfully guided a welfare reform bill, which included work incentives, through the House. The more liberal Senate rejected the bill, offering an indication of the problems Nixon would encounter when he tackled the issue.

Welfare programs had long been a conservative whipping boy, since much of the public was convinced that such programs not only rewarded lazy people and "welfare queens" for not working but also primarily benefited blacks. Although the majority of welfare recipients were white, blacks were found on welfare rolls in disproportionate numbers to their population. In April 1969, Nixon privately "emphasized that . . . the *whole* problem is really the blacks. The key is to devise a system that recognizes this while not appearing to. Problem with the overall welfare plan is that it forces poor whites into same position as blacks."[5]

During the interregnum, a task force headed by Richard Nathan, an adviser to Nelson Rockefeller, considered a variety of approaches to welfare reform, recommending, among other things, a minimum federal welfare allowance. Three days after Nixon took office, he established the Council on Urban Affairs, with Daniel Patrick Moynihan as its executive secretary. According to White House aide Martin Anderson, this "charming Irish rogue," who knew his way around the federal bureaucracy, while most of the president's staff "was almost wholly virgin in the ways of Washington," began to develop a radical welfare reform program inconsistent with Republican principles. Moynihan enlisted the support of HEW secretary Finch, who had a "reputation for being easily persuaded."[6] Anderson told a friend, "It would curl your hair if you knew what some people around here are proposing."[7] After all, Nixon had proclaimed to a cheering crowd in his acceptance speech the previous August, "What we need are not more millions on welfare rolls, but more millions on payrolls."[8]

The key to Moynihan's welfare reform initiative was a negative income tax, although it would not be labeled as such in the final legislation. As early as 1943, conservative economist Milton Friedman had supported a negative income tax, especially for low-income workers who had unstable earnings. By 1968, over sixty nations employed some sort of negative income tax, or family allowance, to provide a direct safety net for the poor. In the summer of 1968, more than 1,000 American economists signed a petition calling for a guaranteed annual income. But 62 percent of Americans, according to one poll the next year, opposed the idea, and even Lyndon Johnson had found it too radical.

During the first three months of the administration, Moynihan and his allies, including Nelson Rockefeller from the New York governor's mansion, clashed with Arthur Burns and his allies over the shape of welfare reform, with the conservatives opposing the reform on both philosophical and fiscal grounds. Ehrlichman mediated between the two groups in such a manner that the final plan reflected many of his own views. Nixon became more involved in the nuts and bolts of the program than in any other domestic program during his tenure. He finally backed the Moynihan approach, designed in good measure by holdover Johnson officials in HEW and supported by Ehrlichman. Because the issue had engendered so much bitterness and backbiting in the White House, he could not bring himself to inform Burns that Moynihan had won; he left that unpleasant task to Ehrlichman.

Nixon supported Moynihan's program for a variety of reasons: the impact of New York City welfare scandals that hit the newspapers in January, Moynihan's urging him to become a Disraeli, his own personal sympathy for the working poor, and especially the idea that reform would weaken the federal bureaucracy. He asked Moynihan, "Will FSS [Family Security System] get rid of social workers?" Moynihan replied, "It will wipe them out."[9] The administration also was affected by a 21 April 1969 Supreme Court decision that struck down residency requirements for welfare.

Nixon announced his Family Assistance Plan (FAP) on 8 August 1969 in a nationally televised address that also dealt with a new job-training program, revamping of the OEO, and New Federalism or federal revenue sharing. (Secretary of Defense Laird had suggested the name Family Assistance Plan because the original name, Family Security System, sounded too "New Dealish."[10]) The FAP proposed a national income floor for a family of four of $1,600 per year plus a food-stamp allotment, a program Nixon had recommended for expansion on 6 May. The $1,600 payment was lower than comparable payments that existed in all but six states at the time, but the states would be free to offer supplements beyond the minimum. Further, as Nixon underscored, "outside earnings would be encouraged, not discouraged. . . . those who work would no longer be discriminated against." A provision for discounting wages earned beyond the $1,600 would have permitted a working family of four to receive federal funds up to a combined maximum of $3,920 in wages and FAP.

Nixon's program would have made 13 million more Americans eligible for federal aid. He also proposed that states pay a minimum sum to the aged, blind, and disabled on their welfare rolls. He sweetened this bitter pill for conservatives when he included provisions that encouraged able-bodied welfare recipients to work, linked FAP to dismantling of the OEO, and offered to share more tax revenues with the states under New Federalism.

The initial response was positive. Sixty-five percent of those who knew about FAP approved of it, according to one poll, as did 81 percent of those who sent telegrams and letters to the White House. Ninety-five percent of editorials praised the plan, which seemed to combine welfare reform, attractive to Republicans, with income redistribution, attractive to Democrats.

Opposition soon developed from conservative Republicans and, unexpectedly, from liberal Democrats who should have been pleased with the federalizing of welfare, the providing of aid to the working poor, and the setting of minimum standards. One problem was that despite Bryce Harlow's admonitions, Nixon had not consulted with Congress in advance about his revolutionary new program. Moynihan had a more sinister explanation: "You know the libs will never forgive Richard Nixon for this. And you know why? Because he's done what they wouldn't do, what they wouldn't *dare* do. And they can't stand that."[11]

George Wiley, head of the National Welfare Rights Organization (NWRO), claimed that the "Family Annihilation Plan" was "anti-poor and anti-black" and demanded a floor of $5,500.[12] The Americans for Democratic Action, the National Council of Churches, and many welfare agencies announced their opposition as well, primarily because the floor was too low and the plan was punitive to those who refused to work.

Nixon sent his bill to Congress on 3 October 1969. The House approved it on 16 April 1970 by 243 to 155, with supporters including 141 Democrats and 102 Republicans. But even at that juncture, it was clear that the bill would face rough going in the Senate. On 1 May 1970, the Senate Finance Committee sent it back to the White House with instructions to increase benefits for poor families. By then, Nixon was no longer enthusiastic about FAP, which suggests that he might have been more interested in public relations than genuine reform. Or he might have been exasperated with Democratic criticism, which he had not expected. Haldeman reported on 13 July that Nixon "wants to be sure it's killed by Democrats and that we make big play for it, but don't let it pass, can't afford it."[13] On 20 November 1970, the Senate Finance Committee, dominated by southern Democrats, voted ten to six against FAP, and when it was not included in the Social Security bill, the House refused to go to conference, thereby killing both FAP and Social Security increases for 1970. Another casualty was HEW secretary Finch, who physically collapsed on 18 May 1970, burned out in good measure because of the energies he had expended on FAP.

After almost a year and a half of debate and much tinkering with the original plan, Moynihan felt that "it was not likely that as many as a dozen United States senators understood the bill."[14] Despite this initial defeat, Nixon listed FAP first among his domestic programs in the 1971 State of the Union Address. But although he submitted it to Congress two more times, he did not spend as much time or energy on it, was less willing to compromise, and finally, in February 1973, declared it dead, even though he referred to it again in his 1974 State of the Union Address. Paradoxically, George McGovern may have hammered the final nail in FAP's coffin when the public greeted with derision his 1972 campaign proposal to offer poor people $1,000 cash payments. Nixon blamed Congress, conservatives, and "the damn social workers" for the failure of his program, which despite the relatively low federal floor, represented a promising solution to some of the problems of the welfare system.[15]

Congress did approve, in October 1972, that part of Nixon's welfare program that dealt with supplemental security income (SSI). This important measure, which went into effect in 1974, provided for a federally guaranteed monthly income of up to $210 per couple for the aged, blind, and disabled and protected Medicaid recipients from loss of eligibility. The 6.2 million citizens eligible for this aid (4.6 million elderly and 1.6 million blind and disabled) became the first recipients, aside from veterans, of a federally guaranteed income.

In addition, during Nixon's first term, Social Security benefit rates increased by 51 percent, Medicare and Medicaid benefits increased from

$7.8 billion to $11.5 billion, and total federal outlays for the elderly increased 71 percent. Even factoring in inflation, these increases were substantial. Nixon also approved automatic cost-of-living increases in Social Security in 1972 to help recipients keep up with inflation, although he later regretted their inflationary aspect. Beginning in FY 1971–72 and continuing through the rest of his administration, spending on all human resources programs (some of which were indirectly military related) exceeded defense spending for the first time since World War II.

This record, which made Nixon an even bigger spender on social programs than Lyndon Johnson, does not tell the entire story. Nixon truly intended to eliminate those Great Society programs he perceived to be wasteful, inefficient, and administered by a left-wing bureaucracy. He wanted "to get resources to people in need and then to let them run their own lives."[16] His primary target was the OEO, the Johnson administration's chief agency in its War on Poverty. Nixon was convinced that "the poverty program has been a miserable failure" and was a target for "vivisection," in Pat Buchanan's colorful word.[17] But as the president discovered, it proved difficult to vivisect a large government program that had supporters in Congress, in the bureaucracy, and among influential sectors of the population.

For example, he also wanted to phase out Johnson's Model Cities Program, but Moynihan and HUD secretary George Romney, who soon became its champion, rallied support by demonstrating how the program fit into the administration's revenue-sharing plans and its overall decentralized approach. Although not an especially successful program, Model Cities was of symbolic importance, since it represented a major commitment from Washington to the cities. During his first administration, Nixon reluctantly approved $2.3 billion for Model Cities, a figure not far from that which had been projected by the Johnson administration. In 1974, Model Cities finally disappeared, swallowed up as part of the revenue-sharing program.

OEO appeared to be an easier target, considering the controversial reputation it had earned during the previous administration, especially its Legal Services and locally controlled Community Action Programs (CAPs). In March 1969, Nixon ordered, "no increases in any poverty program until more evidence is in." Further, he wanted "some action taken immediately to clean up this [OEO] outfit. (Moynihan objects but Burns thinks it is essential and I agree.)"[18] Nixon's first OEO director was Donald Rumsfeld, who had been told that his job was to oversee the transferring of the viable programs to the departments and maintaining, at best, a scaled-down office as "an instrument of innovation and social experimentation" to run pilot programs.[19] As the president told the nation on 19 February 1969 in an address announcing his intention to continue OEO, at least through 1970, but to transfer many programs to other agencies, he found its "greatest value is as an initiating agency . . . an 'incubator.'"

Even some of OEO's allegedly viable programs faced dismantling—for example, Head Start, after a 1969 Westinghouse Learning Corporation report suggested that children in the program were not doing as well as expected. Nixon was ambivalent, however, about doing away with CAPs, fearing that the employees of those grassroots agencies who would lose their jobs might end up "blowing up cities."[20] He evinced similar ambivalence when he discovered that $752 million had been spent on providing 861,000 jobs in the Summer 1969 Youth Program, wondering, "Is this huge amount really worth what it accomplishes? It's a pretty big bribe unless it leaves permanent results."[21]

Rumsfeld streamlined OEO and transferred some programs to other departments, but he could not completely gut the agency, even had he been willing to do so. Following his decision to promote Rumsfeld to White House counselor in December 1970, Nixon appointed Howard Phillips to run the agency, but only as acting director, so that he would not have to submit his name for congressional confirmation. According to Fred Malek, Phillips was "an idealogue, not a manager, he went about tearing apart his agency with unconcealed glee."[22] Malek told Haldeman after the 1972 election that, as the administration's chief talent scout, he would fill OEO positions with people who were "known quantities who are committed to decimating OEO" and who were "100 percent responsive to the White House."[23]

By 1973, OEO had shrunk considerably, with Head Start transferred to HEW; the Job Corps ("a boondoggle" to Nixon), or what was left of it after he closed fifty-nine centers, to Labor; and Manpower Training to local governments under the provisions of the 1973 Comprehensive Employment and Training Act (CETA).[24] But he was prevented from completely destroying the agency by a 1973 federal district court order, which ruled that the president could not discontinue a program if Congress had provided for its continuance in multiple-year authorizations. That same judge ruled that Nixon had to submit the nomination of Phillips to the Senate for confirmation because Phillips had been holding his position unlawfully; acting directors usually were appointed for less than thirty days because of death, emergency, or illness of the director.

Nixon also opposed federal housing programs, which he labeled "a waste of $90 billion of taxpayer's money" since the New Deal.[25] After having failed to convince Congress to accept a program whereby people living in the projects would be able to buy their own apartments, he decided in 1973 to refuse to ask for any more money for new federal housing.

He did, however, increase spending for education, including developing a National Student Loan Association for college students from low-income families and a Career Education Program for community colleges. Spending for elementary and secondary schools also increased during his administration. Nixon displayed his concern for the preschool population as well when on 9 April 1969 he announced the establishment of the Office of Child Development and reiterated his 19 February call for a "national commitment to providing all American children an opportunity for healthful and stimulating development during the first five years of life." Although this office did not accomplish very much, the federal commitment was at least of symbolic importance.

Nixon also introduced in 1971 the National Health Insurance Partnership program, which included government support for private-employer-related health insurance, health insurance for low-income families, and health maintenance organizations (HMOs). His plans, which did not extend to establishing a national health care system, were nonetheless the most sweeping proposals to date for government assistance to private health care systems. The end goal was to guarantee that every citizen had access to health care.

In a related vein, Nixon proposed to increase federal grants for medical students. Like FAP, Nixon's health care program, which was reintroduced in Congress in 1973, failed because of an alliance between conservatives, led by the American Medical Association (AMA), and liberals, who felt that the program did not go far enough. The powerful AMA also pressured him early in his administration to withdraw the appointment of Dr. John Knowles as assistant secretary for health at HEW because he was too liberal.

On 5 February 1974, Nixon tried one last time to promote a health plan. That day, in a public address, he alluded to his family's problems caring for his tubercular brother, which was, "from a financial standpoint, a disaster." He did not want to see "other families of modest means . . . driven, basically to bankruptcy because of the inability to handle medical care problems of a catastrophic type."

Although his innovative health care program was never adopted, in 1971, Nixon became the first president to commit the government, through huge increases in federal funding, to a war on cancer, optimistically predicting a cure within five years. As with so many other aspects of his presidency, there was a catch: Nixon insisted that it be called the "President's Cancer Program," with a good "PR program," along with "some good slogans."[26]

In other health-related measures, Nixon signed the Coal Mine Safety and Health Act in December 1969 and the more important Occupational

Safety and Health Administration (OSHA) Act one year later. At least 14,000 American workers died each year because of job-related accidents, and more than 2 million were injured on the job. Congress established OSHA to improve safety and health conditions in the workplace. Under Nixon, not surprisingly, the agency tended to lean toward industry a bit more than critics from the labor movement thought was desirable.

The administration also sponsored a White House Conference on Food and Nutrition in December 1969, headed by Dr. Jean Mayer, who had been hired as special consultant in August. Mayer's conference endorsed Democratic legislation that expanded the food-stamp and school-lunch programs beyond administration proposals and urged the government to feed all poor children. The conference's recommendation of a federal grant of $5,500 for poor people was soon adopted by the NWRO in its struggle against FAP. Moynihan referred to Mayer and the scientists who participated in the prestigious conference as "ungrateful wretches," and Nixon was "ashamed" of the "terrible" affair.[27]

Mayer's conferees were not the only advocates of more food aid to the poor. Secretary of Agriculture Hardin was another who took seriously Nixon's call in the spring of 1969 to end hunger in America, testifying in Congress in support of bills that the administration found too costly. Nixon did have a positive program to feed the hungry, including the aforementioned increase in the food-stamp program and an extension of the free-lunch program, guaranteeing by January 1971 a free lunch to all poor schoolchildren in America. But Nixon preferred to keep those programs low-key so as not to upset his budget-balancing conservative allies. By 1973, the administration began moving aggressively to hold down costs in the burgeoning food-stamp and school-lunch programs.

Roger Egeberg, the distinguished assistant secretary for health and scientific affairs at HEW from 1969 to 1971, who advocated even more federal involvement in health care programs and medical training, was not enthusiastic about the administration's efforts in his area. In a 1970 interview, the outspoken medical administrator complained that "the White House just doesn't appreciate, doesn't know what is going on in the health field," and he "just couldn't get through to Ehrlichman."[28]

As in so many other areas, the administration's problems stemmed from its going further in a human services area than most observers expected but not far enough to please the liberals. Ehrlichman recognized this when he commented in April 1970 that although the administration had compiled an admirable record in that area, "We are presenting a picture of illiberality, repression, close-mindedness and lack of concern for the less fortunate."[29] Yet an examination of the record of a Republican president presumably elected to demolish the New Deal supports Elliot Richardson's view that his administration promoted "creative legislation even in the field of human social concerns."[30]

The Great Society did not disappear during Nixon's years in the White House. The number of Americans below the poverty level, which stood at 17.3 percent in 1965 and had fallen to 12.1 in 1969, hovered around 12 percent in 1973. Cash transfers to the poor increased from $22.4 billion in 1965 to $34.3 billion in 1972; even more impressively, in-kind transfers increased from $10.8 billion in 1969 to $26.6 billion in 1974.

Not coincidentally, Nixon had introduced his general revenue-sharing (GRS) proposal with his antipoverty programs on 8 August 1969. Calling it the New Federalism (which became part of the "New American Revolution" in 1971), the president touted it as "a gesture of faith in America's state and local governments and in the principle of democratic self government." It was necessary because of "the loss of faith" in the federal government, which had become "increasingly remote . . . overcentralized and overbureaucratized," and "unresponsive as well as inefficient."

Although most Republicans were displeased by the continuation of Great Society programs, Nixon promised to redesign them so that the states rather than federal bureaucrats would make decisions about how the programs would operate on the local level. Workforce training programs, for example, were not new, but the 1973 CETA was, in that, as Nixon noted on 23 December, "funds to provide these services will, for the first time, be made available to State and local governments without any Federal strings."

As early as 1958, then Representative Melvin Laird had proposed revenue sharing. Some of Johnson's advisers had been attracted to the concept in 1964, as had Republican governors Romney and Rockefeller. Nathan's task force prepared papers on the issue during the interregnum. As Nixon began to centralize power in the White House, he also decentralized power that had been concentrated in the federal bureaucracy. He understood the paradox when he noted, "Bringing power to the White House [was necessary] in order to dish it out."[31]

It was not an easy sell to a Democratic Congress and its allies in the bureaucracy, even after Nixon declared that New Federalism would be revenue neutral—there would be no cuts in overall appropriations. Democrats were legitimately concerned about the possibility that state and local governments might use human services and urban development funds for projects that would not assist urban poor. The resultant conflict with Congress over revenue sharing was so long and bitter that Nixon seemed to have lost interest in the program until Ehrlichman, its main champion in the White House, convinced him to persevere. In his 1971 State of the Union Address on 4 February, the president revisited the issue, calling for $5 billion worth of tax revenues to be returned to the states as a form of rebate and another $10 billion worth of existing programs to be shifted from Washington to the states, "which would work out their own tailor-made formulas for distributing revenues." The administration was interested in giving states more control over such "distributive" or service issues as education, labor, and health, while reserving welfare, energy, and the environment—"non-distributive" or cash-transfer issues—for Washington.[32] In terms of public relations, Nixon urged Ehrlichman to "find a way to present our Revenue Sharing Proposals which will appeal to those who are part of the "Tax Revolt."[33] However sold, GRS was popular; 77 percent of Americans polled in January 1971 favored the concept.

On 20 October 1972, less than three weeks before the election, Nixon signed into law the State and Local Fiscal Assistance Act, which established a program for matching state and federal funds involving $16 billion over the administration's next three budgets. After the popular bill passed the House by a 223-to-185 margin and the Senate by a vote of 64 to 20, Ehrlichman crowed, "We really passed this over their dead bodies."[34] By the time the program ended in 1986, the federal government had distributed $83 billion directly to the states and to local governments. The money went primarily for urban and rural social services programs, education, worker training, and transportation. Speaking for many conservatives, Pat Buchanan complained that Nixon's GRS did not reduce the size of government, that no funds were really returned to taxpayers, and that most of the money ended up in the hands of Democratic mayors and governors.

Not until the Reagan administration was the decentralization of GRS linked to budget and program cutting. Nixon himself favored the budget-cutting approach, particularly in his second term, but Watergate made it difficult for him to concentrate on much else. For example, in the spring of 1974, the memos to Nixon from director of OMB Roy Ash, who was working on a conservative redirection of the revenue-sharing system, went unread.

Nixon's post office reform did not remove the Post Office Department from Washington, but it did go a long way toward removing the department from Washington politics and patronage. In 1967, Lyndon Johnson had appointed a Presidential Commission on Postal Reorganization that recommended in June 1968 that the Postal Service become a nonprofit government corporation. A lame duck by that time, Johnson had lost interest in pursuing the issue. Nixon followed up with his own Citizen's Committee for Postal Reform, headed by Thruston Morton and former Democratic postmaster general Lawrence O'Brien. Postmaster General

Winton Blount, a strong advocate of reform, helped convince Nixon of its necessity, despite the warning from Bryce Harlow that he was "committing hara-kiri" by taking away patronage from Republicans.[35] Most of the committee's recommendations became Nixon's Postal Service Act of 1969, announced to the nation on 27 May. This act removed the Post Office Department from the cabinet to become the independent, self-supporting U.S. Postal Service, owned by the federal government.

Before the act became law in 1970, Nixon had to confront wildcat postal strikes in late March of that year. On 23 March, he was compelled to send the military into New York City to restore postal service before a settlement was reached on 2 April.

Nixon took office just as the modern environmental movement was taking off. As in so many other areas, he reluctantly approved progressive legislation, which generally reflected a position slightly to the left of center, or "striking a balance," in the words of John C. Whitaker, one of his chief environmental advisers.[36] Such a position pleased neither the business community nor the leaders of the movement.

The publication of Rachel Carson's *Silent Spring* in 1962 played the same catalytic role in the environmental movement as did Betty Friedan's *The Feminine Mystique* in sparking the women's movement. In addition, Paul Ehrlich's *The Population Bomb* (1968) sold 3 million copies in paperback, while the Club of Rome's headline-attracting *The Limits to Growth* (1972) sold 4 million and was translated into thirty languages.

Americans did not need books to tell them that their air and water had become increasingly polluted by lead in gasoline, phosphates in detergents, and mercury and other chemicals. Popular concerns about the environment were heightened in sensational fashion on 28 January 1969 when the Union Oil Company's offshore oil rigs in Santa Barbara began leaking crude oil. For two weeks, the oil fouled 200 miles of telegenic coastline. The sight of oil-covered seabirds dying by the thousands attracted widespread sympathy. After the media quoted the president of Union Oil, somewhat inaccurately, as saying, "I'm amazed at the publicity for the loss of a few birds," public outrage escalated.[37] Later that year, Americans were shocked when the filthy Cuyahoga River in Ohio literally caught fire.

When pollsters first began asking environmental questions in 1965, 28 percent of Americans expressed concern about air pollution and 35 percent worried about water pollution. By 1970, those numbers had increased to 69 and 74 percent, respectively. In May 1969, only 1 percent of those polled thought that the environment was the greatest domestic problem. By 1971, that number had risen to 25 percent.

Even though Nixon had rarely been asked to explain his environmental policy during the campaign, the administration had to respond to public pressure, symbolized by the first Earth Day held on 22 April 1970. (The fact that the date was Lenin's birthday was not lost on some antienvironmentalists, who saw the movement as an anticapitalist plot.) The activity grew out of a call to action from Senator Gaylord Nelson (D-Wisc.) in 1969. On Earth Day, which may have involved as many as 3 million Americans, more than 10,000 high schools and 2,000 colleges held environmental programs; Congress adjourned to permit its members to participate in teach-ins and moratoriums; Fifth Avenue in New York City was auto free, and Nelson Rockefeller rode a bicycle in Central Park; members of the White House staff helped clean up the Potomac; folksingers Pete Seeger and Phil Ochs sang with 5,000 at the Washington Monument, "All we are saying, is give Earth a chance"; and women students at an Indiana University rally threw birth-control pills to the crowd. Earth Day was the largest single nationwide protest in American history.

Although members of the cabinet, including Interior Secretary Walter Hickel and 1,000 of his employees, took part in the activities, Nixon did not directly involve himself in Earth Day, even though he issued proclamations that week celebrating National Archery Week and National Boating Week. Moreover, a few days later, he asked the Interior Department to approve legislation to construct the controversial Alaskan oil pipeline.

Nixon had never been especially interested in the environment, except for parkland. He told Ehrlichman, the environmentalist in the White House, that the movement was "overrated," that it served the "privileged," and was "crap" for "clowns."[38] In 1972, he observed that "people don't give a shit about the environment."[39] Appealing to his business constituency, he asserted, "In a flat choice between smoke and jobs, we're for jobs," and he worried that environmental concerns might "be used sometimes falsely and sometimes in a demagogic way basically to destroy the system."[40] Yet he could not ignore the widespread demands coming from leaders of both parties for federal action to clean up the air and the water. The front-runner for the Democratic nomination for the presidency in 1972, Maine senator Edmund Muskie, was a leading environmentalist. Nixon instructed Ehrlichman, "Just keep me out of trouble on environmental issues."[41]

One of his pre-presidential task forces, headed by prominent environmentalist Russell Train, had recommended the establishment of a cabinet-level interagency environmental office. On 29 May 1969, Nixon appointed his science adviser, Lee DuBridge, to head up the Environmental Quality Council (EQC) in the White House. Dissatisfied with the EQC's progress fashioning a comprehensive environmental program, Nixon shifted the responsibility to Ehrlichman in the summer of 1969, who set up a separate task force, first led by Egil Krogh and then, in August, by John Whitaker. The task force, which recommended the establishment of a separate Department of Natural Resources, was responsible for most of the thirty-six environmental initiatives Nixon announced in his 1970 State of the Union Address.

He had earlier signed the Endangered Species Act on 5 December 1969, an ambitious program to protect wildlife. Further, he signed on 1 January 1970 the National Environmental Policy Act, originally a 1968 initiative of Senator Jackson's. The act established a Council on Environmental Quality (CEQ) in the White House that reported annually to Congress and also mandated environmental-impact statements for all federal projects. In signing the act, Nixon warned, "unless we move on it now, believe me, we will not have an opportunity to do it later."

Congress eagerly began work on Nixon's environmental initiatives in 1970, most notably his proposal submitted in July calling for an Environmental Protection Agency (EPA) and a National Oceanic and Atmospheric Administration (NOAA). Both the administration and Congress recognized the need to centralize federal environmental programs; at the time, forty-four agencies in nine departments dealt with the environment. In the bill Nixon signed on 2 December 1970, the EPA received responsibility for monitoring federal water quality and pesticides from Interior and air pollution control and solid waste management from HEW, among many other functions. Congress, however, put NOAA in the Commerce Department, rejecting Nixon's request to make it an independent agency.

Nixon's choices to head the EPA—first William Ruckelshaus, an assistant attorney general, and then Russell Train—turned out to be forceful leaders who pursued environmentalist agendas somewhat in advance of those of the Oval Office. The administration insisted that the EPA's environmental policies be subjected to a cost-benefit analysis from OMB. This led to frequent conflicts, which Nixon and Ehrlichman had to mediate, between the two agencies, as well as conflicts between the EPA and the Agriculture Department and the automobile industry. On one occasion in 1971, Nixon wrote to Ehrlichman, "I don't believe Train's analyses get me an *honest* report (*not* by an environmentalist)."[42]

Nixon approved the 1970 Clean Air Act Amendments, which significantly strengthened the 1967 Clean Air Act, although not as much as Muskie, one of the bill's chief sponsors, had hoped. The amendments called for automobile manufacturers to decrease carbon monoxide and hydrocarbon emissions to at least 90 percent of 1970 levels by 1975 and mandated the EPA to establish national air-quality standards for emissions from stationary sources and to set up tougher enforcement procedures. Auto executives, who viewed the bill as too harsh on their industry, contended that they could not develop the technology needed to solve the emissions problem in the time given. But when they appealed for relief, as was their right under the bill, Ruckelshaus was not sympathetic. The energy crisis in 1974 permitted Nixon, who had never been enthusiastic about the emissions-control program, to relax the timetable.

The American business community, supported by Secretary of Commerce Maurice Stans, claimed that it was trying to do its part to clean up the environment. Stans also stopped granting licenses to American whalers in 1970 and set up a short-lived National Industrial Pollution Control Council.

The administration earned kudos from some environmentalists for its Coastal Zone Management Act of 1972, designed to protect estuaries; characteristically, the act was not quite as progressive as Senator Jackson's original bill. In addition, as chair of the Property Review Board, Bryce Harlow gave the states thousands of acres of federal land for parkland. By the fall of 1976, the program resulted in the transfer of 80,232 acres of land to the states, which in turn developed 642 new parks, many near cities. Nixon wanted city dwellers to share more fully in the nation's park programs. To that end, his administration sponsored the development of the Gateway National Recreation Area in New York City and the Golden Gate National Recreation Area in San Francisco.

The United States hosted the second World Conference on Parks at Grand Teton National Park in the summer of 1972, out of which grew the UNESCO Convention Concerning the Protection of the World Cultural and Natural Heritage. In November 1973, the United States became the first nation to ratify the convention. Nixon also signed an international Ocean Dumping Convention in 1972 and called for U.S.-Soviet cooperation on environmental issues at the Moscow summit that same year.

At home, the administration approved a Family Planning Services and Population Research Act in 1970, although Nixon was leery of programs that might support abortion, sex education, and contraception; another Endangered Species Act in 1973; the Safe Drinking Water Act of 1974; the Marine Mammal Protection Act of 1972; and the Noise Control Act of 1972 and extended the Solid Waste Disposal Act of 1965. After being taken to court late in 1972, the administration finally agreed to a DDT ban in the United States, although American manufacturers could still sell the pesticide abroad.

Environmentalists were unhappy, however, when on 25 November 1970 Nixon fired their ally at the Interior Department, Walter Hickel, along with six of his aides. But Hickel was fired less for his environmental policies than for his disloyalty during the Cambodian invasion and for his independent and obstreperous behavior. The environmentalists also were unhappy over Nixon's approval of a supersonic airplane, the SST, which they claimed would damage the ozone layer, and of the Alaskan pipeline. But he did cancel plans for a jetport in Miami and for a cross-Florida canal. The canal issue reveals Nixon's balancing act on the environment, as John Whitaker told the president how its cancellation made up for the SST and the pipeline: "You can't out Muskie Muskie," but you can toss the conservationists "raw meat" from time to time.[43]

The administration's generally positive record on the environment took a blow when the president vetoed the Clean Water Act of 1972 on 17 October. His own CEQ had reported in 1971 that 90 percent of the watersheds in America were "moderately" polluted. Still, Nixon suspected that the Democrats were trying to embarrass him by forcing him to veto a bill they knew was too costly. He wanted to "attack pollution in a way that does not ignore other very real threats to the quality of life, such as spiraling prices and increasingly onerous taxes." In 1971, he had established a Quality-of-Life Review that applied a cost-benefit calculation to environmental measures.

Nixon was willing to spend $6 billion on the Clean Water Act—four times more than he had requested in 1969—but not the $24 billion in the Democrats' bill. Congress overrode his veto by a 52-to-12 vote in the Senate and a 247-to-23 vote in the House. After Assistant Attorney General William Rehnquist gave him the constitutional go-ahead, Nixon impounded most of the funds Congress had approved in the act. He claimed that he had the constitutional right not to spend money authorized by Congress if it would lead to higher prices or taxes. He was the first president to make that argument. Considering the general issue in 1969, Rehnquist had contended that the "existence of such a broad power is supported by neither reason nor precedent."[44]

This was Nixon's most famous impoundment, but not the only one. Other presidents, particularly Franklin Roosevelt and Lyndon Johnson, had done a good deal of impounding, but none had used the tactic as extensively. Nixon impounded between 17 and 20 percent of all controllable expenditures from 1969 through 1972. By 1973, he had impounded funds for more than 100 programs. He impounded funds even when legislation explicitly warned him not to do it, and he impounded funds not only for specific projects but also for entire programs he hoped to terminate.

In 1974, Congress passed a Budget and Impoundment Control Act by a vote of 75 to 0 and 401 to 6, which made it very difficult for future presidents to impound funds. Under the act, which Nixon opposed, the president had to obtain congressional approval when he planned not to use all of his budget authority, and it provided a mechanism by which Congress could release funds that the president had impounded. The act also established the Congressional Budget Office (CBO) as a counterbalance to the executive branch's OMB. On 18 February 1975, in *Train v. New York City*, the Supreme Court ruled that the president did not have the inherent right to impound.

Some of the environmental issues with which Nixon dealt, such as automobile and factory emissions, endangered species, and the Alaskan oil pipeline, were intimately related to energy policy. And here, the administration, along with most Americans, was rather slow to address the impending energy crisis. Despite the implications for energy policy, Nixon did not mention that subject in his February 1970 environmental policy statement.

In 1960, the United States imported 19 percent of its oil. By 1970, that figure had crept up to 24 percent, and it would reach 38 percent in 1974. One-third to one-half of the imported oil came from the Middle East. Although early in 1970 a cabinet task force recommended alterations in the nation's energy policy, particularly to reform the import quota system that permitted oil companies to maintain high prices and control supply, Nixon refused to tinker with the system, which had kept energy prices low and consumption high. When a State Department official recommended instituting a policy of conservation, if only to improve the nation's balance of payments, Ehrlichman responded, "Conservation is not in the Republican ethic."[45]

However, in 1971, Nixon became the first president to submit an energy program to Congress. He called for more research and development to produce clean energy sources, encouraged expansion of nuclear power programs, and asked for authorization to create a federal energy agency. Although Congress took no action on those requests, the administration initiated several modest programs on federal lands and on the continental shelf to increase energy production while protecting the environment and also began the process of deregulating the natural gas industry to encourage new exploration.

The administration evinced little concern about the new Libyan regime's ability to bully the oil companies into raising prices in 1970 or OPEC's unprecedented assertiveness when it forced price increases in 1971. Both events demonstrated that the oil companies had begun to lose control over pricing decisions. Nixon commented after his reelection in 1972, "Energy won't get the public attention it deserves until people run out of it, and then they'll blame the government."[46] Shortly after he made that comment, several areas of the country were hit by energy shortages that led to the closing of schools and factories. Nixon finally took action on 18 April 1973 in an important energy address in which he ended the oil import quota, partially decontrolled natural gas prices to encourage exploration, called for approval of the Alaskan oil pipeline, and again encouraged the development of nuclear power, promising that "if our energy resources are properly developed, they can fill our energy requirements for centuries to come."

Charles DiBona, who worked with Ehrlichman on the speech, was the White House's chief energy adviser. On 29 June 1973, Nixon established an Energy Policy Office headed by former Colorado governor John Love, with DiBona as his chief of staff. On 4 December 1973, that structure became the Federal Energy Office, run by William Simon as an "energy czar" with immense authority. His office became, in turn, the congressionally authorized Federal Energy Agency on 7 May 1974.

In the speech in which he announced Love's appointment, Nixon again asked Congress for a cabinet-level department for energy and natural resources, announced a new $10 billion research and development program, and, for the first time, launched "a conservation drive to reduce anticipated energy resources across the Nation by 5 percent over the next 12 months." The federal government would cut its energy use by 7 percent, a mandate he formalized in a memorandum to all federal agencies to reduce the air-conditioning in their buildings, relax dress standards, cut back on business trips, and take other conservation measures. Despite those actions, the nation confronted sporadic energy shortages during the summer, which led Nixon to go to the people again. In September, concerned about the possibility of energy shortages in the winter and not foreseeing the October 1973 war, he prodded Congress to move more rapidly on his energy proposals.

Then came the war and the Arab oil boycott, when, as William Simon later wrote, Americans realized "for the first time that this country had lost its energy independence."[47] On 7 November, Nixon again spoke to the nation about energy, calling for "Project Independence," whereby the United States would become energy self-sufficient by 1980. His new program to meet the energy crisis included conservation, reduction in speed limits to fifty miles per hour, the halt of industrial conversion from coal to oil, cutbacks in air flights, reductions of 15 percent in the supply of heating oil, and a speedup in the licensing of nuclear power plants.

He announced additional programs on 25 November, beginning with a 15 percent cutback on gasoline to provide for adequate heating oil and the closing of filling stations on Sundays. After reiterating his earlier proposals, he called for the "curtailment of ornamental outdoor lighting for homes and the elimination of all commercial lighting except that which identifies places of business" during the upcoming Christmas season. Nixon, who disliked rationing from his experiences during World War II, nonetheless quietly ordered the printing of energy ration stamps, just in case they were needed.

Not everyone was pleased with the administration's measures during the crisis. Truckers grumbled about speed limits, while others were troubled by a rise in the number of accidents involving automobiles and children walking to school, a product of the extension of daylight saving time through the winter. And almost everyone complained about waiting in line to buy expensive gasoline, in what Simon called a "psychology of hysteria."[48]

The key to the president's program was to reduce gasoline consumption through federal allocation strategies. John Love's early recommendation was to "allocate the reduced quantities of gasoline to the retail level and force a reduction in demand by permitting customers to wait in lines at . . . stations."[49] The administration never revealed that it wanted people to have to queue up in order to reduce demand. Those waiting in the long gas lines blamed the Arabs, and sometimes the oil companies, for their plight.

The problem was not only supply but also cost as OPEC raised the price of oil over a five-month period from $4 to $12 a barrel. Consequently, on 19 January 1974, Nixon urged Congress to enact immediately a windfall-profits tax and promised that federal monitors would be vigilant in investigating price gouging. But he vetoed a bill on 6 March that would have cut back the price of oil, believing that such a measure would discourage domestic production. Despite Nixon's rhetorical concern about windfall profits, the oil companies' profits rose by 57 percent in 1973 compared with 1972 and rose 76 percent during the first quarter of 1974.

The Arab nations lifted their embargo in mid-April, and the energy crisis was over. That is, there was no longer a supply problem. However, since OPEC did not lower its prices, the unprecedented spike in the cost of gasoline and heating oil soon had a major negative impact on the economies of almost all the nations in the world, including the United States.

The oil price shock compounded economic problems for the United States, which had been struggling with inflation and unemployment since the beginning of the Nixon administration. It was Nixon's misfortune to be confronted by the most serious economic problems since the depression. When he took office, unemployment stood at 3.5 percent and inflation was approaching 5 percent; the comparable figures for 1974 were 5.6 percent and 8.7 percent. Those numbers might confirm that "Nixonomics," a term coined by Democratic economist Walter Heller in July 1969, had failed to control those two key indicators of national economic health. Moreover, during Nixon's presidency, the gross domestic product increased an average of only 1.9 percent a year, the lowest figure for any president from Truman through Bush. Taking into consideration other economic variables such as the growth of the federal budget, the growth in the national debt, and taxes as a share of gross domestic product, Nixon's economic record ranked him seventh of the nine presidents from 1945 through 1993, with only Carter and Bush finishing lower.[50]

Such an analysis masks the huge economic perturbations during the Nixon administration and tells us precious little about the ability of presidents in general to alter the economic hands they are dealt. All modern presidents realize that their reelection depends in good measure on pocketbook issues. They understand that they are incapable of truly "managing" the economy and that events such as the Vietnam and the October 1973 wars, which had significant negative ramifications for the U.S. economy, were exogenous factors that could not be controlled. Nonetheless, presidents institute a variety of strategies relating to monetary and fiscal policy that at least have a chance of temporarily slowing unhealthy economic trends before the next election cycle. So it was with Nixon, who, despite the apparent weakness of his overall record when examined from the perspective of 1974, easily won the approval of voters in 1972 for the way he was managing the economy.

He was not especially interested in economics. In one conversation he commented, "I don't give a shit about the lira."[51] He did remember how the conservative economics of the Eisenhower administration in 1959–1960 may have cost him the election in 1960. His advisers, the "Troika"—Paul W. McCracken, head of the CEA; Treasury Secretary David Kennedy; and director of the Bureau of the Budget Robert Mayo, joined monthly in a "Quadriad" by William McChesney Martin of the Federal Reserve—were moderate conservatives or, as one CEA member labeled them, "conservative men with liberal ideas."[52] That same label applied to Labor Secretary George Shultz, who came to play a central role in the administration's economic affairs, and, to a lesser extent, counselor Arthur Burns, who left the administration in early 1970 to replace Martin as head of the Federal Reserve. Herbert Stein, who took over from McCracken as head of the CEA in January 1972, added the first woman to the council, Marina von Neumann Whitman.

Despite their shared moderate conservatism, Nixon's advisers were split between those who favored tinkering with fiscal policies (the Keynesians) and those who favored tinkering with monetary policies (the [Milton] Friedmanites). Nixon himself initially leaned toward the latter group, phoning Friedman from time to time for advice. But at bottom, he was a pragmatist. As he told his colleagues, "Whenever political considerations are not present we can afford to look at things purely from an economic standpoint. But that will not be often."[53]

Nixon was pleased to ship Burns off to the Federal Reserve in 1970 for several reasons. First, he would not have to listen to his lectures anymore.

Frank and Hannah Nixon with Harold, Donald, and Richard in 1917. (Courtesy of Whittier College)

ELECT

RICHARD M.
NIXON
WORLD WAR II VETERAN
YOUR
CONGRESSMAN

YOUR VETERAN CANDIDATE

Dick Nixon is a serious, energetic individual with a high purpose in life—to serve his fellow man. He is a trained scholar, a natural leader and a combat war veteran. He has acquired the "human touch" the hard way—by working his way through college and law school; by sleeping in fox-holes, sweating out air raids; by returning from war confronted with the necessity of "starting all over again."

There is in Richard Nixon's background much that is typical of the young western American. There are the parents from the mid-west, the father who has been street car motorman, oil field worker, citrus rancher, grocer. There is the solid heritage of the Quaker faith; the family tradition of Work—and Service.

The effects of this background show in Richard Nixon. He has worked in a fruit packing house, in stores, as a gas station attendant. He has made an outstanding success of his law practice. He played college footba[...] tains an inte[...]

Of course[...] are Mrs. Ri[...] Patrick's Da[...] Mrs. Nixon i[...] worked for t[...] husband wa[...] Pacific. Lik[...] the Nixons r[...] tion compri[...] the savings[...]

Mr. and [...] this year. I[...] looking for a[...] taking care [...] veterans' aff[...] for Whittie[...] ilies; (5) be[...] (6) they hav[...] NIXON [...]

r New[...]

ᴵCH[...]

MR. AND MRS. RICHARD M. NIXON AND PATRICIA

"I pledge myself to serve you faithfully;

To act in the best interests of all of you;

To work for the re-dedication of the United States of America as a land of opportunity for your children and mine;

To resist with all my power the encroachments of foreign isms upon the American way of life;

To preserve our sacred heritage, in the name of my buddies and your loved ones, who died that these might endure;

To devote my full energies to service for you while opposing regimentation of you;

To remain always humble in the knowledge of your trust in me."

Launching a political career in 1946 in the first of many controversial and hard-hitting campaigns. (Courtesy of Whittier College)

Chief Justice Earl Warren administering the oath of office on 20 January 1969 as President Johnson, Pat Nixon, and Vice President Humphrey look on. (National Archives)

One of Nixon's heroes, French President Charles de Gaulle, addresses remarks to the president and his aides (left to right) Bob Haldeman, John Ehrlichman, Henry Kissinger, and William Rogers on 1 March 1969 as the Americans prepare to leave France. (National Archives)

Greeting troops in South Vietnam on 30 July 1969 during a trip to the combat zone. (National Archives)

Explaining in a televised address on 30 April 1970 why it was necessary to invade Cambodia to interdict the Ho Chi Minh Trail and capture COSVN. (National Archives)

The president of the United States meets the premier of China, Mao Zedong, in Beijing on 29 February 1972. (National Archives)

With Soviet leader Leonid Brezhnev aboard the presidential yacht *Sequoia* on 19 June 1973 during the Russian's visit to the United States. (National Archives)

The very private president spent a good deal of time working alone in his office in the Executive Office Building as well as the Lincoln Sitting Room in the residence, as was the case on 6 December 1971. (National Archives)

On the beach at the vacation White House in San Clemente on 13 January 1971. (National Archives)

Left to right: John Mitchell, J. Edgar Hoover, and John Ehrlichman in the White House consider law-enforcement issues with the president on 26 May 1971. (National Archives)

Meeting with Elvis Presley and Egil Krogh in the Oval Office on 13 December 1970 to consider the entertainer's offer of assistance in the war on drugs. (National Archives)

Warren Burger addressing a press conference on 21 May 1969 after the president announced his nomination to become chief justice of the Supreme Court. (National Archives)

The nation's number-one football fan with Washington Redskins coach George Allen and his players. (National Archives)

Two days before Tricia's Rose Garden wedding on 12 June 1971, the micromanager of the White House examines the work of a carpenter laying a subcarpet for the big event. (National Archives)

Somewhat formally dressed for a Kennedyesque beach stroll, the always proper president at San Clemente on 9 January 1971. (National Archives)

Spiro Agnew on the campaign trail on 23 September 1972. (National Archives)

Left to right: Henry Kissinger, Gerald Ford, and Alexander Haig meet with the president in the Oval Office on 13 October 1973 to discuss Ford's nomination as vice president. (National Archives)

The president reluctantly announcing the release of tape transcripts in a televised address on 29 April 1974. (National Archives)

The Nixon family—(left to right) Edward F. Cox, Tricia, Pat, Julie, and David Eisenhower—maintaining a stiff upper lip on 7 August 1974, moments after the president told them that he was going to resign. (National Archives)

A teary farewell to the White House staff on 9 August 1974. (National Archives)

The Nixon Presidential Library and Birthplace is dedicated on 19 June 1990 with three other presidents in attendance—(left to right) Ronald Reagan, who relied on Nixon's Silent Majority for his victory in 1980, George Bush, who served as UN ambassador and as head of the RNC for Nixon, and Gerald Ford, Nixon's handpicked successor. (National Archives)

More important, he assumed that he could exercise more control over the Fed with Burns at the helm than with Martin. When Nixon nominated Burns in October 1969, he ordered him, "You see to it: no recession."[54]

He expected his former adviser to avoid recession by relaxing the tight-money policy, a point he made at Burns's swearing-in ceremony, much to the economist's displeasure. Although the proud and confident Burns was more helpful to Nixon than Martin had been, his independent streak irked the administration. Nixon was so exasperated on one occasion that in order to "put some heat" on him, he instructed Colson to leak a totally unfounded story to the media that Burns had asked OMB for a 50 percent raise. Colson performed the dirty trick for the president, even though he thought that it was a "dumb idea."[55]

As befits someone emotionally and intellectually committed to a laissez-faire approach, Nixon's first major economic move was to jettison the informal wage-price guidelines established during the Kennedy presidency. Further, he did not think much of the Johnson administration's practice of "jawboning," or using the government's power of persuasion to keep wages and prices down.

In 1969, more concerned about inflation than unemployment, he was willing to see unemployment rise from 3.5 percent to 4 percent or higher if that is what it took to curb inflation. He did not mention that trade-off when he announced his 1969 fiscal program on 12 April, referring to inflation as "the most disguised and least just of all the taxes that can be imposed." Eisenhower had once predicted that Nixon would be a one-term president because he would unwisely devote his energies to fighting inflation. In an attempt to control inflation, Nixon recommended continuing Johnson's income tax surcharge and excise taxes on phones and automobiles, promised to control spending, and supported the Federal Reserve's tight monetary policy.

He reluctantly approved the Tax Reform Act of December 1969, in which Congress had responded to some of his April requests. The act contained provisions for a minimum income tax for wealthy people who were avoiding paying taxes, the removal of some citizens below the poverty line from the tax rolls, and a repeal of the 7 percent investment tax credit. His Troika had recommended a veto because of the measure's inflationary provisions. But it contained several items that Nixon approved of, and it was popular. He felt that he could not defend a veto, since "you can't explain economics to the American people," even though he considered the bill "an attorney's paradise."[56]

Burns, who understood the international dimensions of America's economic problems, tried to convince Nixon to consider a devaluation of the dollar, but the president was even less interested in international economics than in national economics. "I do not want to be bothered with international monetary matters," he ordered in March 1970.[57] Nixon did not mention international economics in public during his first eighteen months in office. One Treasury Department aide commented on this policy, which ignored the overvaluation of the dollar and the balance-of-payments problem: "The implicit assumption or hope was that we could muddle through."[58]

Despite the fact that his 1969–70 budget produced a $3.2 billion surplus (the only time between 1965 and 1998 that a president could make such a claim), and despite the fact that the Federal Reserve raised interest rates from 6.75 percent in December 1968 to 8.5 percent the following June in an attempt to curb inflation, by the end of 1969, the economy, which had not been much of a problem for Nixon when he took office, became a serious one indeed. The nation was entering its first real recession since 1959. And this one was difficult to understand, since it was marked by stagflation, rising unemployment, and rising inflation, a situation that the dominant Keynesian economic model suggested was unlikely if not impossible. Ironically, just as it appeared that the model was no longer useful, Nixon told an interviewer early in 1971, "Now I am a Keynesian."[59]

The mild recession that began in 1970 saw unemployment hit 6 percent in January, real GNP drop by $3.5 billion, and businesses experience a credit squeeze that produced a record number of bankruptcies. In addition, the jump in inflation from 4.7 to 6.1 percent during 1969 was the highest in a decade. To add to these troubles, in 1970 the economy was buffeted by a three-month-long General Motors strike in the fall, and business confidence was weakened by the Penn Central Railroad's default on tens of millions of dollars of bonds in June, followed by a declaration of bankruptcy. Nixon's policy of fiscal restraint had failed. One of the first to recognize the seriousness of the problem was Burns, who (belying his conservatism) recommended that the administration adopt an incomes policy. For their part, as early as the fall of 1969, Shultz and McCracken pointed out that the Fed's tight-money policy had failed to curb inflation.

By the beginning of 1970, Nixon became less concerned about inflation than about the general state of the economy, especially the rise in unemployment, which was approaching the highest level in nine years. Now, he would "pay lip service to inflation but [warned] don't let it run danger of a recession."[60] He blamed the situation on the economy he had inherited from Johnson. In March he also identified Burns as one of the problems; he might even have to "take the Fed on publicly."[61] He told Ehrlichman, his liaison with Burns, that the chief of the Federal Reserve was "too cautious"—if you want moderate expansion, ask him for a lot more.[62] Later that year, he commented at a meeting directly, "We'll take inflation if necessary—can't take unemployment."[63]

On 17 June 1970, Nixon announced several new but still voluntary measures to solve the problems of a weakening economy, rising unemployment, and inflation. These included the establishment of the National Commission on Productivity, a Government Procurement and Regulations Review Board, the voluntary incomes policy, and the announcement that the CEA would issue inflation alerts. That summer, in the Economic Stabilization Act of 1970, in what appeared at the time to be a meaningless gesture, Congress gave the president authority to stabilize prices, rents, wages, and salaries, never expecting that a Republican president would institute wage and price controls.

Nixon's most important economic policy initiative in 1970 was to appoint former Texas governor and Democrat John Connally to replace David Kennedy at the Treasury Department. Connally had impressed Nixon with his work in 1969 on the Ash commission on government reorganization. A strong, colorful, and assertive leader, he quickly became the most powerful and influential member of the cabinet, rumored to be Nixon's choice to replace Spiro Agnew in 1972. Much more of an activist and a pragmatist on the economy than most of Nixon's advisers, Connally claimed that the president "had given me almost carte blanche authority"[64]—and this to a man who proudly claimed, "I was not an economist; I had really never studied monetary affairs."[65] Early in 1971, Nixon and Connally began talking to each other about wage and price controls.

But Nixon had not yet decided to become the first president to introduce peacetime controls. He continued to rely on other measures first, including trying to "lift" the "psychology which pervades the buying public" during the 1970 Christmas shopping season with positive statements about the economy, jawboning Big Steel to partially roll back a price increase in January 1971, and suspending the Davis-Bacon Act (dealing with wage floors for federal contractors) in February.[66] His 1 February 1971 economic report to Congress began, "1970 was the year in which we paid for the excesses of 1966, 1967, and 1968." He then announced a new expansionist program that would have the federal government spend for programs as if the nation were at full employment. The days of the budget-balancing Republicans were at an end. Under such a program, the Defense Department bought a two-year supply of toilet paper in an attempt to stimulate the economy by the 1972 election, a product of Nixon's order to "kick Laird in the ass."[67]

But nothing seemed to work. He later wrote, "The first months of 1971 were the lowest point of my first term as President. . . . It seemed possible that I might not even be renominated for reelection in 1972."[68] During the second quarter of 1971, the economy grew at a 2.9 percent rate, while unemployment stood at 6 percent. Wages had been increasing at an average of 10 percent a year; the wholesale price index had risen 5.2 percent in nine months.

The nation's international economic position was also deteriorating rapidly. The nationalistic Connally had once said, "My view's that the foreigners are out to screw us, and therefore it's our job to screw them first."[69] The main problem was the overvalued dollar and the consequent balance-of-payments deficit. Kennedy and Johnson had dealt with several crises in this area, with the fear always present that someday the Europeans and Japanese, who held $7 for every $1 of gold in Fort Knox, might begin buying gold. As part of the international economic regime that the British and Americans had set up since the end of World War II, gold was artificially undervalued at $35 an ounce.

CIEP head Peter Peterson's secret April 1971 report, "The United States in the Changing World Economy," brought home to Nixon the looming international crisis. Peterson pointed out that the American share of world exports had decreased from 18.2 percent in 1960 to 15.4 percent in 1970, attributing this to the decline in U.S. productivity and the undervalued currencies of the increasingly affluent Europeans and Japanese, which made it easier for them to sell goods in the United States.

During the post–World War II period, the United States had developed much of its international economic policy in terms of its security needs, including massive spending on NATO and in Vietnam. The maintenance of a strong and viable Europe and Japan was central to containment, even if that meant adopting policies detrimental to the American economy. In 1971, the administration, led by Connally, began thinking about fashioning an international economic policy that enhanced the American economy. The issue became more pressing as the 1972 election neared.

Aside from the Peterson report, several other international events helped convince Nixon of the need for drastic action. From 1896 to 1970, the United States had always maintained a trade surplus. Things began to change in 1971, when Washington ran a trade deficit of $804 million during the second quarter. In May, Bonn floated its currency, an act that led to an increase in the value of the mark, followed by more dollars flowing into German and other European treasuries. In an even more serious démarche on 9 August, London informed the Treasury Department that because of its own financial problems, it would convert $3 billion of its dollar reserves to gold. The previous month, wholesale prices had increased 0.7 percent, the highest spike since 1955. In addition, to remain solvent, the mammoth Lockheed corporation had to be bailed out by congressional loans, backed by the free-marketeer Nixon.

With the American economy poised to tumble even farther than it had during his first two and a half years in office, Nixon gathered his economic team at Camp David on 13 August for a secret meeting to resolve the related international and national economic crises. The president—the nation's number-one football fan and employer of gridiron analogies—disliked Ohio State University's celebrated, conservative three-yards-and-a-cloud-of-dust approach to victory; according to Herbert Stein, he "always believed in throwing the long bomb."[70] In this case, he had to keep his momentous policy decisions secret to foil stock manipulations. That is why he made his announcement on a Sunday, even though he knew that he irritated viewers by preempting the popular *Bonanza* television program.

On 15 August 1971, Nixon announced his New Economic Policy (NEP). (Once he found out that the original NEP was Lenin's, he quickly dropped the phrase from his lexicon.) NEP's centerpiece was a ninety-day freeze on wages, prices, and profit margins under the authority that Congress had granted the president the previous August. Connally would chair the Cost of Living Council to monitor the freeze. The treasury secretary was pleased with the vigilance of his agents, who went so far as to compel Detroit's Sheraton Cadillac Hotel to stop replacing ten-cent locks on men's room toilets with twenty-five-cent locks.

Nixon, who, along with most of his aides, still did not approve philosophically of wage and price controls, later admitted that he had instituted them for political reasons. In the long run, he contended, they were wrong, because "the piper must always be paid."[71]

In addition to the ninety-day freeze, the president lifted the excise tax on automobiles to encourage sales; announced spending cuts, in part by delaying revenue sharing and cutting government personnel by 5 percent; and reinstated the investment tax credit. Those were the issues that mattered most to his American audience. Nixon astounded the rest of the world when he also announced that the United States was closing the gold window, in effect going off the gold standard and permitting the dollar to float; he expected the dollar to lose value and make it easier for Americans to export. On top of the "devaluation" (a word he did not use because it suggested weakness), he instituted a temporary 10 percent surcharge on imports in another measure to help the country's trade balance. In 1974, in a judgment that could have cost the Treasury $500 million, the Customs Court ruled that the surcharge was invalid. The following year, however, the Court of Customs and Patent Appeals upheld the legality of Nixon's action under provisions of the Trading with the Enemy Act.

The immediate public reaction to NEP was positive, with 73 percent of those polled approving of wage and price controls. Wall Street seemed pleased as well, as the Dow-Jones average jumped almost thirty-three points on Monday, 16 August, the largest one-day increase in history to that point. The Europeans and the Japanese were disturbed by NEP, which immediately sent shock waves through their economies. They were especially upset by the fact that although allies, they had received little if any advance warning. And they howled about the 10 percent import surcharge, which the administration described as a temporary measure to ensure that the Europeans would not devalue their currencies as well.

After failing to reach agreement in Rome at the end of November to reorder the international economic system, the major financial powers gathered in Washington two weeks later, where they confronted a plain-spoken, undiplomatic John Connally, who remarked, "I have sometimes heard the accusation that I have become a sort of bully boy on the manicured playing fields of international finance."[72] He convinced or perhaps bullied the Europeans and the Japanese to accept a devaluation of the dollar averaging about 8 percent against their currencies. In exchange, in the Smithsonian Agreement of 18 December 1971, Connally agreed to eliminate the 10 percent surcharge and to drop the "buy American" provisions of the investment tax credit, while exacting a promise from the allies to consider removing trade restrictions. A week earlier, Nixon had virtually guaranteed the success of the meeting when he convinced France's President Pompidou to accept an 8.6 percent revaluation of the franc in exchange for Nixon's agreement to increase the price of gold to $38 an ounce.

The Smithsonian arrangement helped the United States in the short run as its balance-of-payments deficit declined from $29.8 billion in 1971 to $10.4 billion in 1972. In March 1973, after the United States devalued the dollar by an additional 11 percent, the fixed-rate system based on the 1944 Bretton Woods agreement officially died. Nixon's gamble had succeeded—the United States remained the leader of the Western alliance, and the allies had accepted the new loose system as a necessary reform.

On the home front, his wage and price freeze also seemed to be a success, at least in the short run. On 7 October 1971, Nixon announced that wholesale prices had declined in September more than in any month over the previous five years, while the price of industrial commodities had declined for the first time in seven years. He was gratified to receive thousands of letters from Americans who "put their country's interest above their personal interest in fighting this battle" against inflation.

But Nixon had given little thought to what was going to happen after the freeze ended on 13 November. CEA chief Herbert Stein admitted, "We had no plan for getting out of . . . the ninety-day freeze."[73] He and his colleagues hurriedly cobbled together a Phase II program, announced that same night, which called for the appointment of a citizens' Price Commission to establish yardsticks to restrain prices, as well as a citizens' Pay Board that would permit modest but not inflationary raises. That is, wages and prices would no longer be frozen, but the government would not allow them to rise too high. Those boards established a series of highly complex guidelines permitting yearly price increases of 2 to 3 percent and yearly pay increases up to 5.5 percent. During its first two weeks in business, the Price Commission received 400,000 inquiries about its rules.

Phase II ended in January 1973. While they were in operation, the boards permitted scores of major exceptions to their guidelines. The exceptions on the price side caused AFL president George Meany and two other labor members on the Pay Board to quit in protest in March 1972. Nixon was upset about "all those free breakfasts I gave that son of a bitch" while he was trying to win his political support.[74]

Nor was the president pleased with the behavior of business. Commenting on a Business Council's July 1972 cautious view of the economy, he noted, "It is no wonder that the soft headed chief execs in the business community are putty in the hands of the dese and dose labor guys."[75] When the automakers sought to raise prices on their 1973 models higher than the guidelines suggested, Nixon complained, "If their selfishness prevails over their good sense, then they can go to hell—and that is exactly where McGovern would send them."[76] Nixon had always preferred small businesspeople to the *Fortune* 500. This preference partly explains why the antitrust division of the Justice Department under Richard McLaren was far more active than Republican big businesspeople and Secretary of Commerce Maurice Stans had anticipated. There were, of course, at least two important politically driven exceptions to Justice's antitrust thrust: the ITT case and the Newspaper Preservation Act, both of which are discussed later.

During 1972, the Federal Reserve System adopted expansionist policies that led to a mini-boom in the run-up to the 1972 election. Arthur Burns denied having introduced such policies merely to help reelect Nixon. A year before the election, Nixon wrote to Burns urging an expansionist policy, pointing out, "I cannot think of one election where inflation had any effect whatever in determining the result."[77] From August 1971 through August 1972, the consumer price index rose by only 2.9 percent, and average pay increases declined from 8 percent to below 6 percent. GNP had run at an annual rate of 8.9 percent during the second quarter of 1972. Unemployment figures showed only marginal improvement, dropping from 5.9 percent in 1971 to 5.6 percent in 1972, but that was better than an increase in joblessness before the election. Considering the radical overheating of the economy that Nixon's 1972 policies produced in 1973, his more restrained 1971 policies might have been more effective in the long term. But they would not have jump-started the economy before the 1972 election.

Despite these good economic numbers, Nixon suspected, as always, that the bureaucracy was trying to sabotage his programs. After the Bureau of

Labor Statistics (BLS) issued a disappointing report in October, Nixon feared "they may have jobbed us—on this last report before the election."[78] On another occasion, he ordered the BLS to stop holding news conferences to announce monthly unemployment figures, but that did not stop the Joint Economic Committee of Congress from releasing the same figures.

Wilbur Mills assisted Nixon's reelection bid when he pushed through Congress a bill, which the president signed in October, to increase Social Security payments by a whopping 20 percent. At least for a while in the fall of 1972, many Americans were pleased with Nixon's handling of the economy, even though Nixon himself was never comfortable with the "liberal" approach he embraced to win a second term.

A safely reelected Nixon ended Phase II of his economic program on 11 January 1973, after confronting considerable opposition from within his administration, led by George Shultz, and from outside the White House, led by organized labor. Phase III retained controls on food, health care, and construction but relied on voluntary compliance from all other sectors. Under Phase III, the Pay Board and Price Commission were abolished. The Cost of Living Council assumed their tasks, which now included receiving quarterly reports from businesses *after* they raised prices. In addition, Nixon returned to more traditional policies on 30 January, when he "put restraining Federal expenditures at the top of the list of economic policies for 1973." On 29 March, speaking out against congressional attempts to increase his budget, he told Americans, "This is not a battle between Congress and the President. It is your battle. It is your money, your prices, your taxes I am trying to save."

Phase III was a failure. The stock market greeted its announcement with a steep drop, while wholesale prices soared, especially for meat and grains, affected by the Soviet grain deal. At the end of March, Nixon ordered the Cost of Living Council to place a ceiling on the price of beef, pork, and lamb. This did not halt the organization of a successful nationwide beef boycott, which attracted the support of 25 percent of American consumers. Between the summer of 1972 and the fall of 1974, the price of grain more than tripled.

On 13 June 1973, Nixon announced another price freeze, this time for sixty days on all items except unprocessed agricultural products at farm levels and rents. Shultz, who later said that "no one should aspire to manage the economy," offered to resign after the enactment of the freeze, with which he disagreed.[79] It was a disaster, producing, among other things, the slaughter of 43,000 baby chickens in full view of television cameras, because poultry farmers found it too expensive to raise them. One month later, Nixon announced Phase IV, which lasted until April 1974. This program maintained a price freeze (with exceptions granted for cost increases) until 12 August, after which only food prices would be frozen, while the rest of the economy would be slowly decontrolled. During August, food prices rose at an annual rate of 60 percent.

The nervous administration intervened in the international grain trade for the first time since the 1940s when it embargoed soybean exports on 27 June 1973 because of high prices. The Republican administration violated the sanctity of contracts when it announced that only 50 percent of the contracts signed before 27 June would be permitted to go through. The embargo, which irritated the Japanese, ended in September after record fall harvests, which should have been anticipated, quickly brought down the price. Nixon had told the nation on 13 June, "We will not let foreign sales price meat and eggs off the American table."

Agricultural interests opposed many of Nixon's policies in their sector. During much of the postwar era, administrations invariably tried to please rural voters. But by the early 1970s, the political significance of those voters had declined because of the decline of the family farm and the growth of urban and suburban areas. In 1966, the rural districts together constituted 83 percent of an absolute majority in the House; by 1973, that number had fallen to 60 percent. The Nixon administration may have been the first to develop agricultural policy primarily in terms of its impact on domestic and international economic policy and national security.

Whatever approach he adopted, Nixon's economic policies appeared to be failures. His last treasury secretary, William Simon, claims that he told the president "over and over again" that they were "insane."[80] But few economists could devise any better policies as the nation confronted rising energy costs and unprecedented stagflation. Certainly Nixon had tried just about every possible approach since 1969, beginning that year with a budget surplus. In 1970, the goal was a balanced full-employment budget; in 1971, a covert full-employment budget in deficit; in 1972, an overt full-employment budget with a deficit; in 1973, a balanced full-employment budget; and in 1974, a balanced budget.

During the first three months of 1974, the GNP dropped by the greatest amount since 1958, and inflation was running at an annual rate of 14.5 percent. From 1971 through 1974, it had risen at an average annual rate of 6.6 percent. In addition, in 1974 the United States lost its number-one position in international standard-of-living indices. Yet one has to sympathize with Nixon and his colleagues; they had inherited an unprecedented situation not of their own making, were bereft of new tools or insight to deal with their problems, and naturally were worried about reelection and their margins in Congress.

It is quite likely that a Democratic administration, backed by a Democratic Congress, would have adopted many of the Nixon administration's approaches toward the economy and even toward the Great Society and the environment. But it is difficult to imagine a Democratic administration dealing with those problems in such a cynical and completely political fashion. Yet by looking at what Nixon accomplished in domestic and economic policy, and not what he said about those issues, one can understand why observers in the year 2000 might label him the last liberal president.

8

★ ★ ★ ★ ★

A PRIVATE PRESIDENT'S
PUBLIC RELATIONS

Bob Haldeman, whose White House days were dominated by seemingly endless hours of conversation with Richard Nixon, considered his boss to be "the strangest man I ever met."[1] Henry Kissinger found this career politician to be a "painfully shy" man who had a good deal of "insecurity with personal encounters."[2] Nixon himself once confided to a reporter that he was "fundamentally relatively shy" and that he could not "really let my hair down with anyone."[3] His shyness and difficulty interacting with people affected the way he ran the White House.

For one thing, Nixon disliked meetings where he might have to meet new people and make small talk. When forced into such situations because of presidential responsibilities, he sometimes appeared awkward or put his foot in his mouth. He once tried to do away with the time-honored practice of having new ambassadors present their credentials to the president because he felt uncomfortable on such occasions, which he also considered a waste of his valuable time.

Nixon also preferred talking on the phone to seeing people in person. Early in 1971, an apparently lonely president asked White House aide Charles Colson for a list of important people who liked him whom he could call from time to time. Among those on the list were Robert Dole, Gerald Ford, Ronald Reagan, George Meany, Pearl Bailey, Bob Hope, John Wayne, and, from the athletic world, Green Bay Packers quarterback Bart Starr, Detroit Tigers right fielder Al Kaline, and Washington Redskins coach George Allen.

215

Nixon was an ardent sports fan. He offered advice on plays to Allen, an old friend from earlier days in Los Angeles; appeared on television during halftime at an Arkansas football game; and spent the busy 24–25 June 1972 weekend at Camp David (after the Watergate break-in) with son-in-law David making up his own baseball all-star teams, as he had promised at a 22 June press conference. He had been offered the opportunity in 1965 to become the head of either major league baseball or the players' association. "If I had a second chance and could choose to be a politician or go into sportswriting . . . I would have taken the writing," he remarked in 1992. "I love the game, love the competition."[4]

Nixon knew most of the major league baseball players' batting averages because he had a photographic memory. In preparation for a speech or even a meeting, his aides would prepare extensive briefing papers, talking points, and anecdotes, which he would rehearse and commit to memory so that he could convey the impression of speaking extemporaneously.

Nixon made most of his key decisions alone, often in his hideaway in the EOB, with his "silent yellow pad" his "closest friend," according to Leonard Garment.[5] After he made the momentous 1970 Cambodian decision, he confided to a reporter, "You listen to everybody's argument, but then comes the moment of truth. Then I sit alone with my yellow pad and I write down on one side the reasons for doing it and on the other reasons for not doing it. I do this before every important decision."[6]

Nixon generally arrived at the Oval Office to sit behind his "Woodrow Wilson" desk between 7:30 and 8:00 in the morning. He had been able to retrieve the desk of one of his great heroes from his old vice-presidential office in the Senate. He soon discovered that for years he had been laboring under a misapprehension—the desk actually belonged to Henry Wilson, who had been Grant's vice president.

In 1970, he could reach directly from the phones on his desk only three people: Haldeman, Kissinger, and Ehrlichman. In contrast, the far more sociable and garrulous Lyndon Johnson, for whom a phone was almost an extension of his body, could contact sixty people from his desk. While Nixon prepared for the day's activities, his domestic advisers and the NSC staff met separately at 7:30. At 8:00, Haldeman held a meeting in his office, which usually included Ehrlichman, Kissinger, Harlow, and later Shultz when he came into the White House. Nixon met with Haldeman alone at 9:00, with Kissinger joining them in the Oval Office soon after.

The president's formal schedule began about 9:30 and ran until noon. Nixon, who generally ate the same lunch at his desk—a canned Dole pineapple ring with a scoop of cottage cheese, Rye Krisp, and skim milk—boasted that he spent only five minutes eating breakfast and lunch when he dined alone. Usually, he had no formal appointments from noon until 2:00. He often ended his day talking to Kissinger, Ehrlichman, Haldeman, and later Colson at about 6:00 and then went up to work alone in the Lincoln Sitting Room before having a simple family dinner in the residence, often Salisbury steak with gravy. On days when he needed solitude, he retreated to his EOB office.

Nixon enjoyed talking about a wide variety of subjects to his aides, especially to the discreet Haldeman, who often preferred to get on with his own busy schedule rather than listen to the president's musings. He spent approximately 70 percent of his staff time with Haldeman. Despite the inordinate amount of time they spent together, the two men were not intimates. Nixon had no intimates among the White House staff, although he did attempt to be kind to them and their families. He instructed his staff on many occasions to be especially considerate to the White House service people; he had heard horror stories about how impolite Johnson's family and aides had been to the butlers, servers, and ushers. Nixon felt a bond with those from lower stations in life.

While polite, he rarely engaged many of his middle- to lower-level staff or White House service people in conversation, however. One Domestic Council aide complained "that very few people on the staff, especially the younger members highly touted in the press, have ever had the chance to have a chat with him."[7]

One of the reasons Nixon spent so much time with trusted aides like Haldeman, Ehrlichman, Colson, and Kissinger and so little time with others was that he was generally uncomfortable with most people, particularly when they became involved in disputes with one another. He preferred to receive their arguments in writing so that he could come to a decision without having to offend them in person. Even Garment, his old friend and former law partner, rarely saw Nixon alone.

Richard Nixon never forgot his relatively humble roots, contending proudly that he was the first president in office since Truman who did not own stocks and bonds. His net worth when he became president was over $500,000, but most of that came from the value of property he owned on Fisher Island in Florida. He also never forgot the manners his mother had taught him, tucking his napkin in his collar while he ate or placing a towel on the hassock in his EOB office so as not to dirty it. He almost always wore a coat and tie and demanded that his aides appear in comparable formal clothing in his presence. On one occasion, he organized a Kennedyesque photo opportunity, strolling along the beach near his San Clemente vacation White House—wearing shoes.

After Haldeman told him about the film *The Candidate*, in which politicians wore American flags in their lapels, he began wearing one and ordered his staff to do likewise. One of his sartorial edicts proved to be a failure. Disappointed by the lack of pomp at the White House compared with European presidential mansions, he asked a designer to create new uniforms for the White House police that "included double-breasted white tunics, trimmed with gold, gold buttons, and a stiff military hat with a high crown and plume."[8] The press corps greeted the uniforms with derision when they first appeared on 27 January 1970, likening them to Ruritanian costumes from a Sigmund Romberg operetta. The White House police force soon went back to its original uniforms.

Nixon was a hard worker. He once described his "brutal schedule" over a four-day period in March 1970, when he slept about four hours a night, going to bed at 11:00 or 12:00, waking at 2:00, when he did his "clearest thinking," working two to three hours, and then going back to sleep until 7:30.[9] His aides knew that they could expect a call from the president anytime after midnight. Later, much was made of the fact that Bob Woodward and Carl Bernstein in *The Final Days* reported that the Nixons had not slept in the same bedroom for twenty years. But this was not necessarily a sexual matter. Pat Nixon explained, "Nobody could sleep with Dick. He wakes up during the night, switches on the light, speaks into his tape recorder or takes notes—it's impossible."[10]

Nixon found so little time for sleep because he spent so much time micromanaging the White House. No detail escaped him as he gave orders to gardeners, ushers, sommeliers, orchestra leaders, chefs, and protocol officers. For example, on one occasion he instructed an aide, "I don't want salad served as a separate course at a state dinner of eighty people or less."[11] In another, more amusing incident, he told Haldeman to eliminate soup from all state dinners because "men don't really like soup" and it took too much time to serve.[12] Manolo Sanchez, his valet, confided to Haldeman that the president had issued his edict because he was so clumsy that he could not eat soup without spilling it on his tie.

Ehrlichman claimed that the president spent half his time on the "nonsubstantive aspects of the presidency."[13] After more than a year in office, for example, he asked Haldeman to look into the problem of the "pretty uncomfortable" chairs in the Cabinet Room.[14] Further, he usually checked the seating charts for formal White House dinners. This was a formidable task, considering that during his first three years alone he entertained 109,000 guests at state dinners. On one occasion when he was forced to invite Katherine Graham of the *Washington Post* to a dinner, he ordered Haldeman to seat her at a faraway table with no VIPs for companions. But he did understand the "symbolism" of inviting members of the other party to some functions, although he instructed Ehrlichman to keep liberal Democrats off guest lists.[15]

Performers who were Democrats posed another problem. Many were not especially eager to appear at the Nixon White House, especially after 1972, and Nixon tried to make certain that most musicians and other entertainers at the dinners were Republicans. He occasionally recommended groups he had heard at restaurants, and as a former pianist, he often commented on the pieces that should be presented. He complained once because a pianist played "esoteric" music instead of the expected Chopin, particularly the "Polonaise," which "audiences understand."[16]

Many great classical musicians, Democrat or not, appeared at "Evenings at the White House" or state dinners, with Rudolph Serkin playing at a dinner for artist Andrew Wyeth, Isaac Stern and Leonard Bernstein entertaining Golda Meir, and Eugene List playing for Ethiopian emperor Haile Selassie. Nixon was pleased when even the *New York Times* approved of the high quality of music at the White House—his musicians, he boasted, "make the Johnson years appear almost barbaric and the Kennedy years very thin indeed."[17]

Nixon's tastes ran to the classics. In planning for a dinner to honor Duke Ellington's seventy-first birthday in April 1969, he told Haldeman he wanted to have "all the jazz greats, like Guy Lombardo."[18] He found contemporary rock music "subtle, insidious," and full of "double entendres."[19] Speechwriter Ray Price described the president as "aggressively square," like most adult Americans, at a time when more than 300,000 young people turned out at Woodstock, the rock "Festival of Life" held seventy miles northwest of New York City in August 1969.[20] Rock diva Janis Joplin commented on the memorable weekend when "Woodstock Nation" was born: "We used to think of ourselves as little clumps of weirdos. But now we're a whole new minority group."[21]

Nixon recognized the cultural importance of Elvis Presley, who had little to do directly with Janis Joplin, the Rolling Stones, Jimi Hendrix, and their ilk. Presley appealed directly to Nixon for a meeting to discuss the problems of the "drug culture, the hippie elements, the SDS, Black Panthers etc." and offered to "be of any service" to the country. He thought that he could influence young people if the president appointed him a "Federal Agent at Large." Understanding Presley's popularity among many of his own adult constituents, Nixon agreed to meet him on 21 December 1970. The entertainer told the president that the "Beatles had been a real force for anti-American spirit" and explained how he could be helpful with hippies and other young people in pushing an antidrug message.[22] Nixon was distressed about the rise in the use of marijuana and wondered why "all the Jews seem to be the ones that are for liberalizing the regulations on marijuana."[23] Such comments reveal his penchant for conflating liberals and liberal causes with Jews.

Like many Americans, Nixon strongly opposed drug usage but saw nothing wrong with the use of alcohol. In fact, after he left the presidency, aides reported that he had often drunk to excess. During the sixties, Ehrlichman had been convinced that "Nixon's drinking could cost him any chance of a return to public life."[24] Part of Nixon's problem was that he could not drink when he was tired; "one beer," Haldeman observed, "would transform his normal speech into the rambling elocution of a bowery wino." But Haldeman never saw him drunk when he was president.[25] Others in the White House, however, including Kissinger, who talked about "my drunken friend," maintain that the president, who enjoyed martinis, drank to excess on occasion, especially in the evening.[26] Barry Goldwater had "seen him drunk only twice. He's really a wonderful fellow when he drinks. I wish he'd done more drinking when he was President."[27]

Whether he was ever drunk when president, Nixon did enjoy fine wine. He had developed an expertise in New York during the sixties. He knew enough to look down his nose at several recent Bordeaux vintages that the White House had purchased and tried to sell them off. And, surprising for such a nationalist, he had a "standing instruction that California wine is never to be served at State Dinners—especially those for Europeans."[28] When California wine had to be served for a function, he stated his preferences for specific wineries and vintages, but he rarely drank wine from his home state. Instead, he had private stocks of Chateau Lafite Rothschild and Chateau Margaux that waiters, hiding the labels behind napkins, served to him, while his guests and aides drank decent but hardly comparable vintages.

Whatever the menu or the music, politics was never very far from Nixon's mind at White House functions. Haldeman noted, "The President feels that both the Worship Services as well as the Evenings at the White House should be used for political opportunities."[29] Nixon was a religious man who knew that the president had to look religious, but regular Sunday churchgoing posed a security problem. Thus he introduced periodic ecumenical White House worship services and told Colson to invite, among others, "rich people with strong religious interest."[30] Nixon also invited Catholics and evangelicals, who often were Democrats, to the services. Along with those services, he used flights on *Air Force One* to reward or court political contributors, instructing Haldeman to identify a person of "high rank," perhaps Harlow, Haldeman, Ehrlichman, or youth adviser and former University of Oklahoma football coach Bud Wilkinson, to "be along to talk to the VIPs" he invited to accompany him.[31]

Considering the fact that a good deal of what he did was politically motivated, Nixon grudgingly became something of a patron of the arts. After all, as he noted in November 1972, "The arts are not our people," and "We should dump the whole culture business."[32] Early in his administration, Garment, in particular, convinced him that it was good politics to assist the arts. As Nixon instructed Ehrlichman and Haldeman in 1969, "let's do it (But *no* modern art in the White House!)."[33]

He had a strong aversion to modern art. On one occasion, he ordered Garment to have an abstract sculpture on the lawn of the nearby Corcoran Gallery removed to someplace where he would not have to look at it every day. It ended up in an obscure spot near Hain's Point. He also wanted to get rid of "atrocious objects," the "horrible modern art in some of our embassies."[34] Consequently, the State Department felt compelled to take down much of the modern art from the walls of the American embassy in Paris on the eve of Nixon's February 1969 visit. Despite the president's personal distaste for such art, Garment and Moynihan helped keep alive a 1966 bill for the establishment of the Hirshhorn Museum, a modern-art museum, on the Mall. Conservatives tried to halt the building of the museum because they objected to the agreement that permitted benefactor Abraham Hirshhorn not only to have his name on the museum but also to appoint the first director. The museum, which opened in 1974, soon became one of the more important modern-art museums in the country.

Even more significant, on 10 December 1969, after being prodded by Garment, Nixon asked Congress to increase funding for the National Endowment for the Arts (NEA) and the National Endowment for the Humanities (NEH). By the time he left office, the NEA's budget had increased from $12 million to $81 million, and the NEH's budget had risen from $11 million to $72 million. He justified his requests because "the attention and support we give the arts and the humanities—especially as they affect our young people—represent a vital part of our commitment to enhancing the quality of life for all Americans." He was especially interested in bringing the arts to all regions of the United States.

Nancy Hanks, an active and politically skilled appointee who took charge of the NEA in the fall of 1969, also promoted the democratization of the arts. Her encouragement of the development of local art institutions led to an increase in the nation's professional orchestras from 58 in 1965 to 110 in 1975, while the number of opera companies increased from 27 to 45 and the number of dance companies from 37 to 157 during the same period. Ronald Berman, a conservative academic who took over the NEH in 1971, presided over a comparable expansion.

Although a supporter of Hanks, Garment feared that the expansion of the NEA, with more and more artists and writers receiving grants, could lead to political controversy. This occurred in 1974 when Erica Jong, who received a $5,000 grant from the NEA in 1973, published her sexually explicit novel *Fear of Flying*.

Closer to home, Pat Nixon spent a good deal of time enhancing the quality of the White House collection of furniture and art through the Committee for the Preservation of the White House. She was ably assisted by Clement E. Conger, the knowledgeable White House curator. During her tenure, the White House acquired 65 new paintings and 156 original pieces of furniture, and 14 rooms were redecorated and refurnished.

Nixon was not as enthusiastic about promoting the development of public television and radio. The Public Broadcasting System (PBS), founded in 1967, had its federal subvention raised from $5 million in 1969 to $31 million, out of a total budget of $158 million, three years later. By 1972, it had established a 233-station television network, which produced, among other popular shows, *Sesame Street* and *The Great American Dream Machine*. National Public Radio made its first appearance in 1970.

Perceiving public television and especially public radio as too liberal, the administration schemed to gain control of their main funding and coordinating agency, the Corporation for Public Broadcasting (CPB). In 1972, Nixon vetoed Congress's bill appropriating $155 million for the CPB, an action that caused its chief, John Macy, and several others to resign. The following year, Nixon approved a two-year $110 million appropriation for the CPB. One problem he faced, according to Ehrlichman, was that by slashing the network's appropriation too deeply, it "will cut 'Sesame Street' and leave [newsmen Martin] Agronsky and [Sander] Vanocur in place."[35] Ralph Rogers, a Republican who took over PBS in 1973, fought the president's attempts to rein in public broadcasting, noting, "People like me couldn't believe that any President of the United States could say no to the people of the United States, who own the air, that they could not discuss public affairs on the air."[36]

Both Nixon and Vice President Agnew spoke often of the decline in morality in the United States, expressing concern about pornography and obscenity and other assaults against traditional values. During their term in office, popular culture seemed to shift away from those values, with Hollywood films becoming more and more explicit, as exemplified by the steamy 1973 Marlon Brando feature *Last Tango in Paris*. At the same time, gay Americans began coming out of the closet to demand equal rights, symbolized by the pitched battle between homosexuals and police at the Stonewall Inn in Greenwich Village in June 1969. In 1974, much to the distress of cultural conservatives, the American Psychological Association declared that homosexuality was not a psychological disorder.

When the National Commission on Obscenity and Pornography, appointed during the Johnson administration, finally produced its report, Nixon announced that "American morality is not to be trifled with. The Commission . . . has performed a disservice, and I totally reject its report." In a public statement on 24 October 1970, he refused to accept the notion that "the proliferation of filthy books and plays has no lasting harmful effect on a man's character" and vowed never to accept the commission's recommendation for "the repeal of laws controlling smut for adults."

Nixon did not say such things merely to make political points with the majority of the population that opposed the commission's conclusions; he felt strongly about the issue, which to him was just another example of how the liberal media and intellectuals were leading the nation astray. He complained, "When you have to call on the nation to be strong on such things as drugs, crime, defense, our basic national position, the educated people and the leader class no longer has any character and you can't count on them. We can only turn for support to the noneducated people."[37]

But he did not always practice what he preached, as Americans learned from the infamous "expletives deleted" in the transcripts of the White House tapes. Nixon occasionally used profanity, although many of the deleted expletives were words like "damn." Gerald Ford claims to have been shocked by the tapes, having never heard Nixon "use intemperate language."[38] The rather puritanical Nixon may have used more expletives than he preferred because that was the way he thought the "boys" in political backrooms talked. In any event, he was nowhere as colorful and imaginative in his use of profanity as his predecessor. Of course, LBJ never claimed to be a choirboy. In many ways, Nixon's use of ethnic slurs was more profane than his use of four-letter words.

The first lady, however, was a model of propriety, aptly described by Mamie Eisenhower as "the Rock of Gibraltar."[39] Although she always supported her husband in public, she was not happy being a politician's wife. She once wrote, "You think people in the movie business are competitive. They may be competitive but they are not mean. In politics, they are the most vicious people in the world."[40] In the aftermath of the humiliating experience of the Checkers speech in 1952, she thought she had extracted a promise from her husband to leave politics after the vice presidency. When he ran for president in 1960, she allegedly told him, "If you ever run for office again, I'll kill myself."[41]

But she carried on, playing her role well, appealing to women as a competent, attractive, middle-class helpmate to her husband. A political asset, she had been chosen the "Outstanding Homemaker" of 1953, "Mother of the Year" in 1955, and the "Nation's Ideal Wife" in 1957. Like her husband, she was an intensely private person who rarely showed much emotion in public. Critics among the sophisticated set labeled her "Plastic Pat," but those people did not represent the Nixon constituency.

The Nixons rarely touched each other in public. According to one journalist, the president considered her "like just a piece of furniture" and often forgot she was there.[42] On occasion, he appeared to treat her less than generously, such as on the night before he resigned, when he told a congressional group, "I have a wonderful family and a pretty good wife."[43] The next day, in his farewell to his staff, he offered tributes to most members of his family but did not mention his wife. After the Nixons left the White House, stories began to circulate that she was not only extremely depressed but, during the last few years, had also started to drink heavily. Her former aides vigorously denied those rumors.

As first lady, she visited 23 countries and 107 American cities during the first term, while daughter Tricia traveled to 3 countries and 65 cities and daughter Julie to 4 countries and 84 cities. After her husband was safely reelected, she delegated more of her hostess and traveling responsibilities to Julie, even though the White House had been pleased with the "warm and appealing" face she put on the first family.[44] She never publicly embraced feminism, but she supported the ERA, lobbied her husband to put a woman on the Supreme Court, and was quietly pro-choice on the abortion issue. Like most first ladies, she promoted a special cause. Hers was "voluntarism," but she was somewhat less active than Jacqueline Kennedy and Lady Bird Johnson.

Not surprisingly, she developed a "natural adversary relationship" with the president's staff, particularly the forceful Haldeman.[45] This was not unprecedented; the East and West Wings of the White House had frequently come into conflict during previous administrations. The president's West Wing, according to a member of her staff, simply "discounted" the East Wing, where first ladies traditionally had their offices, despite the fact that Mrs. Nixon, who had used her secretarial skills throughout her husband's career, put in unusually long hours personally answering mail and planning functions.[46]

The president often complained that his wife was not getting the publicity that she—and he—deserved. Early in his second term, he asked press secretary Ron Ziegler to take over the task of publicizing her many "unprecedented" activities opening up the White House to "all people of all races." He wanted the wire services to run "a story with regard to how much has been done over the past four years in terms of the number of people, number of receptions."[47]

The most exciting family reception was the gala White House wedding of Tricia Nixon to Edward F. Cox on 12 June 1971, the first to be held in the Rose Garden and the eighth of a president's daughter held at the mansion.

Although the wedding went off without a snag despite some rain, it produced a mini-brouhaha with the *New York Times*. Jean Hewitt, the food editor, tried to make a miniature replica of the six-foot-tall, 300-pound wedding cake with a recipe supplied by White House chef Henry Haller. She reported that there was something wrong with the recipe, since her cake turned out to be "mush on the outside and soup on the inside," leaving her oven a "mess." On a second try, the cake turned into "porridge."[48] Tricia defended Haller, pointing out, "It takes a real gourmet cook. I think a few people need cooking lessons."[49] The problem involved the difficulty of adapting the recipe for a 300-pound cake to one for a 1-pound cake.

The previous April, Tricia's White House tea for Finch College alumni almost went awry. Finch alumna Grace Slick of the acid-rock group the Jefferson Airplane not only brought Yippie leader Abbie Hoffman as her date but also planned to lace the punch with LSD hidden under her fingernails. Hoffman had recently boasted in a Buffalo speech that he had "fucked Kim Agnew," the thirteen-year-old daughter of the vice president who was rumored to be supportive of the peace movment.[50] A journalist whom Slick and Hoffman had tipped off about their LSD plot revealed it to White House security guards, who barred the couple from the tea.

The president, along with family members and aides, frequently went to Camp David for weekends, where he enjoyed swimming and bowling. He filled in the White House indoor swimming pool, but he did so to provide adequate offices for the press. His staff prevailed on him not to make a lawn out of the White House tennis court.

For longer vacations, the presidential entourage traveled to either Key Biscayne, Florida, or San Clemente, California. For almost two decades, Nixon had been coming to Key Biscayne, where he first rented a three-bedroom bungalow from Senator George Smathers (D-Fla.), adjacent to the home of his closest friend, Bebe Rebozo. After the 1968 election, he purchased the Smathers bungalow and another for $250,000, which, with Rebozo's home, became a presidential compound. Key Biscayne was not too far from industrialist Robert Abplanalp's island in the Bahamas, where Rebozo and the president also spent a good deal of vacation time.

In March 1969, Nixon purchased another vacation home, this time in San Clemente. He raised part of the money for the $340,000 purchase by selling his Fisher Island holdings. "La Casa Pacifica," near the area where he had courted Pat, once belonged to a Democratic politician who had hosted poker parties for Franklin Roosevelt. Nixon told a reporter, "I have never lived in a house like this, you know."[51] Despite its fourteen rooms, beachside location, and glorious views of the Pacific, Andrei Gromyko found it "not especially luxurious. It was even rather modest." The Soviet delegation had to be jammed into every nook and cranny during Brezhnev's

1973 visit.[52] Nixon's modest tastes carried over to his favorite San Clemente restaurant, the Hole in the Wall Restaurant, an extremely casual Mexican eatery.

Referring obliquely to the previous administration's credibility problems at his first news conference, Herbert Klein, Nixon's director of communications, announced, "Truth will be the hallmark of the Nixon administration."[53] Confident when making that statement, Klein later regretted it, considering the relationship that soon developed between the administration and the media. More than most presidents, Nixon was concerned about the media and the way they portrayed his activities. His misfortune was to arrive on the scene during the early days of adversarial journalism.

Like all presidents, he worried about leaks, especially in the national security area. In May 1961, following the failed Cuban émigré invasion at the Bay of Pigs, he had warned, "The concept of a return to secrecy in peacetime demonstrates a profound misunderstanding of the role of a free press as opposed to that of a controlled press. The plea for secrecy could become a cloak for errors, misjudgments, and other failings of government."[54] Once in office, he quickly changed his tune to the point where, in 1972, he drafted a National Secrets Act that would have made the publication of national security material a criminal offense.

Behind this concern lay Nixon's long-standing fundamental antagonism to the press, which he maintained was reciprocated in kind. On 12 December 1968, he warned his cabinet officials and their wives, "The time will come when they run lies about you, when the columnists and editorial writers will make you seem to be scoundrels or fools or both and the cartoonists will depict you as ogres . . . let the criticism roll off your back."[55] Despite his long and bitter experience with the press, he soon found it impossible to accept his own sound advice.

Late during his first year in office, he asserted that "75% of these guys [the press] hate my guts. The [sic] don't like to be beaten." He claimed that they never forgave him for his prosecution of Alger Hiss and they resented his coolness under pressure in Caracas in 1958 and Moscow in 1959, his victory in 1968, and especially his Silent Majority speech, when they took "the biggest beating."[56] On another occasion, he thought as many as 35 percent of the journalists were decent but the rest "have no intention whatever to be fair whenever they are able to get away with unfair coverage."[57]

In fact, Nixon had received fairly favorable press during most of his career, beginning with the role the Los Angeles Times played in 1946. In 1960, he led Kennedy in editorial endorsements by 54 to 15 percent; in 1968, he led Humphrey by 60.8 to 14 percent; and in 1972, he led McGovern by 71.4

to 5.3 percent.[58] Such numbers did not alter his impression that liberal journalists from a handful of nationally influential publications and networks were biased against him. A content analysis of items on presidents in *Time* and the *New York Times* and on CBS from 1954 through 1978 reveals that even considering the general trend toward more unfavorable coverage of presidents over the period, Nixon received the most unfavorable coverage.

Following his famous "last" press conference the morning after the 1962 California gubernatorial election, Nixon claimed to have been "delighted" with his performance; "I finally told those bastards off, and every God-damned thing I said was true."[59] He was especially antagonistic to the nationally influential, New York and Washington-based media: the *New York Times, Washington Post*, CBS, NBC, ABC, *Time*, and *Newsweek*. He felt that they were far too liberal and insular, out of touch with the rest of America. At the same time, recognizing their influence among elites, he desperately sought their approval. Thus, he was extremely pleased whenever they found something good to say about him.

His concern about the power of Jewish Americans may have had something to do with his hatred of the eastern-based national media. At the time of his presidency, almost all of his seven targeted media outlets were owned or edited by Jewish Americans. In 1973, he complained to Anatoly Dobrynin about the Jewish lobby and how the mass media that opposed him were run by "essentially the same Jewish circles."[60] One of his closest friends and the only nonfamily member that Julie and Tricia referred to as "uncle," Elmer Bobst, the head of Warner-Lambert, was a raving anti-Semite who wrote to Nixon in 1972, "most all of them [newspeople] are Jews, and Jews have troubled the world from the very beginning." Bobst warned, if the country falls apart, it will be because of "the malicious action of Jews in complete control of our communications." Nixon underlined that last phrase and instructed Rose Mary Woods, in the margin, "Note!"[61]

Ray Price asserted that the complaints aired by Nixon and his staff were by and large accurate. He accused the media of being too powerful, inaccurate, biased, self-righteous, sloppy, insular, and generally antigovernment. Speechwriter James Keogh resigned from the White House to prepare a defense of the administration's views, which was published in 1972 as *President Nixon and the Press*.

The Nixon papers and tapes fairly brim over with constant attempts to have the media "effectively discredited."[62] Typical was his order to Haldeman in April 1972: "The discrediting of the press must be our major objective over the next few months." He could not "emphasize too strongly" that issue.[63]

Nixon set out to combat the press with a variety of offenses and defenses. The most important was to develop a positive image through sophisticated public-relations operations directed from the White House around or over the heads of his enemies in the media. He explained that a president "must try to master the art of manipulating the media."[64] Colson boasted that by 1972, the White House came "as close to managing the news as you can do."[65] Nixon admitted that he was not happy that the "concern for image must rank with concern for substance," but it was a "fact of life."[66] If Mitchell's public theme was watch what we do, not what we say, Nixon's private theme was that what people think you are doing is more important than what you are doing. Kissinger thought that "the conviction that Nixon's standing depended less on his actions than on their presentation was a bane of his administration."[67] Speechwriter David Gergen reported, "We had a rule in the Nixon operation that before any public event was put on his schedule, you had to know what the headline out of that event was going to be."[68]

One way to control the media was to limit potentially hostile journalists from gaining access to the president. Nixon had adopted this approach during the 1968 campaign. While president, he held the fewest number of press conferences of any president from Hoover through Carter, averaging eight per year during his first term and only five per year during his second term. Kennedy, for example, averaged twenty-two press conferences a year. Early in 1970, Nixon instructed Haldeman to limit press conferences to five or six a year because of the time and effort that went into their preparation and also because of the risk of making a critical mistake in answering a question. To a complaint about the infrequency of his press conferences, Nixon responded on 10 December 1970, "I think the American people are entitled to see the President and to hear his views directly and not to see him only through the press."

Nixon's relative inaccessibility backfired as journalists became extremely aggressive at the daily briefings conducted by press secretary Ron Ziegler. Ziegler rarely gave them much useful information, even though the 1966 Freedom of Information Act (FOIA) permitted them to make greater demands than ever on a press secretary. Colson described him as "absolutely programmable. I mean, Ziegler was like Charlie McCarthy."[69] The harsh nature of their encounters with the media reinforced for Nixon and his aides the media's innate hostility toward them.

While avoiding press conferences, Nixon made more prime-time television appearances than any president from Kennedy to Bush. He addressed the nation on thirty-two occasions; in contrast, Johnson made only fifteen such appearances. In one of his many historic firsts, in February 1970, he became the first president to veto a bill on prime-time television when he explained to the nation why he could not accept an HEW appropriations bill. He also changed the time of his State of the Union Address from 12:30 P.M. in 1970, when it drew only 22.5 million viewers, to 9 P.M. in 1971, when it attracted an audience of 51.1 million. And he changed the time of his televised press conferences to 9 P.M., which, aside from being in prime time, made it difficult for print journalists to get their stories into the morning papers. In 1973, he broke precedent by dividing the State of the Union message into four parts, which he then presented separately in written form to Congress in order to keep his programs constantly in the headlines for a one-month period.

In 1971, he told the National Association of Broadcasters, "I am the world's living expert on what television can do for a candidate and what it can do to a candidate."[70] In January of that year, he had created a White House Television Office, headed by Mark Goode, and became the first president to employ a full-time producer. Nixon made so many appearances on television that the Democrats applied to the FCC to gain equal time to respond under the "fairness doctrine." The Democratic National Committee (DNC), despite a brief period when CBS offered free time for a "Loyal Opposition" program, was generally unsuccessful with the networks and in the courts in obtaining comparable access to the airwaves to answer what it claimed were the president's partisan charges. For example, between January 1969 and August 1971, Nixon delivered fourteen televised addresses and held fifteen news conferences, carried free on all the networks; the Democrats were able to make only three rebuttal appearances, and none was carried on all the networks.

The FCC ruled in 1970 that the fairness doctrine did apply to the president's Vietnam speeches but held that the networks could choose the Democrats' spokespersons. The commission also ruled that when the president appears before the nation to announce an action, he is behaving in a nonpartisan manner and the fairness doctrine does not apply. FCC head Dean Burch, a Nixon appointee, controlled a working majority that favored the White House's position on most issues. Burch and Colson worked closely on many of the administration's media problems. For example, Burch met with network presidents after the 1970 election to deal with Nixon's charges that their election-night coverage had been unfair to Republicans, and he threatened more FCC regulation unless they changed their approach. The administration's cause was aided by a May 1973 Supreme Court ruling that neither the Communications Act nor the First Amendment required broadcasters to accept even *paid* editorial advertising.

Later in life, Nixon worried about the way television had come to dominate American politics. "What makes good television," he asserted in 1990, "often makes bad policy. . . . Public debate is conducted increasingly in slogans and one-liners."[71]

Nixon offered his aides public-relations tips on how best to feature him. Five days into his presidency, he told Ehrlichman to get out the word that "RN has wit, is kind to his staff, that he works long hours, that people in the Cabinet and Security Council and all who come to see him are immensely impressed by his ability to preside over a meeting, to grasp a subject, that he reads an immense amount of material etc."[72] But he also realized his problems, noting that "I've got to put on my nice-guy hat and dance at the White House . . . but let me make it clear that's not my nature."[73]

To send out his promotional messages, he established the "Five O'Clock Group" of high-level aides who met daily to plan and evaluate public-relations policies. On one day alone, 22 September 1969, he dictated nine separate memos to Haldeman on public-relations issues, one of which called for impressing the public with his "hard work, dignity, programs, world leader restoring respect for the United States."[74] Several months later, he told his advisers to "build a mythology re the P[resident]," pointing out that even though Taft was a better president than Theodore Roosevelt, Roosevelt has been recorded as greater than Taft because of the way he developed his mythology.[75] In 1971, Haldeman was still concerned that Nixon's "courage, boldness, and guts has not come through."[76] But even Haldeman thought that Nixon spent too much time on his image; "it would work a lot better if he would quit worrying about it and just be President."[77]

Nixon and his aides also tried to appeal to what they called "Metro America" by showcasing attractive members of their administration. Magruder compared young White House aide Martin Anderson to Mel Laird—"he's got more *hair*, a Ph.D., a sexy wife, drives a Thunderbird, and lives in a high rise apartment."[78] Magruder also singled out an obscure, young, attractive White House counsel named John Dean as a possible model for the administration.

Nixon constantly looked for opportunities to appear on television in one or another precedent-shattering activity, whether it was the first visit to a communist country or talking to men on the moon. Many of his speeches began, "This is the first time in history that . . ." When on 20 July 1969 Neil Armstrong and Edwin "Buzz" Aldrin announced that "the Eagle has landed" on the moon and that the *Apollo 11* mission had been successful, the president called them: "Hello Neil and Buzz, I am talking to you by telephone from the Oval Office in the White House, and this certainly has to be the most historic telephone call ever made from the White House." The *New York Times* criticized the president for "sharing the stage with the astronauts."[79] Although Nixon had been a promoter of space missions in the Eisenhower administration, the *Apollo 11* mission was a result of President Kennedy's promise to land a man on the moon by the end of the decade and thus beat the Russians in the space race.

When the astronauts splashed down in the South Pacific on 24 July, Nixon met them aboard the *Hornet* to announce, "This is the greatest week in the history of the world since Creation," a comment that caused even his good friend Billy Graham to gently criticize the president for hyperbole. Far less well-publicized was the fact that for budgetary reasons, the administration would soon cut back on the space program, opposing the building of a space station (although approving the development of a space shuttle in 1972), the manned exploration of Mars, and the Saturn program. But in 1969, the administration and the United States received a good deal of favorable publicity as the astronauts toured the world with their moon rocks. When *Apollo 12* landed on the moon in November, however, the public-relations activities were much more low-key, in part because there were no live transmissions from the moon due to the failure of the television cameras in the landing vehicle.

One major problem with his press and public-relations campaigns, as Nixon saw it, was that his director of communications, his old friend Herbert Klein, proved to be too friendly with the journalists he was supposed to be manipulating. In September 1969, Haldeman made Jeb Stuart Magruder Klein's deputy to bring a harder, more aggressive edge to press relations. In early 1971, Colson, Nixon's ablest expert in hardball politics, took over most of Klein's responsibilities. By then, Klein had become, as Ehrlichman writes, "among the walking dead." But characteristically, Nixon found it impossible to fire his friend, even though he thought, "He just doesn't have his head screwed on."[80] Finally, in July 1973, Klein left the administration and was replaced by Kenneth Clawson, who had been one of Colson's assistants. White House ombudsman Clark Mollenhoff felt that "if Nixon had paid attention to Herb Klein it would have been a different presidency."[81] Compared with Klein, most of the aides who handled public relations for the president had limited experience in caring for and feeding the national press.

Klein, Ziegler, Buchanan, Colson, Chapin, Safire, Clawson, and others met frequently to plan public-relations strategy. Every Nixon program had to be accompanied by a detailed plan for public relations. For example, they tried to sell Vietnamization with "Cocktails with Clawson" functions. The revenue-sharing program announced in the 1971 State of the Union message had a "game plan" that ran 158 pages. In an example of the magnitude of these activities, from November 1970 through January 1971, the Office of Communications sponsored 465 speakers on various programs.

More specifically, from 19 January 1970 through 11 March 1970, the State Department dispatched 14 speakers who appeared on 269 television stations and 35 radio stations in 40 cities in 24 states. Similarly, during two weeks in April 1971, the White House sent out 16 separate mailings to 146,000 groups, publications, and individuals on such issues as the environment and abortion. During 1970, Nixon himself sent out 50,000 letters over his signature. The traffic went both ways, of course. During the 1969–1971 period, he received 6 million letters, cards, and telegrams, which led to over 700,000 responses, most of which were printed cards.

Throughout his administration, Nixon emphasized the need to get his message out beyond Washington and New York to places where the media were far more friendly. Thus, he gave a special briefing to eastern media executives on 18 June 1971 in Rochester, New York, and one for midwestern executives in Kansas City on 6 July 1971. Other approaches included the "device of controlled leaks" to the *Washington Star* in an attempt to cut into the circulation of the *Washington Post*.[82] Colson once wrote to Malek that "the Army [should] take over *The Washington Post* . . . immediately after the Army took over, we should have [columnist] Hobart Rowen beheaded" and Ben Bradlee and others tried as war criminals.[83] Colson referred to the army again when he told Haldeman, "I hate the [New York] *Times* as much as anyone else and would like to be in the first wave of Army shock troops going in during the second term to tear down their printing presses."[84]

The administration also periodically kept unfriendly journalists from the *Post* and other media outlets out of press pools on trips and forbade administration officials to meet with them. In May 1970, for example, Nixon ordered that "*no one* from the White House staff under any circumstances is to answer any call or see anybody from the *New York Times* except for [Robert] Semple" for at least sixty days.[85] Ziegler, Klein, Colson, and others constantly compiled lists of journalists who could be counted on and much longer lists of journalists to be wary of. There was more to the offensive against individual journalists than merely freezing them out of interviews and other functions. Nixon once tried to cancel the press credentials of Kandy Stroud of *Woman's Wear Daily*, whom he referred to as a "kike girl," and requested Treasury Secretary John Connally to order tax audits of every member of the family of *Los Angeles Times* publisher Otis Chandler.[86]

CBS correspondent Daniel Schorr, whom Nixon privately asserted has "been against us for years," was a special target of the administration.[87] After Schorr discovered in the fall of 1971 that someone had ordered a full FBI field audit on him, the administration issued the unbelievable explanation that it had simply been following normal procedures since he was being considered for a post in the Interior Department. Schorr was just one of several anti-Nixon journalists whose phones were tapped, IRS returns examined, or activities monitored.

Nixon kept track of the media with the most elaborate monitoring service of any president in history. Mort Allin, who worked under Buchanan, was in charge of providing the president with daily media surveys that sometimes were as long as fifty single-spaced pages. Overall, Allin's office produced over 15,000 pages of news summaries between 1969 and 1974. He and his staff culled editorials and columns from about fifty newspapers and forty magazines. They also reported on the television networks' evening news shows, as well as talk shows hosted by Merv Griffin, Johnny Carson, and Dick Cavett. Although claiming objectivity, the media monitors often looked for items to reinforce the president's biases. Moreover, few if any of those making the evaluations had any training in journalism or the sociology of public opinion, so when they evaluated television, for example, they rarely commented on the visual aspects of the news reports. In another context, Nixon once complained, "I've never been able to get anybody in my press operation who understood the power of television."[88]

The president, Buchanan, Allin, and the others involved took inordinate pride in the comprehensiveness and objectivity of these surveys. Nixon made marginal notes directly on them, ordering Haldeman and others to take action against unfair publications. During his first year in office, Nixon's marginalia produced over 300 specific Haldeman action memoranda. For a while, Magruder produced a "Weekly Report of Little Lies Corrected and News Summary Notations" to keep track of how well the president's orders had been carried out.

The proposed Vanderbilt University Television Archive represented another way for the White House to monitor or even threaten the networks. Nixon was pleased that the university was going to tape all network newscasts and make them available for public scrutiny. Buchanan felt that if the networks knew that someone was taping their biased material for posterity, the archive could serve as an "inhibiting factor."[89] Consequently, they searched for ways to raise funds quietly to support the project. Colson contended that the news that "TV journalists can be held accountable . . . has had a shock impact on the networks . . . [which] have decried it as horrendous censorship."[90]

In actions that were more threatening to the media, the Justice Department brought antitrust suits against newspapers such as the *Washington Post* that owned television stations and against NBC, ABC, and CBS because they monopolized prime time and fostered unfair competition. Hollywood studios supported the television suits because they would deny the networks the right to produce their own feature films. In 1980, the networks agreed to limit their control over film production.

The administration pressured the networks, Colson maintained, not to make them pro-Nixon but just "to offset their anti-Nixon bias." He described how he and the president "chortled over how he had twisted their tails" when, armed with a variety of licensing threats, he met with the three network presidents in 1970. Colson was especially proud that he bullied CBS chair William Paley to compel White House correspondent Dan Rather to behave more fairly. He boasted to Haldeman, "The harder I pressed them (CBS and NBC) the more accommodating, cordial, and almost apologetic they become."[91] At the same time, Clay Whitehead, the director of the White House Office of Telecommunications, encouraged local television stations not to carry the allegedly biased national network news programs.

The administration was not alone in assaulting the media during the early seventies. In July 1971, after 181 members of the House of Representatives voted for a resolution to censure CBS president Frank Stanton for not supplying outtakes of the network's controversial documentary "The Selling of the Pentagon," Don Riegle observed how "their spite for the networks stops just short of hatred."[92]

In June 1969, the administration gave serious thought to identifying friends who might buy the *Washington Star* or start up a new Republican morning daily. That fall, H. Ross Perot talked to a Nixon aide about buying a Washington paper. Later that year, Nixon met with friendly journalist Ralph de Toledano to encourage him to buy a news service that would support the administration. Nixon was also pleased to hear rumors in February 1970 from Billy Graham that a southwestern group was thinking of buying CBS and in September that Graham, Thomas E. Dewey, and others were also considering buying a network.

The administration did have friends in the media. Colson boasted that he was able to plant tough questions on *Meet the Press* for Alexander Heard, Nixon's own adviser on campus problems, and "very embarrassing questions" for Nixon's rival for the 1972 Republican nomination, California representative Pete McCloskey.[93] Similarly, when someone like Henry Kissinger did not like what *Time* reporter Jerrold Schecter was writing, he went directly to the editor, Henry Grunwald, who sometimes reined in putatively anti-Nixon journalists.

Although the White House operated its own private polling operations, Nixon, like several other presidents, was also able to plant questions with national pollsters and to obtain advance information about their results, first with the Gallup organization and then even with the Democratically oriented Harris organization. Nixon met with Louis Harris during the summer of 1971 in attempt "to load some of the questions so as to develop the answers we want (that is the answers he [Nixon] wants), especially regarding the environment."[94]

In her 1971 book *The News Twisters*, journalist Edith Efron, using a pseudoscientific content analysis, contended that the media were unfair to Nixon. Behind the scenes, the White House staffers tried to make the book a success by buying up copies from those bookstores used by bestseller compilers. Later, Haldeman told Nixon that Magruder was worried "that there was a monumental problem if word ever got out that he had doled eight thousand dollars out to buy Edith Efron books . . . to try to get it on the best seller list."[95]

Other media friends included the owners of several large newspapers chains such as Scripps-Howard, Cox, and Hearst, who wanted to jointly operate more than one paper in a city in violation of antitrust laws. In June 1969, a Justice Department official testified in Congress against the newspaper chains. Although agreeing that the "Justice Department is technically correct in its position," Nixon supported the Newspaper Preservation Act of 1969, which permitted joint operating agreements, because those in favor of the bill "are for the most part on our side."[96]

To keep the media honest, and also to create a favorable image of himself and his policies, Nixon called for the creation in 1969 of a nationwide system of Republican respondents to the "biased" media, organized through the RNC, who would flood magazines and newspapers with letters to the editor. The idea came from a program Pat Buchanan had organized in 1967. Buchanan boasted that, on one occasion, "six of the seven letters published in one *Look* issue were our team's attacks on an anti-RN article."[97]

Under the program, Magruder directed one full-time White House employee who wrote fifty to sixty letters a week signed by Republicans and sent to magazines, newspapers, television and radio stations, and individual journalists who got under the president's skin, especially at press conferences. On one typical occasion after *Time* and *Newsweek* criticized his Vietnam policy, Nixon instructed Haldeman, "Have your ltrs team give them Hell—we *must keep our Silent Majority group involved*."[98] This operation did not always run smoothly. In one week in August 1971, of fifty-one letters sent out, only six were published.

The attempt to influence opinion through this network by sending thousands of letters and telegrams to the president congratulating him on a speech or policy was also important. The news media often reported the tone of letters coming to the president, unaware that many of them had been part of the RNC campaign. On occasion, the president apparently forgot about the origin of many of the letters and telegrams received at the White House as he preened privately among his colleagues about his success with the public.

Of all Nixon's dealings with the media, the most important revolved around the *Pentagon Papers*, which Egil Krogh felt "caused the downfall of the administration."[99] In the summer of 1967, Secretary of Defense Robert S. McNamara, concerned about the way the Vietnam War had turned out, commissioned an internal study called "History of U.S. Decision Making Process on Vietnam Policy." Completed in January 1969, the forty-seven-volume study, based on Pentagon documents, received a "Top Secret–Sensitive" classification. The fifteen copies of the *Pentagon Papers* were not meant to circulate beyond the Defense Department. But one of the experts who worked on the project, Daniel Ellsberg, used a copy from the Rand Corporation, where he was employed, to make other copies and then tried to interest legislators and newspapers in making the material public. He wanted Americans to understand how they had been deceived and misled by the Kennedy and Johnson administrations. Ellsberg was a former hawkish Marine turned dove and a former student of and assistant to Henry Kissinger at Harvard. He had served as an adviser to those who put together NSSM-1 on Vietnam early in the administration.

The *New York Times* began printing excerpts from the Pentagon study on 13 June 1971, surprising both the public and the White House. Nixon, who considered what Ellsberg had done "despicable and contemptible," agreed with Laird that 95 percent of the material could have been declassified, but he worried about the other 5 percent and how it might jeopardize national security.[100] Laird's assistant, David Packard, "couldn't find a damn thing in them on security."[101] Nixon also worried that if foreign governments knew that their secret exchanges might turn up in the press, they would have a difficult time dealing honestly and discreetly with the United States.

Behind Nixon's reaction to the Ellsberg leak was his experience with Alger Hiss, a subject that came up frequently in conversations with his aides throughout his administration. He was forever reminding them to read that chapter in *Six Crises*. The papers in the Hiss case, like the papers in this case, were not that important; "the key thing [was] that we got across the point that Hiss was a spy, a liar, and a Communist" through a campaign to discredit him publicly.[102]

Nixon and his aides at first took some consolation from the fact that the material, concentrating on the Kennedy and Johnson years, was critical of the Democrats. Haldeman suggested that they refer to the documents as the "Kennedy/Johnson Papers."[103] Nixon preferred to take it easy on Johnson and "nail the Kennedy elite, Harvard, Eastern Establishment" as responsible for the Vietnam mess.[104]

Kissinger was livid from the start, demanding a vigorous response from the administration. Embarrassed about his relationship to Ellsberg as well as the fact that he himself had undertaken secret Vietnam missions for the Johnson administration, Kissinger, knowing his boss all too well, warned that if he did not act, "It shows you're a weakling, Mr. President."[105] Through the week of 13 June, egged on by Kissinger, Nixon became more and more angry at the *Times*. The administration succeeded in briefly obtaining a restraining order against the newspaper on 15 June, but then the even more despised *Post* began publishing the material until it too was temporarily restrained. After several courts issued mostly favorable decisions supporting the papers, both the government and the *Times* asked for immediate Supreme Court review on 25 June. From the Office of Legal Counsel, William Rehnquist advised the president that he had a strong case.

On 30 June, the Supreme Court ruled by a six-to-three vote that the newspapers could continue to print the documents. In a minor victory for the administration with possible major ramifications, the Court did not rule out the idea of prior constraint in future cases. Erwin Griswold, the solicitor general of the United States who reluctantly argued the case, later admitted that "no harm was done by publication of the *Pentagon Papers*."[106] Even the study's titular author, Robert McNamara, advised the *Times* to proceed with publication.

After losing the case in the Supreme Court, the administration went after the leaker Daniel Ellsberg and his associate, Anthony J. Russo, with a vengeance, to reassure foreign governments and to discourage other leakers. On 28 June, Ellsberg and Russo were indicted for theft of government property and unauthorized possession of defense documents. But before allowing the judicial process to bring Ellsberg to account, the administration set out to destroy him by leaking unfavorable material about his personal life to the media. When the FBI proved reluctant to involve itself in tapping or otherwise surveilling Ellsberg, the administration launched a private operation.

Ehrlichman pulled together a White House Special Investigations Unit under David Young and Egil Krogh, who recruited G. Gordon Liddy and E. Howard Hunt. They set up office in Room 16 of the EOB and placed a "Plumbers" sign on their door—they were going to take care of leaks. Their first task was to break into the Los Angeles office of Ellsberg's psychiatrist, Dr. Lewis Fielding. Although they did break in on 3 September after some amateurish derring-do, they did not find Ellsberg's file.

The president had ordered a general offensive against Ellsberg—"I want him exposed . . . I don't care how you do it but get it done." But he claimed that "I do not believe I was told about the break-in at the time."[107] Dean reported that Krogh told him that Nixon did order the break-in, while Haldeman quotes the president as saying, "maybe I did order that break-in."[108] In any event, Nixon claimed that it was important, for national security purposes, to see what else Ellsberg might have in his possession. His real motivation, however, was to find material to discredit Ellsberg in the press, to "leak stuff all over the place," just as he did in the Hiss case, which "was won in the papers."[109]

The administration's antagonism toward Ellsberg knew no bounds. Hunt even organized a group of toughs to beat him up while he was speaking on the steps of the Capitol on 3 May 1972 during May Day demonstrations. The gang did beat up some of the demonstrators but never got to Ellsberg.

Ellsberg's trial began on 8 January 1973 before Judge W. Matthew Byrne. Nixon tentatively offered the vacant job of FBI director to an interested Byrne in early April. Later that month, the judge learned of the Fielding break-in and illegal NSC wiretaps, and when the White House refused to provide information about those activities, he dismissed the case against Ellsberg on 11 May. The administration was in the midst of the Watergate crisis, which involved some of the same personnel as in the Fielding break-in. Nixon insisted on the cover-up of the Watergate break-in in part because he feared that an investigation of that operation would turn up evidence of the Fielding break-in, in which he was directly involved.

Those were not the only break-ins that ultimately made headlines. Immediately after the publication of the *Pentagon Papers*, Nixon and his advisers also planned to break into the Brookings Institution, where several of Ellsberg's colleagues and Democratic foreign policy experts worked. As early as the spring of 1969, one Nixon aide worried about "suspicious" stuff going on at Brookings, where a "shadow cabinet" had allegedly formed.[110] Several months later, Clark Mollenhoff expressed concern about "anti-Nixon conspiracies" going on at the Washington think tank.[111] A year before the *Pentagon Papers* case, Tom Huston talked about breaking into Brookings to search for classified material held by the "government-in-exile," with Nixon urging, "Goddammit, go and get those files. Blow the safe and get it."[112]

In order to blackmail Lyndon Johnson into supporting him on the *Pentagon Papers* case, Nixon wanted his men to break into Brookings to find secret documents concerning his predecessor's alleged political motivation for engineering a bombing halt just before the 1968 election. Colson and Liddy drew up a plan to stage a fire in the building, arrive in a fire truck before the real firefighters showed up, and break into the safes. Ehrlichman squelched the "Trojan horse" fire-engine scheme, in another example of Nixon ordering actions that his aides ignored.[110]

The conflict over the *Pentagon Papers*, won in court by the *Times* and the *Post*, emboldened the newspapers, particularly the *Post*, to become even more aggressive in investigating wrongdoing in the Nixon administration. The media, according to historian Stanley Kutler, emerged from the confrontation with "a new confidence and sense of legitimacy," as "the people's paladin" against the government.[114] Although no one suspected it at the time, the *Pentagon Papers* case was the beginning of the end for the Nixon administration.

9

★ ★ ★ ★ ★

THE ROAD TO REELECTION

Early during their first terms, presidents begin thinking about reelection. Richard Nixon was no different, except that he came into office with a $1,668,000 surplus from his 1968 run, which he immediately began to use for personal political projects. He tried to add to that war chest in a variety of ways, as when he asked Bebe Rebozo to raise funds on the sly from multimillionaire J. Paul Getty so that the president, and not the RNC, could "retain full control of their use."[1] Nixon ultimately controlled more than $2 million in private funds, some of which had been laundered through banks. He did not use those funds to pay for the aboveboard expenses incurred during his reelection campaign. For those expenses, he raised $40 million by 1972; in contrast, the RNC raised only $4 million for its campaigns. In a nation where registered Democrats outnumbered Republicans, the president, who tried to play down his party affiliation, was not interested in sharing his largesse.

But there was no doubt that he was a Republican. Aside from setting up a separate fund-raising apparatus for 1972, his first order of political business in 1969 was to try to wrest control of Congress from the Democrats in 1970, or at least weaken them sufficiently to enhance his own chances to develop a domestic program that would leave him in good shape for 1972.

Nixon could not command much cooperation from Congress during his first two years in office. That was to be expected from the Democrats, but it was a bit surprising from the Republicans, considering that the president had been a member of both houses and an indefatigable campaigner for his party.

Bryce Harlow, Nixon's experienced assistant for congressional affairs, did his best to maintain good relations with Capitol Hill but admitted, "Nixon respected the Congress as an institution but he was not often impressed by its individual members."[2] Gerald Ford's aide Robert Hartmann more directly articulated this problem: "Nixon could not hide his disdain for the Congress and he had treated some individuals in Congress very badly."[3] Of his enemies in Congress, Nixon vowed to Colson, "One day we will get them—we'll get them on the ground where we want them. And we'll stick our heels in, step on them hard and twist."[4]

Ford explained that Nixon was so much more "enamored with foreign policy than domestic policy" that he left congressional affairs to an "evil group" composed of Haldeman, Ehrlichman, and Colson. That triumvirate, which Ford blames in good measure for Watergate as well, did its best to "insulate" the president from Congress and, though claiming to be talking for Nixon, did not always represent his views.[5] "They were obnoxious when it came to dealing with Congress," Ford complained, and, even worse, had no real political experience.[6] The genial Harlow did not get along very well with them either.

At bottom, Nixon's problems related to his disinterest in domestic issues and his general distaste for personal interactions outside his circle of intimates. He was uncomfortable having to ask legislators directly for their support on a bill. Members of Congress, especially Republicans, wanted to meet the president more frequently than he preferred, or at least wanted to be consulted by his aides more frequently about administration initiatives. For example, in April 1969, Labor Secretary George Shultz announced the closing of fifty-nine Job Corps centers without giving advance warning to those legislators in whose districts they were located. Even conservative Republicans were upset about the lack of notice. Republicans again were unhappy over Nixon's 1970 veto, without consultation, of the popular Hill-Burton Hospital Construction Program. In this case, even HEW Secretary Elliot Richardson did not know about the veto.

During the two-month period of the Cambodian crisis in 1970, Harlow met only once with the president. He told Haldeman that Congress believes "our crowd thinks Congressmen generally are toads."[7] Such complaints continued into the next year. Congressman John Anderson of Illinois informed Haldeman, "House Republicans want to be consulted more frequently than in the past during the developmental stages of the President's legislative proposals."[8] That same month, Congressman Tom Pelley (R-Wash.) told Harlow's assistant to tell Ehrlichman that "you don't return your telephone calls or answer . . . mail," and that Ehrlichman was the "biggest obstacle to good White House Congressional relations."[9]

Even if Nixon had maintained cordial relations with Congress, he still had to deal with Democratic majorities in both houses during his tenure. Democratic House majorities ranged from 243–192 during 1969–1971 to 255–180 during 1971–1973 to 242–192 during 1973–1975; their Senate majorities ranged from 58–42 to 54–44 to 56–42 (two senators represented third parties in 1971–1975) for the same years.

From 1969 through 1970, Harlow attempted to create a working coalition that would support at least some of the administration's initiatives. Every Wednesday afternoon from 1:30 to 4:30 he held court in House Minority Leader Ford's office, listening to legislators' concerns. Working with conservative southern Democrats to create a coalition on many issues, he was more successful in the House, where Joe Waggoner (D-La.) was especially helpful, than in the independent Senate, where he encountered problems even with Republicans. In fact, Nixon was often most upset with moderate Republican senators such as Maryland's Charles Mathias, New York's Charles Goodell, and Ohio's William Saxbe, all three of whom he ordered "cut off" from White House connections in the fall of 1969, along with Illinois' Charles Percy, an "opportunist" running for the 1976 presidential nomination.[10] In contrast, on foreign relations, Nixon could depend on Democratic senators such as Thomas Dodd of Connecticut, who on at least one occasion received from Murray Chotiner canned questions to ask Nixon at a meeting with congressional leaders.

Nixon also crossed swords with William Proxmire (D-Wisc.), the gadfly of the Senate, who was always on the lookout for government mismanagement. Ernest Fitzgerald, a Pentagon procurement specialist, informed the senator about cost overruns on the new C-5A cargo plane in 1968. The new administration harassed and finally fired the "whistleblower" after the president ordered, "Get rid of that son of a bitch."[11] Fitzgerald, whose suit against the president was dismissed by the Supreme Court in 1982, nevertheless received $142,000 from Nixon as part of a pretrial settlement.

Prefiguring the party switches that followed the astounding Republican congressional victories in 1994, from December 1972 through March 1973, at least forty congressional Democrats, including Waggoner, negotiated with their counterparts about what sort of deals they might obtain if they switched parties to give the Republicans a majority in the House. By the 1972 election, their political and social agendas had moved far closer to Nixon's than to those of the Democratic Party of George McGovern. After learning about this potentially revolutionary development, a handful of liberal Republicans contemplated switching to the Democrats.

Any possible realignment fell apart when Senator Ervin opened the Watergate hearings in March 1973. From that point on, Nixon, having lost much of his "clout with Congress," had virtually no opportunity to promote a legislative program.[12] The vigor with which Congress pursued the Watergate investigations had a good deal to do with the strong personal dislike that many Democrats and quite a few Republicans harbored toward Nixon and the arrogant way the White House had dealt with them during the first term. They were particularly upset about the lengths to which Nixon had gone, following his immediate predecessors' lead, in expanding the "imperial presidency." In April 1973, for example, Attorney General Kleindienst announced that there were no limits on the president's right to withhold material from Congress under executive privilege when disclosure "would impair the proper exercise of his constitutional functions."[13]

Even before Watergate, Congress tried to level the playing field. On 14 December 1970, Nixon attempted to pocket veto the Family Practice of Medicine Bill that had passed both houses by the vetoproof margins of 346 to 2 and 64 to 1. In response, Congress went to court to win a judgment that the president could not use the Christmas recess as part of the pocket-veto period, and the bill became law on 25 January 1970.

In October 1971, the legislators again counterattacked; for the first time ever, Congress rejected in entirety the Foreign Aid Authorization Bill. In addition, they took Nixon to court again in 1973 and won a major victory in *Minnesota Chippewa Tribe v. Carlucci,* forcing the president to appoint members to the National Advisory Council on Indian Education, authorized under the Indian Education Funds Bill. The judge ruled that the president had to "take care that the laws be faithfully executed" as stipulated in Article II of the Constitution.[14]

Congress did not always prevail. That same year, Senator Walter Mondale (D-Minn.) failed to reduce the size of the Domestic Council and to cut its appropriations. He contended that the White House had been initiating too much policy on its own without congressional legislation or public scrutiny. Approaching the issue differently in 1973, Congress did not renew the Reorganization Act of 1939, which had made it easier for a president to reorganize the executive branch of government. And, as recounted earlier, Congress somewhat restored the balance by passing the Budget and Impoundment Control Act of 1974.

The War Powers Act of 1973 was Congress's greatest triumph against the imperial presidency. During the Johnson administration, the Senate Foreign Relations Committee, led by Senator Fulbright, began considering legislation to restrain the president from involving the United States in undeclared wars without congressional approval. In 1969, in an augury of things to come, the Senate passed a nonbinding National Commitments Resolution by a vote of seventy to sixteen, asserting that an American commitment to a foreign power needed the affirmative action of both the executive and the legislative branches.

With Nixon reeling from Watergate during 1973, Congress enacted the War Powers Resolution that made it mandatory for the president to report to Congress within forty-eight hours of committing U.S. forces to a combat theater and to return to Congress for permission to maintain troops in that theater after sixty days. Many of those who voted for the bill did not think it especially well crafted, a judgment shared by constitutional lawyers. But its supporters viewed it as a necessary protest against the way Nixon—and Johnson—had involved the United States in a full-scale undeclared war.

Nixon vetoed the bill on 24 October 1973, complaining that it represented an "unconstitutional and dangerous" denial of the president's proper role in the international sphere. Two weeks later, after the Watergate-related "Saturday-Night Massacre" had weakened him, Congress overrode his veto.

Nixon's reelection strategy depended on increasing his natural constituency, which Kevin Phillips had called "the emerging Republican majority." Two other pundits, Richard M. Scammon and Ben J. Wattenberg, described that constituency in their influential 1970 book *The Real Majority* as "unyoung, unpoor, and unblack."[15] Nixon and his aides were impressed with their approach, especially since Wattenberg was a noted Democratic political analyst. Attorney General John Mitchell gleefully proclaimed in 1969, "This country is going so far right you are not even going to recognize it"; he was appealing to a new conservative majority fed up with the liberals' political and social agenda.[16]

By the 1970s, much of Middle America lived in the increasingly economically and politically powerful Sun Belt states: North and South Carolina, Georgia, Florida, Tennessee, Alabama, Mississippi, Arkansas, Louisiana, Oklahoma, Texas, New Mexico, Arizona, Nevada, and California. It was not entirely coincidental that in 1973 the heads of the Democratic and Republican Parties, the Wallace movement, and the Young Democrats and Young Republicans came from Sun Belt states, and nine of the seventeen standing Senate committees were headed by people from that region. Of the almost 500 names on one of John Dean's lists of targets for IRS audits, only 5 percent were from Sun Belt states, aside from California. To bring matters full circle, two-thirds of Nixon's aides who were indicted or convicted came from the Sun Belt.

In July 1969, speechwriter William Safire recommended that the White House organize a nationwide support group of "Middle Americans" who were "God-fearing, tax-paying good people" who would represent the "silent center," not the Right.[17] Safire's memo prompted the formation of a secret Middle American Committee whose membership included Buchanan, Anderson, Huston, Keogh, Mollenhoff, and Dent. Nixon, however, did not like the term Middle American because he did not "think that people like to be known as such."[18] Instead, the terms Silent Majority and Silent Center soon replaced Middle Americans. That December, the Middle American Committee contemplated using H. Ross Perot's United We Stand movement as the basis for a foundation "to support a moderately conservative course" in which the White House would "secure some degree of control over Perot's activities," even though it would allow the feisty Texas millionaire to think that it was his movement. The idea, which never came to fruition, would have had Perot putting up $10 million, a sum that the administration would match.[19]

Nixon also seriously considered calling for a convention to create a new political party to embrace the Silent Majority of Americans from the right and center of the political spectrum. He would run for president on the new party's ticket in 1972, with John Connally as his vice-presidential candidate. At the least, he hoped that the Republican Party would change its name to the Conservative Party. Although nothing ever came of them, Ehrlichman contends that "these dreams were real."[20] Eisenhower had earlier toyed with the idea of creating a new centrist party.

Not found in great numbers in the Sun Belt, socially conservative, blue-collar, working-class Democrats who were distressed about their party's approach to race, crime, and cultural issues were another prominent target for the Republicans. During the 1970 congressional campaign, Nixon underlined parts of a Colson memo that, after pointing out that Leonard Woodcock, head of the United Auto Workers (UAW), was a "socialist," recommended that the White House "cultivate local leaders who are strongly patriotic, anti-student and keenly aware of the race question (witness: Warren, Michigan and the Wallace core in the UAW)."[21] (Warren was a blue-collar Detroit suburb that had once been a Democratic stronghold.)

The administration did not entirely ignore national union leadership. Colson, the administration's labor expert, enjoyed a close covert relationship with Jay Lovestone, the foreign policy specialist on the AFL board, to the point where Lovestone sent Christmas gifts to Colson's secretary and Colson sent cigars to Lovestone. Lovestone periodically offered Colson intelligence on union policies, and Colson shared classified FBI and other government files with Lovestone about radicals in the unions. On one occasion, Colson wrote, "I shouldn't be sending this so please keep it confidential or destroy it after you and your friends have seen it."[22] Colson's connections to labor paid off in 1972 when the AFL leadership remained neutral in the presidential race. He promised Lovestone, "As long as Richard Nixon is in the White House, George Meany always has a friend here," whereas he characterized George McGovern as an "arrogant son of a bitch, [who] in my opinion, is a traitor [who] should be running from the gallows."[23]

The administration enjoyed its greatest success in the labor field with the International Brotherhood of Teamsters, whose head, Frank Fitzsimmons, according to Colson, "regards himself as our house labor man."[24] Nixon solidified the relationship when he commuted former Teamster president Jimmy Hoffa's prison term on 23 December 1971, even though parole boards had unanimously rejected his appeals on three occasions. Nixon's action was legal, but one investigative journalist maintained that he and the Teamsters were engaged in a political "conspiracy."[25] Colson admitted that he exercised influence, through John Dean, with the Justice Department to "take care of your friends" in the union.[26]

During the 1968 campaign, Nixon had told William Loeb of the *Manchester Union Leader*, a Hoffa ally, that he would release Hoffa in exchange for Teamster support. In June 1971, Nixon became the first president since FDR to speak before the Teamsters' annual convention. The union endorsed him in the 1972 election.

Many urban union members were also Catholic. For generations, Catholics had favored Democrats over Republicans, supporting Humphrey by a 59 to 33 percent margin in 1968. To capture the Catholic vote, Nixon relied heavily on social issues such as his opposition to abortion and pornography and his support for state aid to parochial schools. On the first two issues, he was a true believer. Characteristic of this approach was his April 1971 directive making it more difficult for service personnel to obtain abortions in military hospitals; his public letter to New York's Terence Cardinal Cooke outlining his antiabortion views in 1972; and his support, against his solicitor general's judgment, for the filing of an amicus brief in *Lemon v. Kurtzman*, a parochiaid (government financial support for religious schools) case that the Supreme Court rejected by an eight-to-zero vote. By the time the 1972 election came around, Nixon could claim the loyalties of a majority of Catholic voters.

Nixon worried, however, about George Wallace's appeal to many of the same blue-collar people he was courting. He first tried to ruin Wallace with corruption charges. A Justice Department investigation of the Wallace family turned up a probable case of bribery against Gerald Wallace, George's brother. Murray Chotiner leaked that information to Jack Anderson, who published it in a column in April 1970. When the leak did not do the trick, Nixon tried to eliminate his Alabama rival by secretly helping Albert Brewer, Wallace's opponent in the 1970 *Democratic* gubernatorial primary.

He later referred to the $400,000 in cash his bagmen had delivered to Brewer's agents as "Republican revenue sharing." His generous party "had a little bit more than we needed and we shared it with them."[27] The revenue did not help. Wallace won the governor's race and thus was poised to challenge Nixon in 1972.

During the fall of 1970, Nixon appealed over and over to the Silent Majority in his attempt to weaken the Democrats in Congress in the 1970 elections. He instructed his aides to play down the administration's handling of the economy, which was under assault from the Democrats, and instead "Emphasize—anti-Crime—anti-Demonstrations, anti-Drug, anti-Obscenity—Get in touch with the mood of the country which is fed up with the Liberals. This stuff is dynamite politically."[28] Magruder, who worked with Colson on the campaign, later admitted, "It was a totally negative approach, one that combined the national fear of increased crime with undertones of racism."[29] In addition, he toyed with the idea of trying to infiltrate Republican operatives into Common Cause to encourage the creation of a third party on the Democrats' left or perhaps create "a front that sounds like the SDS to support Democratic candidates."[30]

He settled on sending the vice president out on the hustings that fall to play the same role Nixon had played for Eisenhower in the 1954 election. While Agnew would play the partisan role, Nixon would take a European tour and remain above the fray. He instructed Agnew to attack the Democrats as "Radiclibs" in order to convince moderates to vote Republican. Colson called for even tougher actions, so tough that even Chotiner thought he was going too far. Colson, for example, spread false rumors about Senator Joseph Tydings (D-Md.) that may have contributed to his defeat.

During the campaign, to counter the better-financed Republicans, the Democrats enacted legislation to limit television campaign spending to $5 million. Nixon vetoed the bill, contending that it represented a violation of free speech. Well-heeled candidates, of whom there were many more Republicans than Democrats, were thus free to purchase unlimited time for increasingly negative advertisements.

Despite the advertisements and Agnew's hard-hitting speeches, the Republicans were not doing as well in the early October polls as they had expected. On 10 October, Nixon decided to campaign in person, making appearances in twenty-three states during the last two weeks of the election. His most memorable appearance was in San Jose, California, on 29 October. There, in Safire's words, the nation witnessed "a mob attack upon a U.S. President—unique in our history."[31] Demonstrators had surrounded the auditorium where the president was speaking, chanting, among other things, "One, Two, Three, Four—We don't want your fuckin' war." After leaving the auditorium, Nixon jumped on the hood of his limousine and flashed the demonstrators the "V" sign in a calculated attempt to provoke them. He "could not resist showing them how little respect [he] had for their juvenile and mindless ranting."[32] Rowdies in the crowd responded by throwing rocks, flags, and candles, some of which struck the presidential motorcade as it beat a hasty retreat.

The next night, Nixon discussed the unprecedented incident in a speech in Anaheim, declaring, "It is time for the great silent majority of Americans to stand up and be counted. And the way you can stand up and be counted is not to answer in kind. You don't have to resort to violence. You don't have to shout down speakers. You don't have to shout four-letter words." All they had to do was "go to the polls and vote . . . for those men who will stand with the President."

On election eve, his advisers put together a film of another tough speech he had delivered in Phoenix on 31 October in which he referred to the "violent thugs" who had attacked him. But the grainy and amateurish film, featuring an angry and mean-spirited president, did not help the party. What made matters worse was the Democratic reply, a slick and calm presentation "starring" Senator Muskie, a gentle Lincolnesque figure who stood in stark contrast to the aggressive president.

On 4 November, Nixon proclaimed "victory" because Republican congressional losses were less than what might have been expected in an off-year election. Privately, he was disappointed. The Democrats raised their total vote margin over the Republicans from 1.1 million in 1968 to 4.5 million in elections in which they gained nine House seats, lost two in the Senate, and gained eleven governorships. The fact that the Senate moved slightly to the right, with the defeat of Nixon's Republican opponent Charles Goodell by James Buckley in New York and the replacement of two dovish Democrats (Albert Gore of Tennessee and Tydings) by more hawkish senators, represented one bright spot for the administration.

Harry Dent reported to the president that they had "avoided big losses" and that the social issue "blunted the economic issue, but "we do not have a stunning array of achievements to show what we have done materially for the people, especially their pocketbooks."[33] Nixon thought that he *had* accomplished much during his first two years, taking pride in the Cambodian incursion, an open White House, the dignity and respect the country received abroad, and his hardworking, open-minded approach to his job.

Yet something had gone wrong. There were lessons to be learned from the 1970 election as the administration began planning for 1972. Above all, a better game plan was needed to enhance Nixon's image, lead to a better economy, produce a successful legislative program, improve congressional relations, tone down Agnew's rhetoric, and shake up the cabinet. Foremost among the candidates for removal from the cabinet were the contentious Hickel and Romney and the ineffective Kennedy.

But Nixon's new game plan was slow going into operation. In February 1971, polls showed Muskie leading him by 43 to 40 percent; in May, the gap widened to 47 to 39 percent. Moreover, Pete McCloskey, an antiwar Republican congressman from California, called for Nixon's impeachment, an act that led the president to order Haldeman to "get a movement calling for his recall going."[34]

In January 1971, to aid in the ensuing campaign, Nixon selected Robert Dole, a conservative Kansas senator, to head the RNC. Dole later commented ascerbically, "The Republican Party was not only not involved in Watergate, but it wasn't involved in the nomination, the convention, the campaign, the election or the inauguration."[35] In March 1971, the Committee to Reelect the President opened its doors in Washington. William Safire, Nixon's accomplished wordsmith who named the organization, assumed that it would be known as CRP. He never anticipated that the media would adopt the unfortunate acronym CREEP.

The 1970 campaign experience taught Nixon that he had to spend his time on domestic politics more efficiently. A month after the election, he told Ehrlichman that he no longer wanted to meet with Jewish groups, "where we have nothing to gain at all. . . . We will continue to get 8 to 10% of the Jewish vote and there is nothing that I can do that will get more." Although he also did not expect much support in the African American community, he recognized that "presidential responsibility requires symbolic actions be taken," such as occasionally meeting with its leaders. He felt a similar responsibility to Native Americans. In contrast, the president anticipated making gains among Hispanics, especially Cubans, and among Italians and Eastern Europeans, with the "Poles at the top of the list."[36] He followed up this strategy several months later, explaining that "we're going to quit meeting with the people that are against us, and playing to the issues such as consumers, environment, youth, press, business elite, intellectuals, volunteers, etc."[37]

At the same time, Nixon stepped up his intelligence campaigns against possible Democratic rivals for 1972. Even though he was not a serious candidate, Senator Edward Kennedy (D-Mass.) was a special target for the administration. The senator's controversial involvement in the death of Mary Jo Kopechne off Chappaquiddick Island on 18 July 1969 contributed to a marked decline in his political stature. Jack Caulfield of the White House security detail dispatched Anthony Ulasewicz, a private investigator, to Chappaquiddick to see what dirt he might turn up. Caulfield, who paid Ulasewicz from the off-the-books White House political war chest, told Ehrlichman that he was compiling "evidence [that] will become part of our growing file of ammunition for use when and if it becomes necessary."[38] Colson, who was from Massachusetts, was the "case officer" in charge of Kennedy intelligence.

In December 1970, Colson was able to place a photograph of Kennedy dancing with a European princess in the *National Enquirer*. "The President *loved* that picture," reported Haldeman; "it stuck a knife into a Kennedy: one hundred points on the Oval Office chart."[39] Nixon was interested in intelligence on Kennedy "for [the] personal slant," while he was interested in intelligence on Muskie and the other Democratic contenders for the political slant.[40]

Concerned because Kennedy had come back to lead all potential Democratic candidates in May 1971 polls, Nixon ordered a more or less permanent tail on the senator. Wearing a red wig and thick glasses and employing a speech-alteration device supplied by the CIA's Technical Services Division, E. Howard Hunt took charge of surveilling the senator. His operation became much easier in 1972 when, in the wake of the assassination attempt on George Wallace, the president planted spies in the Secret Service detail dispatched to protect Kennedy. Nixon chortled, "We might just get lucky and catch this son of a bitch. Ruin him for 76. It's going to be fun."[41]

In a related effort to ruin Edward Kennedy, the White House attempted to destroy the reputation of John Kennedy. Nixon asked Secretary of State Rogers to declassify documents that had been held "much longer than necessary for the maintenance of our national security" and then ordered NSC staffers to help with the declassification in order to turn up embarrassing material on the Kennedy administration.[42] This interest in the rapid declassification of diplomatic documents contradicted the administration's position on the *Pentagon Papers* affair only four months earlier.

After Nixon's operatives could not turn up legitimate evidence of Kennedy family malfeasance, Colson instructed Hunt to forge documents that would make it look like President Kennedy had been directly implicated in the 1963 assassination of South Vietnamese president Ngo Dinh Diem. Colson then arranged for publication of the material in *Life* magazine in the fall of 1971, but at the last minute, the magazine's editors decided not to run the story. Material from the forged documents was used by a former CIA operative who was interviewed on an NBC "White Paper" on 23 December 1971.

Wallace posed an even greater threat than Kennedy. After having failed to stop him from winning the Alabama governorship in 1970, Nixon concentrated on keeping him in the Democratic Party. As a third-party candidate in 1968, he may have taken away as many votes from Nixon as he had taken from Humphrey. Polls suggested that he might hurt Nixon even more in 1972.

Wallace and Nixon enjoyed a rapprochement beginning in 1971. On 12 January 1972, the Justice Department dropped its investigation of Wallace's brother. The next day, Governor Wallace announced that he was going to run as a Democrat. Although no conclusive proof links the two events, and although one of Wallace's aides did go to jail as a result of the investigation, Nixon, Haldeman, and Ehrlichman had discussed the outlines of some sort of deal with Wallace as early as February 1971.

During the early Democratic primary campaigns, Dent fed a Wallace consultant polling information and offered campaign advice. The White House hoped that Wallace and Senator George McGovern (D-S.D.) would come in first and second in the primaries, a result that would lead the more centrist and electable Democrats to withdraw before the convention.

On 15 May 1972, Arthur Bremer shot Wallace at a campaign appearance in Laurel, Maryland. A seriously wounded and paralyzed Wallace dropped out of the race. The deranged Bremer had originally planned to assassinate Nixon in Ottawa on 14 April when the president was on a state visit. Although he saw the president six times that day, Bremer never was able to get a clear shot at him.

Nixon ordered Colson to send an investigator to Bremer's apartment to identify the assassin's political orientation and to plant material suggesting that he was a Democrat. By the time the disguised E. Howard Hunt arrived at the apartment, the FBI had sealed it off. Even though Hunt was unable to plant incriminating evidence, Colson leaked erroneous information to friends in the press that Bremer was a left-winger with ties to McGovern and Kennedy. The White House did obtain Bremer's diary, which contained no such information, and ordered the FBI not to mention its existence.

Even after Wallace abandoned the primaries, Nixon feared that he still might run on a third-party ticket. Accordingly, Nixon's agents gave Wallace $750,000 to keep his staff together as a sort of bribe, offered to fly him to the Republican convention in a C-147 hospital plane, and had Billy Graham and John Connally try to convince him to endorse Nixon. The efforts to obtain Wallace's endorsement failed, but at least he remained neutral in the contest between Nixon and McGovern.

In another scheme to weaken the Democrats, Nixon mused in October 1971 about encouraging Jesse Jackson to form a fourth party by offering to pay him $1 a vote. Unbeknownst to the civil rights leader, the president thought about creating an artificial Jackson boomlet in the media to "get his ego going," and then when he ran, promising him an "incentive bonus" of perhaps $10,000 per percentage point.[43] That scheme never developed beyond the talking stage.

The major thrust of the administration's meddling in Democratic politics involved McGovern. Pat Buchanan argued that "McGovern is our candidate. . . . He could be painted as a left-wing radical candidate, the Goldwater of the Democratic Party"; thus "we must do as little as possible . . . to impede McGovern's rise."[44] When McGovern became the first Democrat to announce for the presidency in January 1971 (the earliest declaration of candidacy in history), he appeared to be a very long shot. A year later, although the odds had closed a bit, he still seemed an unlikely winner against either Muskie or Humphrey. But even without Nixon's "support," McGovern enjoyed advantages that few foresaw at the time.

After the disastrous 1968 convention, his party selected McGovern to head a reform commission to draw up new procedures for electing delegates. Although the word "quota" never appeared in the commission's final report, McGovern suggested that it recommended "a de facto quota system" for those underrepresented at the 1968 convention.[45] That system produced a convention that had 38 percent women delegates, 23 percent young people, 15 percent blacks, and an astonishing 39 percent with postgraduate degrees. As one Democratic congressman lamented, "I don't think those people represent the mainstream of the party."[46]

In addition, many more states added primaries between 1968 and 1972. Fifty-seven percent of the Chicago delegates had been chosen by state parties; four years later, that number dropped to 18 percent. The reforms played into Nixon's hands, increasing the influence of liberal activists, who were still resentful over the 1968 campaign and intent on getting back at the Democratic establishment.

The administration did not rely on the Democratic reforms alone to produce the weakest nominee. CREEP engaged in a well-orchestrated campaign of "dirty tricks" the likes of which had never been seen before in any modern American election, including Nixon's 1946 and 1950 campaigns. House Democratic leader "Tip" O'Neill (D-Mass.) considered the president's reelection campaign a "new kind of dirty politics," despite Nixon's contention that "I played by the rules of politics as I found them."[47] Haldeman, who later explained that all they did was "hassle them like they hassle us," pointed to previous campaigns in which Democratic dirty trickster Dick Tuck gave Republican candidates a hard time.[48] But Tuck's handful of relatively harmless pranks hardly compared with the campaign waged by CREEP's "black advance" men, in what McGovern labeled after the election "just about the dirtiest, meanest campaign in this nation's history."[49]

In the Nixon Presidential Library's display on the 1972 presidential election, McGovern is singled out for the dirty tricks his campaign played on Nixon. In fact, in the winter of 1973, confronted by the Watergate scandal, the administration went on the counteroffensive to attack the Democrats' 1972 campaign of "libel and slander" as well as their links to radical demonstrators.[50]

Former attorney general John Mitchell, who ran CREEP, was often disconcerted by personal problems revolving around his wife, Martha, an alcoholic who was a journalist's delight because of her frequent impolitic remarks. Dwight Chapin, from Haldeman's staff, joined CREEP in the fall of 1971 to help Magruder organize the campaign; Colson assisted, often independently, from the White House. Chapin's chief operative was Donald Segretti, who, with twenty-eight agents in seventeen states, forged documents, leaked false statements, and canceled Democratic candidates' appearances. Segretti, whose name means "secrets" in Italian, was an old college friend of Chapin's and Ziegler's at the University of Southern California, where the three took pleasure in campus political intrigue they referred to as "ratfucking."

The president's lawyer, Herbert Kalmbach, paid Segretti from the White House's private funds. Although Nixon did not know of each specific operation, he approved of the general thrust of the program, the import of which he later dismissed as "chicken shit."[51] Ed Rollins, a Republican electoral consultant who worked on the 1972 campaign, explained that the job requirements for CREEP included a "total lack of campaign experience, zero common sense, and a knack for irritating even the most loyal Nixon supporters and staffers by being a total asshole."[52] Others agreed with this analysis. CREEP attorney G. Gordon Liddy and security agent E. Howard Hunt considered the Segretti operation to be "sophomoric."[53]

Some of his tricks did seem sophomoric, such as ordering thousands of pizzas to be delivered to Democratic Party headquarters. Others were more sinister. For example, CREEP agents, trying to sound like African Americans, called New Hampshire voters in the middle of the night asking them to vote for Senator Muskie. In another attempt to weaken Muskie, CREEP operatives distributed cards at a Wallace rally that read, IF YOU LIKED HITLER YOU'LL LOVE WALLACE. The flip side of the card carried the message VOTE MUSKIE.

At Nixon's suggestion, Colson, whom the president praised for having "the balls of a brass monkey," organized a group calling itself "Democrats for Muskie and Busing."[54] Colson also took pride in such activities as rigging a phone poll on Washington radio station WTOP concerning Nixon's handling of the war. During the New Hampshire primary, Ken Clawson of the White House press office was most likely responsible for sending a letter to the *Manchester Union Leader* that falsely charged Muskie's wife with using the derogatory term "Canuck." Muskie defended his wife's honor in an emotional speech in front of the *Union Leader* building, during which he appeared to shed tears. Some voters expressed concern about a man running for president who cried so easily.

CREEP knew how to get to the Maine senator because one of its operatives was Muskie's driver. Nixon received private campaign strategy documents directly from the Muskie team "obtained through covert sources."[55] Muskie did, however, take the New Hampshire primary by a 46 to 37 percent margin over McGovern. But he faltered in Florida a week later, coming in fourth with 9 percent, while George Wallace won with 41 percent.

During the Florida campaign, Republican agents mailed forged letters under the heading "Citizens for Muskie," accusing Washington senator Henry Jackson, a rival for the nomination, of having an illegitimate child and having been arrested on homosexual charges, while also claiming that Hubert Humphrey had been arrested on a drunk-driving charge. After these and related activities turned up in the Watergate investigations, Segretti was indicted on three counts of distributing illegal campaign literature and was sentenced to four and a half months in jail. One of Segretti's aides received a nine-month term, while Chapin received a ten- to thirty-month term for making false statements to a grand jury about his relationship to Segretti. Buchanan engaged in a legal "prank" when he had "Black Vice President" bumper stickers made up for distribution in inner-city ghettos.

All these successful illegal and extralegal campaign intelligence and counterintelligence activities and dirty political tricks pale in their long-term significance to one failed operation—the break-in at Democratic National Committee headquarters in the Watergate apartment and commercial complex in Washington during the early-morning hours of 17 June 1972. Tipped off by a night watchman, district police apprehended five men wearing surgical gloves and carrying tear-gas fountain pens, walkie-talkies, and new $100 bills, apparently attempting to plant electronic surveillance equipment in the DNC offices. The police quickly discovered two other men coordinating the operation from the Howard Johnson Hotel across the street.

Four of the men inside the Watergate were Cubans who had worked for the CIA, one of whom, Eugenio Martinez, was still officially on the agency's payroll. The fifth, James McCord, was a former CIA agent who was chief of security for CREEP. The two men across the street were Hunt, who had worked on security issues for the White House, and Liddy, who, along with Hunt, had been involved with the White House Special Investigations Unit (the "Plumbers") until the fall of 1971, when he left to become counsel to CREEP's finance committee. On 19 June, two energetic and aggressive young reporters from the *Washington Post*, Bob Woodward and

Carl Bernstein, wrote a story about the links between the break-in and the White House, links turned up in the police investigation of Hunt and Liddy's hotel room. That same day, White House press secretary Ron Ziegler referred to the break-in as "a third-rate burglary attempt."[56] Three days later, the president assured the nation at a press conference that "the White House has had no involvement in this particular incident."

Technically speaking, that may have been true, but the break-in was part of a secret CREEP information-gathering campaign code-named "Gemstone." On two occasions in the spring of 1972, Liddy, prodded by John Dean to develop political intelligence programs, had presented to campaign chief Mitchell, second-in-command Magruder, and Dean a wide variety of operations for which he needed $1 million. Liddy, an assertive former FBI agent, was, according to another CREEP official, "a Hitler but at least he's our Hitler." Mitchell, who had a difficult time saying no to any of his aides and who was preoccupied with his ill wife, told Liddy to "tone it down a little" and lower the costs.[57] On 29 March 1972, he finally approved Liddy's new seven-point program that would cost only $250,000. The seventh point was a break-in at the DNC.

Liddy's operatives first broke into the DNC on 28 May, after abortive attempts on the two previous nights, and photographed documents and planted listening devices on the phones of DNC chair Lawrence O'Brien and executive director of the Association of State Democratic Chairmen R. Spencer Oliver. Returning on 17 June apparently to remove or perhaps improve on the bugs, the burglars were caught. Liddy's team had also tried and failed to break into McGovern's headquarters late in May.

To this day, it remains uncertain what Liddy and Hunt were looking for at the DNC, and no one has claimed direct responsibility for ordering the break-in. Even Colson, who apparently told all that he knew about Nixon's White House after he became a born-again Christian, did not know what the operation was all about, aside from trying to discover what the Democrats were up to and what O'Brien may have had on the Republicans.

As early as March 1970, Nixon had expressed interest in establishing "Operation O'Brien."[58] His concerns did not just involve political intelligence. Millionaire industrialist Howard Hughes had paid O'Brien, then a lobbyist, a retainer of $100,000 a year as one of his clients. The president may have thought that O'Brien had information about Hughes's 1956 $205,000 loan to Nixon's brother, Donald. That loan may have led then Vice President Nixon to influence an IRS ruling favorable to Hughes's enterprises. Worried about the political damage his "poor damn, dumb brother" might do to him, Nixon had asked the CIA to keep him under surveillance almost as soon as he became president.[59] When the agency refused, Ehrlichman ordered the Secret Service to accept the task.

Furthermore, Nixon had received an illegal contribution of $100,000 from Hughes through Bebe Rebozo after the 1968 campaign. O'Brien could have learned about the contribution through his Hughes connection. Nixon may have feared as well that the Democrat had information linking him to anti-Castro plots, again through a convoluted Hughes connection, and perhaps that O'Brien had documents relating to the ITT scandal that involved the administration's efforts to assist in the corporation's conflict with the antitrust division of the Justice Department. In January 1971, Nixon told Haldeman, the "time is approaching when L. O'Brien is held accountable for his retainer with Hughes."[60] Even after the break-in, Nixon continued his offensive against O'Brien and ordered an IRS investigation, hoping not only to find something on him—"hardly anyone is really clean" when it comes to taxes—but also to glean political intelligence from O'Brien's subpoenaed files.[61]

O'Brien later revealed that he had no secret documents concerning the Hughes loan or contribution. He also reported that his personal apartment had been burglarized on two occasions and documents had been stolen. He labeled as "preposterous" the theory promoted by Haldeman and others that the Democrats knew about the Watergate break-in in advance and set CREEP up for the 17 June arrests.[62]

In September 1971, Hank Greenspun, publisher of the *Las Vegas Sun*, revealed that he had information in his safe relating to the 1968 Hughes contribution that had been stolen by Robert Maheu, a renegade former Hughes official. Greenspun, who was a friend of Jack Anderson, claimed that someone broke into his office in August 1972. Liddy had included intelligence operations against Greenspun in his Gemstone plan.

Conspiracy theorists offer other possible explanations. E. Howard Hunt was a friend of Bob Bennett, the head of the public-relations firm Robert R. Mullen Company and the son of Senator Wallace Bennett (R-Utah). The Mullen Company took over the Hughes account when O'Brien returned to politics. The company was most likely working with the CIA. Hughes was the agency's largest civilian contractor. Because of this linkage, several analysts concluded that Hunt, perhaps with McCord, was engaged in a CIA plot either to gather its own intelligence or even to bring down the Nixon administration by purposefully botching the DNC break-in.

A somewhat more far-fetched theory revolves around John Dean, whom Gerald Ford considered a "young man on the make" in the Nixon White House.[63] Dean, who knew about the break-in, also allegedly knew that somewhere in DNC headquarters, perhaps Oliver's desk, was a little black book with the names of high-priced call girls who had been referred to visiting Democratic officials. Heidi Rikan, a prominent madam who had done business with the DNC, was not only a friend of Dean's fiancee,

Maureen Biner, but had also shared Biner's address for a while. According to this theory, Dean organized the break-in to erase all traces of his fiancee's name from the black book, where she may have been listed under the code name "Clout."

Whatever the reason, the break-in appeared to be if not a third-rate burglary then merely one failure among the many successful CREEP and White House operations to guarantee a Nixon victory. The president brushed off its potential impact four days after the arrests, noting, "I think the country doesn't give much of a shit when somebody bugs somebody else, you see."[64]

It is difficult to determine the impact of the administration's extensive and unprecedented intelligence, counterintelligence, and dirty-tricks campaigns on the Democratic Party's nomination process. After a relatively weak showing in New Hampshire and his failure in Florida, Muskie faded quickly. Soon, the two most successful candidates in the primaries were Wallace and McGovern. Following Wallace's withdrawal from the race in May, the way was clear for McGovern, especially after he won the California primary in June, to take the nomination on 14 July at the Democratic Party convention in Miami.

McGovern, whom Robert Kennedy once called "the most decent man in the Senate," was an uncharismatic former World War II bomber pilot with a Ph.D. in history who had served the Kennedy administration as director of the Food for Peace program and had been senator from South Dakota since 1963.[65] Coming from the left wing of his party, he was an outspoken opponent of American involvement in Vietnam but by no means the radical he eventually came to be painted by Republicans. Nixon considered him "guilty by association by bringing in Abbie Hoffman, Jerry Rubin, Angela Davis. We should get a maximum number of pictures of rowdy people around McGovern, while we go for the all-out-square America."[66]

The senator hoped to defeat Nixon by "appealing to the decency and common sense of the American people," but after Hugh Scott's label began to stick to him—"The candidate of the 3 A's: acid, abortion, and amnesty"—he found it difficult to win over mainstream America, even right and centrist Democrats.[67] The candidate was not helped by the chaotic Democratic Convention, where "passions ran high" among the stop-McGovern forces and where McGovern regretted that television viewers "saw a lot of aggressive women . . . militant blacks . . . long-haired kids."[68] Delegates nominated thirty-nine people for vice president, including Martha Mitchell and Mao Zedong. The long, drawn-out process of nominating a vice president resulted in the Democratic standard-bearer having to deliver his acceptance speech to a very small television audience at 2:48 in the morning on 15 July. His theme was "come home America. . . . From a conflict in Indochina which maims our ideals as well as our soldiers. . . . From military spending so wasteful it weakens the nation. . . . From the waste of idle hands to the joy of useful labor, come home America."[69]

Most modern presidential candidates have received a "bounce" in the polls after their conventions. McGovern's numbers fell. And so began a campaign that for national campaign manager O'Brien was the "three worst months of my life . . . a nightmare."[70]

Aside from his other problems, McGovern left the convention with a ticking time bomb, his running mate Senator Thomas Eagleton of Missouri. A week after the convention ended, Jack Anderson wrote a column revealing that Eagleton had earlier suffered a nervous breakdown for which he had received shock therapy. Several days later, McGovern's press secretary issued a statement under the candidate's name proclaiming he was "1,000 percent for Tom Eagleton." Because of the chaos at the convention, McGovern had made only a perfunctory check of his running mate's record, and Eagleton had not volunteered information about his medical history. Four days after his 1,000 percent affirmation—after it turned out that many Americans were nervous about having someone like Eagleton the proverbial heartbeat away from the presidency—McGovern pressured him to withdraw. The abrupt reversal undermined McGovern. He felt that the Eagleton affair "destroyed any chance" of his being elected.[71]

McGovern had an even more humiliating experience when he tried to find a replacement for Eagleton. Refused by virtually all prominent candidates, McGovern settled on R. Sargent Shriver, Johnson's head of the OEO, who was married to Edward Kennedy's sister Eunice.

Far behind in the polls from the start, McGovern's chances became even dimmer as voters read about his inefficient and mismanaged campaign. Although almost all the journalists who followed McGovern liked him personally and almost all of them voted for him, they tried to be as unbiased as possible in their coverage. Moreover, the Democratic nominee's campaign was the only game in town for aggressive reporters searching for gossip about internal conflict. Like many incumbents, Nixon practiced a remote Rose Garden strategy, venturing out from the White House on only five occasions and rarely meeting with the press.

The press was not McGovern's main problem. Just as many liberal Democrats had refused to work for or even endorse Hubert Humphrey in 1968, many moderate and conservative Democrats sat out McGovern's campaign. For example, although Lyndon Johnson ultimately tepidly supported McGovern, Billy Graham claimed that the former president used him as a conduit to give Nixon campaign advice. Further, even though he had broken with the administration over wage and price controls, George Meany told Nixon that he would sit out the election. The powerful union chief refused to spend any of the AFL-CIO's $6 million campaign fund on McGovern's election.

McGovern has subsequently complained that no one listened to him when he warned on 4 October 1972 that the "Nixon Administration is the most corrupt Administration in our national history."[72] On 29 August 1972, referring to a fictitious John Dean internal investigation on Watergate, Nixon had assured a news conference, "I can state categorically that no one in the White House staff, no one in this administration, presently employed, was involved in this very bizarre incident. . . . What really hurts is if you try to cover it up." During the campaign, the administration successfully contained and covered up the Watergate scandal, despite the fact that Hunt, Liddy, and the five burglars were indicted on 15 September. The administration was helped immeasurably when U.S. District Court chief judge John J. Sirica announced a gag order until after the election, when the case would be heard.

On 20 June, after learning from the *Washington Post* about James McCord's link to the White House, O'Brien had filed a $1 million damage suit against CREEP on behalf of the Democratic Party that could have resulted in the Democrats gaining access to CREEP's files in discovery. One week after Sirica's gag order, U.S. District Court judge Charles R. Richey sealed the depositions taken in the O'Brien investigation and postponed hearing the case until after the election. Dean later testified that Richey had consulted with the administration about the break-in during the period in question.

Congress posed a greater threat of exposing the Watergate affair before the election. At the end of August, the chairman of the House Banking and Currency Committee, Wright Patman (D-Tex.), demanded hearings to examine the murky financial dealings surrounding the Watergate principals that had begun to appear in the press. The administration set about to frustrate Patman, relying on House Minority Leader Ford. On 15 September, Nixon told Haldeman and Dean that "Jerry is really got to lead on this. . . . He's got to really lead . . . tell Eh[rlichman] to get [Garry] Brown [R-Mich.] in and Ford in, and then they can all work out something."[73] As part of his strategy, Nixon refused to permit his aides to appear before the committee and then blocked Patman's attempt to obtain subpoena power to compel their testimony. A coalition of Republicans and southern Democrats composed a twenty-to-fifteen majority to deny Patman subpoena power. As a result, no one of significance showed up at his hearings. Colson reported, "I talked to Ford directly [about the Patman strategy]. It was pure politics." But Ford denied during his vice-presidential confirmation hearings that he had discussed the committee's activities with the White House.[74]

In September, only 52 percent of those polled had ever heard of Watergate, despite periodic news items appearing in the *Washington Post* and the *New York Times*. Most Americans, and in fact, most journalists, had concluded that it was of little interest, especially considering the Sirica and Richey rulings and the failure of the Patman committee to shed light on the matter. During the late summer of 1972, only 15 of the 430 reporters in Washington worked on the Watergate story, only NBC assigned a reporter to the story full-time, and the *Chicago Tribune* ran no Watergate story on its front pages until the end of August. *Washington Post* publisher Katherine Graham asked her editor, "If this is such a good (blank) story, where is the rest of the press."[75]

The administration's assault against the press had something to do with why most newspapers and television stations paid scant attention to Watergate. On one occasion, Colson convinced CBS chair William Paley to shorten the second part of a series on Watergate. For its efforts to pursue the story, the *Washington Post* became the administration's special target. The president told Haldeman and Dean on 15 September that the *Post* is "going to have problems. . . . The main thing is the *Post* is going to have damnable problems out of this one. They have a television station . . . and they're going to have to get it renewed."[76] And sure enough, when renewal time came around in January, the only license challenges among thirty Florida stations up for renewal were directed at the two *Post*-owned stations. Those challenges affected the value of the corporation's stock.

The threats were even more direct. John Mitchell warned the *Post*'s Carl Bernstein early in October that publisher "Katie Graham's gonna get her tit caught in a big fat wringer if that's [a Watergate story] published."[77] After Nixon left the presidency, Bob Woodward presented Graham with a wooden laundry wringer as a memento of the occasion.

By the end of the campaign, newspaper publishers had endorsed Nixon by a 753-to-56 count. No wonder a frustrated George McGovern lost his patience in Battle Creek, Michigan, when he told a heckler in an airport crowd, "I've got a secret for you. Kiss my ass?"[78]

He would have been even more upset had he known that Nixon ordered Murray Chotiner to lead a three-person team to look for "bad apples" among McGovern's donors and friends and not to "be soft on the Jews."[79] The initiative was part of a program begun in the fall of 1971 to have the

IRS investigate big Jewish contributors to the Democrats. One problem, according to Nixon, was that "the IRS is full of Jews."[80]

In July 1970, Tom Huston had complained to Haldeman that "we don't have any reliable political friends at IRS."[81] Nixon finally removed the unresponsive head of the agency, Randolph Thrower, a Republican, in early 1971 and replaced him with Johnnie Walters. Dean told Walters that he had a "firm requirement and responsibility" to make investigations for the administration.[82] Those to be investigated were political opponents whose names appeared on several different updated "enemies lists" or, as one staffer referred to them, "bad guys list[s]."[83]

Although administration defenders explained that such lists were maintained merely to make certain that the wrong people did not get invited to the White House, Nixon clearly did not have that in mind when he asked Haldeman in November 1970 to compile a list of opponents in the media, the arts, Congress, and the eastern establishment and to develop "an intelligent program . . . to take them on."[84] Among the hundreds of people who appeared on lists compiled by Dean, Colson, Huston, and others were entertainment figures Bill Cosby, Paul Newman, Barbra Streisand, and Gregory Peck; journalists Mort Kondracke, Richard Rovere, and Tom Wicker; academics Arthur Schlesinger, Jr., J. Kenneth Galbraith, and Yale president Kingman Brewster; New York Jets quarterback Joe Namath; and scores of Democratic politicians. Also making the lists were organizations such as the Ford Foundation.

Conceding that this activity was "sleazy and sophomoric," speechwriter Ray Price claims that Nixon never saw the lists and that the IRS, especially when Shultz was secretary of the treasury, resisted pressure to audit enemies.[85] In fact, when Dean told the president in September 1972 that Shultz was not being cooperative with his IRS investigations, Nixon threatened that after the election "the whole Goddamn bunch [IRS would] go out" and that Shultz would be "out as Secretary of the Treasury."[86]

Whether Nixon ever saw the lists, he was aware that the IRS's Special Services staff did investigate many of his "enemies" among the 8,500 individuals and 2,900 groups and institutions targeted by the administration. Nixon wanted to "use our power" with the IRS the same way the Democrats had used the agency against him and other Republicans (as he claimed—to some degree correctly).[87]

Nixon's path to the nomination was relatively easy. He faced token opposition from the Left from Pete McCloskey and from the Right from Ohio representative John Ashbrook. McCloskey, whom Buchanan portrayed as a "Democratic tool" backed by "New York Jewish money and California fat cat money," peaked in New Hampshire when he took 20 percent of the vote.[88]

The White House meticulously managed a four-day coronation ceremony at its Miami convention in August. According to Nixon aide David Gergen, campaign organizers "actually provided, down to the minute, a script for the whole convention," including "spontaneous" demonstrations and moments for applause.[89] Further, the media-savvy Republicans established a format that forced the networks to carry their propaganda films. Few Americans seemed concerned when the script was leaked to the press before the convention took place.

During 1971 and into 1972, Nixon talked frequently of wanting to drop Vice President Agnew, whom he considered a bothersome lightweight, for John Connally. Haldeman told the outspoken Agnew early on, "The President does not like you to take an opposite view at a cabinet meeting or say anything that can be construed to be mildly not in accord with his thinking."[90] Nixon preferred to keep him out of his sight, sending him on meaningless foreign trips. On a one-month Asian tour, Agnew was able to play golf thirteen times. Yet the colorful vice president was so popular with the Silent Majority that Nixon found it expedient to select him as his running mate once again. But, he maintained, "he's not the one for '76 but we may be stuck w/him—We will not help him."[91]

Antiwar protesters and other radicals appeared in Miami Beach to mar the well-orchestrated proceedings, with the police compelled to use tear gas against them on 23 August. The "Last Patrol" of more than 1,000 VVAW members created the largest stir, particularly Ron Kovic, Bobby Muller, and Bill Wyman, three disabled veterans who were able to get into the auditorium to stage a brief protest, shouting "Stop the Bombing, Stop the War." The Secret Service quickly ejected them before the script needed to be altered. Throughout the campaign, when unruly dissenters confronted Nixon or his surrogates with shouts and chants, they were often thrown out of meeting halls extralegally, either by the local police or by campaign staffers, who in many cases violated the protesters' First Amendment rights.

In his acceptance speech on 23 August, delivered according to the script in prime time, Nixon responded to McGovern's "come home America theme" with, "To those millions who have been driven out of their home in the Democratic party we say come home . . . not to another party, but . . . to the great principles we Americans believe in together . . . members of a new American majority bound together by our common ideas."

Nixon left the convention holding a 69 to 30 percent lead over McGovern in the polls. In an attempt to win as massive a victory in November as possible, preparatory to introducing his "New American Revolution" that would loosen the liberals' stranglehold on the political system, Nixon went well beyond the usual fund-raising techniques to swamp the Democrats, especially with television and radio advertising.[92] In addition, he opposed the party check-off provision on IRS forms in the Tax Reform Act of 1971 that would have enhanced the public financing of elections and helped the perennially broke DNC. He approved the provision for the 1976 election, too late to help McGovern. During the 1972 campaign, the South Dakota senator raised $38 million to Nixon's $60 million.

On 7 February 1972, Nixon did sign a Federal Election Campaign Act, which limited expenditures for media (a provision ruled unconstitutional in *Buckley v. Valeo* in 1976), placed ceilings on contributions by candidates and their families, and provided for disclosure of contributors' names. The law was to become effective on 7 April. During the sixty-day interval, CREEP operatives raised $20 million. They also backdated checks that came in after the disclosure deadline.

In the most elaborate fund-raising program in presidential election history to that date, Kalmbach and his aides not only established a "tithing" system for companies doing business with the government but also advised them how to skirt campaign finance laws. Kalmbach, for example, told soon-to-become New York Yankees owner and head of the American Shipbuilding Company George Steinbrenner how much was expected of him— $100,000—and also how to circumvent the campaign finance laws by making his contribution appear as thirty-three individual contributions of $3,000 from his employees. For participating in that activity, Steinbrenner received a $15,000 fine, and the baseball commissioner suspended him from team ownership for two years. Kalmbach received a six- to eighteen-month sentence for such activities, and former secretary of commerce Maurice Stans, chair of CREEP's financial committee, received a fine. Stans and Mitchell were acquitted of charges that they accepted $250,000 from financier Robert Vesco in exchange for assistance with the Securities and Exchange Commission, which was investigating his affairs. Among other corporations found guilty of making illegal contributions were American Airlines, Goodyear, Braniff Airlines, Ashland Oil, Phillips Petroleum, Gulf Oil, and Minnesota Mining and Manufacturing.

In an even more celebrated case of apparently trading campaign contributions for political favors, the administration's policy on price supports for milk seemed to have been influenced by the promise of a large contribution from the Milk Producer's Association. On 11 March 1971, Secretary of Agriculture Hardin announced that there would be no change in the current price-support policy. Nixon met with milk lobbyists on 23 March. Two days later, Hardin reversed the policy to permit a support hike. Nixon, who considered the dairymen's organization the "best and most efficient lobby in America," maintained that he reversed Hardin's decision because it was the "right thing to do."[93] He explained at a press conference on 17 November 1973 that he had raised the price supports because "Congress put a gun to our head" and would have overridden any veto of its own more generous bill to increase them.

CREEP collected $85,000 from the dairymen's lobby before the price increase and $322,500 from the lobby after the increase was announced. Campaign aides explained to the lobbyists how to "launder" their gifts by designating them to dummy committees. After an investigation and a trial, Connally, Hardin, and most of the others involved were cleared of criminal charges.

Jack Anderson broke an even more sensational story in February 1972 during Richard Kleindienst's confirmation hearings to become attorney general. The muckraking columnist published a memo from Dita Beard, a lobbyist for the ITT corporation ("a total bitch," according to Nixon), that outlined a deal made by the Justice Department the previous July to go easy on an antitrust case in exchange for a contribution to the city of San Diego to help finance the Republican convention.[94] The FBI could not confirm administration charges that the letter was a forgery. An ailing Beard, interviewed in her hospital room by the ubiquitous E. Howard Hunt wearing a disguise, denied authorship of the memo.

Nixon, who considered Richard McLaren, the head of the antitrust division, a "son-of-a bitch" captive of the antitrusters, opposed the suit against ITT.[95] Asserting on 19 April 1971 that "there is not going to be any more antitrust actions as long as I am in this chair," Nixon pressured Mitchell to settle with the corporation and drop the suit.[96] ITT had already won three cases against the government in lower courts, and the final settlement represented a compromise that led to some divestiture. The scandal led the Republicans to move the convention to Miami Beach. Kleindienst, who misled the Senate during his confirmation hearings, pleaded guilty to a misdemeanor for not having testified fully about his contact with the president concerning the ITT suit. The first former attorney general to have pleaded guilty to a crime received a one-month suspended sentence and a fine that was also suspended.

In previous campaigns, contributors were often rewarded with ambassadorships, but in no previous campaign was this activity undertaken with a specific price for each posting. Nixon asserted in the summer of 1971 that "anybody who wants to be an ambassador must at least give $250,000."[97] Dr. Ruth Farkas, when told by Kalmbach how much her husband, a department store magnate, would have to contribute, complained, "Isn't two hundred and fifty thousand an awful lot of money for Costa Rica?"[98] She was happy to pay $300,000 for Luxembourg. Senator Gale W. McGee (D-Wyo.) made light of the affair, noting, "The money—that's par for the course. It used to be a cheaper price—but that's Nixon's inflation."[99] Nonetheless, in 1974, Kalmbach pleaded guilty to promising federal employment for contributions and received a six-month sentence that ran concurrent with his other sentence. He may have overpromised; as late as April 1973, an aide reported that he "continue[d] to get extensive pressure from heavy contributors who had expected some kind of indication by now as to whether they would be nominated as Ambassadors."[100]

While collecting funds from supporters, the administration targeted particular regions and groups for special attention during 1972 in a "Departmental Responsiveness" program.[101] As part of the program, staffers convinced the chair of the EEOC not to pursue a suit against the University of Texas, ordered the Labor Department to award a $2.2 million grant to a Texas group dealing with migrant labor, and introduced a "Key State Unemployment Project" to increase federal jobs in electoral vote–laden states such as California.

Moreover, Nixon's economic program had improved things just in time for the election. The first new hefty Social Security checks were sent out in October, whereas the payroll tax increase to pay for them did not appear in wage earners' paychecks until January. Continuing the themes of the 1968 election, Nixon explained in the spring of 1972 that the "'gut' issues would be crime, busing, drugs, welfare, inflation."[102] Taking note of Wallace's strength in the North, he told Ehrlichman to "zero in on the busing issue," especially in Michigan, and announced his support for a constitutional amendment against busing that he knew had no chance of being approved.[103] Farmers were pleased with the Russian grain deal announced during the summer of the election year. And while there were still more registered Democrats than Republicans, Nixon's campaign literature rarely mentioned his party affiliation. McGovern played down his party affiliation as well.

A confident Nixon appealed once again to the Silent Majority on 21 October: "I have seen the will of the majority in action, responding to a call to responsibility, to honor, and to sacrifice. . . . I speak with pride of the 'new majority' that is forming not around a man or a party but around a set of principles that is deep in the American spirit."

When Kissinger announced on 26 October that "peace is at hand" in Vietnam, he took away the hapless McGovern's only real issue. On 7 November, Nixon and Agnew won the election by a 61 to 38 percent margin in the popular vote and lost only Massachusetts and the District of Columbia in the electoral college. In 1973, when the administration began to unravel over the Watergate affair, automobile bumper stickers began to appear proclaiming, "Don't blame me, I'm from Massachusetts."

Despite Nixon's smashing victory, the Republicans lost two seats in the Senate and gained only twelve in the House. (Two of the Democratic seats in the House were won by Andrew Young from Georgia and Barbara Jordan from Texas, the first African Americans elected from the South since Reconstruction.) Of course, the administration had devoted most of its energies and its overflowing war chest to CREEP, not the RNC. The Democratic majorities on Capitol Hill would make it difficult for Nixon to pull off his vaunted New American Revolution in 1973. Although not recognized at the time, those majorities proved to be crucial to sustain the vigorous prosecution of the variety of charges against the president that came to be known as Watergate. In an eerie prefiguration of investigations during the Clinton administration, the majority Democrats were able to fend off Republican demands to investigate all campaign dirty tricks and illegal fund-raising, despite the fact that Humphrey and Muskie, among others, had accepted tainted contributions.

But in November 1972, in the wake of Nixon's greatest political victory, no one gave much thought to Watergate. In a few short months, the president—and the American people—would have to confront the seventh and most serious crisis of Nixon's public life.

10

★ ★ ★ ★ ★

WATERGATE

Richard Nixon claimed to thrive on crises. However, once he surmounted them, he could not enjoy his success. Such was the case following his smashing 1972 electoral triumph. The morning after the election, Nixon met first with Haldeman, Ehrlichman, and his other chief aides, and then with cabinet secretaries. Instead of reveling in the moment, and characteristic of his inability to directly fire anyone, the president, after talking perfunctorily about the great projects ahead, had Haldeman ask everyone for their formal resignations. Nixon planned a wholesale reorganization of government on his way to creating the New American Revolution during his second term. The first step was to take control of the government from the bureaucrats. He lashed out that same day: "Mitchell was captured by the bureaucacy.... Rogers was totally captured.... Mel Laird, he didn't change anybody.... The people who ran the Pentagon before are still running the goddam Pentagon. ... HEW, the whole damn bunch. ... Let's remember the VA—Clean those bastards out. ... Take that Park Service, they've been screwing us for years. Rog Morton won't get rid of that son-of-a-bitch. But he's got to go."[1]

Nixon later realized that suddenly calling for everyone's resignation in the wake of his overwhelming victory was "a mistake" because it created a morale problem.[2] Bryce Harlow wished that Nixon had spoken to him the day after the election. Haldeman, Ehrlichman, and Nixon "were up there planning the future of the Administration as though they were in Berchtesgaden. I had the feeling they had lost their bearings."[3] Although Nixon acted rashly in asking for everyone's resignation so swiftly after winning the election, this was no impetuous decision. He had promised the previous March "the most comprehensive and carefully planned . . . reorganization since the executive was first constituted in George Washington's administration 183 years ago."[4]

On 27 November, Nixon explained to the nation his approach to recruiting for his second administration. History had shown that "a second administration usually lacks . . . vitality . . . because when an individual . . . holds any position in Government, after a certain length of time he becomes an advocate of the status quo; rather than running the bureaucracy, the bureaucracy runs him." Between 28 November and 22 December, Nixon announced fifty-seven resignations and eighty-seven other personnel decisions, which included the nomination of six new cabinet officials. Most interesting, he dispatched White House staffers to departments in undersecretary or assistant secretary roles, including Krogh to the Treasury, Whitaker to Interior, and Frank Carlucci to HEW. In all, the administration assigned over 100 people from the White House, OMB, and CREEP to departments in another attempt to gain control of the bureaucracy. The trouble, according to Ehrlichman, was that even those loyalists "go off and marry the natives."[5] After shaking up the departments, four months into his second term, Nixon still complained, "We have no discipline in this bureaucracy. We never fire anybody. We never reprimand anybody. . . . We always promote the sons-of-bitches that kick us in the ass."[6]

Aside from changes in personnel, Nixon also hoped to reduce the size of government by slashing the budget 6.5 percent in 1973–74 and 16.3 percent the following year in "a historical turning point."[7] In part, this reflected a return to a less expansive economic policy with which he was more philosophically comfortable. But he seriously believed in the need to cut the number of federal employees, which had grown from 2.4 million to 3 million since 1961. He hoped to eliminate 4,250 executive department positions in 1973–74 and earmark another 1,696 for reduction the next fiscal year. A good number of those proposed reductions came from OEO and other areas of the executive branch he expected to dismantle.

Nixon also wanted to implement the Ash commission recommendation to reduce the eleven departments to seven—and from those seven to create four super secretaries who would spend half their time in the White House and half their time in their new consolidated departments. They would run departments of Community Development (HUD), Human Resources (HEW, Labor), Economic Affairs (Transportation, Commerce), and Natural Resources (Agriculture, Interior). But before Nixon could present his dramatic reorganization plan to Congress, his two chief domestic aides,

Haldeman and Ehrlichman, were forced to resign, and he became immobilized by the Watergate affair. At that point, according to Alexander Haig, who replaced Haldeman as chief of staff, everything "shuddered to a halt" for a month or so while the White House reorganized itself.[8] The administration never recovered from the departures of Haldeman and Ehrlichman. It certainly became a more disorderly operation, even with the strong-willed Haig in charge, as aides ignored the instructions of their preoccupied president and tried to "advance their own agendas."[9]

During his second administration, Nixon had also planned to expand the management role of the OMB. To accomplish this task, he appointed Roy Ash to head the office, with Fred Malek as his second in command. Ash's importance increased after Ehrlichman's resignation, when Ken Cole, who took over the Domestic Council, proved to be no match for Ash in administrative infighting. Ash viewed himself as the dominant figure on domestic affairs during Nixon's last twelve months in office. Haig claims that he, not Ash, was the "point man" in charge of domestic politics and that while the OMB director was "creative," he was not a "bare-knuckle" politico. More important, Haig maintains that Nixon "could not stand him."[10]

In 1973, concerned about the growth in power of the OMB, Congress passed a bill requiring senatorial approval for Ash's and Malek's positions. Nixon's veto of the bill was sustained. In 1974, in a compromise of sorts, Congress accepted Nixon's right to appoint Ash and Malek but insisted that future OMB appointments had to be approved by the Senate.

Nixon's most important staff change in 1973 was his nomination of Kissinger in August to replace Rogers at the State Department. Kissinger also maintained his portfolio at the NSC. The president had been prepared to fire him at the end of 1972, because he believed that Kissinger had disobeyed instructions during the Vietnam negotiations and had also leaked information to friends in the media. Further, Kissinger had participated in an interview, which he later called "the single most disastrous conversation I ever had with any member of the press," in which, referring to himself, he stated, "Americans admire the cowboy leading the caravan alone astride his horse, the cowboy entering the village or city alone on his horse. Without even a pistol, maybe."[11] When Nixon read the interview, he told Colson, "He's going back to Harvard; that's where he belongs. I've put up with everything I am going to put up with. This is the end."[12]

Above all, Nixon was displeased that Kissinger had eclipsed him in popularity. The national security adviser had his own statue in Madame Tussaud's London Wax Museum, and Miss Universe finalists had designated him "the most outstanding world figure." But Kissinger was saved by Watergate. By the time Nixon was prepared to replace him, preferably with John Connally or Kenneth Rush, the president was so weakened by the scandal that the firing of the most popular and seemingly indispensable member of his administration became impossible. Instead, Nixon appointed Kissinger to Rogers's post, telling the world at a press conference that he would be the first secretary of state since World War II who did not part his hair in the middle. He also could have said that he was the first secretary of state who spoke with a foreign accent. Nixon once told Israeli prime minister Golda Meir, "We both have Jewish foreign ministers." She replied, "Yes, but mine [Abba Eban] speaks English without an accent."[13]

In staffing his second administration, Nixon searched for candidates who fit into "New Majority categories."[14] These included representatives from labor, Italians, Poles, and Hispanic Americans, who were supporting Republicans in ever-increasing numbers. On Nixon's orders, his inaugural planners made certain that such people were in evidence on the reviewing stand, with eleven old people, twelve blacks, ten veterans, nine labor figures, and thirteen ethnics alloted positions.

John Scali, an Italian American who became UN ambassador, and Peter Brennan, an Irish American labor leader who became secretary of labor, reflected this approach. This new quota system proceeded "at the cost of alienating Cabinet officers and agency heads." By the end of July 1973, the White House was "again staffing positions with the best candidates available" without much concern for their ethnicity.[15] William Simon was a case in point. Nixon had opposed Shultz's decision to make Simon deputy secretary of the treasury in 1972, saying, "I don't want any more of those Eastern Cadillac liberals."[16] Yet Nixon appointed Simon head of the Federal Energy Office in late 1973 and secretary of the treasury when Shultz left in May 1974.

Even with the wholesale reorganization and staffing changes, Nixon did not feel completely comfortable with his victory. Displeased with his press coverage, he directed his public-relations people to write or commission several monographs on the campaign, including one called "The Dirtiest Campaign in History against a President." They would point out that "RN [ran](one of the cleanest campaigns in history)."[17]

But all this was far off when Nixon strode to the podium at the Capitol to take the oath of office on 20 January 1973. Signaling the end of big government, he announced "the time has come to turn away from the condescending policies of paternalism—of Washington knows best. . . . Government must learn to take less from people so that people can do more for themselves." And then, sounding like his old nemesis John F. Kennedy, he proclaimed, "let each of us ask—not just what will government do for me, but what can I do for myself?"

He did not have much of an opportunity to bring about the New American Revolution. From 8 through 30 January, the seven men indicted for the Watergate burglary were on trial. The four Cubans and E. Howard Hunt pleaded guilty; a jury found Liddy and McCord guilty. On 7 February, the Senate voted to establish a select committee to investigate Watergate. The next day at a White House breakfast, a still confident Nixon told his cabinet and staff, "Seventy-three can be and should be the best year ever."[18]

Almost as soon as the words were out of his mouth, his administration began to unravel. During his abbreviated second term, Nixon still played an active role on the international scene, with the two Russian summits, involvement in the October 1973 war, and foreign travels. At home, however, Congress, the media, and the nation soon became obsessed with the Watergate break-in, his apparent cover-up, and a variety of other related activities that John Mitchell labeled "White House horrors" in Senate testimony. In 1971, Safire had written a memo to Haldeman, with a copy to Dean, asking, "Why don't we make more of the fact that ours is a scandal-free Administration?"[19] Over the next eighteen months, the Nixon administration would be revealed to be the most scandal-ridden administration in American history. And those scandals did not involve merely the looting of the public treasury by public officials, as had occurred during the Grant and Harding administrations, or the irresponsible and reckless sexual peccadilloes of John F. Kennedy and Bill Clinton. They revolved around a variety of illegal and extralegal political actions directed by the president and his chief assistants, including the former attorney general of the United States, that attempted to subvert the American political system.

In a defense of the administration, Victor Lasky wrote *It Didn't Start with Watergate*, a book replete with examples of other presidents committing many of the same crimes and misdemeanors that Nixon committed, including illegal wiretapping and using federal agencies for political intelligence.[20] But whereas some presidents participated in some of those illegal activities much of the time, and others did almost all of them on occasion, none of them committed all the illegal acts that constituted Watergate all the time.

Another defense of the administration revolves around special measures the White House must take to protect national security during wartime. According to John Taylor, who was director of the Nixon Library,

Nixon was a "war president." The nation was under siege from within and without, and he had to act accordingly to protect national security.[21]

Conceding errors in judgment during the Watergate affair, Nixon himself points to his overall record with pride. "We did all the big things right and we screwed up the goddam little things," he told actor Jimmy Cagney after he left the presidency.[22] To Nixon, the break-in, the cover-up, and the hard-ball politics were insignificant compared to his overall performance as president. James Roosevelt told Rose Mary Woods that "everything they ever accuse him of, Father did twice as much of." Another old New Dealer, Thomas Corcoran, remarked, "The trouble with your fellows is that they're always writing memos. When we did those things we never put it on paper."[23] Nor did they put it on tape.

The problem of defending the administration is compounded by the existence of those infamous tapes on which the president suggests or approves illegal schemes, often in an extremely crude and vindictive fashion. It is difficult after listening to the tapes or reading the transcripts to emerge with much admiration for Richard Nixon as a person. His predecessor, a notoriously foul-mouthed, dissembling, bullying politician, also taped many of his conversations. Yet Lyndon Johnson sounded like a principled and good-humored gentleman compared with the perpetually dark and hateful Nixon.

Nixon's defenders contend that one should not take literally much of what he said on the tapes; he was merely blowing off steam and thinking out loud, as demonstrated by the fact that many of his orders were not carried out. But some of those orders were carried out, and saying that he was merely blowing off steam does not excuse the racial and religious slurs that littered his conversations.

His foul language was another problem. Although he rarely if ever used the "f" word in private conversation, he did use other profanities such as "shit" and "son of a bitch" frequently. During the 1960 presidential debates, he had attacked former President Truman for using intemperate language in public and promised that as president he would set a higher standard. Nixon did speak decorously in public as president, never for a moment imagining that his private, locker-room conversations would ever be heard.

Nixon was not the first to covertly tape conversations in the White House. Franklin Roosevelt had a device hidden in a lamp on his desk in the Oval Office that he used occasionally, mostly before 1941, to maintain a more accurate historical record. Truman made a few test recordings but had his system dismantled. Eisenhower did a bit more taping, explaining, "There are some guys I just don't trust in Washington, and I want to have myself protected so that they can't later report that I said something else."[24] Nixon, who found out about Eisenhower's system in 1954, was one of those whom the president taped. Kennedy selectively taped more than 200 hours of White House conversations, unbeknownst to most of those taped. Johnson maintained a taping system in the Oval Office and the Cabinet Room, about which several of his aides had knowledge.

After Nixon toured the White House in December 1968, he ordered Johnson's system dismantled. However, he had second thoughts and set up his own taping system on 16 February 1971. From then until 18 July 1973, roughly 4,000 hours of presidential meetings and phone conversations were taped from the Oval Office, the Cabinet Room, the Lincoln Sitting Room, the EOB, and Camp David.

Nixon began to tape primarily because of difficulties he encountered trying to keep accurate records of his conversations. He did not like the idea of having a note taker at important meetings, because he felt that such a person might inhibit aides and guests from talking freely. But records were needed. In June 1970, Haldeman had asked the respected and versatile linguist Vernon Walters, then a military attaché in Paris, if he would take notes at Nixon's meetings. Walters refused the job. Had he accepted, the president might not have had to resort to the taping system.

Nixon later explained that he needed the tapes for "my own record of the presidency."[25] Johnson had told him how useful his taping system had been in the preparation of his memoirs. Nixon may have been concerned about the sort of history his "rival," Henry Kissinger, would be writing after he left the administration. In a related vein, Nixon most likely felt that the tapes could serve as a way to keep his guests and aides honest, perhaps even to blackmail them, in a political sense, were they to cross him. He may also have seen some pecuniary advantage in owning what would become an extremely valuable historical artifact. The December 1969 Tax Reform Act had eliminated the deduction presidents could take for depositing their personal papers in archives. It did not mention tapes. Finally, three psychobiographers claim that he ordered the taping "to collect proof of adoration and power—as supplies for his narcissism."[26] Whatever one may think of that interpretation, the tapes fairly brim over with aides continually singing his praises and the notoriously insecure Nixon consistently seeking those praises.

The only people who knew about the taping system were Haldeman, his aides Larry Higby and Alexander Butterfield, and the Secret Service. Because Nixon was so physically clumsy—an absolute "klutz," according to Higby—the systems in the Oval Office, the EOB, and Camp David were sound-activated.[27] This meant that many conversations Nixon might not have wanted to tape were taped. It also explains why on some occasions he could be seen talking quietly into a curtain or a wall to avoid the ubiquitous machines that continued to run. But he did not muffle his voice often enough, as can be seen in the narrative of the Watergate scandal that follows, much of which is based on taped conversations. The tapes offer irrefutable evidence of the crimes and misdemeanors in which President Nixon was involved.

On 17 June 1972, the day of the break-in, Nixon was vacationing in the Bahamas on Walker's Cay, owned by his wealthy friend Robert Abplanalp. When he first read about the break-in in the *Miami Herald* on 18 June, he thought it was "preposterous." However, he "could not muster much moral outrage over a political bugging."[28] Although several of his aides later claimed that one should not dismiss the possibility that he knew about or even ordered the break-in, the evidence suggests otherwise.

Once Nixon discovered the links between the burglars, CREEP, and the White House, he, along with Dean, Haldeman, and Ehrlichman, began to cover up the affair. He explained, "My motive was pure political containment. And political containment is not a corrupt motive."[29] He had many reasons to organize a cover-up, not the least of which was to protect his reelection chances. In addition, he expressed concern about protecting his old friend John Mitchell, whom he suspected had ordered the break-in. Four days after the arrests, he told his aides that although it would be best to come out with the truth or to make Liddy the fall guy, "If it involved Mitchell, then I would think that you couldn't do it, just because it would destroy him."[30] On 1 July, Mitchell resigned from CREEP, allegedly to care for his ailing wife.

Although Nixon never admitted it, the *Pentagon Papers* affair may have been at the bottom of the cover-up. He did know about the attempt to smear Ellsberg and either ordered or knew about the break-in at Ellsberg's psychiatrist's office. Once he discovered that some of those involved in Watergate were also involved in illegal Plumbers' activities, he feared that unless they maintained their silence, his presidency would be threatened. According to Nixon, the payments to them, which appeared to be hush money, were for "humanitarian purposes."[31]

The cover-up began to take shape when Nixon met with Haldeman on 20 June. Their taped conversation includes an eighteen-and-a-half-minute gap that caused a good deal of controversy when it later came to light. The strategy over the next few weeks involved keeping the White House out of the affair, limiting the investigation to the simple burglary, and paying money to assist those arrested with their legal defenses and to ensure their silence. On the last issue, Nixon mused as early as 20 June about getting Bebe Rebozo to find some way to raise funds for the four Cuban Americans who had been arrested on 17 June.

By the time Nixon and his colleagues began to try to contain the investigation, it had already gone too far. The FBI had traced some of the money the burglars had carried to a Miami bank, one link in a scheme to launder funds donated to CREEP through Mexican banks. In an attempt to call off the FBI, Haldeman explained to Nixon on 23 June, on what was later labeled the "smoking-gun" tape, how both Mitchell and Dean had hatched a plan—"the only way to solve this . . . is for us to have [deputy CIA director Vernon] Walters call [L.] Pat[rick] Gray [acting FBI chief] and just say, 'Stay the hell out of this . . . this is ah, business here we don't want you to go any further on it.'"[32] Nixon approved the cover story that the Cuban burglars had been involved in CIA activities in Mexico and had links to the 1961 Bay of Pigs invasion. Any release of information about the burglars' activities beyond the break-in would jeopardize national security and, according to Nixon, "be very unfortunate for the CIA." When Haldeman told Richard Helms about the problem, the CIA director exclaimed, "The Bay of Pigs had nothing to do with this! I have no concern about the Bay of Pigs."[33]

National security was not at stake here. The CIA's only involvement with the burglars involved the technical assistance that Hunt's friends in the agency had provided for the Ellsberg break-in and other intelligence gambits. Nixon's fraudulent employment of national security constituted his first major involvement in an illegal scheme to curtail the Watergate investigation. On 6 July, Nixon warned that it could hurt him if his aides "try to cover for subordinates." The next day, he explained that the "cover-up is how I got Truman," and on 19 July he warned again, "If you cover up, you're going to get caught."[34]

Even though Helms told Haldeman on 22 June that the agency was not involved with Watergate, Haldeman insisted that he instruct Walters to tell the FBI to halt its investigations into the money trail. The next day, a reluctant Walters met Gray in his FBI office and told him that their investigations might touch on CIA activities. The plan worked for a little more than a week, but the FBI agents on the case did not follow through. Gray had to inform Nixon on 6 July that his underlings were trying to "mortally wound you" by working with the CIA on Watergate.[35] As for the CIA, Helms, who had not done all that he could to contain the investigation, ended up being fired by Nixon after the election and was sent off to be ambassador to Iran.

Equally important in the president's illegal activities were attempts to silence the burglars by paying them off or even promising them clemency. During several meetings on 26 June, Dean asked Walters to pay the burglars' salaries if they ended up in jail, a request that Walters rejected. That rejection led the administration to look elsewhere for hush money. On

29 June, Kalmbach informed Stans, CREEP's finance chief, that he was "on a special mission on a White House project and I need all the cash I can get."[36] When Stans offered to write him a check, Kalmbach insisted on cash. Over the next few months, Stans, Fred C. LaRue (another CREEP official), and Haldeman provided over $350,000 to Kalmbach, most of which went to E. Howard Hunt's wife, Dorothy, to pay for bail, lawyers' fees, and "income replacement" for the seven men arrested on 17 June. When Dorothy Hunt died in a plane crash on 8 December 1972, she was carrying $10,000 in cash in her handbag.

Anthony Ulasewicz, who had worked for the White House as a private investigator primarily on the Edward Kennedy "case," was Kalmbach's bagman. Ulasewicz, Colson, and Jack Caulfield, among others, pressured the burglars to remain silent, promising not only monetary payments but also possible presidential clemency. As early as 8 July, Nixon raised the issue of pardoning the burglars, along with antiwar protesters then in prison. On 30 June, he blurted out, "I'll pardon the bastards."[37] One month later, he said, "Well . . . they have to be paid. That's all there is to that. They have to be paid."[38] Nixon later admitted, "It now seems certain that I knew Colson was sending messages of reassurance to Hunt through his lawyer and maybe I knew about the other reassurances."[39] But throughout, he claimed that he was only trying to "contain" and not cover up the Watergate investigation.[40]

Dean, whose former mother-in-law had once tried to obtain a clerkship for him with Judge Sirica, was at the center of the containment effort. Dean still had close ties at the Justice Department, where he had been before coming over to the White House in 1971. He warned Henry Petersen, the head of the Criminal Division, "I don't believe the White House can stand a wide-open investigation . . . there are all kinds of things over there that could blow up in our face."[41] The White House also made it clear to Attorney General Kleindienst that it wanted the Watergate investigation to involve only the simple break-in, nothing more. Following the indictment of the seven burglars on 15 September, the department announced that it had no information that anyone else was involved in the affair.

Petersen and Earl Silbert, Jr., the U.S. attorney in charge of the investigation who wanted to expand its scope, were apparently honest if "naive" public servants who accepted the White House's request to limit the investigation to the original seven men.[42] Whatever their own private suspicions, they had to obey Kleindienst, who was in close contact with the White House throughout the fall of 1972.

Dean and Petersen met frequently during that period, sharing information about the case, learning about the sorts of questioning going on at the grand jury, and then sharing that information with Mitchell and others who were going to appear before the grand jury. Dean had assured Petersen that "anything you tell me will not be passed on."[43] Dean later told Nixon that "Petersen is a soldier. He kept me informed. He told me when we had problems, where we had problems and the like."[44]

Dean enjoyed an even closer working relationship with acting FBI director Gray. After Hunt was arrrested, Dean broke into his White House safe and removed incriminating items, including files on Ellsberg and Edward Kennedy and fake State Department cables from the abortive *Life* magazine scheme. Dean then gave them to Gray, explaining that although they had nothing to do with Watergate, they "should not see the light of day."[45] Gray kept them at his home for six months and then burned them.

When the government investigation seemingly ended with the conviction of the seven Watergate burglars at the end of January 1973, it appeared that Nixon had put the affair behind him. But several events occurred over the next few months that revealed that the Watergate investigations had only just begun.

First of all, congressional Democrats organized to investigate the break-in and other Republican campaign abuses. Tip O'Neill confided to Speaker of the House Carl Albert in January that the Republicans "did too many things. Too many people know about it. There is no way to keep it quiet. The time is going to come when impeachment is going to hit this Congress."[46] In the Senate, Majority Leader Mansfield urged the head of the Senate Judiciary Committee, Sam Ervin, a respected constitutional expert, to lead the call for an investigation of Watergate. On 7 February, the Senate voted seventy to zero to establish a select committee to conduct the investigation. Over the objections of the three Republicans on the seven-person panel, the Democrats decided to limit the investigations to Watergate and related Republican campaign abuses. Armed with a memo from former FBI official William Sullivan, the White House had hoped that the committee would investigate Johnson's and other Democrats' political uses of the FBI all the way back to Franklin Roosevelt. Four of the committee members, three Democrats and one Republican, had received questionable campaign contributions themselves.

At its peak, the Senate Select Committee on Presidential Campaign Activities, or the Ervin committee, as it came to be known, employed ninety-seven people. Nixon complained that with the White House able to spare fewer than ten staffers for the defense against not only the Senate but also the continuing Justice Department investigations, "We were like a high school team headed into the Super Bowl."[47] The administration's original strategy, according to Nixon, Haldeman, and Ehrlichman, was to "discredit the hearings," which they felt were overly partisan, and to "cooperate publicly but quietly destruct."[48]

Nixon consulted frequently with the senior Republican member of the committee, Howard Baker (R-Tenn.), on ways to keep the hearings as brief and as sketchy as possible. On 9 April, Ehrlichman told Nixon, "Baker was a lot of help—in fact Baker was of enormous help through this thing today."[49] However, the Tennessee senator and minority counsel Fred Thompson were unable to contain the scope of the investigations. Their efforts were impeded, in part, by one of the three Republican panelists, Lowell Weicker of Connecticut, who was an especially independent member of the party. The Ervin committee held thirty-seven days of hearings from 17 May to 7 August. During that period, the television networks covered more than 300 hours of testimony.

The administration took another blow during the seemingly unrelated senatorial confirmation hearing for L. Patrick Gray to become the permanent head of the FBI. Gray foolishly blurted out on 28 February that he had given Dean full access to the FBI's investigative reports of the Watergate affair, including permitting him to sit in on the bureau's interviews with suspects, and that he had also discussed the proceedings with Ehrlichman. Two weeks later, Gray confirmed that he had met with Dean thirty-three times to discuss Watergate. Although Nixon had instructed Gray before the hearings, "As far as the Watergate, I'd rather throw it all out there and not be defensive," the White House was furious with his gratuitous admissions.[50] Gray had opened a Pandora's box that made it even more difficult for the administration to limit the legislative and judicial investigations to the burglars and their immediate bosses at CREEP. As for Gray, the White House gave up on his nomination. Ehrlichman instructed Dean, "Let him hang there: let him twist slowly, slowly in the wind."[51] Gray asked that his name be withdrawn from consideration on 5 April.

Trying to make the best of a bad situation, at a press conference on 15 March, Nixon referred to "information from the FBI that may have been provided in the line of their duties to a member of the White House staff." He also introduced what became his defense over the next seventeen months, invoking executive privilege to bar Dean or other White House aides from testifying before the Ervin committee. Ironically, four years earlier, in dealing with a request for information from a committee investigating Johnson's OEO, Nixon had ordered, "I want a memorandum to go out to all Cabinet officers and also to other agencies in government indicating that it is a policy of this Administration to be as cooperative with Congress and particularly with investigating committees as we can, and if information is requested it should generally be furnished."[52]

The Gray fiasco was a minor problem compared with that posed by James McCord five days later. In a letter addressed to presiding judge John J. Sirica on 19 March 1973, McCord, who was awaiting sentencing, revealed that "political pressure was applied to the defendants to plead guilty and remain silent." McCord asserted further that witnesses had perjured themselves and that "others in the Watergate operation were not identified" during the trial in January. He also emphasized that the CIA was not involved in the affair.[53] McCord, an agency loyalist, may have blown the whistle because of the way the administration had used the CIA to block the investigation. He wrote his letter to Sirica even though "several members of my family have expressed fear for my life if I disclose knowledge of the facts in this matter."[54]

On 23 March, before he sentenced the seven Watergate defendants, Judge Sirica, a tough law-and-order Republican who had earned the nickname "Maximum John," read McCord's letter in open court. Sirica had always suspected that there was more to the Watergate affair than the federal prosecutors had presented at the trial. For him, the letter was the key to unlocking the remaining secrets of the break-in and its aftermath.

After issuing maximum sentences to the defendants—thirty-five years for Hunt, forty years for the Cubans, and twenty years for Liddy—Sirica urged the defendants to cooperate with the several Watergate investigations. He hoped that his stiff sentences would encourage others beyond McCord to talk to the prosecutors and the Senate committee.

On 27 February, Nixon held the first of a series of important meetings with Dean, the chief administrator of the cover-up, to plan strategies. He had not met with Dean to discuss the matter since the previous fall. His young counsel outlined to him how the congressional, Justice Department, and press investigations were closing in on the Oval Office. On 21 March, he told Nixon, "We have a cancer within, close to the Presidency, that is growing. It is growing daily. It's compounded, growing geometrically."[55] He explained how witnesses had perjured themselves and about the involvement of Mitchell, Haldeman, and Ehrlichman in the original plan. Nixon already knew most of these details.

That same day, in considering Hunt's demands for more money to maintain his silence, Nixon commented, "We could get that . . . you could get a million dollars. And you could get it in cash. I, I know where it could be gotten."[56] One place might be from Republican fund-raiser Thomas Pappas, who asked in return only that the ambassador to Greece, whom Nixon was about to recall, be maintained in Athens. For Nixon, that was "no problem."[57] The president raised the issue of Hunt's blackmail thirteen times during the 21 March conversation, without directly telling Dean to raise the money and give it to Hunt and the others. Nixon later feared that Dean secretly taped the incriminating conversation.

Aside from trying to keep the original seven quiet, Nixon began to worry about what his own aides might say to investigators. He suborned perjury when he coached Haldeman and Dean, "You can say 'I don't remember.' You can say 'I can't recall. I can't give any answer to that that I can recall.'"[58] He also came close to obstructing justice when, two months later, he told Haldeman that for him, Ehrlichman, and "even that pour [sic] damn dumb John Mitchell," there would be "a total pardon."[59]

On 30 March, McCord revealed to the Ervin committee that Liddy and Hunt had told him that Magruder, Mitchell, Dean, Haldeman, Colson, and others approved of or knew about the break-in. Three days later, Dean's attorney informed Watergate prosecutors that his client was prepared to talk to them about what he knew about the affair, including the Ellsberg break-in, Hunt's safe, and Ehrlichman's, Haldeman's, and Nixon's involvement in the hush money and cover-up schemes. By this time, Dean, who feared that Nixon and his two chief aides would make him the scapegoat, began thinking about arranging the best deal for himself with the prosecutors.

Eight days later, Magruder told his attorneys that he was prepared to tell the prosecutors about his earlier perjury before the grand jury during the summer of 1972 and how Liddy, Dean, and Mitchell had had prior knowledge of the break-in. Other key figures in the cover-up quickly asked their attorneys to negotiate deals with prosecutors before their testimony lost its value.

For a few days, it appeared that the damage might be limited to CREEP, with Mitchell, or "the big enchilada," as Haldeman called him, taking the fall for the White House.[60] That sort of containment was no longer an option. Neverthless, as late as 4 April, a Gallup poll revealed that Nixon still enjoyed a hefty "approval-rating" margin of 60 to 33 percent. Events happened so quickly that two weeks later, a despondent Nixon mused to Kissinger, "Maybe we'll even consider the possibility of, frankly, just throwing myself on the sword—and letting Agnew take it."[61]

On 15 April, Dean, whom Nixon had considered a "pretty good gem" as recently as 2 March, told the president that he was talking to the prosecutors.[62] Two days later, the president announced that he would permit his aides to testify at the Ervin committee hearings. Over the days that followed, Nixon recognized that Haldeman and Ehrlichman would be closely linked to the Watergate scandals by their colleagues who had already begun talking. Thus, on 30 April, he announced to a nationwide television audience that he was accepting the resignations of Haldeman, Ehrlichman, and Kleindienst, all of whom he praised. He also announced that Dean had resigned and that he had nominated Elliot Richardson to be attorney general and had "instructed him that if he should consider it appropriate, he has the authority to name a special supervising prosecutor." As for his own role, "Until March, I remained convinced that the denials were true and that the charges of involvement by members of the White House staff were false." However, he admitted that they were "people whose zeal exceeded their judgement." But they had not broken any laws.

Haldeman's and Ehrlichman's forced resignations left the White House in a shambles. It was also a personally wrenching decision for a shaken Nixon, who, in a surprising display of emotion, and perhaps affected by a few drinks, blurted out to Haldeman as he asked him to resign, "I love you, as you know. . . . Like my brother."[63] He told his daughter Julie that night, "I hope I don't wake up in the morning."[64]

Bit by bit, the administration was falling apart. On 11 May, Judge W. Matthew Byrne dismissed charges against *Pentagon Papers* leakers Daniel Ellsberg and Anthony Russo because of government misconduct, including the Fielding break-in. Three days later, a House subcommittee revealed that the government had spent as much as $10 million on Nixon's vacation White Houses, a charge made worse by a subsequent revelation that he had paid little or no federal or state income taxes since he became president. He was able to pay as little as $878 in taxes in 1971 by backdating a gift of vice-presidential papers, which permitted him a huge write-off. (Lyndon Johnson had advised him about the tax deduction, albeit not about the backdating.) The financing of the San Clemente property itself, with a loan from Robert Abplanalp, raised further questions about suspicious tax manipulations. Finally responding to these charges on 17 November, Nixon assured Americans, "People have got to know whether or not their president is a crook. Well, I am not a crook." In April 1974, the Joint Congressional Committee on Taxation ruled that he owed the IRS $432,787.13 in back taxes, a sum that he never paid in full.

The Ervin committee began its hearings on 17 May with extremely damaging testimony from McCord, Ulasewicz, Stans, Caulfield, and Magruder. In an attempt to limit the damage, the president issued a 4,000-word statement on 22 May in which he asserted, "I took no part in, nor was I aware of, any subsequent efforts that may have been made to cover up Watergate." He also denied having prior knowedge of the break-in, offering anyone clemency, raising hush money, trying to implicate the CIA, authorizing his aides to commit illegal acts, or knowing anything about the Ellsberg break-in until recently. Haig, one of the president's staunchest defenders, later wrote that of the seven itemized denials, six were lies.[65] Nixon was digging a deeper and deeper hole. In that same 22 May statement, he also acknowledged the 1969 wiretappings, the aborted Huston Plan, and the Plumbers' activities, explaining them as justified by the need to protect national security.

Four days earlier, Archibald Cox, a distinguished Harvard Law School professor and a former U.S. solicitor general, had accepted Attorney General Richardson's invitation to become a special prosecutor, the first in American history. He was not Richardson's first choice; among those who refused the daunting challenge of taking on the president were Leon Jaworski and Warren Christopher. Congressional leaders, who had enacted special legislation to create this new position, had earlier informed the White House that Richardson would not be confirmed as attorney general until a special prosecutor was in place.

Cox was a Democrat with close ties to the Kennedys. His great-grandfather, William Evarts, had successfully defended Andrew Johnson during the first presidential impeachment trial in American history. The special prosecutor's office—or the "Coxsuckers," as the White House referred to it—armed with a budget of almost $3 million and given wide latitude by Richardson to explore matters well beyond the original break-in, went to work on Mitchell's White House horrors with a zeal that infuriated the president. Nixon later complained, "No White House in history could have survived the kind of operation Cox was planning."[66] Seven of Cox's eleven senior appointees had worked for a Kennedy.

By the time they began their investigations, the special prosecutor's staff was able to profit from the groundwork laid by the increasingly more aggressive and independent Justice Department prosecutors and the Ervin committee. Cox had hoped to convince Ervin to halt his hearings, or at least keep them off television, so that future prosecutions would not be jeopardized. Ervin rejected Cox's request, and Sirica upheld the senator's position on 12 June.

Dean appeared before the committee on 25 June (immediately after the Nixon-Brezhnev summit) for the first of his five days of riveting testimony, beginning with a 246-page statement. Ervin found him a "most impressive and convincing witness."[67] Not only had Dean taken scores of documents from the White House to support his presentation, but he had something close to a photographic memory that enabled him to recall conversations almost verbatim. Explaining that he had been personally in charge of the cover-up and that he had attended the key White House meetings on 23 June 1972 and 21 March 1973, Dean placed Nixon at the epicenter of the conspiracy. His testimony led Senator Baker to pose the now famous question, "What did the President know and when did he know it?"[68]

Others who testified, including Haldeman, an especially contentious Ehrlichman, and Mitchell, refuted Dean's account. Nixon had made provisions to pay for Haldeman's and Ehrlichman's legal defense with money from Rebozo's war chest. Privately, Larry Higby had told the Ervin committee that Dean was "trying to save his ass and screw everyone else."[69] For several weeks that summer, the entire case seemed to rest on one question: whom to believe, John Dean or the president of the United States? The president refused to provide the committee with records it had requested that might have cleared up some issues. On 7 July, Nixon wrote to Ervin (whom he considered "an old fart") and claimed executive privilege once again because "no President could function if the private papers of his office, prepared by his personal staff, were open to public scrutiny."[70]

The papers were one issue—the tapes were another. On 13 July, Donald G. Sanders, a member of the minority counsel's team, asked White House aide Alexander Butterfield, "Do you know of any bases for the implications in Dean's testimony that conversations in the President's office are recorded?" Butterfield replied, "I was hoping you fellows wouldn't ask that."[71] Three days later, Butterfield testified in public about the taping system. Now it was possible to learn whether Dean was telling the truth and what the president knew and when he knew it.

On 17 July, Ervin announced that he wanted the president's relevant tapes. The next day, Cox made a similar request. Nixon responded on 23 July that he would not release them and that, in any event, they "are entirely consistent with what I know to be the truth and what I have stated to be the truth." One of his lawyers, Charles Alan Wright, a distinguished constitutional scholar, claimed in a letter to Cox that the president had the "inherent" right to withhold such materials and, more importantly, that Nixon was Cox's superior.[72] The day he received the response, Ervin issued a subpoena on behalf of his committee for the tapes, the first time since 1807 that a congressional committee had subpoenaed a president. Three days later, responding to a subpoena issued by Judge Sirica on Cox's request to obtain tapes of nine specific conversations, Nixon maintained that "the President is not subject to compulsory process from the courts." It was now up to Sirica and the higher courts of appeal to resolve the conflict.

But that was not the entire story. At the time the existence of the tapes became public, Nixon was in Bethesda Naval Hospital with a serious case of viral pneumonia. His aides and other advisers met at his bedside to discuss their options, which included destroying the tapes. Haig's old boss Joseph Califano (a Democrat); Fred Buzhardt, the president's chief lawyer in the case; Nelson Rockefeller; and Kissinger, among others, recommended that the president destroy the tapes, contending that they were his private property. Connally advised Haldeman, "For heaven's sake, tell the President to go on and burn the rest [aside from the subpoenaed] of these tapes. . . . Have a bonfire on the south lawn."[73]

White House counsel Leonard Garment disagreed, warning that if Nixon destroyed "evidence," Garment would resign and go public with his objections.[74] Thinking that the tapes might contain evidence to help clear himself, Haldeman also urged Nixon not to burn them. Nixon needed little prodding on this matter. Sealing his fate, he decided not to destroy the tapes, because he too felt that he could use them to exonerate himself and also because he thought that he could win the legal right to withhold all or parts of them. Had Nixon burned the tapes, he would have suffered a good deal of criticism, but he might have survived the impeachment investigation. He later commented that he had received "bad advice" from his lawyers and "should have destroyed them."[75]

The tapes not only contained several "smoking guns" but also revealed to the nation that in private its president was a profane and nasty fellow who behaved in a manner unbecoming his office. Nixon seriously blundered by failing to permit his lawyers to listen to the tapes before seeking advice on their disposition.

On 31 July, Robert Drinan (D-Mass.) introduced an impeachment resolution in the House. It was never voted on, the Democratic leadership having concluded that it could not pass at that juncture. The polls revealed that Americans were almost evenly split in their attitudes toward the president.

But a few weeks later, Nixon's favorable poll figures had plummeted to 31 percent. The decline can be attributed not only to the several ongoing investigations but also to the media's coverage of those investigations. During the spring and summer of 1973, the Watergate story finally became front-page news throughout the nation. Woodward and Bernstein, relying for confirmation of their stories on a mysterious informant, allegedly a White House insider code-named "Deep Throat," regularly turned up new material and, along with other investigative reporters, received leaks from the Justice Department and congressional investigators. In turn, those investigators often picked up leads from stories in the *Washington Post, Los Angeles Times,* and *New York Times,* among other newspapers.

At the end of August, Sirica ruled that the White House should turn over to him the nine tapes requested by Cox. Nixon appealed the decision to the U.S. Court of Appeals, which on 12 October ruled five to two against him, ordering both sides to work out an arrangement by which national security could be protected and the tapes released.

As the case made its way through the courts, the administration confronted another unprecedented scandal that resulted in Vice President Spiro Agnew's resignation on 10 October. As Baltimore county executive and then as governor, Agnew had received more than $100,000 in kickbacks for public-works contracts. This practice became the subject of a grand jury investigation late in 1972. Agnew later claimed that although he had accepted political contributions, he had never taken kickbacks. Whatever they were called, while vice president, he had received payments owed for 1968 contracts. The Justice Department's investigation of Agnew made the front pages on 7 August 1973. After Attorney General Richardson told Haig that he had an "open-and-shut case" that included forty indictable crimes, Haig and Buzhardt strongly advised the vice president to resign.[76] Richardson agreed, fearing that with Nixon's impeachment a possibility, Agnew could become president.

On 20 September, after what a U.S. attorney labeled "the most momentous plea bargaining in United States history," Agnew prepared to resign.[77] But when a Justice Department official leaked to a reporter, "We've got the evidence. We've got it cold," Agnew changed his mind and dug in his heels.[78]

On 25 September, he requested Speaker Albert to have the House consider his case, just as it had considered a comparable case against Vice President John C. Calhoun in 1826. The Constitution, he claimed, prohibited the indictment or conviction of a vice president in a criminal court. Nixon himself worried that should Agnew be indicted, he might be as well.

With no support from the administration, little interest in Congress in trying him, and limited defense funds, Agnew reconsidered and resigned on 10 October. As part of his plea-bargaining agreement, he pleaded nolo contendere to one charge of income tax evasion, for which he received three years of unsupervised probation and a $10,000 fine. Several of his coconspirators received prison sentences. The IRS then billed him for $150,000 in back taxes, an amount he raised through a loan from his friend, entertainer Frank Sinatra. The first vice president in history to resign, Agnew "felt totally abandoned" by the administration.[79] He claimed that although Nixon called him on eight separate occasions between 1973 and 1994, he had refused to return his calls. A civil court in 1981 determined that Agnew had solicited $147,000 in bribes while a county executive and governor, $17,500 of which he received while vice president.

From a tactical perspective, Nixon appears to have mishandled the Agnew affair. Had he urged his vice president to insist on the time-consuming impeachment route, he might have been able to take the pressure off his own impeachment investigation. Moreover, Agnew as vice president was a form of insurance policy against presidential impeachment—who in Congress would vote to remove Nixon only to have Agnew become president?

Following Agnew's resignation, Nixon moved quickly to find a replacement. He instructed Gerald Ford and Hugh Scott to ask Republicans in the House and Senate, and George Bush to ask Republicans at the RNC, to present ranked lists of three nominees. Rockefeller led the polls in the Senate and the RNC, and Ford led in the House. Rockefeller was too strong a personality for Nixon and, more important, like another possible candidate, Ronald Reagan, represented an extreme wing of the party. John Connally, Nixon's own favorite, could not have been confirmed in the Senate. Nixon introduced Gerald Ford as his choice three days after Agnew's resignation.

A moderately conservative politician, Ford was well liked by Republican leaders and a favorite among Democrats as well. He was also not much of a political threat to the Democrats in 1976. Ford was considered so unpresidential as to serve as anti-impeachment insurance for Nixon, although he was certainly a more plausible president than Agnew. Nonetheless, in June 1974, the president asked Rockefeller in the Oval Office, "Can you imagine Jerry Ford sitting in this chair?"[80]

In discussing the nomination, Ford assured Nixon that he would not run in 1976 and would support Connally. During confirmation hearings, Ford also told the Senate Rules Committee that he had "no intention of seeking any public office in nineteen seventy-six" and that Nixon was "completely innocent."[81] Despite a covert attempt by a handful of Democrats to block Nixon's vice-presidential appointments until his removal from office in order to make Speaker of the House Carl Albert president, the Senate confirmed Ford on 27 November by a 92-to-3 vote, and the House by 387 to 35 on 6 December. The nation had employed the Twenty-fifth Amendment for the first time.

The administration did not give Ford very much to do aside from chairing the moribund Domestic Council when Nixon was not available, heading the new Commission on the Right of Privacy, and making the rounds at fund-raising functions. A glance at his weekly briefing file of executive branch activities reveals that most of the time, under "recommended participation" for Ford, the president's men wrote "none."[82] More valuable as the president's cheerleader, Ford traveled around the country loyally—and blindly—supporting Nixon's claims of innocence. During his eight months as vice president, he addressed 500 groups in 40 states, held 50 press conferences, and gave 80 interviews. As late as 24 July 1974, he "could say from the bottom of my heart that the President of the United States is innocent."[83] Of course, he was not shown the transcripts of tapes or any documents relating to the affair until the final days.

A Massachusets rabbi, Baruch Korff, impressed with Nixon's activities on behalf of Soviet Jews, also joined the cheerleaders. On 29 July 1973, he paid for newspaper advertisements announcing a National Citizen's Committee for Fairness to the President, which, after Nixon left office, became the Nixon Justice Fund. Although Korff's initiative was spontaneous, he soon received help from the RNC and from White House aide S. Bruce Herschensohn. Korff's committee established 231 chapters and raised more than $350,000 to help defray the president's legal fees. There is a certain irony here that among those most involved in his defense were two Jewish Americans.

Agnew's resignation and the wrangling over the tapes occurred during the crises-filled period of the October 1973 war. With one bleary eye on the Middle East and the other on Watergate, Nixon told Elliot Richardson that "Brezhnev would never understand it if I let Cox defy my instructions."[84] During the most difficult period of the crisis, both Kissinger and Haig were convinced that the Russian leader was acting boldly because he thought that Nixon had been immobilized by Watergate.

As the Court of Appeals deadline for a settlement of the tapes issue approached, Nixon floated a proposal to Cox through Richardson in which he would agree to provide a summary of the nine tapes to Judge Sirica. Senator John Stennis would have access to the original tapes to authenticate the summaries. At this point, Cox was looking for a compromise but was unwilling to accept the proposal because it was conditional on his promise not to ask for any more tapes or related documents. Nixon made it a take-it-or-leave-it offer. When Cox rejected it, the president expected him to resign. Instead, he appeared at a press conference on 20 October to explain his position to a sympathetic nation.

That night, in what came to be called the "Saturday Night Massacre," Nixon announced that Cox had been fired by the third in command at the Justice Department, Robert Bork, and that he had abolished the special prosecutor's office. That same night, Haig and Bork ordered the FBI to seal Cox's offices. Attorney General Richardson and his second in command, William Ruckelshaus, had resigned rather than carry out Nixon's order to fire Cox. As Richardson explained in his letter of resignation, he had "specified that he [Cox] would have 'full authority' for determining whether or not to contest the assertion of 'Executive Privilege.'"[85] Nixon commented privately, "I'm not surprised that pious bastard cares more for his ass than for his country."[86]

The sacking of Cox produced a firestorm of outrage. In his defense, Cox framed the issue in stark terms: "Whether we shall continue to be a government of laws and not of men is for Congress and ultimately the American people" to decide.[87] Within twenty-four hours of Cox's dismissal, the White House and Congress received 150,000 telegrams, the largest such outpouring ever. Ten days later, the total reached 450,000 telegrams and mailgrams, almost all of which opposed the firing, and many of which demanded simply, "Impeach Nixon." The president of the ABA assailed Nixon's attempt "to abort the established processes of justice," while delegates to the annual AFL-CIO convention unanimously approved a resolution calling for Nixon's impeachment.[88] The editor of *Time*, a magazine that never ran editorials, took the unprecedented step of writing one to demand Nixon's resignation. (That same magazine later made Judge Sirica its "Man of the Year" for 1973.) In the wake of the Saturday Night Massacre, the Gallup poll revealed that Nixon's approval rating had dropped to 17 percent. On the Tuesday and Wednesday following the massacre, reprentatives and senators introduced forty-four Watergate-related bills, twenty-two of which called for an impeachment investigation. Many legislators concluded that Nixon had fired Cox because he had something serious to hide.

The proposed Stennis compromise that Cox had rejected was dead. Ervin refused to accept it on 23 October. Facing anger, outrage, and widespread calls for his resignation, Nixon was now in full retreat. That same day, Nixon's attorney Charles Wright told Sirica that he would hand over the subpoenaed tapes to him. But even that concession caused problems when, on 9 and 12 November, White House counsel Fred Buzhardt testified that two of the tapes did not exist. More shocking, the White House revealed nine days later the eighteen-and-a-half-minute gap on the tape of the crucial 20 June 1972 conversation between Nixon and Haldeman. Although the reason for the gap has never been explained—Haig referred in court testimony to "some sinister force" being responsible—most Americans agreed with the conservative *National Review* that "believers in the accidental theory could gather for lunch in a phone booth."[89] Public suspicions would have increased had it been known that when a subpoenaed dictabelt tape failed to show up, Nixon told Haig, "all we have to do is create another one."[90]

The White House eventually handed over the seven existing tapes to Sirica on 26 November. He immediately sent three to the new special prosecutor, while he vetted the other four for national security matters. On 31

October, the president had reestablished the prosecutor's office and named Leon Jaworski, a Nixon Democrat from Texas and a former ABA president, to replace Cox. Nixon promised him even more independence than Cox, agreeing that he could be removed only with the approval of six of eight specified House and Senate leaders. But Jaworski would not be Nixon's only worry.

The day before Jaworski's appointment, the House Judiciary Committee, by a straight party vote of twenty-one to seventeen, granted chairman Peter Rodino (D-N.J.) broad subpoena powers in its upcoming impeachment investigation. He also received a budget of $1 million and a staff of 106 (among them a recent Yale Law School graduate named Hillary Rodham), all of whom worked under chief counsel John Doar, a former head of the Civil Rights Division of the Justice Department. At its height, Nixon's legal team, which had to deal with both the House's and Jaworski's investigations, employed fifteen lawyers. Early in January, he named James St. Clair head of his Watergate defense. St. Clair had far more experience in criminal cases than his predecessor Charles Wright.

With its broad mandate, and armed with materials from the investigations of the Ervin committee, Cox, and the Justice Department that had been made public, as well as new information from Jaworski, the House committee began examining the charges against Nixon in executive session. Jaworski's evidence was essential to the proceedings—800 pages of documents, 13 tape recordings, and a 60-page report or "road map" to the evidence.

The long bill of particulars against the president included his possible involvement in obstruction of justice, conspiracy to obstruct justice, conspiracy, conspiracy to misuse government agencies, cover-ups, illegal wiretaps, destruction of evidence, election fraud, forgery, perjury, money laundering, bribery, financial misdealings, break-ins, the Huston Plan, offers of clemency, providing political favors for contributions, failure to fulfill the oath of office, failure to answer subpoenas, interference with federal prosecutors, obstruction of congressional investigations, the bombing of Cambodia, illegal impounding of funds, and the Agnew case.

After hearing the first of the tapes sent to the prosecutors for use at the grand jury, Jaworski became convinced that Nixon was guilty of illegal activities that could lead to his removal from office. In December, he had urged Haig to tell the president to hire a top-flight criminal attorney for the months ahead.

On 1 March 1974, a Washington grand jury hearing the special prosecutor's case indicted Haldeman, Ehrlichman, Mitchell, Mardian, Colson, Gordon Strachan, and Kenneth W. Parkinson for participating in the cover-up. Jaworski kept secret at the time the fact that Nixon had been named an unindicted coconspirator by the grand jury by a nineteen-to-zero vote. A week later, Ehrlichman, Colson, Liddy, and others were indicted for the Fielding break-in. Egil Krogh, also involved in that break-in, had earlier pleaded guilty to conspiracy to violate civil rights, saying that "I cannot in good conscience assert 'national security' as a defense."[91]

The House Judiciary Committee subpoenaed forty-two additional tapes on 11 April; a week later, Jaworski subpoenaed sixty-four tapes, which he needed for the trials resulting from the grand jury indictments. Rather than comply with the subpoenas, Nixon announced on 29 April that he would supply the Judiciary Committee with edited transcripts of the tapes and permit them to be made public. He told the nation, "Never before in [the] history of the Presidency have records that are so private been made public. In giving you these records—blemishes and all—I am placing my trust in the fairness of the American people." Although the 1,254 pages of edited transcripts contained a good deal of embarrassing material, including scores of presidential "expletives deleted," they proved to be both inaccurate and selective. Their innacuracy was demonstrated in July when the House Judiciary Committee released its own version of the tapes. As for their tone, Senator Hugh Scott considered the taped conversations a "shabby, disgusting, immoral performance by all those involved."[92]

When Sirica rejected the transcripts as an inadequate response to his original subpoena and called again for the tapes themselves, St. Clair appealed to the Court of Appeals. Jaworski then asked the Supreme Court to bypass the lower court and hear the case in an "imperative public importance" brief. Although the Court had taken this action only twice since World War II, on 31 May it agreed to hear the case of *United States of America v. Richard M. Nixon, President* on 8 July, with Justice Rehnquist recusing himself. Originally, the Court had voted two to six against expedition, but Justice William Brennan had been able to convince four colleagues to agree to hear the case because of the overriding need to resolve the Watergate crisis quickly.

As the nation awaited the outcome of the momentous case, more and more opinion leaders, and especially members of Congress, began to call for Nixon's resignation. In April, *Playboy* magazine printed excerpts from Bernstein and Woodward's *All the President's Men*, which became an instant best-seller when it was published in June. In early July, the House Judiciary Committee released 4,000 pages of evidence it had amassed in closed session during the previous months. Rumors abounded that some Republicans on the committee, as well as conservative southern Democrats on whom the president counted, were leaning toward impeachment.

At the same time, Nixon had just completed a triumphal world tour. Several million people turned out to hail him in Alexandria and Cairo, enthusiastic crowds greeted the first president ever to visit Israel, and the Soviets laid out the red carpet for the summit. Nixon displayed a good deal of personal courage as he persevered on the gruelling trip despite a painful case of phlebitis, the same malady that almost took his life in the fall. He was so ill that when he refused to get off his feet to prevent a blood clot, his personal doctor, Walter Tkach, remarked, "the President has a death wish. He won't take my advice."[93]

Nixon was far more popular abroad in the summer of 1974 than he was at home. On 8 July, James St. Clair argued before the Supreme Court that Nixon did not have to surrender the tapes because the doctrine of the separation of powers gave him absolute immunity from revealing his private discussions; only the president can decide what he must surrender to the other branches of government. St. Clair also invoked national security issues and hinted in oral argument that Nixon might not obey a Supreme Court order. In rejoinder, Jaworski contended that the public interest outweighed the vague and extraconstitutional claim of executive privilege, that Nixon had waived that claim in any event when he released the edited version of his tapes, and that a conspirator could not claim such a privilege. Commenting on another matter in 1969, Nixon had himself contended that executive privilege "must be very narrowly construed."[94]

On 24 July, in an eight-to-zero decision written by Chief Justice Burger, the court upheld the doctrine of executive privilege for the first time in U.S. history—but not in this case. The Court concluded that "the generalized interest in confidentiality . . . cannot prevail over the fundamental demands of due process of law in the fair administration of criminal justice."[95] Nixon had hoped that even if he lost the case the vote would be a close one, permitting him to disobey the order. Three of the eight justices were his appointees. That night Nixon announced, "I respect and accept the Court's decision."

Even before the release of the tapes, it was clear that the House Judiciary Committee was going to vote to impeach Nixon; the question was the margin of the vote. The six days of televised hearings began on 24 July, the same day the Court issued its opinion. At least 35 million Americans tuned in each day to watch the unprecedented drama. When the committee began deliberating, close to 75 percent of those polled believed in Nixon's complicity in the scandal. By the time the committee completed its work, those polled supported Nixon's impeachment by a 66 to 27 percent margin.

On 27 July, the committee approved the first article of impeachment dealing with obstruction of justice by a vote of twenty-seven to eleven, with six Republicans joining all the Democrats in the majority. Two days later, the committee voted twenty-eight to ten to approve the abuse of power article, with seven Republicans joining all the Democrats, and on 30 July, it voted twenty-one to seventeen in favor of the contempt of Congress article. The committee rejected articles relating to the secret bombing of Cambodia and tax violations by an identical twelve-to-twenty-six tally.

On 5 August, after the White House finally released transcripts of the 23 June 1972 meetings between Nixon and Haldeman, clearly demonstrating that the two had conspired to use the CIA to blunt the FBI's Watergate investigation—the "smoking-gun" tapes—all of Nixon's Republican supporters on the committee announced that they would change their votes to support the first article of impeachment. A teary-eyed Charles Wiggins (R-Calif.), Nixon's chief supporter on the committee, announced, "With great reluctance and deep personal sorrow I am prepared to conclude that the magnificent career of public service of Richard Nixon must be terminated."[96] One of Wiggins's aides complained, "It doesn't vindicate the process to know that the lynch mob lynched the right guy."[97] Wiggins himself was convinced that partisan politics lay behind the drive to impeach. After Nixon resigned, the House accepted the Judiciary Committee's report by a 412-to-3 vote on 22 August.

As for Nixon, those close to him over the eighteen months of the Watergate crisis saw a good deal of the mercurial behavior associated with manic depression. On some occasions, he seemed resilient and combative, but more often than not he appeared sad, unfocused, and melancholy. At a dinner at the White House in December 1973, Barry Goldwater worried about the way he "jabbered incessantly, often incoherently" and "appeared to be cracking."[98]

Just before he explained to the nation why he had to fire Haldeman and Ehrlichman in April 1973, Nixon had confided to speechwriter Ray Price, "Maybe I should resign. . . . If you think I should resign, just write it into the next draft, and I'll do it."[99] Three weeks later, he had asked his daughters, "Do you think I should resign?"[100] But from that point on, Julie Nixon Eisenhower did not discuss resignation with him until 2 August 1974. Nixon did tell Colson in December 1973, "You know that if I am impeached, I'll be wiped out financially—no pension—and now with all I owe in taxes."[101] If he resigned, he stood to claim a $60,000 presidential pension and almost $100,000 for staff expenses.

After the Judiciary Committee's approval of three articles of impeachment, and knowing what was in the smoking-gun tape that the Court was forcing him to release, the president told Haig on 1 August that he was going to resign rather than go through a Senate trial that he was certain to lose, along with his pension. That same day, Haig asked Ford, "Are you ready, Mr. Vice-President, to assume the Presidency in a short period of time?"[102]

The next day, Nixon changed his mind, telling Haig,"let them impeach me. We'll fight it out to the end."[103] At least he wanted to see what happened when the tapes became public and even instructed Price to prepare a speech explaining his decision not to resign. In the speech that was never given, Price was going to have him defend the institution of the presidency: "We must not let this office be destroyed—or let it fall such easy prey to those who would exult in the breaking of the President that the game becomes a national habit."[104]

But in the several days that followed, it became clear that he had no chance of prevailing in the Senate. Barry Goldwater exclaimed, "There are only so many lies you can take and now there has been one too many. Nixon should get his ass out of the White House—today." He told the president that he could count on the votes of twelve to fifteen senators, no more.[105] During the same period, Haig had been carefully orchestrating the situation—"the political equivalent of a military envelopment"—in which he helped Nixon realize that he had to resign.[106] On 6 August, House Judiciary chair Peter Rodino told Robert McClory (R-Ill.) to get a message to the White House, "If he resigns, we can drop all this, the impeachment, the threat of criminal proceedings. If he quits, that's the end of it."[107] That day, Nixon informed Haig and Ziegler, the two people on whom he had relied most during the previous year, that he would deliver a speech on 8 August announcing his resignation effective the next day. He told them, "Well, I screwed up real good, didn't I?"[108] The next day he met with Republican leaders, who told him what he already knew: the situation was hopeless.

On the night before he was to deliver his resignation speech, Nixon summoned Kissinger to the residence, where the two spent three hours talking over their foreign policy triumphs. At one point in the Lincoln Bedroom, a weeping Nixon asked Kissinger to get down on his knees with him to pray in what "was the most wrenching thing" the secretary had ever experienced in his life. Nixon pleaded with him, "please don't ever tell anyone that I cried and that I was not strong."[109]

He was strong on 8 August. In a televised speech at 9 P.M., his thirty-seventh from the Oval Office, he announced his intention to resign at noon the next day. He admitted that "some of my judgments were wrong," but he refused to concede that he had done anything criminal to justify impeachment. He did not even mention the word in his address. Instead, he explained how he could no longer govern because "I no longer have a strong enough political base in Congress." And although "I have never been a quitter . . . as President, I must put the interests of America first." He spent some time on his foreign policy accomplishments, pointing out that "sometimes I have succeeded and sometimes I have failed, but always I have taken heart from what Theodore Roosevelt once said about the 'man in the arena . . . who at the best knows in the end the triumphs of high achievement and who at the worst, if he fails, at least fails while daring greatly.'" Nixon retained his composure throughout, something that had worried Haig and other aides. Only as the red light went off on the television cameras did he, drenched in sweat, begin to shake. A crowd had gathered outside the White House chanting, "Jail to the Chief."

Nixon revealed more of himself the next day when he made his farewell address to his staff. Not having slept, bleary-eyed, sweating, and trembling, he rambled through a variety of intensely personal subjects, beginning with gracious compliments for the staff of "this house [that] has a great heart, and that comes from those who serve." He was proud of them and the fact that "no man or no woman who came into this Administration . . . left it with more of this world's goods than when he came in. . . . Mistakes, yes. But for personal gain, never." He returned again to one of his lifelong heroes, Theodore Roosevelt, explaining, "As you know, I kind of like to read books. I am not educated but I do read books," and he talked about how after Roosevelt had lost his first wife, "He thought the light had gone from his life forever—but he went on." He advised the teary-eyed crowd, "Always give your best, never get discouraged, never be petty; always remember, others may hate you, but those who hate you don't win unless you hate them, and then you destroy yourself."

A few hours later, Nixon left the White House accompanied by Pat and President and Mrs. Ford. The night before, he had remarked to an aide in a phone call, "Some of the best political writing in this century has been done in jail."[110] It was now up to Gerald Ford to determine how Richard Nixon would spend the next few years of his life.

11

★ ★ ★ ★ ★

RUNNING FOR EX-PRESIDENT

A few minutes after noon on 9 August 1974, as Richard Nixon was flying over Missouri on his way into "exile" at San Clemente, Gerald Ford announced in his inaugural remarks, "My fellow Americans, our long national nightmare is over." But that was easier said than done, considering the many questions remaining from the Watergate investigations, the most important of which revolved around the criminal culpability of the former president.

During his vice-presidential confirmation hearings, Ford was not asked directly about a pardon for Nixon. But in commenting about whether he would halt the investigations or prosecutions if he became president, he told the panel, "I don't think the public would stand for it."[1]

After reading the transcript of the smoking-gun tape on 24 July 1974, Fred Buzhardt, Nixon's lawyer, began talking among his colleagues about the possibility of pardons for the Watergate defendants. Before leaving office, Nixon could have legally pardoned all the defendants, as well as himself. Haldeman had suggested to Nixon that he balance Watergate pardons with pardons for antiwar protesters and draft resisters. But the most politically palatable pardon option rested with Ford.

Haig asked to see Ford on 1 August, apparently at Buzhardt's request, who in turn had been prompted by Nixon. At the meeting, with Ford's aide Robert Hartmann in attendance, Haig did not raise the pardon issue. During a second forty-five-minute meeting that day when he was alone with Ford, Haig sketched six different scenarios for the coming weeks. The sixth was that, "according to some on Nixon's White House staff, Nixon could agree to leave in return for an agreement that the new President—Gerald Ford—would pardon him."[2] To punctuate that point, Haig handed Ford memos, drawn up by Buzhardt, on the pardon power and the legal form needed to execute a pardon. Instead of immediately rejecting that option, something he later regretted, Ford told Haig, "I shall need some time to think about this."[3]

In subsequent testimony about the pardon to a House committee on 17 October, Ford explained that he had been "shocked and stunned" by the new information that Haig had brought to him about Watergate on 1 August. That may have been the reason why he had not grasped what Hartmann called "the monstrous impropriety" of Haig's offer.[4] The next day, 2 August, with witnesses present, Ford phoned Haig to tell him that there would be no deal over Nixon's resignation. That same day, Nixon temporarily changed his mind about resigning.

Following the resignation, and despite what he said about the nightmare being over, Ford "wanted to get the issue off my desk in the Oval Office as quickly as possible, so I could concentrate 100 percent of my time on what I thought were the problems of 230 million people at home and abroad."[5] Having concluded that he had been duped and lied to while vice president, Ford had lost almost all respect for Nixon. While he later referred to other presidents as Lyndon Johnson or Jack Kennedy, he always referred to Nixon as "Nixon."[6]

But there was still a human element in his relationship with his former friend. Nixon was in very frail emotional and physical shape during the weeks following his resignation. Senator James Eastland (D-Miss.) told Jaworski of a call he had received from San Clemente—"He was crying." Nixon pleaded, "Jim, don't let Jaworski put me in that trial with Haldeman and Ehrlichman. I can't take anymore." Senate Minority Leader Hugh Scott, no friend of Nixon's, commented during the same period, "The nation has its pound of flesh. It doesn't need the blood that goes with it."[7] Members of the Nixon family also lobbied for a pardon, with David Eisenhower telling Ford that his father-in-law "might go off the deep end."[8]

At a press conference on 28 August, Ford announced that he would not rule out the possibility of granting Nixon a pardon. That day, Leonard Garment, working with Ray Price, sent Ford's counsel, Philip Buchen, a draft pardon document that would bring "a national sigh of relief." Ironically, former Supreme Court justice Abe Fortas, an old enemy of Nixon's, had convinced Garment that a pardon was appropriate. In his covering letter, Garment pointed out, "Most of the country does not want Richard Nixon hounded, perhaps literally to death."[9] He may have been overly optimistic about the public reaction. The outgoing president of the ABA had recently spoken out against a pardon, and the polls reflected public ambivalence on the issue, fluctuating from day to day with the headlines. Sam Ervin also opposed a pardon, contending that Ford should wait until the legal proceedings were completed.

It is unclear whether Ford saw the Garment memo on 28 August, but he did speak with Haig about the pardon, and Haig had seen the memo. After that conversation, Haig assured Garment, "It is going to happen, but not today."[10] Ford apparently made up his mind on 30 August to pardon Nixon. He asked his staff that day, "If eventually, why not now?"[11] He had heard from Jaworski, who also favored a pardon, that Nixon could be tried for as many as ten possible crimes and that it might take over a year to bring the case to trial. Jaworksi's staff was pursuing investigations into obstruction of justice, Nixon's taxes, the Ellsberg break-in, the NSC wiretaps, the political uses of the IRS, campaign contributions from the milk lobby, the FCC challenges to the *Washington Post*'s television stations, the ITT deal, and Rebozo's secret funds. Jaworski also wondered whether Nixon could ever get a fair trial. Nixon's new lawyer, Herbert J. Miller, had written to Jaworski, "Never before in the history of this country have a person's activities relating to possible criminal violations been subjected to such massive publicity, analysis, and debate."[12]

Ford certainly did not want Nixon to go to jail, a likelihood if the case went to trial. He thought the sooner the nation got over Watergate the better: "The hate had to be drained and the healing begun."[13] No doubt the president was also concerned about the difficulty he or any Republican would have running for president in 1976 while Nixon was on trial for one or all of his many Watergate offenses.

As to whether granting a pardon cleared Nixon of guilt, as late as 1995, Ford carried in his wallet an opinion from the 1915 *Burdick* case in which the Supreme Court had ruled that a pardon "carries an imputation of guilt, acceptance, a confession of it."[14] Ford and his staff also knew that if Nixon were pardoned, he could not use the Fifth Amendment to avoid testifying against the other Watergate defendants.

The new president, who had to deal with Nixon's tapes and personal papers, thought that the pardon could be used to convince Nixon to accept Ford's solution to the problem of the ownership and possession of the papers. With these factors in mind, he dispatched a young White House lawyer, Benton L. Becker, to San Clemente to discuss a pardon and the papers and especially to obtain a statement of contrition from the former president that could be made public the same day Ford pardoned him. Haig warned the president, "You'll never get it."[15]

Becker, who flew out to San Clemente accompanied by Herbert Miller, reported back to Ford that Nixon was in terrible shape, appearing with "freakish grotesqueness" to be a man of eighty-five years, and "at times he appeared to drift."[16] But he was focused enough to refuse categorically to offer a statement of contrition. When Becker threatened to return to Washington, Ziegler prepared several different drafts of innocuous statements to meet Ford's requests. Haig had already informed Ziegler that the president was going to pardon Nixon no matter what, so he and the former president could afford to resist Becker's demands. Nixon finally approved a statement in which he admitted that he was "wrong in not acting more decisively and more forthrightly," and that he had made "mistakes and misjudgments" that might lead people to think that he had acted illegally. He now knew that he had handled Watergate in the "wrong way" and that it was a "burden I shall bear for every day of the life that is left to me."[17] Even with that mild statement, Nixon told Julie on 8 September, the day that Ford pardoned him, "This is the most humiliating day of my life."[18]

Speaking from the Oval Office at 11:05 that morning, Ford discussed the "American tragedy [that] could go on and on and on, or someone must write 'The End' to it. I have concluded that only I can do that, and if I can, I must. . . . I feel that Richard Nixon and his loved ones have suffered enough." Further, he doubted whether Nixon could ever get a fair trial or due process. Ford then signed Proclamation 4311 granting "a full, free, and absolute pardon unto Richard Nixon for all offenses against the United States, which he, Richard Nixon, has committed or may have committed or taken part in during the period from January 20, 1969 through August 9, 1974."

For Ford, this was "an unbelievable lifting of a burden." He admitted to having "failed to anticipate the vehemence of the hostile reaction to my decision." The American people "wanted to see him [Nixon] drawn and quartered publicly."[19] Ford's favorability rating in the polls dropped from 71 to 49 percent; mail and telegrams to the White House ran five to one against the pardon. Jerry terHorst, Ford's press secretary, resigned in protest over an act he "felt was ethically wrong."[20] With their eyes on the upcoming congressional elections, most Republicans on Capitol Hill were furious with Ford. Senator Marlow Cook (R-Ky.) complained, "Doesn't he have any sense of timing."[21] As for Senate Democrats, they introduced a resolution on 11 September, which passed by a vote of fifty-five to twenty-four, opposing any more Watergate pardons until the defendants had gone on trial and all their appeals had been exhausted. Several weeks later, Nixon called Ford and offered to give up his pardon if it would make the president's life any easier.

The outcry throughout the nation was so great that Ford took the unprecedented action of volunteering to go before a House Judiciary subcommittee to explain his actions. His appearance on 17 October marked the first time a president had testified in Congress since George Washington.

Explaining his reasons for the pardon and emphatically stating, "There was no deal, period, under no circumstances," Ford testified for two hours, facing gentle and polite questioning. Ford lost the popular vote to Jimmy Carter in the 1976 election by 2 percent. Seven percent of those who responded to exit polls reported that they had voted against Ford because of the pardon.

More Americans might have voted against Ford had they known about Nixon's attempt in the days after his resignation to ship all his presidential papers and tapes to San Clemente. Presidents had established their rights to their personal papers, but in this case, many of those documents would be needed in impending criminal cases. In 1973, Nixon had signed an agreement to donate his presidential papers to the National Archives. The day before he resigned, he changed the deed of gift, retaining sole access to his papers and any photocopying.

On 7 August, Rose Mary Woods had asked William Gulley, a marine sergeant in charge of the White House military office and liaison with former presidents, to begin making arrangements to pack up and ship Nixon's personal property to San Clemente. Two days later, Nixon called Haig from California asking to have his papers flown out to him. That same day, Jerry Jones, an aide Haig had entrusted with the tapes, instructed the White House staff to separate all Ford and Nixon materials, copy what it needed, and get ready to ship everything over the next few days. Gulley, who had advised Nixon to work quickly to retrieve his materials while the Ford White House was in disarray, "started shipping stuff out to San Clemente as fast it fell in my hands." Nixon told a sympathetic Gulley on 11 August, "Look I'm entitled to anything that any former President is entitled to."[22] That included 46 million pages of documents and 950 reels of tape that could fill three fifty-foot boxcars.

On the night of 11 August, Benton Becker happened to see boxes being loaded into an air force truck in the White House driveway. He quickly discovered what was going on, and when the uniformed personnel refused to heed his order to stop loading, he called out the Secret Service to enforce it. He then informed Ford about the shipment then on its way to Andrews Air Force Base and San Clemente. Becker considered the action "the final act of coverup of Watergate."[23] Although Becker did stop the shipment that night, and also halted the destruction of records in the White House burn room, not everyone had gotten the message. On 12 August, Jones was boxing up the tapes to be sent to Nixon when Buzhardt stopped him, because "if we let these tapes out of here, all hell is going to break loose. You and I may go to jail."[24] By that point, 400,000 pounds of material had already been sent to California, and other documents had been burned or shredded. When Nixon found out that the flow of his materials had stopped, he was furious at the Ford White House. "What are those bastards going to do to me?" he fumed.[25]

Nixon not only wanted to control the release of embarrassing tapes and other documents, he also needed them to respond to a subpoena to serve as a witness at the Ehrlichman trial. He expected, correctly, that this would be the first of a series of subpoenas he would be served. In addition, he wanted to be able to review materials for the writing of his memoirs. On 31 August in San Clemente, he met with Irving "Swifty" Lazar, a leading Hollywood agent, to talk about a book contract. When he left the White House, he was in desperate financial shape, considering the back taxes and legal fees he owed. (His Watergate legal fees alone through 1990 ultimately reached $1.8 million.) And he could no longer practice law, having resigned from the California and New York bars. Even after his resignation, Nixon haters in New York instituted disbarment proceedings. Consequently, he was enormously relieved when Lazar sold the rights to his memoirs, based in good measure on 10,000 pages of handwritten personal diaries, for $2.5 million. The book, *RN*, published in 1978, sold 330,000 copies in its first six months, despite generally negative reviews from his "friends" in the press.

After stopping the document airlift from the White House to San Clemente, Ford provisionally decided that all Nixon tapes and documents that had not been subpoenaed would be returned to the former president. A few days later, after hearing from Jaworski and his own legal counsel, he reversed himself. But Ford wanted to resolve the issue that was consuming so much of his time. That is how Becker came to negotiate a deal on his trip to San Clemente to obtain the contrition statement under which Nixon would agree to deposit his papers in the National Archives, although he would maintain title and control access to them and could withdraw them after three years. Under the terms of this agreement, his tapes would be destroyed when he died or by 1984. The so-called Nixon-Sampson (Arthur Sampson, administrator of the General Services Administration) agreement, which was announced the same day as the pardon, favored Nixon but granted him less control over his papers than that of previous presidents. Attorney General William Saxbe had advised Ford that Nixon's papers were his "private property" and that he was "alone as custodian of the materials."[26]

Jaworski strongly opposed the Nixon-Sampson agreement and urged Congress to abrogate it. Several weeks later, Congress passed the Presidential Recordings and Materials Preservation Act of 1974. This left Nixon's records—including the tapes—in the National Archives, which had sole authority to decide how to use them. A Ford aide worried that release of the tapes "will probably lead to the sensational and destructive exposure of President Nixon's dealings," which would embarrass the Republicans, the presidency, and the government itself.[27]

Passage of the Presidential Recordings and Materials Preservation Act did not end the matter, nor did the 1977 Supreme Court ruling upholding the act, which contended that Nixon could not automatically control his papers because his resignation put him "in a different class from all other Presidents."[28] Nixon and his lawyers fought for thirteen years against the release of his tapes and records. Their successful defense or obstructionism, which kept much unflattering material from reaching the public, explains in part why Nixon was able to rehabilitate himself during the 1980s. Starting in 1987, however, the Archives won the right to release papers and, later, tapes. As Nixon feared, those materials did not reflect favorably on his presidency, especially much of the first 200 hours of tapes released in 1996, the transcripts of which were published in *Abuse of Power*, edited by historian Stanley Kutler. The Nixon estate did win a battle in 1998 to compel the Archives to remove all private conversations from the tapes and send them to the Nixon Library. That same year, the estate sued the government for $213 million for the tapes, photographs, and papers seized in 1974.

Despite the 1977 Supreme Court ruling, Nixon did not think that he was in a different class from other presidents. He demanded the same treatment accorded other former presidents, including comparable air-travel accommodations and access to national security materials. On 14 February 1969, Nixon had issued an executive order establishing the Office of Special Assistant to the President for Liaison with Former Presidents, the main task of which was to keep former presidents informed about U.S. policies. Three weeks after he left Washington, Nixon told Gulley that he wanted briefings by NSC personnel, Haig, or Ford's new national security adviser, Brent Scowcroft.

Ford was quite generous with Nixon, agreeing to detail eighteen Secret Service personnel and twenty assistants for which Congress provided $200,000 for expenses and salaries during his first six months at San Clemente. There, Steve Bull, Ron Ziegler, Diane Sawyer, Rose Mary Woods, and Ray Price, among others, worked for Nixon while receiving salaries from the government and expenses up to $40 a day. Nixon's own presidential and congressional pensions totaled $80,000 per year. In addition, during the first two months, the government paid $126,000 for protection, $20,000 for courier flights, and $76,000 for maintenance. Congress, however, did not approve Ford's request for $850,000 for Nixon's transition expenses, settling on $200,000 as a reasonable amount.

Concerned about his status as a former president, worried about his financial situation, and shamed by his resignation and pardon, the exile had to deal with another severe crisis during that first fall in San Clemente, one that almost took his life. On 16 September, he experienced a recurrence of phlebitis, the ailment that had plagued him since 1964. On this occasion, he had to be hospitalized when a blood clot traveled from his left leg to his lung. A second trip to the hospital on 23 October posed an even more serious threat. While recovering from a difficult operation five days later, his blood pressure dropped to 60 over 0 for a brief period. In shock for three hours, Nixon hovered near death. He pulled through, returning to San Clemente on 14 November, in his own words, "a physical wreck; I was emotionally drained; I was mentally burned out. . . . I could see no reason to live."[29] To boost his morale, a compassionate Gerald Ford, who was on a western campaign trip, had visited him in the hospital on 31 October, the only time the two met while Ford was president. During that traumatic fall, depressed and isolated at San Clemente, Pat referred to herself and her husband as "two broken people."[30] They were even more depressed when prominent opinion leaders around the country thought that "Tricky Dick" was feigning near-death illnesses to avoid having to testify during the Watergate trials.

Nixon suffered more blows through 1974 and 1975 as his aides were sentenced in those trials. The Watergate grand jury, having sat for thirty months, completed its work in December 1974. Among those who went to trial and received prison terms were Dean (one to four years); Ehrlichman, Haldeman, and Mitchell (two and a half to eight years, but Sirica reduced their sentences in 1977 to Dean's term); LaRue (six months); Magruder (ten months to four years); Colson (one to three years); Krogh (two to six years); Liddy (six years and eight months to twenty years); McCord (one to five years); and Kalmbach (six to eighteen months). Nixon heard about Mitchell's and several others' sentences while he was enjoying the 1975 Rose Bowl on television.

Nixon hit bottom that holiday period, but he soon began his amazing comeback. On 25 January 1975, he told the visiting Barry Goldwater that the stories that "he was losing his will to live were 'bullshit.'"[31] In March, a Ford aide asked Gulley to see if Nixon would not mind sending the president political advice from time to time. With the code name "The Wizard," Nixon had begun working his way back to political respectability.

That December, without seeking permission from the White House, he accepted an invitation to visit China in February 1976, an action that infuriated Ford and other Republicans. Goldwater thought about invoking the Logan Act against him, saying on television, "As far as I'm concerned

Mr. Nixon can go to China and stay there." He later remarked, "I wouldn't speak to that son of a bitch if he was dying of thirst out in the desert" and later demonstrated his disgust with his old friend by not attending his funeral in 1994.[32]

Nixon's comeback received a temporary setback in 1976 when Woodward and Bernstein published *The Final Days*, a far more sensational book than *All the President's Men*. *The Final Days* dealt with the resignation and Nixon's unstable behavior during that period. The reporters alleged gratuitously that the Nixons, involved in a loveless marriage, had not slept together for twenty years. In July 1976, while reading the book, Pat suffered a stroke from which she never completely recovered.

In the next step on his road to rehabilitation and financial security, Nixon agreed to be interviewed on television in May 1977 by David Frost. For that series of interviews, he was paid $600,000 and 20 percent of related profits, of which $540,000 went to his lawyers. Nixon came up with the interviews-for-money idea when CBS paid Haldeman $100,000 for an interview. Although Frost posed many embarrassing questions in front of an audience that reached 50 million, Nixon more than held his own, particularly when he talked about foreign affairs and the great leaders he had met over the years. But he admitted that he had "let down" his friends and fellow citizens, that he had engaged in a cover-up, and that "I brought myself down. I gave them a sword. And they stuck it in. And they twisted it with relish. And, I guess, if I'd been in their position, I'd have done the same thing."[33] After the series, 44 percent of Americans felt more sympathy for him, 28 percent less.

In November 1978, Nixon traveled to Great Britain to appear at the Oxford Union. He asserted, "Some people say I didn't handle it [Watergate] properly, and they're right. I screwed it up. And I paid the price. *Mea culpa.* But let's get on to my achievements. You'll be here in the year 2000 and we'll see how I'm regarded then."[34] He left the room to a standing ovation.

Audiences were enthralled with his reminiscences and prognostications about foreign policy. He had known almost all of the prominent cold war leaders. Speaking without notes, he displayed a prodigious memory as he pontificated about the great issues of war and peace. He solidified his position by publishing an astounding flurry of books about international relations between 1980 and 1992, almost all of which became best-sellers. During those twelve years, he wrote *The Real War* (1980), *Leaders* (1982), *Real Peace: A Strategy for the West* (1984), *No More Vietnams* (1985), *1999: Victory without War* (1988), *In the Arena: A Memoir of Victory, Defeat, and Renewal* (1990), *Seize the Moment: America's Challenge in a One Superpower*

World (1990), and *Beyond Peace* (1994). Although foreign policy experts did not find the arguments in the books especially interesting or new, his anecdotes about his experiences attracted many readers.

Nixon did not write these books merely to make money. For one thing, he wanted to reestablish himself as the nation's preeminent foreign policy expert. More important, he wanted to continue to exercise some influence over American diplomacy. For example, he was extremely disturbed by Jimmy Carter's overly soft foreign policy, a subject he began speaking about in public in July 1978. That did not stop Carter from inviting him to the White House for a dinner with Chinese leaders the following January. And unlike Ford, Carter was not upset when Nixon went to China that September. By that time, a Gallup poll ranked Nixon among the ten most admired men in the world.

He moved back to New York in 1980, where major opinion leaders and celebrities vied for invitations to dinner at his fashionable brownstone. Nixon's salon was a men-only affair, in part because of the rough language. Following Ronald Reagan's election, Nixon commanded increased influence because his former aides Richard Allen, George Shultz, Caspar Weinberger, William Casey, Lynn Nofziger, and Al Haig (whose appointment he lobbied for) all played major roles in the new Republican administration. However, unlike Carter, Reagan and later George Bush did not invite Nixon to the White House during their terms in office. Nor was he invited to Republican conventions.

In 1981, Nixon joined former presidents Carter and Ford to lead the U.S. delegation to Egyptian president Anwar Sadat's funeral. The sharp-tongued Bob Dole described the trio as "See No Evil, Hear No Evil, and Evil."[35] Despite Dole's acerbic comment, Nixon was by then winning his campaign for ex-president. In November 1982, he organized a reunion in Washington for members of his administration. For most of them, including those who went to jail, all seemed to be forgiven. Yet a Gallup poll released that year revealed the number of Americans who thought that Nixon should have resigned had increased to 75 percent, compared with 65 percent in 1974. In 1987, his "favorable" rating in the polls stood at 39 percent, well below that of Edward Kennedy at 64 percent and Jesse Jackson at 51 percent.

Nixon's comeback could not be complete without the erection of a presidential library. All modern ex-presidents had presidential libraries, but establishing one for Nixon was not easy. In July 1981, the president of Duke University told the most famous alumnus of his law school that he would like to locate the library on his campus. The university's academic council voted down the project by one vote. After other false starts, the Nixon Presidential Library and Birthplace was finally established in Yorba Linda, California, with the original modest home in which he grew up situated on the grounds. Unlike all the other presidential libraries, this was a private library not run by the National Archives. Further, without the Nixon papers, it was more a museum than an archive. Nixon chose the director, who had the sole authority to decide what documents to collect and who could use them. The library, which cost $25 million raised from private funds, opened on 19 July 1990. For the first time in history, four presidents and their wives appeared in public together when Presidents Bush, Ford, and Reagan attended the impressive dedication ceremonies, along with a crowd of 50,000. With state-of-the-art technology and lavish displays, the library saluted Nixon's triumphs and paid scant attention to his failures.

Whatever people may have thought of Watergate and Nixon personally, by the time the library opened, many considered him a wise elder statesman whose ideas about foreign policy, particularly relating to the communist bloc, were worth listening to. Aside from writing books, he spent a good deal of time in the eighties traveling around the world, visiting friends in the East and West, and offering his views in newspapers and on television about the shape of the world. Like the rest of his party, he soured on détente during the Reagan years. However, enthused about the prospects for democracy in the Soviet Union by the end of the decade, he became impatient with George Bush's unwillingness to offer more support to new Russian reformers such as Boris Yeltsin.

During the remaining two years of his life, by cleverly using the media, he once again influenced U.S. Soviet policy. On 25 February 1992, Nixon sent President Bush a memo criticizing his policy toward the Soviet Union and calling for more U.S. aid, loans, and experts to assist the new Yeltsin regime. He sent a similar memo, entitled "How the West Lost the Cold War," to fifty leaders and opinion makers, including Kissinger, Carter's NSC adviser Zbigniew Brzezinski, and influential *New York Times* columnist William Safire, hoping that they would leak it to the press and thereby pressure Bush to act on his recommendations. The memo, which quickly found its way into the columns of the *Times* and *Washington Post*, served as a backdrop and advance publicity for a conference Nixon had organized in Washington on "America's Role in the Emerging World." Running for reelection and engaged in difficult primary contests, Bush felt compelled to accept an invitation to speak at the conference, at which Nixon's views predominated. Based on this gambit, Leonard Garment labeled Nixon "the Magic Johnson" of politics, with flashy moves comparable to those of the professional basketball star.[36]

Although disappointed that Clinton won the election that year, in part because his victory "vindicated . . . anti-Vietnam, draft-dodging, drug-taking behavior," Nixon continued his efforts to influence U.S. foreign policy.[37] Using Clinton campaign aide Dick Morris as liaison, he sent word to the new president that he wanted to talk to him about foreign policy and that a meeting would "buy" the new president a "one-year moratorium" on criticism. He warned Clinton that he was going to write a foreign policy op-ed piece in the *New York Times* on 5 March 1993 that "could be gentle or not so gentle."[38] Clinton agreed to see him in the White House on 8 March; the article on 5 March was gentle. Initially pleased with the brief friendship he developed with Clinton during this period, he soon became disappointed with the new president's grasp of foreign policy.

Pat Nixon died in 1993. Richard Nixon died on 22 April the following year after suffering a severe stroke. He had previously instructed his family not to take dramatic measures in such a situation to prolong his life. Clinton and his wife and all four living ex-presidents and their wives attended his funeral at Yorba Linda on 27 April. Never before in American history had so many first families appeared together at a presidential funeral. In his eulogy, Henry Kissinger quoted Shakespeare, "He was a man, take him for all in all. I shall not look upon his like again." California governor Pete Wilson praised him as "a grocer's son" who was a "fighter of iron will." Billy Graham told the audience, "I never heard him one time criticize a living President who was in office at that time." The most impressive tribute came from Clinton, who mentioned Nixon's contributions to cancer research and the environment, his "wise counsel" on Russia, and how even in his last years, he displayed "an incredibly sharp and vigorous and rigorous mind." Alluding obliquely to Watergate, the president then graciously proclaimed, "May the day of judging President Nixon on anything less than his entire life and career come to a close."[39]

Not everyone was pleased with Clinton's and the other luminaries' tributes to the former president. Former undersecretary of state George Ball, who himself died a month later, considered the Nixon funeral "the most obscene orgy of revisionism that I've seen in this country. Why should they rehabilitate the son of a bitch?"[40]

After more than a decade of popular acceptance as a wise elder statesman, even in death, Richard Nixon arouses strong passions. Those passions help explain, in part, why American historians, many of whom are liberals, have continued to rank his presidency a failure. Furthermore, the infamous tapes confirm what Nixon haters knew all the time—he was a crude, bigoted, and mean-spirited fellow whose entire life seemed to be devoted to destroying real and imagined enemies.

If it is possible to evaluate Nixon's years in the White House without considering his character and the scandals that led to his resignation, then his presidency certainly seems far from a failure. At the least, he can be credited with scores of accomplishments at home and abroad that make those of Democratic contemporaries, Presidents Kennedy and Carter, pale in comparison.

In his own evaluations, Nixon always began with foreign policy. He took pride in the construction of détente with the Soviet Union in the early seventies, which contributed to the process that led to the détente of the mid-eighties and ultimately to the end of the cold war. And while the United States was destined to open relations with the People's Republic of China someday, it took courage and diplomatic dexterity for that inveterate anticommunist to break bread with Mao Zedong and Zhou Enlai.

Nixon also ended the Vietnam War. Here, he deserves more censure than credit for not ending the war sooner and for not fulfilling his promise to establish a peace with honor that could have saved South Vietnam from communism. Such a promise, of course, could not have been fulfilled by any U.S. leader in the early seventies. Even more important, the devious and deceitful ways that he and Henry Kissinger planned and executed their Southeast Asian policies were all too characteristic of their penchant for ignoring the fact that they were operating in a democracy.

It is also difficult to give Nixon much credit for his activities in the Third World, where, among other misadventures, he played a nefarious role in the destabilization of Salvador Allende's government in Chile, and his administration's policies in the Middle East made the outbreak of war in October 1973 more likely. But it is true, as Nixon and Kissinger had hoped, that the Egyptian "victory" created the conditions that led to the Camp David peace accords between Egypt and Israel five years later.

In many ways, Nixon's domestic record, absent Watergate, is more impressive. To be sure, he shares much of the responsibility for progressive legislation with a Democratic Congress with which he was often in mortal combat. Nonetheless, he signed legislation that made him the most environmentally conscious president since Theodore Roosevelt. Among the other initiatives he approved were those ending the draft, giving eighteen-year-olds the vote, establishing OSHA, dramatically increasing federal spending for the arts and humanities and for cancer research, and introducing an unprecedented welfare reform proposal. In addition, despite his racially polarizing rhetoric, it was during Nixon's tenure that segregated schools were finally dismantled in the South.

Like most presidents, he tinkered with the economy for political reasons, even to the point of accepting, against his better judgment, wage and price controls in 1971. Though his quick fix for 1972 temporarily halted the economy's downward spiral—and helped get him reelected—it may have exacerbated the hard times that Americans confronted through the rest of the seventies and into the eighties. Yet Presidents Ford and Carter, and President Reagan during his first term, did not offer any more successful solutions to the nation's structural economic problems than had Nixon.

No matter how Nixon and his defenders would like to avoid the subject, however, there is no way to evaluate his domestic political record without paying considerable attention to what years later he called the "Watergate crap," that "silly, silly thing."[41] Billy Graham suggested that Watergate was "a brief parenthesis in a good man's lengthy political career."[42] His good friend was being charitable. One can easily make a case that Watergate was emblematic of Nixon's behavior throughout his career. After all, he once told Leonard Garment, "You're never going to make it in politics, Len. You just don't know how to lie."[43] Dean Burch claimed, "The man didn't believe in anything. He didn't believe in a religion or principle or anything. He was totally cynical."[44]

Watergate did not begin when CREEP operatives broke into Democratic headquarters in 1972. It began when Nixon took office, armed with his private slush fund, prepared to do battle by fair means and foul against his enemies. Although he felt that he was merely playing political hardball, no president before or after ordered or participated in so many serious illegal and extralegal acts that violated constitutional principles. The wiretapping and surveillance of his enemies in politics and the media, his attempts to replace civil-service bureaucrats with loyal Republicans, his intervention in Democratic primary politics, and his shakedown of corporate America for campaign contributions came close to undermining the entire political system.

When asked by pollsters in 1987 to list twelve major events that most affected their political views, Americans ranked Watergate fourth behind the Vietnam War, Ronald Reagan, and the sixties' assassinations. Watergate's legacies include a distressing decline in American citizens' trust in government and scores of reforms instituted to prevent future Watergates, such as the Budget and Impoundment Control Act of 1974; the 1978 Ethics in Government Act, which provided for the appointment of an independent counsel to investigate White House misdeeds; the 1974 amendments to the Federal Election Campaign Act; the 1974 and 1978 Presidential Materials and Preservation Acts; and several major reforms of the CIA and FBI that grew out of the 1975 congressional hearings on their abuses. Watergate also gave rise to an aggressively intrusive brand of investigative journalism that has made it difficult for any White House since to keep its professional and personal skeletons in the closet.

Much of this might have transpired eventually with or without Richard Nixon. Historian Joan Hoff maintains that Watergate was the natural product of the political system as it existed in the seventies, "a disaster waiting to happen."[45] Perhaps, but one wonders whether it would have happened the way it did on anyone else's watch but Nixon's. His was among the most unusual, controversial, and tragic presidencies in American history. Indeed, his entire career could be described in those terms. Preeminent Nixon biographer Stephen E. Ambrose considers Nixon "Shakespearean like no other American politician."[46] His controversial and wide-ranging political activities from the 1946 congressional campaign to the 1993 "blackmailing" of Bill Clinton continue to engage the interest of those scholars who are able to approach their endlessly fascinating subject with any degree of objectivity. The period from the end of World War II to the end of the cold war was in good measure an age of Nixon.

NOTES

In citing sources in the notes, the following abbreviations have been used:

cf	confidential
co	contested
GFL	Gerald R. Ford Presidential Library
HI	Hoover Institution Archives
NP	Nixon Presidential Materials Project
PDDS	Presidential Decision Directives Series
PH	President's Handwriting
POF	President's Office Files
PPF	President's Personal Files
RNL	Richard Nixon Presidential Library and Birthplace
SF	subject file
WHCF	White House Central Files

PREFACE

1. Quoted in Leon Friedman and William F. Levantrosser, eds., *Watergate and Afterward: The Legacy of Richard M. Nixon* (Westport, Conn.: Greenwood, 1992), p. 36.

CHAPTER 1
TRAIN WHISTLES IN THE NIGHT

1. Richard M. Nixon, *In the Arena: A Memoir of Victory, Defeat, and Renewal* (New York: Simon & Schuster, 1990), p. 75.

2. Stewart Alsop, *Nixon and Rockefeller: A Double Portrait* (Garden City, N.Y.: Doubleday, 1960), p. 196.

3. U.S. Congress, Joint Committee on Printing, *Memorial Services in the Congress of the United States and Tributes in Eulogy of Richard M. Nixon, Late a President of the United States* (Washington, D.C.: U.S. Government Printing Office, 1996), p. 7.

4. Hugh Sidey, "Perspectives on Richard Nixon," in Leon Friedman and William F. Levantrosser, eds., *Politician, President, Administrator: Richard M. Nixon* (Westport, Conn.: Greenwood, 1991), p. 9; Tom Wicker, *One of Us: Richard Nixon and the American Dream* (New York: Random House, 1991), p. xiv; Arkady N. Shevchenko, *Breaking with Moscow* (New York: Knopf, 1985), p. 215.

5. William Safire, *Before the Fall: An Inside View of the Pre-Watergate White House* (Garden City, N.Y.: Doubleday, 1975), p. 8.

6. Monica Crowley, *Nixon Off the Record: His Candid Commentary on People and Politics* (New York: Random House, 1996), p. 204.

7. Alsop, *Nixon and Rockefeller*, p. 184.

8. Richard Nixon, *RN: The Memoirs of Richard Nixon* (New York: Grosset & Dunlap, 1978), pp. 4, 3.

9. Alsop, *Nixon and Rockefeller*, p. 185.

10. Nixon, *In the Arena*, p. 89.

11. Bryce Harlow in Kenneth W. Thompson, ed., *The Nixon Presidency—Twenty-two Intimate Perspectives of Richard M. Nixon* (Lanham, Md.: University Press of America, 1987), p. 8.

12. Roger Morris, *Richard Milhous Nixon: The Rise of an American Politician* (New York: Henry Holt, 1990), p. 118.

13. Jonathan Aitken, *Nixon: A Life* (Washington, D.C.: Regnery, 1993), p. 32.

14. Ibid., p. 44.

15. Stephen E. Ambrose, *Nixon: The Education of a Politician, 1913–1962* (New York: Simon & Schuster, 1987), p. 76; Nixon, *RN*, p. 20.

16. William C. Sullivan with Bill Brown, *The Bureau: My Thirty Years in Hoover's FBI* (New York: Norton, 1979), p. 196.

17. Nixon, *RN*, p. 23.

18. Ibid., p. 26.

19. Ralph de Toledano, *One Man Alone: Richard Nixon* (New York: Funk & Wagnalls, 1969), p. 45.

20. William Costello, *The Facts about Richard Nixon: An Unauthorized Biography* (New York: Viking, 1960), p. 39.

21. Morris, *Richard Milhous Nixon*, p. 284.

22. Nixon to Perry, 12 December 1945, PE 217, Richard Nixon Presidential Library and Birthplace (hereafter RNL), Yorba Linda, California.

23. Nixon, *RN*, p. 35.

24. Ibid., p. 39.

25. Ibid., p. 42.

26. de Toledano, *One Man Alone*, p. 56.

27. Ibid., pp. 164–65.

28. Morris, *Richard Milhous Nixon*, p. 375.

29. Herbert Klein, exit interview, p. 5, Nixon Presidential Materials Project (hereafter NP), National Archives II, College Park, Maryland.

30. Telephone interview with Gerald R. Ford, 15 May 1997.

31. Wicker, *One of Us*, p. 66.

32. Herbert S. Parmet, *Richard Nixon and His America* (Boston: Little, Brown, 1990), p. 169.

33. Christopher Matthews, *Kennedy and Nixon: The Rivalry that Shaped Postwar America* (New York: Simon & Schuster, 1996), p. 64.

34. Nixon, *RN*, p. 81.

35. Richard M. Nixon, *Six Crises* (Garden City, N.Y.: Doubleday, 1962), p. 62.

36. Morris, *Richard Milhous Nixon*, p. 475.

37. Wicker, *One of Us*, p. 76.

38. Ambrose, *Nixon: The Education of a Politician*, p. 210.

39. Morris, *Richard Milhous Nixon*, p. 578.

40. Parmet, *Richard Nixon and His America*, p. 215.

41. Nixon, *RN*, p. 78.

42. Morris, *Richard Milhous Nixon*, p. 617.

43. Matthews, *Kennedy and Nixon*, pp. 123, 74.

44. Costello, *The Facts about Richard Nixon*, p. 7.

45. Aitken, *Nixon*, p. 222.

46. Nixon, *RN*, p. 110.

47. Dwight David Eisenhower, *Mandate for Change, 1953–1956* (Garden City, N.Y.: Doubleday, 1965), p. 165.

48. Costello, *The Facts about Richard Nixon*, p. 104.

49. Stephen E. Ambrose, *Eisenhower*, vol. 1, *Soldier, General of the Army, President-Elect, 1890–1952* (New York: Simon & Schuster, 1983), p. 554.

50. Nixon, *RN*, p. 98; Nixon, *Six Crises*, p. 100.

51. Ronald Steel, *Walter Lippmann and the American Century* (New York: Vintage, 1980), p. 483.

52. Nixon, *Six Crises*, p. 128; Julie Nixon Eisenhower, *Pat Nixon: The Untold Story* (New York: Simon & Schuster, 1986), p. 52.

53. Nixon, *RN*, p. 117.

54. Robert Schulzinger, *A Time for War: The United States and Vietnam, 1941–1975* (New York: Oxford University Press, 1997), p. 58.

55. Robert R. Bowie and Richard Immerman, *Waging Peace: How Eisenhower Shaped Enduring Cold War Strategy* (New York: Oxford University Press, 1998).

56. Costello, *The Facts about Richard Nixon*, p. 276.

57. Interview with Andrew Goodpaster, 26 September 1996, Washington, D.C.

58. Emmet John Hughes, *The Ordeal of Power: A Political Memoir of the Eisenhower Years* (New York: Atheneum, 1963), p. 173; Milton J. Eisenhower, *The President Is Calling* (Garden City, N.Y.: Doubleday, 1974), pp. 325–26; Goodpaster interview.

59. Nixon, *Six Crises*, p. 202; Vernon A. Walters, *Silent Missions* (Garden City, N.Y.: Doubleday, 1978), p. 323.

60. John Lewis Gaddis, *We Now Know: Rethinking Cold War History* (Oxford: Oxford University Press, 1997), p. 179.

61. Nixon, *Six Crises*, pp. 258, 257; Nikita S. Khrushchev, *Khrushchev Remembers: The Last Testament* (Boston: Little, Brown, 1974), p. 207.

62. Michael R. Beschloss, *Mayday: Eisenhower, Khrushchev, and the U-2 Affair* (New York: Harper & Row, 1986), p. 341.

63. Khrushchev, *Khrushchev Remembers*, p. 491.

64. Beschloss, *Mayday*, p. 183.

65. Parmet, *Richard Nixon and His America*, p. 396.

66. Beschloss, *Mayday*, p. 114.

67. Eisenhower to Nixon, 25 September 1963, PPS 324.214, RNL.

68. Eisenhower to Nixon, 28 January 1959, PPS 324.127, RNL.

69. Elliot Richardson, oral history, p. 5, NP.

70. Goodpaster interview.

71. Eisenhower to Nixon, 28 October 1960, PPS 324.145, RNL.

72. Richard Whalen, *Catch the Falling Flag: A Republican's Challenge to His Party* (Boston: Houghton Mifflin, 1972), p. 13.

73. Ibid., p. 14.

74. Ben Bradlee, *A Good Life: Newspapering and Other Adventures* (New York: Simon & Schuster, 1995), p. 211; Lawrence F. O'Brien, *No Final Victories: A Life in Politics from John F. Kennedy to Watergate* (Garden City, N.Y.: Doubleday, 1974), p. 93.

75. Whalen, *Catch the Falling Flag*, p. 14.

76. Wicker, *One of Us*, p. 257.

77. Nixon, *Six Crises*, p. 422.

78. Nixon, *RN*, p. 228.

79. Ibid., p. 239.

80. Nixon to Robert Finch, 16 November 1972, box 16, John G. Veneman papers, Hoover Institution Archives (hereafter HI), Stanford, California.

81. Klein, exit interview, p. 23, NP.

82. Aitken, *Nixon*, p. 305.

83. Ibid., p. 306.

84. John Robert Greene, *The Limits of Power: The Nixon and Ford Administrations* (Bloomington: Indiana University Press, 1992), p. 16.

85. Nixon, *RN*, p. 265.

86. A. James Reichley, *Conservatives in an Age of Change: The Nixon and Ford Administrations* (Washington, D.C.: Brookings, 1981), pp. 53, 57.

87. Lewis L. Gould, *1968: The Election that Changed America* (Chicago: Ivan Dee, 1993), p. 28; Lewis Chester, Godfrey Hodgson, and Bruce Page, *An American Melodrama: The Presidential Campaign of 1968* (New York: Dell, 1969), p. 113.

88. Dan T. Carter, *The Politics of Rage: George Wallace, the Origins of the New Conservatism, and the Transformation of American Politics* (New York: Simon & Schuster, 1995), p. 329; Kenneth O'Reilly, *Nixon's Piano: Presidents and Racial Politics from Washington to Clinton* (New York: Free Press, 1995), p. 281.

89. Theodore H. White, *The Making of the President: 1968* (New York: Atheneum, 1969), p. 290.

90. Whalen, *Catch the Falling Flag*, p. 202.

91. Aitken, *Nixon*, p. 357.

92. Katherine Graham, *Personal History* (New York: Knopf, 1997), p. 409.

93. Nixon, *RN*, p. 315.

94. White, *The Making of the President: 1968*, p. 390.

95. Chester et al., *American Melodrama*, p. 707.

96. Rudy Abramson, *Spanning the Century: The Life of W. Averell Harriman, 1891–1986* (New York: Morrow, 1992), p. 668.

97. John Morton Blum, *Years of Discord: American Politics and Society, 1961–1974* (New York: Norton, 1991), p. 311; Wicker, *One of Us*, p. 292.

98. Jonathan Schell, *The Time of Illusion* (New York: Vintage, 1976), p. 41.

99. Whalen, *Catch the Falling Flag*, p. 212.

100. Joe McGinniss, *The Selling of the President, 1968* (New York: Trident, 1969) p. 39.

101. Ibid., p. 58.

102. Wicker, *One of Us*, p. 366.

103. Steel, *Walter Lippmann*, p. 589.

104. Whalen, *Catch the Falling Flag*, p. 137.

105. Parmet, *Richard Nixon and His America*, p. 506; Safire, *Before the Fall*, p. 48.

106. David M. Barrett, ed., *Lyndon Johnson's Vietnam Papers: A Documentary Collection* (College Station: Texas A & M Press, 1997), p. 786.

107. Gould, *1968*, p. 145.

108. Ilya V. Gaiduk, *The Soviet Union and the Vietnam War* (Chicago: Ivan Dee, 1996), pp. 181–82.

109. Lyndon B. Johnson, *The Vantage Point: Perspectives of the Presidency, 1963–1969* (New York: Holt, Rinehart & Winston), p. 521.

110. Kent G. Sieg, "The 1968 Presidential Election and Peace in Vietnam," *Presidential Studies Quarterly* 26 (fall 1996): 1072.

111. Robert Dallek, *Flawed Giant: Lyndon Johnson and His Times, 1961–1973* (New York: Oxford University Press, 1998), p. 588.

112. McGinniss, *The Selling of the President*, p. 23.

113. Schell, *The Time of Illusion*, p. 17.

CHAPTER 2
ORGANIZING THE WHITE HOUSE

1. Henry Brandon, *The Retreat of American Power* (New York: Dell, 1974), p. 12.

2. Peter N. Carroll, *It Seemed Like Nothing Happened: America in the Seventies* (New Brunswick, N.J.: Rutgers University Press, 1990), p. 31.

3. Katherine Graham, *Personal History* (New York: Knopf, 1997), p. 410.

4. John Anthony Maltese, *Spin Control: The White House Office of Communications and the Management of Presidential News*, 2d ed.(Chapel Hill: University of North Carolina Press, 1994), p. 12.

5. William Safire, *Before the Fall: An Inside View of the Pre-Watergate White House* (Garden City, N.Y.: Doubleday, 1975), p. 265.

6. Samuel Kernell and Samuel L. Popkin, eds., *Chief of Staff: Twenty Five Years of Managing the Presidency* (Berkeley: University of California Press, 1986), p. 183.

7. Tom Wicker, *One of Us: Richard Nixon and the American Dream* (New York: Random House, 1991), p. 446.

8. Herbert G. Klein, *Making It Perfectly Clear* (Garden City, N.Y.: Doubleday, 1980), p. 8.

9. Monica Crowley, *Nixon Off the Record: His Candid Commentary on People and Politics* (New York: Random House, 1996), p. 148.

10. Shirley Anne Warshaw, *Powersharing: White House–Cabinet Relations in the Modern Presidency* (Albany: State University of New York Press, 1996), p. 42.

11. Richard Nixon, *RN: The Memoirs of Richard Nixon* (New York: Grosset & Dunlap, 1978), p. 338.

12. Joan Hoff, *Nixon Reconsidered* (New York: Basic Books, 1994), p. 52.

13. Earl Mazo and Stephen Hess, *Nixon: A Political Portrait* (New York: Harper, 1968), p. 314.

14. Kernell and Popkin, *Chief of Staff*, pp. 214–15.

15. Elliot Richardson, *Reflections of a Moderate Conservative* (New York: Pantheon, 1996), p. 119.

16. Seymour Hersh, *The Price of Power: Kissinger in the White House* (New York: Simon & Schuster, 1983), p. 71n.

17. Henry Kissinger, *White House Years* (Boston: Little, Brown, 1979), p. 32.

18. John Ehrlichman meeting notes, 3 December 1970, HI.

19. Ibid.

20. Robert Alan Goldberg, *Barry Goldwater* (New Haven, Conn.: Yale University Press, 1995), p. 252.

21. Fred Malek to Nixon, 4 November 1971, box 7, Malek papers, HI.

22. Ehrlichman meeting notes, 3 December 1970, HI.

23. A. James Reichley, *Conservatives in an Age of Change: The Nixon and Ford Administrations* (Washington, D.C: Brookings, 1981), p. 63.

24. John Ehrlichman, *Witness to Power: The Nixon Years* (New York: Simon & Schuster, 1982), p. 107.

25. Ehrlichman meeting notes, 19 March 1971, HI.

26. Herbert S. Parmet, *Richard Nixon and His America* (Boston: Little, Brown, 1990), p. 23.

27. Rowland Evans, Jr., and Robert D. Novak, *Nixon in the White House: The Frustration of Power* (New York: Random House, 1971), p. 51.

28. H. R. Haldeman, *The Haldeman Diaries: Inside the Nixon White House* (New York: G. P. Putnam's Sons, 1994), p. 309.

29. Kissinger, *White House Years*, p. 25.

30. John C. Whitaker, "Nixon's Domestic Policies: Both Liberal and Bold in Retrospect," *Presidential Studies Quarterly* 26 (winter 1996): 134.

31. Jeb Stuart Magruder, *An American Life: One Man's Road to Watergate* (New York: Atheneum, 1974), p. 61.

32. Elizabeth Drew, *Washington Journal: The Events of 1973–1974* (New York: Vintage, 1976), p. 394.

33. Nixon to Haldeman, 16 June 1969, box 7, EX FG 6 11-1, Haldeman, Subject Files (hereafter SF), White House Central Files (hereafter WHCF), NP.

34. Michael Medved, *The Shadow Presidents: The Secret History of the Chief Executives and Their Top Aides* (New York: Times Books, 1979), p. 312.

35. Jerry Jones interview, box 1, Hyde and Wayne collection, Gerald R. Ford Presidential Library (hereafter GFL), Ann Arbor, Michigan.

36. Bill Gulley, *Breaking Cover* (New York: Simon & Schuster, 1980), p. 123.

37. Kenneth W. Thompson, ed., *The Nixon Presidency—Twenty-two Intimate Perspectives of Richard M. Nixon* (Lanham, Md.: University Press of America, 1987), p. 132.

38. Safire, *Before the Fall*, p. 464.

39. Tod Hullin to White House switchboard, 10 March 1972, box 6, EX FG 6-11-1, Ehrlichman, SF, WHCF, NP.

40. Frederick V. Malek, *Washington's Hidden Tragedy: The Failure to Make Government Work* (New York: Free Press, 1978), p. 31.

41. Clark Mollenhoff, *Game Plan for Disaster: An Ombudsman's Report on the Nixon Years* (New York: Norton, 1976), pp. 33, 32.

42. Robert Sam Anson, *Exile: The Unquiet Oblivion of Richard M. Nixon* (New York: Simon & Schuster, 1984), p. 239.

43. Robert T. Hartmann, *Palace Politics: An Inside Account of the Ford Years* (New York: McGraw-Hill, 1980), p. 171.

44. Reichley, *Conservatives in an Age of Change*, p. 70; Jonathan Aitken, *Nixon: A Life* (Washington, D.C.: Regnery, 1993), p. 375.

45. Elliot Richardson in Thompson, *The Nixon Presidency*, p. 68.

46. Dan Rather and Gary Paul Gates, *The Palace Guard* (New York: Warner, 1975), p. 87.

47. Haldeman to Ehrlichman, 1 July 1969, contested (hereafter [co]), box 412, Haldeman papers, NP.

48. Colson, oral history, p. 17, NP.

49. Rather and Gates, *The Palace Guard*, p. 331.

50. Colson, exit interview, p. 5, NP.

51. Magruder, *An American Life*, p. 69.

52. Harlow to Haldeman, 10 December 1969 (co), box 55, Haldeman papers, NP.

53. Magruder, *An American Life*, p. 65.

54. Peri E. Arnold, *Making the Managerial Presidency: Comprehensive Reorganization Planning, 1905–1980* (Princeton, N.J.: Princeton University Press, 1986), p. 298.

55. Patrick J. Buchanan, *Conservative Votes, Liberal Victories: Why the Right Has Failed* (New York: Quadrangle, 1975), p. 18.

56. Colson to Haldeman, 5 August 1971 (co), box 273, Haldeman papers, NP.

57. Walter Isaacson, *Kissinger: A Biography* (New York: Simon & Schuster, 1992), p. 133; Bernard Kalb and Marvin Kalb, *Kissinger* (London: Hutchinson, 1974), p. 21.

58. Hersh, *The Price of Power*, p. 20.

59. Interview with Alexander Haig, 24 September 1996, Washington, D.C.

60. Alexander M. Haig, Jr., with Charles McCarry, *Inner Circles: How America Changed the World: Memoirs* (New York: Warner, 1992), p. 205.

61. Interview with Andrew Goodpaster, 26 September 1996, Washington, D.C.

62. John H. Holdridge, *Crossing the Divide: An Insider's Account of Normalization of US-China Relations* (Lanham, Md.: Rowman & Littlefield, 1997), p. 32.

63. Haig interview.

64. Richard M. Nixon, *In the Arena: A Memoir of Victory, Defeat, and Renewal* (New York: Simon & Schuster, 1990), p. 271.

65. John Newhouse, *War and Peace in the Nuclear Age* (New York: Knopf, 1989), p. 212.

66. Bob Woodward and Carl Bernstein, *The Final Days* (Simon & Schuster, 1976), pp. 188, 168, 196.

67. William Shawcross, *Sideshow: Kissinger, Nixon, and the Destruction of Cambodia*, rev. ed. (New York: Touchstone, 1987), p. 101.

68. Nixon, *RN*, p. 433.

69. U. Alexis Johnson with Jef Olivarius McAllister, *The Right Hand of Power* (Englewood Cliffs, N.J.: Prentice Hall, 1984), p. 517.

70. Monica Crowley, *Nixon in Winter* (New York: Random House, 1998), p. 293.

71. Hedrick Smith, *The Power Game: How Washington Works* (New York: Random House, 1988) p. 600.

72. Nixon note to Peter Flanigan and Kissinger on Schmidt to Nixon, 24 March 1969 (co), box 15, President's Personal Files (hereafter PPF), NP.

73. Leonard Garment, *Crazy Rhythm: My Journey from Brooklyn, Jazz, and Wall Street to Nixon's White House, Watergate, and Beyond . . .* (New York: Times Books, 1997), pp. 186, 187.

74. Johnson, *The Right Hand of Power*, p. 519.

75. Kissinger, *White House Years*, p. 887.

76. Hersh, *The Price of Power*, p. 467.

77. Haig interview.

78. Nixon, *RN*, p. 532.

79. Kissinger, *White House Years*, p. 36.

80. Robert M. Gates, *From the Shadows: The Ultimate Insider's Story of Five Presidents and How They Won the Cold War* (New York: Simon & Schuster, 1996), p. 43.

81. Nixon, *RN*, p. 358.

82. Mark Riebling, *Wedge: The Secret War between the FBI and the CIA* (New York: Knopf, 1994), p. 282.

83. Ibid.

84. David Frost, *"I Gave Them a Sword": Behind the Scenes of the Nixon Interviews* (New York: William Morrow, 1978) p. 183.

85. John Robert Greene, *The Limits of Power: The Nixon and Ford Administrations* (Bloomington: Indiana University Press, 1992), p. 134.

86. Taped conversation, 13 April 1971, tape 2, 247-4, NP.

87. Cartha D. DeLoach, *Hoover's FBI* (Washington, D.C.: Regnery, 1995), p. 412.

88. Riebling, *Wedge,* p. 288.

89. Ehrlichman meeting notes, 20 September 1971, HI.

CHAPTER 3
ENDING AMERICA'S LONGEST WAR

1. The words are Leonard Garment's in *Crazy Rhythm: My Journey from Brook-lyn, Jazz, and Wall Street to Nixon's White House, Watergate, and Beyond* . . . (New York: Times Books, 1997), p. 85.

2. Rowland Evans, Jr., and Robert D. Novak, *Nixon in the White House: The Frustration of Power* (New York: Random House, 1971), p. 11.

3. Henry Grunwald, *One Man's America: A Journalist's Search for the Heart of his Country* (New York: Doubleday, 1997), p. 388.

4. Joan Hoff, *Nixon Reconsidered* (New York: Basic Books, 1994), p. 147.

5. Ibid., p. 153.

6. Cyrus L. Sulzberger, *The World and Richard Nixon* (Englewood Cliffs, N.J.: Prentice Hall, 1987), p. 31.

7. David Frost, *"I Gave Them a Sword": Behind the Scenes of the Nixon Interviews* (New York: William Morrow, 1978), p. 165.

8. H. R. Haldeman, *The Haldeman Diaries: Inside the Nixon White House* (New York: G. P. Putnam's Sons, 1994), p. 250; John Ehrlichman, *Witness to Power: The Nixon Years* (New York: Simon & Schuster, 1982), pp. 307–8.

9. John Lewis Gaddis, *Strategies of Containment: A Critical Appraisal of Post-war American National Security Policy* (New York: Oxford University Press, 1982), p. 283.

10. John G. Stoessinger, *Henry Kissinger: The Anguish of Power* (New York: Norton, 1976), p. 14.

11. Andrei Gromyko, *Memoirs* (New York: Doubleday, 1989), p. 283.

12. William Safire, *Before the Fall: An Inside View of the Pre-Watergate White House* (Garden City, N.Y.: Doubleday, 1975), p. 366.

13. H. R. Haldeman with Joseph DiMona, *The Ends of Power* (New York: Times Books, 1978) p. 83; Kenneth W. Thompson, ed., *The Nixon Presidency—Twenty-two Intimate Perspectives of Richard M. Nixon* (Lanham, Md.: University Press of America, 1987), p. 82.

14. Sulzberger, *The World and Richard Nixon,* p. 183.

15. Garment, *Crazy Rhythm,* p. 174.

16. "The Real Richard Nixon," the History Channel, 9 August 1996, Raiford Communications, 1994.

17. Robert B. Reich, *Locked in the Cabinet* (New York: Knopf, 1997), p. 121.

18. Richard M. Nixon, "Asia after Vietnam," *Foreign Affairs* 46 (November 1967): 111–25.

19. Henry Brandon, *The Retreat of American Power* (New York: Dell, 1974), p. 81.

20. Henry Kissinger, *White House Years* (Boston: Little, Brown, 1979), p. 136.

21. Gaddis, *Strategies of Containment*, p. 294.

22. Hoff, *Nixon Reconsidered*, p. 245.

23. Kissinger to Department of State et al., 23 January 1969, box 1, Presidential Decision Directives Series (hereafter PDDS), National Security Archive, George Washington University, Washington, D.C.

24. Rogers to John Leddy, 28 January 1969; Malcolm Toon to Richard F. Pedersen, 13 February 1969, ibid.

25. Arkady N. Shevchenko, *Breaking with Moscow* (New York: Knopf, 1985), p. 199.

26. Stoessinger, *Henry Kissinger*, pp. 50, 77.

27. Kissinger, *White House Years*, p. 969.

28. Tom Wells, *The War Within: America's Battle over Vietnam* (Berkeley: University of California Press, 1994), p. 286.

29. Jeffrey Kimball, *Nixon's Vietnam War* (Lawrence: University Press of Kansas, 1998).

30. Robert Schulzinger, *A Time for War: The United States and Vietnam, 1941–1975* (New York: Oxford University Press, 1997), p. 273.

31. Wells, *The War Within*, p. 463.

32. Don Riegle, *O Congress* (New York: Popular Library, 1972), p. 20, and Riegle to author, 11 November 1990.

33. Haldeman, *Haldeman Diaries*, p. 96.

34. Haldeman, *Ends of Power*, p. 81.

35. Kissinger, *White House Years*, p. 259.

36. Gordon Strahan to Haldeman, 19 April 1971 (co), box 133, Haldeman papers, NP; Haldeman, *Haldeman Diaries*, p. 106.

37. Richard Nixon, *No More Vietnams* (New York: Arbor House, 1985), p. 15.

38. Ibid., pp. 126, 125; Curt Smith, *Long Time Gone: The Years of Turmoil Remembered* (South Bend, Ind.: Icarus Press, 1982), p. 217.

39. Richard Nixon, *RN: The Memoirs of Richard Nixon* (New York: Grosset & Dunlap, 1978), pp. 350–51.

40. Interview with Bui Xuan Ninh, 15 June 1983, New York.

41. Wells, *The War Within*, p. 345.

42. Walter Isaacson, *Kissinger: A Biography* (New York: Simon & Schuster, 1992), p. 246.

43. Roger Morris, *Uncertain Greatness: Henry Kissinger and American Foreign Policy* (New York: Harper & Row, 1977), p. 164.

44. Herbert S. Parmet, *Richard Nixon and His America* (Boston: Little, Brown, 1990), p. 566.

45. Nixon, *RN*, pp. 405, 403.

46. Tad Szulc, *The Illusion of Peace: Foreign Policy in the Nixon Years* (New York: Viking, 1973), p. 158.

47. William Colby with James McCargar, *Lost Victory: A Firsthand Account of America's Sixteen-Year Involvement in Vietnam* (Chicago: Contemporary Books, 1989), p. 331.

48. David Corn, *Blond Ghost: Ted Shackley and the CIA's Crusades* (New York: Simon & Schuster, 1994), p. 194n.

49. Bruce Oudes, ed., *From: The President: Richard Nixon's Secret Files* (New York: Harper & Row, 1989), p. 72.

50. Seymour Hersh, *The Price of Power: Kissinger in the White House* (New York: Simon & Schuster, 1983), pp. 107–08.

51. William M. Hammond, *Public Affairs: The Military and the Media, 1968–1975* (Washington, D.C.: Center of Military History, 1996), pp. 299–300.

52. Ehrlichman meeting notes, 25 April 1970, HI.

53. Hersh, *Price of Power*, p. 191.

54. Kissinger, *White House Years*, p. 495.

55. Morris, *Uncertain Greatness*, p. 147.

56. *New York Times*, 2 May 1970, p. 1.

57. U. Alexis Johnson with Jef Olivarius McAllister, *The Right Hand of Power* (Englewood Cliffs, N.J.: Prentice Hall, 1984), p. 530.

58. Tom Wicker, *One of Us: Richard Nixon and the American Dream* (New York: Random House, 1991), p. 633.

59. Walter J. Hickel, *Who Owns America?* (Englewood Cliffs, N.J.: Prentice Hall, 1971), p. 259.

60. Melvin Small, *Johnson, Nixon, and the Doves* (New Brunswick, N.J.: Rutgers University Press, 1988), p. 204.

61. Julie Nixon Eisenhower, *Pat Nixon: The Untold Story* (New York: Simon & Schuster, 1986), p. 290.

62. Charles W. Colson, *Born Again* (New York: Bantam, 1976), p. 40.

63. Wells, *The War Within*, p. 426.

64. Benjamin F. Schemmer, *The Raid* (London: MacDonald & Jane's, 1977), p. 164.

65. Lucien Vandenbroucke, *Perilous Options: Special Operations as an Instrument of U.S. Foreign Policy* (New York: Oxford University Press, 1993), p. 66.

66. Kissinger, *White House Years*, p. 1002.

67. Hammond, *Public Affairs*, p. 468.

68. Stephen E. Ambrose, *Nixon: The Triumph of a Politician: 1962–1972* (New York: Simon & Schuster, 1989), p. 420.

69. Ibid., p. 428.

70. Buchanan to Haldeman, 14 April 1971 (co), box 180, Haldeman papers, NP.

71. Small, *Johnson, Nixon, and the Doves*, p. 217.

72. Wells, *The War Within*, p. 505.

73. Fred Emery, *Watergate: The Corruption of American Politics and the Fall of Richard Nixon* (New York: Times Books, 1994), p. 37.

74. Vernon Walters, *Silent Missions* (Garden City, N.Y.: Doubleday, 1978), p. 518.

75. Hammond, *Public Affairs*, p. 522.

76. Small, *Johnson, Nixon, and the Doves*, p. 179; Ambrose, *Nixon: The Triumph of a Politician*, p. 511.

77. Nixon, *No More Vietnams*, p. 141.

78. George C. Herring, *America's Longest War: The United States and Vietnam, 1950–1975* (New York: McGraw-Hill, 1996), p. 273.

79. *New York Times*, 27 March 1997, p. B14.

80. Hammond, *Public Affairs,* p. 571.

81. Nixon, *RN,* p. 697.

82. Nguyen Tien Hung and Jerrold L. Schecter, *The Palace File* (New York: Harper & Row, 1986), p. 88.

83. Nixon, *RN,* p. 702.

84. Kissinger, *White House Years,* p. 1400.

85. Hoff, *Nixon Reconsidered,* p. 232.

86. Nixon, *RN,* p. 733.

87. Hung and Schecter, *The Palace File,* p. 392.

88. Ibid., p. 146.

89. Frost, *"I Gave Them a Sword,"* p. 138.

90. Ehrlichman, *Witness to Power,* p. 316.

91. Nixon, *No More Vietnams,* p. 165.

92. John Robert Greene, *The Limits of Power: The Nixon and Ford Administrations* (Bloomington: Indiana University Press, 1992), p. 39.

CHAPTER 4

THE GREAT GAME

1. Willy Brandt, *My Life in Politics* (New York: Viking, 1992), pp. 175, 177.

2. Anatoly Dobrynin, *In Confidence* (New York: Times Books, 1995), p. 245.

3. Arkady N. Shevchenko, *Breaking with Moscow* (New York: Knopf, 1985), p. 164.

4. Ilya V. Gaiduk, *The Soviet Union and the Vietnam War* (Chicago: Ivan Dee, 1996), p. 226.

5. Ibid., p. 205.

6. Joan Hoff, *Nixon Reconsidered* (New York: Basic Books, 1994), p. 189.

7. Nixon to Mitchell, 14 April 1969 (co), box 1, PPF, NP.

8. H. R. Haldeman, *The Haldeman Diaries: Inside the Nixon White House* (New York: G. P. Putnam's Sons, 1994), p. 48.

9. Nixon to Haldeman, Ehrlichman, and Kissinger, 7 August 1969 (co), box 12, FG 1, President, SF, WHCF, NP.

10. Shevchenko, *Breaking with Moscow,* p. 200.

11. Nguyen Tien Hung and Jerrold L. Schecter, *The Palace File* (New York: Harper & Row, 1986), p. 31; Richard Nixon, *RN: The Memoirs of Richard Nixon* (New York: Grosset & Dunlap, 1978), p. 385.

12. Henry Kissinger, *White House Years* (Boston: Little, Brown, 1979), p. 318.

13. Alexander M. Haig, Jr., with Charles McCarry, *Inner Circles: How America Changed the World: Memoirs* (New York: Warner, 1992), p. 251.

14. Keith Nelson, *The Making of Detente: Soviet-American Relations in the Shadow of Vietnam* (Baltimore: Johns Hopkins University Press, 1995), pp. 102–3.

15. Kissinger, *White House Years,* p. 913.

16. Seymour Hersh, *The Price of Power: Kissinger in the White House* (New York: Simon & Schuster, 1983), p. 458.

17. Henry Brandon, *The Retreat of American Power* (New York: Dell, 1974), pp. 263–64.

18. Ibid., p. 463.

19. Melvin R. Laird, "America's Principled Role in World Affairs: A Realistic View of Peace and Freedom," in Robert J. Pranger, ed., *Detente and Defense: A Reader* (Washington, D.C.: American Enterprise Institute, 1976), p. 108.

20. Gerard Smith, *Doubletalk: The Story of the First Arms Limitation Talks* (New York: Doubleday, 1980), p. 468.

21. John G. Stoessinger, *Henry Kissinger: The Anguish of Power* (New York: Norton, 1976), p. 82.

22. Smith, *Doubletalk*, p. 376.

23. Cyrus L. Sulzberger, *The World and Richard Nixon* (Englewood Cliffs, N.J.: Prentice Hall, 1987), p. 44.

24. Stephen E. Ambrose, *Nixon: The Triumph of a Politician: 1962–1972* (New York: Simon & Schuster, 1989), p. 549.

25. Robert D. Schulzinger, "The Rise and Fall of Detente, 1969–1974," in Leon Friedman and William F. Levantrosser, eds., *Cold War Patriot and Statesman: Richard M. Nixon* (Westport, Conn.: Greenwood, 1993), p. 95.

26. Shevchenko, *Breaking with Moscow*, pp. 192–93.

27. Nixon, *RN*, p. 619.

28. Dobrynin, *In Confidence*, p. 274.

29. Kissinger, *White House Years*, p. 1269.

30. Roger B. Porter, *The U.S.-U.S.S.R. Grain Agreement* (Cambridge: Cambridge University Press, 1984), p. 6.

31. Dobrynin, *In Confidence*, p. 289.

32. William Safire, *Before the Fall: An Inside View of the Pre-Watergate White House* (Garden City, N.Y.: Doubleday, 1975), p. 451.

33. U. Alexis Johnson with Jef Olivarius McAllister, *The Right Hand of Power* (Englewood Cliffs, N.J.: Prentice Hall, 1984), p. 593.

34. Sulzberger, *The World and Richard Nixon*, p. 199.

35. John Newhouse, *War and Peace in the Nuclear Age* (New York: Knopf, 1989), p. 243.

36. *Meet the Press*, 10 April 1988.

37. Michael Schaller, "U.S.-China-Japan Relations and the 'Nixon Shocks,'" unpublished paper, p. 1.

38. Gordon H. Chang, *Friends and Enemies: The United States, China, and the Soviet Union, 1948–1972* (Stanford, Calif.: Stanford University Press, 1990), p. 273.

39. Tom Wicker, *One of Us: Richard Nixon and the American Dream* (New York: Random House, 1991), p. 576.

40. Haig, *Inner Circles*, p. 257; Safire, *Before the Fall*, p. 368.

41. Shevchenko, *Breaking with Moscow*, p. 164.

42. NSSM-106, box 3, PDDS.

43. Kissinger, *White House Years*, p. 765.

44. Bruce Oudes, ed., *From: The President: Richard Nixon's Secret Files* (New York: Harper & Row, 1989), p. 294.

45. Robert D. Schulzinger, *Henry Kissinger: Doctor of Diplomacy* (New York: Columbia University Press, 1989), p. 89.

46. Armin H. Meyer, *Assignment Tokyo: An Ambassador's Journal* (Indianapolis: Bobbs-Merrill, 1974), p. 133.

47. J. William Fulbright, *The Crippled Giant: American Foreign Policy and Its Domestic Consequences* (New York: Random House, 1972), p. 162.

48. Nixon, *RN,* p. 559.

49. Richard M. Nixon, *In the Arena: A Memoir of Victory, Defeat, and Renewal* (New York: Simon & Schuster, 1990), p. 13.

50. Nixon, *RN,* p. 563.

51. Kissinger, *White House Years,* p. 1067.

52. Leonard A. Kusnitz, *Public Opinion and Foreign Policy: America's China Policy, 1949–1972* (Westport, Conn.: Greenwood, 1984), p. 138.

53. Richard Brookhiser, "Was It a Bull in China's Shop: Time Will Tell," *New York Observer,* 13 July 1998, p. 5.

54. Nixon to Wayne, 13 January 1972, China folder, America since Hoover Collection, GFL.

55. Rosemary Foot, *The Practice of Power: U.S. Relations with China since 1949* (New York: Oxford University Press, 1995), p. 106.

56. Ad Hoc Group on China Trade memo, 24 March 1972, box 5, PDDS.

57. Foot, *The Practice of Power,* p. 137.

CHAPTER 5
BEYOND THE GRAND DESIGN

1. Abba Eban, *Abba Eban: An Autobiography* (New York: Random House, 1977), p. 464.

2. Leonard Garment, *Crazy Rhythm: My Journey from Brooklyn, Jazz, and Wall Street to Nixon's White House, Watergate, and Beyond . . .* (New York: Times Books, 1997), p. 192.

3. Mohamed Heikal, *The Road to Ramadan* (New York: Quadrangle, 1975), p. 92.

4. Richard Nixon, *RN: The Memoirs of Richard Nixon* (New York: Grosset & Dunlap, 1978), p. 483.

5. Ibid., p. 485.

6. Alexander M. Haig, Jr., with Charles McCarry, *Inner Circles: How America Changed the World: Memoirs* (New York: Warner, 1992), p. 251; interview with Alexander Haig, 24 September 1996, Washington, D.C.

7. Edward R. F. Sheehan, *The Arabs, Israelis, and Kissinger: A Secret History of American Diplomacy in the Middle East* (New York: Thomas Y. Crowell, 1976), p. 26.

8. Eban, *Abba Eban,* p. 498.

9. Sheehan, *The Arabs, Israelis, and Kissinger,* p. 33.

10. Elmo R. Zumwalt, *On Watch: A Memoir* (New York: Quadrangle, 1976), p. 434.

11. Gerald S. Strober and Deborah Hart Strober, eds., *Nixon: An Oral History of His Presidency* (New York: HarperCollins, 1994), p. 153.

12. Matti Golan, *The Secret Conversations of Henry Kissinger: Step-by-Step Diplomacy in the Middle East* (New York: Quadrangle, 1976), p. 49.

13. Ibid., p. 86.

14. Henry Kissinger, *Years of Upheaval* (Boston: Little, Brown, 1982), p. 580.

15. Ibid., p. 583.

16. Haig, *Inner Circles*, p. 415.

17. John Newhouse, *War and Peace in the Nuclear Age* (New York: Knopf, 1989), p. 240.

18. Sheehan, *The Arabs, Israelis, and Kissinger*, p. 33.

19. Haig, *Inner Circles*, p 416.

20. Haig interview.

21. Anatoly Dobrynin, *In Confidence* (New York: Times Books, 1995), pp. 321–22.

22. Ibid., p. 323.

23. Nixon, *RN*, p. 941.

24. Sheehan, *The Arabs, Israelis, and Kissinger*, p. 112.

25. Golan, *Secret Conversations*, p. 251.

26. Walter Isaacson, *Kissinger: A Biography* (New York: Simon & Schuster, 1992), p. 546.

27. Armin Meyer, oral history, p. 56, Oral History Research Office, Columbia University, 1987.

28. Herman Frederick Eilts in Leon Friedman and William F. Levantrosser, eds., *Cold War Patriot and Statesman: Richard M. Nixon* (Westport, Conn.: Greenwood, 1992), p. 143.

29. Isaacson, *Kissinger*, p. 564.

30. Seymour Hersh, *The Price of Power: Kissinger in the White House* (New York: Simon & Schuster, 1983), p. 263.

31. Thomas Powers, *The Man Who Kept the Secrets: Richard Helms and the CIA* (New York: Knopf, 1979), p. 226.

32. Nixon, *RN*, p. 490.

33. Robert D. Schulzinger, *Henry Kissinger: Doctor of Diplomacy* (New York: Columbia University Press, 1989), p. 132.

34. Memo from Inspector General for Latin America, 18 August 1970; memo on Chile, 18 August 1970, pp. 13–14, box 2, PDDS.

35. William V. Broe, memo for the record, 16 September 1970, box 2, Robert K. Wolthius file, GFL.

36. Christopher Andrew, *For the President's Eyes Only: Secret Intelligence and the American Presidency from Washington to Bush* (New York: HarperCollins, 1995), p. 371.

37. John Prados, *Keeper of the Keys: A History of the National Security Council from Truman to Bush* (New York: William Morrow, 1991), p. 319.

38. *New York Times*, 13 September 1998, p. 7wk.

39. H. R. Haldeman, *The Haldeman Diaries: Inside the Nixon White House* (New York: G. P. Putnam's Sons, 1994), p. 53.

40. Kenneth O'Reilly, *Nixon's Piano: Presidents and Racial Politics from Washing-

ton to Clinton (New York: Free Press, 1995), p. 292; Roger Morris, *Uncertain Greatness: Henry Kissinger and American Foreign Policy* (New York: Harper & Row, 1977), p. 131.

41. Mohammad A. El-Khawas and Barry Cohen, eds., *The Kissinger Study of Southern Africa: National Security Memorandum 39* (Westport, Conn.: Lawrence Hill & Co., 1976), pp. 106, 105, 126.

42. Ibid., p. 81.

43. Morris, *Uncertain Greatness*, p. 129.

44. Armin H. Meyer, *Assignment Tokyo: An Ambassador's Journal* (Indianapolis: Bobbs-Merrill, 1974), p. 37.

45. Thomas Zeiler, "Trade War, Cold War: Nixon, Japan, and Protectionism," unpublished paper, p. 7.

46. Ibid., p. 1.

47. Michael Schaller, "U.S.-China-Japan Relations and the 'Nixon Shocks,'" unpublished paper, pp. 11, 12.

48. Ibid., p. 14.

49. Ibid., p. 17.

50. Meyer, *Assignment Tokyo*, p. 269.

51. Zeiler, "Trade War, Cold War," p. 10.

52. Joan Hoff, *Nixon Reconsidered* (New York: Basic Books, 1994), p. 140.

53. Schaller, "U.S.-China-Japan Relations," p. 25.

54. Henry Brandon, *The Retreat of American Power* (New York: Dell, 1974), p. 234; Henry Kissinger, *White House Years* (Boston: Little, Brown, 1979), p. 330.

55. H. R. Haldeman with Joseph DiMona, *The Ends of Power* (New York: Times Books, 1978), p. 161.

56. Robert Bothwell, *Canada and the United States: The Politics of Partnership* (New York: Twayne, 1992), p. 113.

CHAPTER 6
LAW AND ORDER

1. Tom Wicker, *One of Us: Richard Nixon and the American Dream* (New York: Random House, 1991), p. 674.

2. Rowland Evans, Jr., and Robert D. Novak, *Nixon in the White House: The Frustration of Power* (New York: Random House, 1971), p. 213.

3. William Safire, *Before the Fall: An Inside View of the Pre-Watergate White House* (Garden City, N.Y.: Doubleday, 1975), pp. 544–45.

4. Patrick J. Buchanan, *Conservative Votes, Liberal Victories: Why the Right Has Failed* (New York: Quadrangle, 1975), pp. 12–13.

5. Ibid,. p. 17.

6. Safire, *Before the Fall*, p. 134.

7. Richard P. Nathan, "A Retrospective on Richard M. Nixon's Domestic Policies," *Presidential Studies Quarterly* 26 (winter 1996): 155.

8. Richard P. Nathan, *The Plot that Failed: Nixon and the Administrative Presidency* (New York: John Wiley, 1975), pp. 163, 164, 165.

9. John C. Whitaker, "Nixon's Domestic Policies: Both Liberal and Bold in Retrospect," *Presidential Studies Quarterly* 26 (winter 1996): 131.

10. Earl Mazo and Stephen Hess, *Nixon: A Political Portrait* (New York: Harper, 1968), p. 316.

11. Herbert S. Parmet, *Richard Nixon and His America* (Boston: Little, Brown, 1990), p. 530.

12. Wicker, *One of Us*, pp. 300, 302.

13. Paul Charles Light, *The President's Agenda: Domestic Policy Choice from Kennedy to Carter (with Notes on Ronald Reagan)* (Baltimore: Johns Hopkins University Press, 1982), p. 19.

14. Jeb Stuart Magruder, *An American Life: One Man's Road to Watergate* (New York: Atheneum, 1974), p. 73.

15. Nixon memo, 8 March 1970, box 48, Haldeman papers, NP.

16. Light, *The President's Agenda*, p. 59.

17. Aaron Wildavsky in Alexander Bickel, ed., *Watergate, Politics, and the Legal Process* (Washington, D.C.: American Enterprise Institute, 1974), p. 39.

18. Nathan, *The Plot that Failed*.

19. Terry H. Anderson, *The Movement and the Sixties: Protest in America from Greensboro to Wounded Knee* (New York: Oxford University Press, 1995), p. 327.

20. Wells, *The War Within*, p. 448.

21. *The Report of the President's Commission on Campus Unrest* (New York: Arno Press, 1970), p. 289.

22. Parmet, *Richard Nixon and His America*, p. 590.

23. Stephen E. Ambrose, *Nixon: The Triumph of a Politician: 1962–1972* (New York: Simon & Schuster, 1989), p. 261.

24. Wicker, *One of Us*, p. 621.

25. Haldeman to Richard Moore, 23 March 1970 (co), box 4, Haldeman papers, NP.

26. Michael A. Genovese, *The Nixon Presidency: Power and Politics in Turbulent Times* (Westport, Conn.: Greenwood, 1990), p. 90.

27. Genovese, *The Nixon Presidency*, p. 89.

28. Haig to Geoff Shepard, 2 July 1974 (co), box 36, Haig papers, NP.

29. Edward Jay Epstein, "The Krogh File—The Politics of 'Law and Order,'" *The Public Interest* (spring 1975): 119.

30. Nixon to Ehrlichman, 6 March 1973 (co), box 18, Ehrlichman papers, NP.

31. Nixon to Ehrlichman, 28 January 1972 (co), box 20, ibid.

32. Nixon to King, 15 June 1957, PPS 320 10.7.11., RNL.

33. Kenneth O'Reilly, *Nixon's Piano: Presidents and Racial Politics from Washington to Clinton* (New York: Free Press, 1995), p. 311; John Ehrlichman, *Witness to Power: The Nixon Years* (New York: Simon & Schuster, 1982), p. 223.

34. Buchanan, *Conservative Votes, Liberal Victories*, p. 49.

35. Daniel P. Moynihan, *The Politics of a Guaranteed Income: The Nixon Administration and the Family Assistance Plan* (New York: Random House, 1973), p. 157.

36. Dan T. Carter, *From George Wallace to Newt Gingrich: Race in the Conservative Counter-Revolution* (Baton Rouge: Louisiana State University Press, 1996), p. 44.

37. Ehrlichman, *Witness to Power*, pp. 228, 227.

38. Safire, *Before the Fall*, p. 233.

39. Dent to Nixon, 13 January 1970 (co), box 6, President's Handwriting (hereafter PH), President's Office File (hereafter POF), NP.

40. Leon E. Panetta and Peter Gall, *Bring Us Together: The Nixon Team and the Civil Rights Retreat* (Philadelphia: Lippincott, 1971), p. 92.

41. John Robert Greene, *The Limits of Power: The Nixon and Ford Administrations* (Bloomington: Indiana University Press, 1992), p. 45.

42. Harry S. Dent, *The Prodigal South Returns to Power* (New York: John Wiley, 1978), p. 187.

43. Joan Hoff, *Nixon Reconsidered* (New York: Basic Books, 1994), p. 83.

44. Krogh to Larry Higby, 19 June 1970 (co), box 63, Haldeman papers, NP.

45. Bob Woodward and Scott Armstrong, *The Brethren: Inside the Supreme Court* (New York: Simon & Schuster, 1979), p. 315.

46. Burger to Rose Mary Woods, 21 October 1971 (co), box 69, PPF, NP.

47. Ehrlichman meeting notes, 4 December 1969, HI.

48. John Massaro, *Supremely Political: The Role of Ideology and Presidential Management in Unsuccessful Supreme Court Nominations* (Albany: State University of New York Press, 1990), pp. 21, 20.

49. Ibid., p. 81.

50. Ibid., p. 97.

51. Ibid., p. 102.

52. Nixon to Haldeman, 24 November 1969 (co), box 1, PPF, NP.

53. Richard Kleindienst, *Justice: The Memoirs of Attorney General Richard G. Kleindienst* (Ottawa, Ill.: Jameson Books, 1985), p. 118.

54. Parmet, *Richard Nixon and His America*, p. 608.

55. Wicker, *One of Us*, p. 497.

56. Safire, *Before the Fall*, p. 267.

57. Schell, *The Time of Illusion*, p. 81.

58. Massaro, *Supremely Political*, p. 107.

59. Ibid., p. 6.

60. O'Reilly, *Nixon's Piano*, p. 307.

61. Genovese, *The Nixon Presidency*, p. 42.

62. Massaro, *Supremely Political*, p. 115.

63. Ibid., p. 127.

64. James F. Simon, *Independent Journey: The Life of William O. Douglas* (New York: Harper, 1980), p. 401.

65. Woodward and Armstrong, *The Brethren*, p. 77; William O. Douglas, *The Court Years, 1939–1975: The Autobiography of William O. Douglas* (New York: Random House, 1980), p. 362.

66. James Cannon, *Time and Chance: Gerald Ford's Appointment with History* (New York: HarperCollins, 1994), p. 101.

67. Robert T. Hartmann, *Palace Politics: An Inside Account of the Ford Years* (New York: McGraw-Hill, 1980), p. 71.

68. Woodward and Armstrong, *The Brethren*, p. 87.

69. Annotated News Summary, 15 October 1971 (co), box 18, Ehrlichman papers, NP.

70. H. R. Haldeman, *The Haldeman Diaries: Inside the Nixon White House* (New York: G. P. Putnam's Sons, 1994), p. 365.

71. Woodward and Armstrong, *The Brethren*, p. 161.

72. Don Riegle, *O Congress* (New York: Popular Library, 1972), pp. 231, 200.

73. Morgan to Ehrlichman, 24 May 1971 (co), box 11, PH, POF, NP.

74. Nixon to Ehrlichman, 28 January 1972 (co), box 20, Ehrlichman papers, NP.

75. Dan T. Carter, *The Politics of Rage: George Wallace, the Origins of the New Conservatism, and the Transformation of American Politics* (New York: Simon & Schuster, 1995), p. 423.

76. Maurice Stans, *One of the President's Men: Twenty Years with Eisenhower and Nixon* (Washington, D.C.: Brasseys, 1995), p. 69.

77. Donald Carruth, memo, 11 September 1973 (co), box 5, Haig papers, NP; Thomas Kleppe to Henry Paulsen, 27 November 1973 (co), box 7, ibid.

78. Bradley H. Patterson, Jr., oral history, p. 47, NP.

79. Hoff, *Nixon Reconsidered*, p. 93.

80. William Sullivan to Robert Mardian, 15 May 1972, box 12, Mardian papers, HI.

81. Hugh Davis Graham, *Civil Rights and the Presidency: Race and Gender in American Politics, 1960–1972* (New York: Oxford University Press, 1992), p. 192.

82. Hoff, *Nixon Reconsidered*, p. 104.

83. Stephen E. Ambrose, *Nixon: Ruin and Recovery: 1973–1990* (New York: Simon & Schuster, 1991), p. 72.

84. Wicker, *One of Us*, p. 522.

85. Harlow comment on John Campbell memo, no date, folder 3 (co), box 35, HU 2-5, SF, WHCF, NP.

86. Nixon on Rose Mary Woods to Ehrlichman, 20 January 1973 (co), box 8, PPF, NP.

87. Hoff, *Nixon Reconsidered*, p. 109.

88. George Q. Flynn, *The Draft: 1940–1973* (Lawrence: University Press of Kansas, 1993), p. 225.

89. Bruce Oudes, ed., *From: The President: Richard Nixon's Secret Files* (New York: Harper & Row, 1989), p. 539.

90. Nixon to Ehrlichman, 30 November 1970 (co), box 138, Haldeman papers, NP.

91. Bradley H. Patterson, Jr., oral history, p. 32, NP.

92. Hoff, *Nixon Reconsidered*, p. 28.

93. Roger Morris, *Haig: The General's Progress* (Chicago: Playboy Press, 1982), p. 215.

94. Leonard Garment, *Crazy Rhythm: My Journey from Brooklyn, Jazz, and Wall Street to Nixon's White House, Watergate, and Beyond . . .* (New York: Times Books, 1997), p. 200.

95. Nixon to Peter Flanigan, 16 March 1970 (co), box 228, Haldeman papers, NP.

96. Parmet, *Richard Nixon and His America*, p. 632.

97. Charles Colson, oral history 2, p. 5, NP.

98. Jonah Raskin, *For the Hell of It: The Life and Times of Abbie Hoffman* (Berkeley: University of California Press, 1996), p. 201.

99. Nixon to Ehrlichman, 30 November 1970 (co), box 138, Haldeman papers, NP.
100. Stanley I. Kutler, *The Wars of Watergate: The Last Crisis of Richard Nixon* (New York: Norton, 1992), p. 325.

CHAPTER 7
DISRAELI REDUX

1. Herbert Stein, *Presidential Economics: The Making of Economic Policy from Roosevelt to Reagan and Beyond* (New York: Simon & Schuster, 1984), p. 190.
2. Barbara Kellerman, *The Political Presidency: Practice of Leadership* (New York: Oxford University Press, 1984), p. 26.
3. Richard Nixon, *RN: The Memoirs of Richard Nixon* (New York: Grosset & Dunlap, 1978), p. 426.
4. Martin Anderson, *Welfare: The Political Economy of Welfare Reform in the United States* (Stanford, Calif.: Hoover Institution Press, 1978), p. 62.
5. H. R. Haldeman, *The Haldeman Diaries: Inside the Nixon White House* (New York: G. P. Putnam's Sons, 1994), p. 53.
6. Anderson, *Welfare,* pp. 6, 5.
7. Vincent J. Burke and Vee Burke, *Nixon's Good Deed: Welfare Reform* (New York: Columbia University Press, 1974), p. 69.
8. Ibid., p. 110.
9. Stephen E. Ambrose, *Nixon: The Triumph of a Politician: 1962–1972* (New York: Simon & Schuster, 1989), p. 269.
10. Ibid., p. 293.
11. Dan Rather and Gary Paul Gates, *The Palace Guard* (New York: Warner Books, 1975), p. 117.
12. Burke and Burke, *Nixon's Good Deed,* p. 138; Irwin Unger, *The Best of Intentions: The Triumphs and Failures of the Great Society under Kennedy, Johnson, and Nixon* (New York: Doubleday, 1996), p. 319.
13. Haldeman, *Haldeman Diaries,* p. 181.
14. Daniel Patrick Moynihan, *The Politics of a Guaranteed Income: The Nixon Administration and the Family Assistance Plan* (New York: Random House, 1973), p. 552.
15. Herbert S. Parmet, *Richard Nixon and His America* (Boston: Little, Brown, 1990), p. 560.
16. Richard P. Nathan, *The Plot that Failed: Nixon and the Administrative Presidency* (New York: Wiley, 1975), p. 28.
17. Buchanan memo on 18 February 1969 meeting with Republicans (co), box 77, POF, NP.
18. Joan Hoff, *Nixon Reconsidered* (New York: Basic Books, 1994), p. 62.
19. Moynihan, *Politics of a Guaranteed Income,* p. 212.
20. Buchanan notes on 18 February 1969 meeting (co), box 77, POF, NP.
21. Nixon note on Ehrlichman to Nixon, 27 October 1969 (co), box 3, POF, NP.
22. Frederick V. Malek, *Washington's Hidden Tragedy: The Failure to Make Government Work* (New York: Free Press, 1978), p. 52.
23. Malek to Haldeman, 4 December 1972, box 7, Malek papers, HI.

24. Buchanan notes on 18 February 1969 meeting (co), box 77, POF, NP.

25. Unger, *The Best of Intentions*, p. 332.

26. Ken Cole to Nixon, 6 May 1971 (co), box 10, PH, POF, NP.

27. Rowland Evans, Jr., and Robert D. Novak, *Nixon in the White House: The Frustration of Power* (New York: Random House, 1971), p. 236; Ehrlichman meeting notes, 28 December 1969, HI.

28. *New York Times*, 15 September 1997, p. B7.

29. William Safire, *Before the Fall: An Inside View of the Pre-Watergate White House* (Garden City, N.Y.: Doubleday, 1975), p. 470.

30. Richardson, oral history, p. 11, NP.

31. Hoff, *Nixon Reconsidered*, p. 67.

32. Ibid., p. 66.

33. Nixon to Ehrlichman, 14 January 1971 (co) box 18, Ehrlichman papers, NP.

34. Tom Wicker, *One of Us: Richard Nixon and the American Dream* (New York: Random House, 1991), p. 527.

35. Ibid., p. 405.

36. John C. Whitaker, *Striking a Balance: Environment and Natural Resource Policy in the Nixon-Ford Years* (Washington, D.C.: American Enterprise Institute, 1976).

37. Ibid., p. 264.

38. Stanley I. Kutler, *The Wars of Watergate: The Last Crisis of Richard Nixon* (New York: Norton, 1992), p. 78.

39. Taped conversation, 19 April 1972, tape 39, 23–46, NP.

40. Wicker, *One of Us*, p. 515; Michael A. Genovese, *The Nixon Presidency: Power and Politics in Turbulent Times* (Westport, Conn.: Greenwood, 1990), p. 91.

41. Hoff, *Nixon Reconsidered*, p. 23.

42. Nixon note to Ehrlichman on Whitaker to Nixon, 1 July 1971, box 12, PH, POF, NP.

43. Whitaker to Nixon, 18 February 1971 (co), box 272, Haldeman papers, NP.

44. Arthur M. Schlesinger, Jr., *The Imperial Presidency* (Boston: Houghton Mifflin, 1973), p. 237.

45. Peter N. Carroll, *It Seemed Like Nothing Happened: America in the Seventies* (New Brunswick, N.J.: Rutgers University Press, 1990), p. 120.

46. Ibid., p. 121.

47. William E. Simon, *A Time for Truth* (New York: Reader's Digest Press, 1978), p. 2.

48. Simon, *A Time for Truth*, p. 53.

49. Jeffrey M. Nadaner, "The Oil Spigot Runs Dry: An Economic History of the Nixon Administration's Management of the Domestic Petroleum Shortfall of 1973–1974," unpublished paper, p. 3.

50. Richard J. Carroll, *An Economic Record of Presidential Performance: From Truman to Bush* (Westport, Conn.: Praeger, 1995).

51. Joanne Gowa, *Closing the Gold Window: Domestic Politics and the End of Bretton Woods* (Ithaca, N.Y.: Cornell University Press, 1983), p. 136.

52. The title of chapter 5 in Stein, *Presidential Economics*.

53. Allen J. Matusow, *Nixon's Economy: Booms, Busts, Dollars, and Votes* (Lawrence: University Press of Kansas, 1998), p. 16.

54. Wyatt C. Wells, *Economist in an Uncertain World: Arthur F. Burns and the Federal Reserve* (New York: Columbia University Press, 1994), p. 42.

55. Colson, oral history 2, pp. 24, 25, NP.

56. Evans and Novak, *Nixon in the White House,* p. 200; Matusow, *Nixon's Economy,* p. 51.

57. Matusow, *Nixon's Economy,* p. 126.

58. Gowa, *Controlling the Gold Window,* p. 146.

59. Wicker, *One of Us,* p. 551.

60. Matusow, *Nixon's Economy,* pp. 55–56.

61. Wells, *Economist in an Uncertain World,* p. 55.

62. Note on Ehrlichman to Nixon, 3 April 1970 (co), box 6, PH, POF, NP.

63. Ehrlichman meeting notes, 15 December 1970, HI.

64. Hobart Rowen, *Self-Inflicted Wounds: From LBJ's Guns and Butter to Reagan's Voodoo Economics* (New York: Times Books, 1994), p. 66.

65. John Connally with Mickey Herskowitz, *In History's Shadow: An American Odyssey* (New York: Hyperion, 1993), p. 235.

66. Nixon to McCracken, Shultz, and Haldeman, 13 December 1970 (co), box 18, Ehrlichman papers, NP.

67. Matusow, *Nixon's Economy,* p. 189.

68. Nixon, *RN,* p. 497.

69. Rowen, *Self-Inflicted Wounds,* p. 60.

70. Erwin C. Hargrove and Samuel A. Morley, eds., *The President and the Council of Economic Advisors: Interviews with CEA Chairmen* (Boulder, Colo.: Westview, 1984), p. 367.

71. Nixon, *RN,* p. 521.

72. Diane B. Kunz, *Butter and Guns: America's Cold War Economic Diplomacy* (New York: Free Press, 1997), p. 213.

73. Genovese, *The Nixon Presidency,* p. 76.

74. Matusow, *Nixon's Economy,* p. 197.

75. Nixon comments on Peter Flanigan to Nixon, 26 July 1972 (co), box 18, PH, POF, NP.

76. Nixon's note on Rumsfeld to Nixon, 10 August 1972 (co), box 18, PH, POF, NP.

77. Nixon to Burns, 4 November 1971 (co), box 6, PPF, NP.

78. Nixon note on Stein to Nixon, 19 October 1972 (co), box 19, PH, POF, NP.

79. I. M. Destler, *Making Foreign Economic Policy* (Washington, D.C.: Brookings, 1980), p. 57.

80. Simon, *A Time for Truth,* p. 3.

CHAPTER 8
A PRIVATE PRESIDENT'S PUBLIC RELATIONS

1. Gerald S. Strober and Deborah Hart Strober, eds., *Nixon: An Oral History of the Presidency* (New York: HarperCollins, 1994), p. 40.

2. Henry Kissinger, *White House Years* (Boston: Little, Brown, 1979), pp. 11, 143.

3. Stewart Alsop, *Nixon and Rockefeller: A Double Portrait* (Garden City, N.Y.: Doubleday, 1960), pp. 200, 201.

4. William B. Mead and Paul Dickson, *Baseball. The President's Game* (New York: Walker & Co., 1997), p. 140.

5. Leonard Garment, *Crazy Rhythm: My Journey from Brooklyn, Jazz, and Wall Street to Nixon's White House, Watergate, and Beyond* . . . (New York: Times Books, 1997), pp. 111, 110.

6. Henry Brandon, *The Retreat of American Power* (New York: Dell, 1974), p. 95.

7. John L. Campbell to Ehrlichman, 4 November 1969 (co), box 30, Ehrlichman papers, NP.

8. H. R. Haldeman, *The Haldeman Diaries: Inside the Nixon White House* (New York: G. P. Putnam's Sons, 1994), p. 123.

9. Ehrlichman meeting notes, 25 March 1970, HI.

10. Lester David, *The Lonely Lady of San Clemente: The Story of Pat Nixon* (New York: Crowell, 1978), p. 133.

11. Strober and Strober, *Nixon*, p. 86.

12. H. R. Haldeman with Joseph DiMona, *The Ends of Power* (New York: Times Books, 1978), p. 73.

13. John Ehrlichman, *Witness to Power: The Nixon Years* (New York: Simon & Schuster, 1982), p. 266.

14. Bruce Oudes, ed., *From: The President: Richard Nixon's Secret Files* (New York: Harper & Row, 1989), p. 113.

15. Nixon to Ehrlichman, 11 June 1969 (co), box 1, PPF, NP.

16. Oudes, *From: The President*, p. 191.

17. Ibid., p. 421.

18. Haldeman, *Haldeman Diaries*, p. 31.

19. Ehrlichman meeting notes, 23 October 1969, HI.

20. Raymond Price, *With Nixon* (New York: Viking, 1977), p. 119.

21. Terry H. Anderson, *The Movement and the Sixties: Protest in America from Greensboro to Wounded Knee* (New York: Oxford University Press, 1995), p. 278.

22. Oudes, *From: The President*, pp. 192–95.

23. Haldeman, *Haldeman Diaries*, p. 292.

24. Ehrlichman, *Witness to Power*, p. 37.

25. Haldeman, *The Ends of Power*, p. 45.

26. Roger Morris, *Haig: The General's Progress* (New York: Playboy Press, 1982), p. 3.

27. Theodore H. White, *Breach of Faith: The Fall of Richard Nixon* (New York: Atheneum, 1975), p. 272.

28. Oudes, *From: The President*, p. 40.

29. Haldeman to Colson, 13 November 1970 (co), box 86, Colson papers, NP.

30. William Martin, *With God on Our Side: The Rise of the Religious Right in America* (New York: Broadway Books, 1996), p. 98.

31. Nixon to Haldeman, 30 June 1969, box 4, EX FG6-11, Ehrlichman, SF, WHCF, NP.

32. Michael Kammen, "Culture and the State in America," *Journal of American History* 83 (December 1996): 796.

33. Garment to Keogh, 17 February 1969 (co), box 1, PH, POF, NP.

34. Oudes, *From: The President*, p. 86.

35. Ehrlichman to Flanigan, 6 October 1971 (co), box 23, FG 103 [cf], SF, WHCF, NP.

36. *New York Times*, 6 November 1997, p. C24.

37. Haldeman, *Haldeman Diaries*, p. 326.

38. Telephone interview with Gerald R. Ford, 15 May 1997.

39. Julie Nixon Eisenhower, *Pat Nixon: The Untold Story* (New York: Simon & Schuster, 1986), p. 162.

40. Fawn Brodie, *Richard Nixon: The Shaping of His Character* (New York: Norton, 1981), p. 451.

41. Ibid.

42. Strober and Strober, *Nixon*, p. 37.

43. Bob Woodward and Carl Bernstein, *The Final Days* (New York: Simon & Schuster, 1976), p. 441.

44. Colson to Nixon, 19 January 1972 (co), box 5, PPF, NP.

45. Constance Stuart, oral history, p. 11, NP.

46. Gwendolyn B. King, oral history, p. 13, NP.

47. Nixon to Ziegler, 15 March 1973 (co), box 4, PPF, NP.

48. *New York Times*, 2 June 1971, p. 36.

49. Ibid., 6 June 1971, p. 70.

50. Jonah Raskin, *For the Hell of It: The Life and Times of Abbie Hoffman* (Berkeley: University of California Press, 1996), p. 219.

51. Brandon, *The Retreat of American Power*, p. 14.

52. Andrei Gromyko, *Memoirs* (New York: Doubleday, 1989), p. 281.

53. Herbert G. Klein, *Making It Perfectly Clear* (Garden City, N.Y.: Doubleday, 1980), p. 5.

54. Michael Baruch Grossman and Martha Joynt Kumar, *Portraying the President: The White House and the News Media* (Baltimore: Johns Hopkins University Press, 1981), p. 303.

55. James Keogh, *President Nixon and the Press* (New York: Funk & Wagnalls, 1972), pp. 2–3.

56. Ehrlichman meeting notes, 29 December 1969, HI.

57. Tom Wicker, *One of Us: Richard Nixon and the American Dream* (New York: Random House, 1991), pp. 435, 438.

58. Michael A. Genovese, *The Nixon Presidency: Power and Politics in Turbulent Times* (Westport, Conn.: Greenwood, 1990), p. 48.

59. Haldeman, *Ends of Power*, p. 76.

60. Anatoly Dobrynin, *In Confidence* (New York: Times Books, 1995), p. 326.

61. Bobst to Nixon, 9 May 1972 (co), box 188, PPF, NP.

62. William Safire, *Before the Fall: An Inside View of the Pre-Watergate White House* (Garden City, N.Y.: Doubleday, 1975), p. 365.

63. Nixon to Haldeman, 30 April 1972 (co), box 164, Haldeman papers, NP.

64. Richard Nixon, *RN: The Memoirs of Richard Nixon* (New York: Grosset & Dunlap, 1978), p. 354.

65. John Anthony Maltese, *Spin Control: The White House Office of Communica-*

tions and the Management of Presidential News, 2d ed. (Chapel Hill: University of North Carolina Press, 1994), p. 3.

66. Nixon, *RN,* p. 354.

67. Kissinger, *White House Years,* p. 1095.

68. Hedrick Smith, *The Power Game: How Washington Works* (New York: Random House, 1988), p. 405.

69. Maltese, *Spin Control,* p. 24.

70. Newton N. Minow, John Bartlow Martin, and Lee M. Mitchell, *Presidential Television* (New York: Basic Books, 1973), p. 48.

71. Smith, *The Power Game,* p. 704.

72. Nixon to Ehrlichman, 25 January 1969 (co), box 1, PPF, NP.

73. Haldeman, *Haldeman Diaries,* p. 311.

74. Stephen E. Ambrose, *Nixon: The Triumph of a Politician: 1962–1972* (New York: Simon & Schuster, 1989), p. 229.

75. Ehrlichman meeting notes, 2 February 1970, HI.

76. Haldeman memo, 16 April 1971 (co), box 48, Haldeman papers, NP.

77. Haldeman, *Haldeman Diaries,* p. 168.

78. Jeb Stuart Magruder, *An American Life: One Man's Road to Watergate* (New York: Atheneum, 1974), pp. 99–100.

79. Haldeman, *Haldeman Diaries,* p. 74.

80. Maltese, *Spin Control,* p. 92.

81. Ibid., p. 61.

82. Ziegler to Haldeman, 5 December 1972 (co), box 14, Haldeman papers, NP.

83. Hobart Rowen, *Self-Inflicted Wounds: From LBJ's Guns and Butter to Reagan's Voodoo Economics* (New York: Times Books, 1994), p. 79.

84. Colson to Haldeman, 1 June 1972 (co), box 102, Haldeman papers, NP.

85. Nixon to Haldeman, 11 May 1970 (co), box 138, ibid.

86. Dan T. Carter, *The Politics of Rage: George Wallace, the Origins of the New Conservatism, and the Transformation of American Politics* (New York: Simon & Schuster, 1995), p. 413.

87. Taped conversation, 11 November 1971, tape 11, 14–59, NP.

88. Safire, *Before the Fall,* p. 6.

89. Buchanan to Haldeman, 11 November 1969 (co), box 54, Haldeman papers, NP.

90. Oudes, *From: The President,* p. 436.

91. Colson, oral history, pp. 39, 40, NP; Colson to Haldeman, 25 September 1970 (co), box 1, Colson papers, NP.

92. Don Riegle, *O Congress* (New York: Popular Library, 1972), p. 111.

93. Colson to Higby, 16 April 1971 (co), box 77, Haldeman papers, NP.

94. Haldeman to Ehrlichman, 2 August 1971 (co), box 272, ibid.

95. Nixon and Haldeman conversation, 14 April 1973, box 170, PPF, NP.

96. Oudes, *From: the President,* p. 51; Stanley I. Kutler, *The Wars of Watergate: The Last Crisis of Richard Nixon* (New York: Norton, 1992), p. 165.

97. Buchanan to Haldeman, 28 September 1969 (co), box 55, Haldeman papers, NP.

98. Ambrose, *Nixon: The Triumph of a Politician,* p. 325.

99. Wicker, *One of Us,* p. 660.

100. Nixon, *RN*, p. 511.

101. Strober and Strober, *Nixon*, p. 206.

102. Haldeman, *Haldeman Diaries*, p. 303.

103. Haldeman action memo, 15 June 1971, box 112, Haldeman papers, NP.

104. Colson memo on meeting with Nixon, 23 June 1971 (co), box 15, Colson papers, NP.

105. Ambrose, *Nixon: The Triumph of a Politician*, p. 447.

106. David Rudenstine, *The Day the Presses Stopped: A History of the Pentagon Papers Case* (Berkeley: University of California Press, 1996), p. 327; Ben Bradlee, *A Good Life: Newspapering and Other Adventures* (New York: Simon & Schuster, 1995), p. 326.

107. Charles W. Colson, *Born Again* (Old Tappan, N.J.: Chosen Books, 1976), p. 59; Nixon, *RN*, p. 514.

108. Haldeman, *The Ends of Power*, p. 114.

109. Stanley Kutler, ed., *Abuse of Power: The New Nixon Tapes* (New York: Free Press, 1997), pp. 7–8.

110. Bill Casselman to Bill Timmons, 15 August 1969 (co), box 52, Haldeman papers, NP.

111. Mollenhoff to Haldeman, 17 October 1969 (co), box 53, ibid.

112. Fred Emery, *Watergate: The Corruption of American Politics and the Fall of Richard Nixon* (New York: Times Books, 1994), p. 26; Kutler, *Abuse of Power*, p. 3.

113. John Ehrlichman, "Live from the Oval Office," *Newsweek*, 2 December 1996, p. 37.

114. Kutler, *The Wars of Watergate*, p. 111.

CHAPTER 9
THE ROAD TO REELECTION

1. Haldeman to Ehrlichman, 17 February 1969 (co), box 49, Haldeman papers, NP.

2. Bryce Harlow, William A. Syers interviews, GFL.

3. Robert Hartmann interview, GFL.

4. Charles W. Colson, *Born Again* (Old Tappan, N.J.: Chosen Books, 1976), p. 45.

5. Telephone interview with Gerald R. Ford, 15 May 1997.

6. James Cannon, *Time and Chance: Gerald Ford's Appointment with History* (New York: HarperCollins, 1994), p. 94.

7. Harlow to Haldeman, 15 June 1970, box 21, FG 31 [cf], NP.

8. Anderson to Ehrlichman, 4 February 1971, box 5, EX FG6-11, Ehrlichman, SF, WHCF, NP.

9. Timmons to Ehrlichman, 26 March 1971, box 5, EX FG6-11, Ehrlichman, SF, WHCF, NP.

10. Ehrlichman meeting notes, 5 September 1969, HI.

11. Louis Fisher, *Constitutional Conflicts between Congress and the President* (Lawrence: University Press of Kansas, 1997), p. 72.

12. Roy Ash, oral history, p. 20, NP.

13. Arthur M. Schlesinger, Jr., *The Imperial Presidency* (Boston: Houghton Mifflin, 1973), p. 248.

14. Fisher, *Constitutional Conflicts*, p. 28.

15. Richard M. Scammon and Ben J. Wattenberg, *The Real Majority* (New York: Coward McCann, 1970).

16. Jonathan Schell, *The Time of Illusion* (New York: Vintage, 1976), p. 124.

17. Safire to Ehrlichman, 24 July 1969 (co), box 2, PH, POF, NP.

18. Bruce Oudes, ed., *From: The President: Richard Nixon's Secret Files* (New York: Harper & Row, 1989), p. 53.

19. Colson to Haldeman, 3 December 1969 (co), box 41, Colson papers, NP.

20. Vamik D. Volkan, Norman Itzkowitz, and Andrew W. Dod, *Richard Nixon: A Psychobiography* (New York: Columbia University Press, 1997), p. 111.

21. Colson to Haldeman, 14 September 1970 (co), box 7, PH, 9/70, POF, NP.

22. Colson to Lovestone, 16 January 1973, Nixon file, box 360, Jay Lovestone papers, HI.

23. Colson to Lovestone, 31 July 1972, 29 April 1972, ibid.

24. Colson to Nixon, 20 March 1972 (co), box 24, Colson papers, NP.

25. Walter Sheridan, *The Rise and Fall of Jimmy Hoffa* (New York: Saturday Review Press, 1972), p. 534.

26. Colson, oral history 2, p. 21, NP.

27. David Frost, *"I Gave Them a Sword": Behind the Scenes of the Nixon Interviews* (New York: William Morrow, 1978), p. 175.

28. Stephen E. Ambrose, *Nixon: The Triumph of a Politician: 1962–1972* (New York: Simon & Schuster, 1989), p. 374.

29. John Anthony Maltese, *Spin Control: The White House Office of Communications and the Management of Presidential News*, 2d ed. (Chapel Hill: University of North Carolina Press, 1994), p. 123.

30. H. R. Haldeman, *The Haldeman Diaries: Inside the Nixon White House* (New York: G. P. Putnam's Sons, 1994), p. 193.

31. William Safire, *Before the Fall: An Inside View of the Pre-Watergate White House* (Garden City, N.Y.: Doubleday, 1975), p. 332.

32. Richard Nixon, *RN: The Memoirs of Richard Nixon* (New York: Grosset & Dunlap, 1978), p. 492.

33. Dent to Nixon, 19 November 1970 (co), box 397, Haldeman papers, NP.

34. Ambrose, *Nixon: The Triumph of a Politician*, p. 415.

35. Joel K. Goldstein, *The Modern American Vice Presidency: The Transformation of a Political Institution* (Princeton, N.J.: Princeton University Press, 1982), p. 39.

36. Nixon to Ehrlichman, 30 November 1971 (co), box 138, Haldeman papers, NP.

37. Haldeman, *Haldeman Diaries*, p. 280.

38. Caulfield to Ehrlichman, 27 January 1970 (co), box 20, Ehrlichman papers, NP.

39. Christopher Matthews, *Kennedy and Nixon: The Rivalry that Shaped Postwar America* (New York: Simon & Schuster, 1996), p. 289.

40. Taped conversation, 9 April 1971, tape 2, 476–14, NP.

41. *Washington Post*, 8 February 1997, p. A6.

42. Nixon to Rogers, October (?) 1971, box 3, PDDS.

43. Taped conversation, 29 October 1971, tape 11, 607–4, NP.

44. Sam Dash, *Chief Counsel: Inside the Ervin Committee—The Untold Story of Watergate* (New York: Random House, 1976), p. 205.

45. George McGovern, *Grassroots: The Autobiography of George McGovern* (New York: Random House, 1977), p. 148.

46. Peter N. Carroll, *It Seemed Like Nothing Happened: America in the Seventies* (New Brunswick, N.J.: Rutgers University Press, 1990), p. 86.

47. Tip O'Neill with William Novak, *Man of the House* (New York: St. Martin's Press, 1987), p. 281; Richard M. Nixon, *In the Arena: A Memoir of Victory, Defeat, and Renewal* (New York: Simon & Schuster, 1990), p. 41.

48. Gerald S. Strober and Deborah Hart Strober, eds., *Nixon: An Oral History of His Presidency* (New York: HarperCollins, 1994), p. 256.

49. Schell, *Time of Illusion*, p. 295.

50. Haldeman to Dean, 10 February 1973 (co), box 80, Haldeman papers, NP.

51. Stanley I. Kutler, ed., *Abuse of Power: The New Nixon Tapes* (New York: Free Press, 1997), p. 454.

52. Ed Rollins, *Bare Knuckles and Back Rooms* (New York: Broadway Books, 1996), p. 56.

53. J. Anthony Lukas, *Nightmare: The Underside of the Nixon Years*, rev. ed. (New York: Penguin, 1988), p. 154.

54. Jonathan Aitken, *Nixon: A Life* (Washington, D.C.: Regnery, 1993), p. 414.

55. Ehrlichman to Nixon, 1 December 1971 (co), box 15, PH, POF, NP.

56. Fred Emery, *Watergate: The Corruption of American Politics and the Fall of Richard Nixon* (New York: Times Books, 1994), p. 161.

57. Jeb Stuart Magruder, *An American Life: One Man's Road to Watergate* (New York: Atheneum, 1974), pp. 210, 213.

58. Haldeman, *Haldeman Diaries*, p. 134.

59. Fawn Brodie, *Richard Nixon: The Shaping of His Character* (New York: Norton, 1981), p. 442.

60. Emery, *Watergate*, p. 32.

61. Taped conversation, 19 August 1972, tape 47, 176–10, NP.

62. Lawrence F. O'Brien, *No Final Victories: A Life in Politics from John F. Kennedy to Watergate* (Garden City, N.Y.: Doubleday, 1974), p. 342.

63. Gerald R. Ford, *A Time to Heal: The Autobiography of Gerald R. Ford* (New York: Harper & Row, 1979), p. 100.

64. Joan Hoff, *Nixon Reconsidered* (New York: Basic Books, 1994), p. 318.

65. Hunter J. Thompson, *Fear and Loathing: On the Campaign Trail, '72* (San Francisco: Straight Arrow Books, 1973), p. 127.

66. Haldeman, *Haldeman Diaries*, p. 470.

67. McGovern, *Grassroots*, pp. 158, 162.

68. O'Brien, *No Final Victories*, p. 312; Thompson, *Fear and Loathing*, p. 470.

69. *Vital Speeches* (1 August 1972), p. 612.

70. O'Brien, *No Final Victories*, p. 319.

71. McGovern, *Grassroots*, p. 191.

72. Ibid., p. 243.

73. John Robert Greene, *The Presidency of Gerald R. Ford* (Lawrence: University Press of Kansas, 1995), p. 10.

74. Seymour Hersh, "The Pardon: Nixon, Ford, Haig, and the Transfer of Power," *The Atlantic* 252 (August 1983): 58.

75. Ben Bradlee, on "Perspective on Watergate," C-SPAN, 31 March 1997.

76. Katherine Graham, *Personal History* (New York: Knopf, 1997), p. 464.

77. Carl Bernstein and Bob Woodward, *All the President's Men* (New York: Warner, 1975), p. 109.

78. Theodore H. White, *The Making of the President: 1972* (New York: Atheneum, 1973), p. 246.

79. Taped conversation, 13 August 1972, tape 47, 137–12, NP.

80. *Washington Post*, 11 December 1996, p. A8.

81. Oudes, *From: The President*, p. 147.

82. Stanley I. Kutler, *The Wars of Watergate: The Last Crisis of Richard Nixon* (New York: Norton, 1992), p. 106.

83. Joanne Gordon to George Bell, 9 March 1971 (co), box 74, Haldeman papers, NP.

84. Herbert S. Parmet, *Richard Nixon and His America* (Boston: Little, Brown, 1990), p. 576.

85. Raymond Price, *With Nixon* (New York: Viking, 1977), p. 231.

86. Allen J. Matusow, *Nixon's Economy: Booms, Busts, Dollars, and Votes* (Lawrence: University Press of Kansas, 1998), p. 201.

87. Ehrlichman meeting notes, 3 August 1972, HI.

88. Oudes, *From: The President*, p. 346.

89. Maltese, *Spin Control*, p. 96.

90. Spiro T. Agnew, *Go Quietly . . . or Else* (New York: William Morrow, 1980), p. 31.

91. Ehrlichman meeting notes, 14 November 1972, HI.

92. Nixon, *RN*, p. 761.

93. Taped conversations, 5 May 1971, tape 1, 462–13; 23 March 1971, tape 2, 472–22, NP.

94. Taped conversation, 6 March 1972, tape 13, 21–6, NP.

95. Richard Kleindienst, *Justice: The Memoirs of Attorney General Richard G. Kleindienst* (Ottawa, Ill.: Jameson Books, 1985), p. 91.

96. Ambrose, *Nixon: The Triumph of a Politician*, p. 436.

97. *Oakland Press*, 31 October 1997, p. 9.

98. Lukas, *Nightmare*, p. 137.

99. *New York Times*, 22 October 1996, p. B18.

100. Stanton P. Anderson to Haldeman, 3 April 1973 (co), box 174, Haldeman papers, NP.

101. Malek to Ehrlichman, 17 March 1972, box 7, Malek papers, HI.

102. Dan Carter, *From George Wallace to Newt Gingrich: Race in the Conservative Counter-Revolution* (Baton Rouge: Louisiana State University Press, 1996), p. 53.

103. Nixon to Ehrlichman, 17 May 1972 (co), box 24, Ehrlichman papers, NP.

CHAPTER 10
WATERGATE

1. James Cannon, *Time and Change: Gerald Ford's Appointment with History* (New York: HarperCollins, 1994), p. 72.

2. Richard Nixon, *RN: The Memoirs of Richard Nixon* (New York: Grosset & Dunlap, 1978), p. 769.

3. A. James Reichley, *Conservatives in an Age of Change: The Nixon and Ford Administrations* (Washington, D.C.: Brookings, 1981), p. 233.

4. Harold Seidman, *Politics, Position, and Power: The Dynamics of Federal Organization*, 2d ed. (New York: Oxford University Press, 1975), p. 106.

5. Bradley H. Patterson, Jr., *The Ring of Power: The White House Staff and Its Expanding Role in Government* (New York: Basic Books, 1988), p. 257.

6. Richard P. Nathan, *The Plot that Failed: Nixon and the Administrative Presidency* (New York: Wiley, 1975), p. 69.

7. Nixon, *RN*, p. 763.

8. Interview with Alexander Haig, 24 September 1996, Washington, D.C.

9. Roy Ash, oral history, p. 11, NP.

10. Ash, oral history, NP; Haig interview.

11. Henry Kissinger, *White House Years* (Boston: Little, Brown, 1979), p. 1409; John Prados, *Keeper of the Keys: A History of the National Security Council from Truman to Bush* (New York: William Morrow, 1991), p. 310.

12. Gerald S. Strober and Deborah Hart Strober, *Nixon: An Oral History of the Presidency* (New York: HarperCollins, 1994), p. 127.

13. Richard Valeriani, *Travels with Henry* (Boston: Houghton Mifflin, 1979), p. 10.

14. Higby to Malek, 15 September 1972 (co), box 4, Haldeman papers, NP.

15. Jerry Jones to Haig, 31 July 1973 (co), box 1, Haig papers, NP.

16. William E. Simon, *A Time for Truth* (New York: Reader's Digest Press, 1978), p. 7.

17. Nixon enclosure in Buchanan, memo for President's files, 15 November 1972 (co), box 90, POF, NP.

18. William Safire, *Before the Fall: An Inside View of the Pre-Watergate White House* (Garden City, N.Y.: Doubleday, 1975), p. 681.

19. Ibid., p. 15.

20. Victor Lasky, *It Didn't Start with Watergate* (New York: Dial Press, 1977).

21. John Taylor, 24 December 1997, "Retrospective on Watergate," C-Span.

22. Julie Nixon Eisenhower, *Pat Nixon: The Untold Story* (New York: Simon & Schuster, 1986), p. 440.

23. Ray Price in Leon Friedman and William F. Levantrosser, eds., *Watergate and Afterward: The Legacy of Richard M. Nixon* (Westport, Conn.: Greenwood, 1992), p. 249.

24. Stephen E. Ambrose, *Eisenhower*, vol. 2, *The President* (New York: Simon & Schuster, 1984), p. 203.

25. Monica Crowley, *Nixon in Winter* (New York: Random House, 1998), p. 287.

26. Vamik D. Volkan et al., *Richard Nixon: A Psychobiography* (New York: Columbia University Press, 1997), p. 95.

27. Strober and Strober, *Nixon,* p. 38?

28. Nixon, *RN*, p. 628.

29. David Frost, *"I Gave Them a Sword": Behind the Scenes of the Nixon Interviews* (New York: William Morrow, 1978), p. 226.

30. Stanley I. Kutler, ed., *Abuse of Power: The New Nixon Tapes* (New York: Free Press, 1997), p. 55.

31. Ibid., p. 255.

32. Ibid., p. 67.

33. Thomas Powers, *The Man Who Kept the Secrets: Richard Helms and the CIA* (New York: Knopf, 1979), p 201.

34. Ehrlichman meeting notes, 6 July 1972, 7 July 1972, HI; Kutler, *Abuse of Power*, p. 93.

35. Powers, *The Man Who Kept the Secrets*, p. 263.

36. Stanley I. Kutler, ed., *Watergate: The Fall of Richard M. Nixon* (St. James, N.Y.: Brandywine Press, 1996), p. 50.

37. Fred Emery, *Watergate: The Corruption of American Politics and the Fall of Richard Nixon* (New York: Times Books, 1994), p. 195.

38. Kutler, *Abuse of Power*, p. 111.

39. Nixon, *RN*, p. 745.

40. Ibid., p. 773.

41. Emery, *Watergate*, p. 172.

42. John J. Sirica, *To Set the Record Straight: The Break-in, the Tapes, the Conspirators, and the Pardon* (New York: Norton, 1979), p. 84.

43. Sam J. Ervin, Jr., *The Whole Truth* (New York: Random House, 1980), p. 98.

44. J. Anthony Lukas, *Nightmare: The Underside of the Nixon Years* (New York: Penguin, 1988), p. 321.

45. Emery, *Watergate*, p. 197.

46. Jimmy Breslin, *How the Good Guys Finally Won: Notes from an Impeachment Summer* (New York: Viking, 1975), p. 12.

47. Nixon, *RN*, p. 873.

48. Stephen E. Ambrose, *Nixon: Ruin and Recovery: 1973–1990* (New York: Simon & Schuster, 1991), p. 67.

49. Kutler, *Abuse of Power*, p. 299.

50. Emery, *Watergate*, p. 247.

51. Ibid., p. 247.

52. Nixon to Harlow and Ehrlichman, 5 February 1969 (co), box 66, Krogh papers, NP.

53. Kutler, *Watergate*, p. 78.

54. Ibid., p. 77.

55. Ibid., p. 97.

56. Emery, *Watergate*, p. 263.

57. Kutler, *Abuse of Power*, p. 218.

58. *Washington Post*, ed., *The Presidential Transcripts* (New York: Delacorte Press, 1974), p. 132.

59. *New York Times Magazine,* 24 August 1997, p. 21.

60. Emery, *Watergate,* p. 283.

61. Kutler, *Abuse of Power,* p. 322.

62. Ibid., p. 218.

63. Ibid., p. 382.

64. Eisenhower, *Pat Nixon,* p. 369.

65. Alexander M. Haig, Jr., with Charles McCarry, *Inner Circles: How America Changed the World* (New York: Warner, 1982), p. 348.

66. Nixon, *RN,* p. 912.

67. Ervin, *The Whole Truth,* p. 161.

68. Stanley I. Kutler, *The Wars of Watergate: The Last Crisis of Richard Nixon* (New York: Norton, 1992), p. 361.

69. Ibid., p. 360.

70. Kutler, *Abuse of Power,* p. 559.

71. Ervin, *The Whole Truth,* p. 187.

72. Emery, *Watergate,* p. 372.

73. John Connally with Mickey Herskowitz, *In History's Shadow: An American Odyssey* (New York: Hyperion, 1993), p. 266.

74. Haig, *Inner Circles,* p. 377.

75. "The Secret White House Tapes," A&E cable network, 30 March 1997.

76. Strober and Strober, *Nixon,* p. 430.

77. Lukas, *Nightmare,* p. 407.

78. Cannon, *Time and Chance,* p. 193.

79. Spiro T. Agnew, *Go Quietly . . . or Else* (New York: William Morrow, 1980), p. 19.

80. Cannon, *Time and Chance,* p. 275.

81. Ibid., p. 236; John Robert Greene, *The Presidency of Gerald R. Ford* (Lawrence: University Press of Kansas, 1995), p. 13.

82. Vice President Ford Weekly Briefings, box 30, Stephen G. McConahey files, GFL.

83. Lukas, *Nightmare,* p. 544.

84. Elliot Richardson, *The Creative Balance: Government, Politics, and the Individual in America's Third Century* (New York: Holt, Rinehart, 1976), p. 39.

85. Kutler, *Watergate,* p. 156.

86. Emery, *Watergate,* p. 399.

87. Ibid.

88. Ibid., p. 404.

89. Haig, *Inner Circles,* p. 433; Kutler, *Watergate,* p. 169.

90. Haig, *Inner Circles,* p. 426.

91. Emery, *Watergate,* p. 421.

92. Elizabeth Drew, *Washington Journal: The Events of 1973–1974* (New York: Vintage, 1976), p. 263.

93. Bob Woodward and Carl Bernstein, *The Final Days* (New York: Simon & Schuster, 1976), p. 214.

94. Mark J. Rozell, *Executive Privilege: The Dilemma of Secrecy and Democratic Accountability* (Baltimore: Johns Hopkins University Press, 1994), p. 64.

95. Kutler, *Watergate*, p. 202.

96. Lukas, *Nightmare*, p. 557.

97. Raymond Price, *With Nixon* (New York: Viking, 1977), p. 290.

90. Barry Goldwater with Jack Casserly, *Goldwater* (New York: Doubleday, 1988), pp. 270, 271.

99. Price, *With Nixon*, p. 101.

100. Eisenhower, *Pat Nixon*, p. 372.

101. Charles W. Colson, *Born Again* (Old Tappan, N.J.: Chosen Books, 1976), p. 179.

102. Greene, *The Presidency of Gerald R. Ford*, p. 3.

103. Haig, *Inner Circles*, p. 487.

104. *New York Times*, 22 December 1996, p. E7.

105. Lukas, *Nightmare*, p. 559.

106. Cannon, *Time and Chance*, p. 314.

107. Robert McClory, "Was the Fix in between Ford and Nixon," *National Review* 35 (14 October 1983): 1265.

108. Emery, *Watergate*, p. 470.

109. Woodward and Bernstein, *The Final Days*, p. 424.

110. Drew, *Washington Diary*, p. 414.

CHAPTER 11
RUNNING FOR EX-PRESIDENT

1. Joel K. Goldstein, *The Modern American Vice Presidency: The Transformation of a Political Institution* (Princeton, N.J.: Princeton University Press, 1982), p. 243.

2. James Cannon, *Time and Chance: Gerald Ford's Appointment with History* (New York: HarperCollins, 1994), p. 293.

3. Ibid., p. 294.

4. Robert T. Hartmann, *Palace Politics: An Inside Account of the Ford Years* (New York: McGraw-Hill, 1980), p. 131.

5. Jack Lessenberry's interview with Gerald Ford, 28 February 1995, p. 9, GFL.

6. Ron Nessen, *It Sure Looks Different from the Inside* (Chicago: Playboy Press, 1978), p. 36.

7. Leon Jaworski, *The Right and the Power: The Prosecution of Watergate* (New York: Reader's Digest Press, 1976), pp. 222, 223.

8. Robert Sam Anson, *Exile: The Unquiet Oblivion of Richard M. Nixon* (New York: Simon & Schuster, 1984), p. 46.

9. Garment to Buchen, 28 August 1974, box 32, Buchen papers, GFL.

10. Ron Nessen to Dick Cheney and John Marsh, 30 January 1976, box 127, Nessen papers, GFL.

11. Hartmann, *Palace Politics*, p. 259.

12. Miller to Jaworski, 4 September 1974, box 28, Buchen papers, GFL.

13. Gerald Ford, *A Time to Heal: The Autobiography of Gerald R. Ford* (New York: Harper & Row, 1979), p. 161.

14. Ibid., p. 164.

15. John Robert Greene, *The Presidency of Gerald R. Ford* (Lawrence: University Press of Kansas, 1995), p. 49.

16. Becker memo, 9–27 September 1974, box 2, Benton L. Becker papers, GFL.

17. Stanley I. Kutler, ed., *Watergate: The Fall of Richard M. Nixon* (Westbury, Conn.: Brandywine Books, 1997), p. 213.

18. Julie Nixon Eisenhower, *Pat Nixon: The Untold Story* (New York: Simon & Schuster, 1986), p. 433.

19. Ford, *A Time to Heal*, p. 178.

20. Cannon, *Time and Chance*, p. 385.

21. William Timmons to Ford, 10 September 1974, box 27, PH, GFL.

22. Bill Gulley, *Breaking Cover* (New York: Simon & Schuster, 1980), pp. 229–30, 116.

23. "The Secret White House Tapes," A&E cable network, 30 March 1997.

24. Cannon, *Time and Chance*, p. 360.

25. Anson, *Exile*, p. 31.

26. Saxbe to Ford, 6 September 1974, box 32, Buchen papers, GFL.

27. Phillip Areeda to Ford, 2 December 1974, box 7, Timmons papers, GFL.

28. Herbert S. Parmet, *Richard Nixon and His America* (Boston: Little, Brown, 1990), p. 647.

29. Richard M. Nixon, *In the Arena: A Memoir of Victory, Defeat, and Renewal* (New York: Simon & Schuster, 1990), p. 25.

30. Eisenhower, *Pat Nixon*, p. 443.

31. Barry Goldwater with Jack Casserly, *Goldwater* (New York: Doubleday, 1988), p. 282.

32. Robert Alan Goldberg, *Barry Goldwater* (New Haven, Conn.: Yale University Press, 1995), pp. 292–93, 154.

33. David Frost, *"I Gave Them a Sword": Behind the Scenes of the Nixon Interviews* (New York: William Morrow, 1978), pp. 272, 269.

34. Jonathan Aitken, *Nixon: A Life* (Washington, D.C.: Regnery, 1993), p. 547.

35. Stephen C. Ambrose, *Nixon: Ruin and Recovery: 1973–1990* (New York: Simon & Schuster, 1991), p. 545.

36. Marvin Kalb, *The Nixon Memo: Political Responsibility, Russia, and the Press* (Chicago: University of Chicago Press, 1994), p. 77.

37. Monica Crowley, *Nixon Off the Record: His Candid Commentary on People and Politics* (New York: Random House, 1996), p. 137.

38. Kalb, *The Nixon Memo*, pp. 145, 147.

39. U.S. Congress, *Memorial Services in the Congress of the United States* (Washington, D.C.: U.S. Government Printing Office, 1996), pp. 5, 10, 13, 11, 12.

40. James A. Bill, *George Ball: Behind the Scenes in U.S. Foreign Policy* (New Haven, Conn.: Yale University Press, 1997), p. 47.

41. Monica Crowley, *Nixon in Winter* (New York: Random House, 1998), pp. 6, 158.

42. Billy Graham, *Just As I Am: The Autobiography of Billy Graham* (New York: HarperCollins, 1997), p. 456.

43. Leonard Garment, *Crazy Rhythm: My Journey from Brooklyn, Jazz, and Wall*

Street to Nixon's White House, Watergate, and Beyond . . . (New York: Times Books, 1997), p. 115.

44. Jimmy Breslin, *How the Good Guys Finally Won: Notes from an Impeachment Summer* (New York: Viking, 1975), p. 54.

45. Joan Hoff, *Nixon Reconsidered* (New York: Basic Books, 1994), p. 341.

46. "CBS News Sunday Morning," 26 January 1997.

BIBLIOGRAPHICAL ESSAY

The amount of archival and printed materials available on the life and presidency of Richard Nixon is overwhelming. It includes roughly four thousand hours of tapes, of which only a small portion is currently available, and millions of documents, some of which, because of the Watergate crisis, were declassified and released to the public much earlier than those of other administrations. The Nixon legal team's incessant litigation against the National Archives may have resulted, in the long run, in the delayed release of other documents that otherwise would have been made public much sooner. Aside from the papers and tapes (which are more complete for domestic politics than for foreign policy), the Nixon Presidential Materials Project in the National Archives in College Park, Maryland, also contains oral histories and exit interviews from Nixon officials such as Charles Colson, Herbert Klein, Roy Ash, and Elliot Richardson. Several other officials, including Robert Mardian, Kenneth Rush, Fred Malek, and John Veneman, have deposited their papers in the Hoover Institution Archives at Stanford, California. The library also has copies of John Ehrlichman's invaluable meeting notes.

Joan Hoff tells the tangled story of the disposition of the papers and tapes of the Nixon presidency in "Researcher's Nightmare: Studying the Nixon Presidency," *Presidential Studies Quarterly* 26 (winter 1996): 259–75. Hoff is the editor of the microfiche series *Papers of the Nixon White House* (Bethesda, Md.: University Publications of America, 1988–). Some of those papers can be found in Bruce Oudes, ed., *From: The President: Richard Nixon's Secret Files* (New York: Harper & Row, 1989).

As of this writing, the Nixon Presidential Library and Birthplace in Yorba Linda, California, remains a brilliantly conceived state-of-the-art museum with a relative handful of pre- and postpresidential papers. Most of Nixon's prepresidential papers had previously been deposited in the National Archives regional archive at Laguna Niguel, California. The Richard Nixon Oral History Project at California State University, Fullerton, conducted 191 interviews between 1969 and 1972 devoted to Nixon's life to 1946.

As with all presidencies, the key printed source is *Public Papers of the Presidents of the United States, Richard Nixon*, 5 vols. (Washington, D.C.: U.S. Government Printing Office, 1970–1975). Useful in the series, as well, is the 1974 volume on Gerald R. Ford's presidency that was published in 1975. The Gerald R. Ford Presidential Library in Ann Arbor, Michigan, contains material relating to the pardon, documents the Ford administration inherited from the Nixon administration (including correspondence with President Thieu), and oral interviews. For Nixon's press conferences, see *The Nixon Presidential Press Conferences* (New York: Coleman Enterprises, 1978).

Noteworthy printed document collections dealing with foreign policy are *Declassified Document Series* (Woodbridge, Conn.: Carrollton Press, 1976–) and the Woodrow Wilson Center's *Cold War International History Project Bulletin*. The National Security Archive's Presidential Decision Directives Series at George Washington University contains materials relating to national security obtained through requests for declassification under the Freedom of Information Act.

An early guide to Nixon's career, Howard F. Bremer, ed., *Richard M. Nixon, 1913–* (Dobbs Ferry, N.Y.: Oceana Publications, 1975), offers a chronology, documents, and bibliographical aids but is marred by typographical errors. Somewhat more up-to-date are the Nixon entries in *The American Presidency: A Historical Bibliography* (Santa Barbara, Calif.: ABC-CLIO Information Services, 1984) and Fenton J. Martin and Robert U. Goehlert, *American Presidents: A Bibliography* (Washington, D.C.: Congressional Quarterly Press, 1987). In a new resource category that is bound to grow, Graphix Zone has produced "Nixon: The CD-ROM," which features photographs, essays, transcripts, and over 70,000 pages of documents.

Nixon has written in detail about his life and presidency in *Six Crises* (Garden City, N.Y.: Doubleday, 1962) and *RN: The Memoirs of Richard Nixon* (New York: Grosset & Dunlap, 1978). The eight books he wrote after his memoirs, including *The Real War* (New York: Warner, 1980), *Leaders: Profiles and Reminiscences of Men Who Have Shaped the Modern World* (New York: Warner, 1982), and *In the Arena: A Memoir of Victory, Defeat, and Renewal* (New York: Simon & Schuster, 1990), offer revealing autobiographical information. Even after his death, new Nixon commentaries on his career and contemporary politics, based on freewheeling conversations with his assistant during the last years of his life, appeared in Monica Crowley, *Nixon Off the Record: His Candid Commentary on People and Politics* and *Nixon in Winter* (New York: Random House, 1996, 1998). "The Real Richard Nixon," based on 1994 interviews with Nixon conducted at his library, premiered on the History Channel in 1996 and is available from Raiford Communications.

Among the more valuable—and balanced—biographies of Nixon's entire life are Stephen E. Ambrose's near-definitive three volumes, *Nixon: The Education of a Politician, 1913–1962, Nixon: The Triumph of a Politician, 1962–1972*, and *Nixon: Ruin and Recovery, 1973–1990* (New York: Simon & Schuster, 1987, 1989, 1991); Herbert S. Parmet, *Richard Nixon and His America* (Boston: Little, Brown, 1990); and Tom Wicker, *One of Us: Richard Nixon and the American Dream* (New York: Random

House, 1991). Nixon is treated favorably by Jonathan Aitken, to whom he granted rare interviews for *Nixon: A Life* (Washington, D.C.: Regnery, 1993). Roger Morris is not so kind in the first volume of his biography, which takes Nixon to 1952, *Richard Milhous Nixon: The Rise of an American Politician* (New York: Henry Holt, 1990).

Nixon has been a favorite of psychobiographers, but the most serious study is Fawn Brodie's *Richard Nixon: The Shaping of His Character* (New York: Norton, 1981). Others include Bruce Mazlish, *In Search of Nixon: A Psychobiographical Inquiry* (New York: Basic Books, 1972); David Abrahamsen, *Nixon vs. Nixon: An Emotional Tragedy* (New York: Farrar, Straus & Giroux, 1977); and Vamik D. Volkan et al., *Richard Nixon: A Psychobiography* (New York: Columbia University Press, 1997). In a class by itself is Garry Wills's brilliant quasi-psychobiography and rumination on American life and culture, *Nixon Agonistes: The Crisis of the Self-Made Man* (New York: New American Library, 1971).

Several early campaign biographies offer useful tidbits, including Ralph de Toledano, *One Man Alone: Richard Nixon* (New York: Funk & Wagnalls, 1969); Earl Mazo and Stephen Hess, *Nixon: A Political Portrait* (New York: Harper & Row, 1968); and Stewart Alsop, *Nixon and Rockefeller: A Double Portrait* (Garden City, N.Y.: Doubleday, 1960). Decidedly antagonistic is William Costello, *The Facts about Richard Nixon: An Unauthorized Biography* (New York: Viking, 1960). New material appears in Christopher Matthews's sprightly *Kennedy and Nixon: The Rivalry that Shaped Postwar America* (New York: Simon & Schuster, 1996).

Julie Nixon Eisenhower wrote a serious book about her mother, *Pat Nixon: The Untold Story* (New York: Simon & Schuster, 1986), which offers unique perspectives on the presidential years. Lester David, *The Lonely Lady of San Clemente: The Story of Pat Nixon* (New York: Crowell, 1978), is more of a potboiler. The Nixons are compared with other first families in Gil Troy, *Affairs of State: The Rise and Rejection of the Presidential Couple since WWII* (New York: Free Press, 1997).

For Nixon's presidential years, useful interviews appear in Kenneth W. Thompson, ed., *The Nixon Presidency—Twenty-two Intimate Perspectives of Richard M. Nixon* (Lanham, Md.: University Press of America, 1987), and Gerald S. Strober and Deborah Hart Strober, eds., *Nixon: An Oral History of His Presidency* (New York: HarperCollins, 1994). Many of those who appeared in these volumes, along with historians, offer papers and comments in the three volumes in the Hofstra University presidential series on Nixon: Leon Friedman and William F. Levantrosser, eds., *Politician, President and Administrator: Richard M. Nixon, Cold War Patriot and Statesman: Richard M. Nixon,* and *Watergate and Afterward: The Legacy of Richard M. Nixon* (Westport, Conn.: Greenwood, 1991, 1992, 1993).

Joan Hoff, who interviewed Nixon for her provocative *Nixon Reconsidered* (New York: Basic, 1994), sees much to admire in his domestic policies. She also edited the special edition of *Presidential Studies Quarterly* 26 (winter 1996) on "The Nixon Presidency." Two solid studies of the presidency are Michael A. Genovese, *The Nixon Presidency: Power and Politics in Turbulent Times* (Westport, Conn.: Greenwood, 1990), and John Robert Greene, who made good use of interviews in *The Limits of Power: The Nixon and Ford Administrations* (Bloomington: Indiana University Press, 1992). Valuable contemporary journalistic accounts are Rowland

Evans, Jr., and Robert D. Novak, *Nixon in the White House: The Frustration of Power* (New York: Random House, 1971); Dan Rather and Gary Paul Gates, *The Palace Guard* (New York: Warner Books, 1975); and Jonathan Schell, *The Time of Illusion* (New York: Vintage, 1976).

Insiders with informed perspectives are Richard P. Nathan, *The Plot that Failed: Nixon and the Administrative Presidency* (New York: Wiley, 1975), and A. James Reichley, *Conservatives in an Age of Change: The Nixon and Ford Administrations* (Washington, D.C.: Brookings, 1981). Somewhat more sensational is the Nixon chapter in Ronald D. Kessler, *Inside the White House: The Hidden Lives of the Modern Presidents and the Secrets of the World's Most Powerful Institution* (New York: Pocket Books, 1995), and Michael Medved, *The Shadow Presidents: The Secret History of the Chief Executives and Their Top Aides* (New York: Times Books, 1979).

General histories that include the Nixon presidency are Peter N. Carroll's perceptive and lively *It Seemed Like Nothing Happened: America in the 1970s* (New Brunswick, N.J.: Rutgers University Press, 1990); John Morton Blum, *Years of Discord: American Politics and Society, 1961–1974* (New York: Norton, 1991); James T. Patterson, *Grand Expectations: The United States, 1945–1974* (New York: Oxford University Press, 1996); and Michael S. Sherry, *In the Shadow of War: The United States Since the 1930s* (New Haven, Conn.: Yale University Press, 1995). See also E. J. Dionne, Jr., *Why Americans Hate Politics* (New York: Simon & Schuster, 1991).

Many of the key figures in the Nixon administration have written about their experiences, with the most important source being H. R. Haldeman's unique *The Haldeman Diaries: Inside the Nixon White House* (New York: G. P. Putnam's Sons, 1994). For material left out of the printed version, see the CD-ROM *The Complete Multimedia Edition of the Haldeman Diaries* (Santa Monica, Calif.: Sony Electronic Publishing Company, 1994). Haldeman's earlier memoir written with Joseph DiMona, *The Ends of Power* (New York: Times Books, 1978), still merits attention. His colleague John Ehrlichman, one aide who was critical of Nixon, published *Witness to Power: The Nixon Years* (New York: Simon & Schuster, 1982).

Speechwriter William Safire wrote one of the most complete and literate memoirs, *Before the Fall: An Inside View of the Pre-Watergate White House* (Garden City, N.Y.: Doubleday, 1975); fellow speechwriter Raymond Price recalls his days in the White House in *With Nixon* (New York: Viking, 1977). Public relations are the main subject of Herbert G. Klein's *Making It Perfectly Clear* (Garden City, N.Y.: Doubleday, 1980) and of Watergate conspirators Jeb Stuart Magruder, *An American Life: One Man's Road to Watergate* (New York: Atheneum, 1974) and Charles W. Colson, *Born Again* (Old Tappan, N.J.: Chosen Books, 1976). That subject is also touched on by Nixon's liberal adviser Leonard Garment in his entertaining and painfully introspective *Crazy Rhythm: My Journey from Brooklyn, Jazz, and Wall Street to Nixon's White House, Watergate, and Beyond . . .* (New York: Times Books, 1997).

Other aides whose memoirs must be examined are Harry S. Dent, *The Prodigal South Returns to Power* (New York: John Wiley & Sons, 1978); Patrick J. Buchanan's polemical *Conservative Votes: Liberal Victories: Why the Right Has Failed* (New York: Quadrangle, 1975); and Clark R. Mollenhoff, *Game Plan for Disaster: An Ombudsman's Report on the Nixon Years* (New York: Norton, 1976). For photographs and anecdotes, see White House photographer Ollie Atkins's *The White House Years:*

Triumph and Tragedy (Chicago: Playboy Press, 1977). Billy Graham, who often served Nixon (and other presidents) as an informal adviser, wrote about his experiences in *Just as I Am. The Autobiography of Billy Graham* (New York. Harper-Collins, 1997).

Cabinet members' memoirs of value are Maurice Stans, *One of the Presidents' Men: Twenty Years with Eisenhower and Nixon* (Washington, D.C.: Brasseys, 1995); Elliot Richardson, *The Creative Balance: Government, Politics, and the Individual in America's Third Century* (New York: Holt, Rinehart, 1976) and *Reflections of a Radical Moderate* (New York: Pantheon, 1996); Walter J. Hickel, *Who Owns America?* (Englewood Cliffs, N.J.: Prentice Hall, 1971); Richard Kleindienst, *Justice: The Memoirs of Attorney General Richard G. Kleindienst* (Ottawa, Ill.: Jameson Books, 1985); John Connally with Mickey Herskowitz, *In History's Shadow: An American Odyssey* (New York: Hyperion, 1993); and William E. Simon, *A Time for Truth* (New York: Reader's Digest Press, 1978). John Mitchell appears as a major character in Wizola McLendon, *Martha: The Life of Martha Mitchell* (New York: Random House, 1979). See also James Reston, Jr., *Lone Star: The Life of John Connally* (New York: Harper & Row, 1989).

Spiro T. Agnew wrote his angry memoir *Go Quietly . . . or Else* (New York: William Morrow, 1980), which can be read with the favorable John R. Coyne, Jr., *The Impudent Snobs: Agnew vs. the Intellectual Establishment* (New Rochelle, N.Y.: Arlington House, 1972), and the unfavorable Richard M. Cohen and Jules Witcover, *A Heartbeat Away: The Investigation and Resignation of Vice President Spiro T. Agnew* (New York: Viking, 1974).

Other political memoirs and biographies that touch on Nixon are Barry Goldwater with Jack Casserly, *Goldwater* (New York: Doubleday, 1988); Robert Alan Goldberg, *Barry Goldwater* (New Haven, Conn.: Yale University Press, 1995); Tip O'Neill with William Novak, *Man of the House* (New York: St. Martin's Press, 1987); Don Riegle, *O Congress: A Diary of the Years 1971–1972* (New York: Popular Library, 1972); and Lawrence F. O'Brien, *No Final Victories: A Life in Politics from John F. Kennedy to Watergate* (Garden City, N.Y.: Doubleday, 1974).

It is impossible to write the history of the Nixon years without consulting the over 2,000 pages of Henry Kissinger's memoirs *White House Years* and *Years of Upheaval* (Boston: Little, Brown, 1979, 1982). But they must be read in conjunction with Robert D. Schulzinger's scholarly appraisal *Henry Kissinger: Doctor of Diplomacy* (New York: Columbia University Press, 1989); Seymour Hersh's critical—and gossipy—*The Price of Power: Kissinger in the White House* (New York: Simon & Schuster, 1983); and the balanced Walter Isaacson, *Kissinger: A Biography* (New York: Simon & Schuster, 1992). Earlier studies of the always fascinating national security adviser include John G. Stoessinger's *Henry Kissinger: The Anguish of Power* (New York: Norton, 1976), which is informed by the author's interviews with his subject; Bernard Kalb and Marvin Kalb's positive treatment *Kissinger* (London: Hutchinson, 1974); NSC aide Roger Morris's nasty *Uncertain Greatness: Henry Kissinger and American Foreign Policy* (New York: Harper & Row, 1977); and Richard Valeriani's anecdote-laden *Travels with Henry* (Boston: Houghton Mifflin, 1979).

U. Alexis Johnson (with Jef Olivarius McAllister) does not approve of much of Nixon's and Kissinger's activities in his memoir *The Right Hand of Power*

(Englewood Cliffs, N.J.: Prentice Hall, 1984), nor does Elmo Zumwalt in *On Watch: A Memoir* (New York: Quadrangle, 1976). The ubiquitous Vernon Walters discusses his work for Kissinger and long association with Nixon in *Silent Missions* (Garden City, N.Y.: Doubleday, 1978). Alexander M. Haig, Jr., with Charles McCarry, offers his often singular view of events in *Inner Circles: How America Changed the World* (New York: Warner, 1982), and Roger Morris displays his dislike for his old NSC colleague in *Haig: The General's Progress* (Chicago: Playboy Press, 1982).

To place the Nixon presidency in context, one can begin with two recent presidential ratings surveys, Arthur M. Schlesinger, Jr., "The Ultimate Approval Rating," *New York Times Magazine*, 15 December 1996, pp. 46–51, and William J. Ridings, Jr., and Stuart B. McIver, *Rating the Presidents: A Ranking of U.S. Leaders from the Great and Honorable to the Dishonest and Incompetent* (Secaucus, N.J.: Citadel Press, 1997). For studies of the presidency in general, all of which consider Nixon, useful are Godfrey Hodgson, *All Things to All Men: The False Promise of the American Presidency* (New York: Simon & Schuster, 1980); Robert Shogan, *The Riddle of Power: Presidential Leadership from Truman to Bush* (New York: Dutton, 1991); Gary King and Lyn Ragsdale, *The Elusive Executive: Discovering Statistical Patterns in the Presidency* (Washington, D.C.: Congressional Quarterly Press, 1988); James David Barber, *The Presidential Character: Predicting Performance in the White House* (New York: Prentice Hall, 1972); and Arthur M. Schlesinger, Jr., *The Imperial Presidency* (Boston: Houghton Mifflin, 1973), which is highly critical of Nixon. For where Agnew places among his cohorts, see Joel K. Goldstein, *The Modern American Vice Presidency: The Transformation of a Political Institution* (Princeton, N.J.: Princeton University Press, 1982).

Examining the seamy side of Washington are Hedrick Smith's *The Power Game: How Washington Works* (New York: Random House, 1988) and Kathleen Hall Jamieson, *Dirty Politics: Deception, Distraction, and Democracy* (New York: Oxford University Press, 1992). Studies of presidential leadership worth examining are Craig Allen Smith and Kathy B. Smith, *The White House Speaks: Presidential Leadership in Persuasion* (Westport, Conn.: Praeger, 1974), with sections on Nixon's rhetoric and the Ford pardon; Charles O. Jones, *The Presidency in a Separated System* (Washington, D.C.: Brookings, 1974); Richard Neustadt's classic *Presidential Power: The Politics of Leadership from FDR to Carter* (New York: Wiley, 1980); and an examination of how presidents get their appointees approved by the Senate, Judith E. Michaels's *The Presidents Call: Executive Leadership from FDR to George Bush* (Pittsburgh: University of Pittsburgh Press, 1997).

Planning and organizing the White House are the subject of Stephen Hess, *Organizing the Presidency* (Washington, D.C.: Brookings, 1988); Richard W. Waterman, *Presidential Influence and the Administrative State* (Knoxville: University of Tennessee Press, 1989); Harold Seidman, *Politics, Position, and Power: The Dynamics of Federal Organization*, 2d ed. (New York: Oxford University Press, 1975); Peri Arnold, *Making the Managerial Presidency: Comprehensive Reorganization Planning, 1905–1980* (Princeton, N.J.: Princeton University Press, 1986), which looks at the Ash reforms, among others; and Paul Charles Light, *The President's Agenda: Domestic Policy Choice from Kennedy to Carter (with Notes on Ronald Reagan)* (Baltimore: Johns Hopkins University Press, 1982). Dealing with special organizational problems are Larry Berman, *The Office of Management and Budget and the Presidency, 1921–1979* (Princeton, N.J.: Princeton University Press, 1979), and I. M. Destler, *President's, Bureaucrats, and Foreign Policy: The Politics of Organizational Reform* (Princeton, N.J.: Princeton University Press, 1974).

The president's relationships with his staff and the executive departments are explored in a book by Nixon personnel expert Frederic V. Malek, *Washington's Hidden Tragedy: The Failure to Make Government Work* (New York: Free Press, 1978); Thomas J. Weko, *The Politicizing Presidency: The White House Personnel Office, 1948–1994* (Lawrence: University Press of Kansas, 1995); Shirley Anne Warshaw, *Powersharing: White House–Cabinet Relations in the Modern Presidency* (Albany: State University of New York Press, 1996); and former Nixon staffer Bradley H. Patterson's *The Ring of Power: The White House Staff and Its Expanding Role in Government* (New York: Basic Books, 1988). Richard L. Cole and David A. Caputo's "Presidential Control of the Senior Civil Service: Assessing the Strategies of the Nixon Years," *American Political Science Review* 73 (June 1979): 399–413, is valuable. Helpful as well is the transcript of a PBS television program, Samuel Kernell and Samuel L. Popkin, eds., *Twenty-five Years of Managing the Presidency* (Berkeley: University of California Press, 1986).

For Nixon's early political career, particularly his role as a leading anticommunist, see Richard Gid Powers, *Not without Honor: The History of American Anti-Communism* (New York: Free Press, 1995); David Caute's more critical *The Great Fear: The Anti-Communist Purge under Truman and Eisenhower* (New York: Simon & Schuster, 1978); Whitaker Chambers's celebrated autobiography *Witness* (New York: Random House, 1952); Sam Tanenhaus, *Whitaker Chambers* (New York: Random House, 1997); Alger Hiss, *In the Court of Public Opinion* (New York: Knopf, 1957); Bert Andrews, *A Tragedy of History: A Journalist's Confidential Role in the Hiss-Chambers Case* (Washington, D.C.: R. B. Luce, 1962); Robert J. Stripling, *The Red Plot against America* (Drexel Hill, Pa.: Bell, 1949); Allan Weinstein, *Perjury: The Hiss-Chambers Case* (New York: Knopf, 1978); and Athan Theoharis, ed., *Beyond the Hiss Case: The FBI, Congress and the Cold War* (Philadelphia: Temple University Press, 1982).

Greg Mitchell provides a lively and exhaustive account of Nixon's senatorial campaign in *Tricky Dick and the Pink Lady: Richard Nixon vs. Helen Gahagan Douglas—Sexual Politics and the Red Scare* (New York: Random House, 1997). Nixon's vice presidency is covered in memoirs by Dwight David Eisenhower, *Mandate for Change, 1953–1956* and *Waging Peace, 1956–1961* (Garden City, N.Y.: Doubleday, 1963, 1965); Milton Eisenhower, *The President Is Calling* (Garden City, N.Y.: Doubleday, 1974); Emmet John Hughes, *The Ordeal of Power: A Political Memoir of the Eisenhower Years* (New York: Atheneum, 1963); and Sherman Adams, *First Hand Report: The Story of the Eisenhower Administration* (New York: Harper & Brothers, 1961). It is covered in secondary accounts beginning with the definitive Stephen E. Ambrose, *Eisenhower*, vol. 2, *The President* (New York: Simon & Schuster, 1984), and Clarence G. Lasby, *Eisenhower's Heart Attack: How Ike Beat Heart Disease and Held on to the Presidency* (Lawrence: University Press of Kansas, 1997). For Republican politics during the era, Richard Norton Smith, *Thomas E. Dewey and His Times* (New York: Simon & Schuster, 1982), is helpful.

The epochal 1960 election began a series of best-selling works for influential journalist Theodore H. White with *The Making of the President: 1960* (New York: Pocket Books, 1961). Other sources for the election are Edmund F. Kallina, *Courthouse over White House: Chicago and the 1960 Presidential Election* (Orlando: University Presses of Florida, 1987), and Sidney Kraus, ed., *The Great Debates: Background, Perspective, Effects* (Bloomington: Indiana University Press, 1962).

For the background of the 1968 campaign and the nature of the 1960s, see Allen J. Matusow, *The Unraveling of America: A History of Liberalism in the 1960s* (New York: Harper & Row, 1984); Terry H. Anderson, *The Movement and the Sixties: Protest in America from Greensboro to Wounded Knee* (New York: Oxford University Press, 1995); David Farber, *The Age of Great Dreams: America in the 1960s* (New York: Hill & Wang, 1994); Todd Gitlin, *The Sixties: Years of Hope, Days of Rage* (New York: Bantam, 1987); David Steigerwald, *The Sixties and the End of Modern America* (New York: St. Martin's Press, 1995); David Chalmers, *And the Crooked Places Made Straight: The Struggle for Social Change in the 1960s* (Baltimore: Johns Hopkins University Press, 1996); and David Burner, *Making Peace with the 60s* (Princeton, N.J.: Princeton University Press, 1996).

Among the most significant books on the New Left are Kirkpatrick Sale, *SDS* (New York: Random House, 1973); Tom Bates, *Rads: The 1970 Bombing of the Army Math Research Center at the University of Wisconsin and Its Aftermath* (New York: HarperCollins, 1992); Jonah Raskin, *For the Hell of It: The Life and Times of Abbie Hoffman* (Berkeley: University of California Press, 1996); and Roger Rosenblatt, *Coming Apart: A Memoir of the Harvard Wars of 1969* (Boston: Little, Brown, 1997). The President's Commission on Campus Unrest, *Report* (New York: Arno Press, 1970), contains useful data and analysis.

For the rise of the Right, Charles Murray's attack on the liberal paradigm, *Losing Ground: American Social Policy, 1950–1980* (New York: Basic Books, 1984), is a good place to begin before turning to George H. Nash, *The Conservative Intellectual Movement in America since 1945* (New York: Basic Books, 1976); Mary C. Brennan, *Turning Right in the Sixties: The Conservative Capture of the GOP* (Chapel Hill: University of North Carolina Press, 1995); Godfrey Hodgson, *The World Turned Right Side Up: A History of the Conservative Ascendancy in America* (Boston: Houghton Mifflin, 1996); and John A. Andrew III, *The Other Side of the Sixties: Young Americans for Freedom and the Rise of Conservative Politics* (New Brunswick, N.J.: Rutgers University Press, 1997).

Two books that influenced the Nixon administration were Kevin Phillips, *The Emerging Republican Majority* (New York: Arlington House, 1969), and Richard M. Scammon and Ben J. Wattenberg, *The Real Majority: An Extraordinary Examination of the American Electorate* (New York: Coward-McCann, 1970). Kirkpatrick Sale covers similar territory in *Power Shift: The Rise of the Southern Rim and Its Challenge to the Eastern Establishment* (New York: Random House, 1975).

For Nixon from the 1962 gubernatorial race to the presidency, see Jules Witcover, *The Resurrection of Richard Nixon* (New York: G. P. Putnam's, 1970). Theodore H. White, as usual, covered the 1968 election in *The Making of the President: 1968* (New York: Atheneum, 1969), but this time he had serious competition from the more profound Lewis Chester, Godfrey Hodgson, and Bruce Page, *An American Melo-*

drama: The Presidential Campaign of 1968 (New York: Dell, 1969). Joe McGinnis uncovered the deceit that lay behind some of the tactics employed by Nixon campaigners in *The Selling of the President, 1968* (New York: Trident, 1969); an insider's memoir, Richard Whalen's *Catch the Falling Flag: A Republican's Challenge to His Party* (Boston: Houghton Mifflin, 1972), is even more critical. Other useful books on that campaign are Lewis L. Gould, *1968: The Election that Changed America* (Chicago: Ivan Dee, 1993), and George Rising, *Clean for Gene: Eugene McCarthy's 1968 Presidential Campaign* (Westport, Conn.: Praeger, 1997), as well as the political sections of Jules Witcover, *The Year the Dream Died: Revisiting 1968 in America* (New York: Warner, 1997).

Vietnamese politics on the eve of the election attracted considerable attention from Kent G. Sieg, "The 1968 Presidential Election and Peace in Vietnam," *Presidential Studies Quarterly* 26 (fall 1996): 1062–80; Robert Dallek, *Flawed Giant: Lyndon Johnson and His Times, 1961–1973* (New York: Oxford University Press, 1998); and Carl Solberg, *Hubert Humphrey: A Biography* (New York: Norton, 1984). The most up-to-date analysis, including sensational information about the FBI's bugging of Spiro Agnew, is Catherine M. Forslund, "Woman of Two Worlds: Anna Chennault and Informal Diplomacy in U.S.-Asian Relations, 1950–1990 (Ph.D. dissertation, Washington University, 1997). For the participants themselves, see David M. Barrett, ed., *Lyndon B. Johnson's Vietnam Papers: A Documentary Collection* (College Station: Texas A & M Press, 1997); Lyndon Baines Johnson, *The Vantage Point: Perspectives of the Presidency, 1963–1969* (New York: Holt, Rinehart & Winston, 1971); Anna Chennault, *The Education of Anna* (New York: Times Books, 1980); and Bui Diem with David Chanoff, *In the Jaws of History* (Boston: Houghton Mifflin, 1987).

For the foreign policy of the Nixon administration, William Bundy offers a solid, balanced, but ultimately critical analysis in *Tangled Web: The Making of Nixon's Foreign Policy, 1968–1974* (New York: Hill & Wang, 1998). Other studies are Seyom Brown, *The Crises of Power: An Interpretation of United States Foreign Policy during the Kissinger Years* (New York: Columbia University Press, 1979); Coral Bell, *The Diplomacy of Detente: The Kissinger Era* (New York: St. Martin's Press, 1977); Robert J. Litwak, *Detente and the Nixon Doctrine: American Foreign Policy and the Pursuit of Stability, 1969–1976* (New York: Cambridge University Press, 1984); C. L. Sulzberger's laudatory *The World and Richard Nixon* (Englewood Cliffs, N.J.: Prentice Hall, 1987); and Richard C. Thornton's odd tale of conspiracy, *The Nixon-Kissinger Years: The Reshaping of American Foreign Policy* (New York: Paragon House, 1989). The chapter on Nixon in John Prados, *Keeper of the Keys: A History of the National Security Council from Truman to Bush* (New York: William Morrow, 1991), is revealing.

Journalistic accounts written during or just after the Nixon administration that still must be consulted are Henry Brandon, *The Retreat of American Power* (New York: Dell, 1974), and Tad Szulc, *The Illusion of Peace: Foreign Policy in the Nixon Years* (New York: Viking, 1973).

The Nixon administration's foreign policy figures prominently in Thomas M. Franck and Edward Weisband, *Foreign Policy by Congress* (New York: Oxford University Press, 1979), as well as in Cecil V. Crabb, Jr., and Kevin V. Mulcahy,

Presidents and Foreign Policy Making: From FDR to Reagan (Baton Rouge: Louisiana State University Press, 1986). Paula Stern concentrates on the relationship between legislators and White House staffers in *Water's Edge: Domestic Politics and the Making of American Foreign Policy* (Westport, Conn.: Greenwood, 1979).

To understand the way Nixon and Kissinger dealt with the Vietnam War, as well as the view from Hanoi, it is essential to examine Jeffrey Kimball's massive and meticulously researched *Nixon's Vietnam War* (Lawrence: University Press of Kansas, 1998). Tai Sung An, another perceptive Hanoiologist, has much to offer in *The Vietnam War* (Madison, N.J.: Fairleigh Dickinson University Press, 1998). The two best books on the war in general are Robert Schulzinger, *A Time for War: The United States and Vietnam, 1941–1975* (New York: Oxford University Press, 1997), and George C. Herring, *America's Longest War: The United States and Vietnam, 1950–1975* (New York: Knopf, 1996). Blema S. Steinberg uses a psychological approach in *Shame and Humiliation: Presidential Decision Making in Vietnam* (Pittsburgh: University of Pittsburgh Press, 1996).

For the military aspects of the war, see Jeffrey J. Clarke, *Advice and Support: The Final Years, 1965–1973*, The United States Army in Vietnam series (Washington, D.C.: U.S. Army Center for Military History, 1988); Ronald H. Spector, *After Tet: The Bloodiest Year in Vietnam* (New York: Free Press, 1993); Richard A. Hunt, *Pacification: The American Struggle for Vietnam's Hearts and Minds* (Boulder, Colo.: Westview, 1995); Karl J. Eschmann, *Linebacker: The Untold Story of Air Raids over North Vietnam* (New York: Ivy Books, 1989); Lewis Sorley, *Thunderbolt! From the Battle of the Bulge to Vietnam and Beyond: General Creighton Abrams and the Army of His Time* (New York: Simon & Schuster, 1992); and Shelby L. Stanton, *The Rise and Fall of an American Army: U.S. Ground Forces in Vietnam, 1965–1973* (Novato, Calif.: Presidio Press, 1983). The North Vietnamese side is covered in Cecil B. Currey, *Victory at Any Cost: The Genius of Vietnam's General Vo Nguyen Giap* (Washington, D.C.: Brasseys, 1997), and Bui Tin, *Following Ho Chi Minh: The Memoirs of a North Vietnamese Colonel* (Honolulu: University of Hawaii Press, 1995).

For the Sontay raid, see Lucien Vandenbroucke, *Perilous Options: Special Operations as an Instrument of U.S. Foreign Policy* (New York: Oxford University Press, 1993), and Benjamin Schemmer, *The Raid* (London: MacDonald & Jane's, 1977). William Colby (with James McCarger) offers his insider's view of the Phoenix Program in *Lost Victory: A Firsthand Account of America's Sixteen Year Involvement in Vietnam* (Chicago: Contemporary Books, 1989), a self-serving account that must be balanced with Dale Andrade, *Ashes to Ashes: The Phoenix Program and the Vietnam War* (Lexington, Mass.: Lexington Books, 1990). Seymour Hersh uncovered the My Lai massacre and then wrote about the cover-up in *My Lai 4: A Report on the Massacre and Its Aftermath* and *Cover Up* (New York: Random House, 1970, 1972). David Anderson skillfully edited the proceedings of a 1994 conference in *Facing My Lai* (Lawrence: University Press of Kansas, 1998).

Public opinion and the antiwar movement are covered in William M. Hammond's volume, based in part on classified materials, *Public Affairs: The Military and the Media, 1968–1973* (Washington, D.C.: U.S. Army Center of Military History, 1996); Melvin Small, *Johnson, Nixon, and the Doves* and *Covering Dissent: The Media and the Anti-Vietnam War Movement* (New Brunswick, N.J.: Rutgers University Press, 1988, 1994); Charles DeBenedetti with Charles Chatfield, *An American Ordeal: The Antiwar Movement of the Vietnam Era* (Syracuse, N.Y.: Syracuse University Press, 1990); Tom Wells, *The War Within: America's Battle over Vietnam* (Berkeley: University of California Press, 1994); and John E. Mueller, *War, Presidents, and Public Opinion* (New York: John Wiley & Sons, 1973). For a perceptive account of polling, see Andrew Z. Katz, "Public Opinion and Foreign Policy: The Nixon Administration and the Pursuit of Peace with Honor in Vietnam," *Presidential Studies Quarterly* 27 (summer 1997): 496–513. Adam Garfinkle's polemical *Telltale Hearts: The Origins and Impact of the Vietnam Antiwar Movement* (New York: St. Martin's Press, 1995) attacks the movement as ineffective and counterproductive. For military dissent, see Richard R. Moser, *The New Winter Soldiers: GI and Veteran Dissent during the Vietnam Era* (New Brunswick, N.J.: Rutgers University Press, 1996).

Useful on the peace negotiations are Allen E. Goodman, *The Lost Peace: America's Search for a Negotiated Settlement of the Vietnam War* (Stanford, Calif.: Hoover Institution Press, 1978), and Nguyen Tien Hung and Jerrold L. Schecter, *The Palace File* (New York: Harper & Row, 1986). Linebacker II is considered in Martin F. Herz, *The Prestige Press and the Christmas Bombing, 1972: Images and Reality in Vietnam* (Washington, D.C.: Ethics and Public Policy Center, 1980), and Mark Clodfelter, *The Limits of Air Power: The American Bombing of North Vietnam* (New York: Free Press, 1989). For the period after the 1973 peace agreement, see Frank Snepp, *Decent Interval: An Insider's Account of Saigon's Indecent End Told by the CIA's Chief Strategy Analyst in Vietnam* (New York: Random House, 1977); Arnold Isaacs, *Without Honor: Defeat in Vietnam and Cambodia* (Baltimore: Johns Hopkins University Press, 1983); Stuart Herrington, *A Peace with Honor? An American Reports on Vietnam, 1973–1975* (Novato, Calif.: Presidio Press, 1983); Gareth Porter, *A Peace Denied: The United States, Vietnam, and the Paris Agreement* (Bloomington: Indiana University Press, 1975); and P. Edward Haley, *Congress and the Fall of South Vietnam and Cambodia* (Rutherford, N.J.: Fairleigh Dickenson University Press, 1982).

The voluminous literature on the POW-MIA issue includes H. Bruce Franklin, *MIA or Mythmaking in America* (New Brunswick, N.J.: Rutgers University Press, 1993); Malcolm McConnell with Theodore G. Schweitzer III, *Inside Hanoi's Secret Archives: Solving the MIA Mystery* (New York: Simon & Schuster, 1995); and Mark Sauter and Jim Saunders, *The Men We Left Behind: Henry Kissinger, the Politics of Deceit, and the Tragic Fate of the POWs after the Vietnam War* (Washington, D.C.: National Press Books, 1993).

For another legacy of the war, see John Hart Ely, *War and Responsibility: Constitutional Lessons of Vietnam and Its Aftermath* (Princeton, N.J.: Princeton University Press, 1993); Louis Fisher, *Presidential War Power* and *Constitutional Conflicts between Congress and the President,* 4th ed. (Lawrence: University Press of Kansas, 1995, 1997); and Francis D. Wormuth and Edwin Firmage, *To Chain the Dogs of War: The War Power of Congress in History and Law* (Urbana: University of Illinois Press, 1989).

U.S. involvement in Cambodia is the subject of William Shawcross, *Sideshow: Kissinger, Nixon, and the Destruction of Cambodia,* rev. ed. (New York: Touchstone, 1987); Keith William Nolan, *Into Cambodia: Spring Campaign, Summer Offensive, 1970* (Novato, Calif.: Presidio Press, 1970); and Ben Kiernan, *How Pol Pot Came to Power*

(New York: Routledge, 1987). The secret war in Laos is examined in Norman Hannah, *The Key to Failure: Laos in the Vietnam War* (Lanham, Md.: Madison Books, 1987); Timothy N. Castle, *At War in the Shadow of Vietnam: U.S. Military Aid to the Royal Lao Government, 1955–1975* (New York: Columbia University Press, 1993); Roger Warner, *Back Fire: The CIA's Secret War in Laos and Its Link to the Vietnam War* (New York: Simon & Schuster, 1995); Jane Hamilton-Merritt, *Tragic Mountains: The Hmong, the Americans, and the Secret Wars for Laos, 1942–1992* (Bloomington: Indiana University Press, 1992); and Keith William Nolan, *The Story of Dewey Canyon II/Lam Son 719* (Novato, Calif.: Presidio Press, 1986).

The best sources for Nixon's Soviet policy are Keith L. Nelson, *The Making of Detente: Soviet-American Relations in the Shadow of Vietnam* (Baltimore: Johns Hopkins University Press, 1995); Raymond L. Garthoff, *Detente and Confrontation: American Soviet Relations from Nixon to Reagan* (Washington, D.C.: Brookings, 1985); and a documentary collection, William Burr, ed., *The Kissinger Transcripts: The Top Secret Talks with Beijing and Moscow* (New York: New Press, 1999). Other studies of value are Richard W. Stevenson, *The Rise and Fall of Detente: Relaxations of Tensions in U.S.-Soviet Relations, 1953–1984* (London: Macmillan, 1985); Dan Caldwell, *American-Soviet Relations from 1947 to the Nixon-Kissinger Grand Design* (Westport, Conn.: Greenwood, 1983); and William G. Hyland, *Mortal Rivals: Superpower Relations from Nixon to Reagan* (New York: Random House, 1987). For relations with Germany, see Martin J. Hillenbrand, *Fragments of Our Time: Memoirs of a Diplomat* (Athens: University of Georgia Press, 1998), and James K. Sutterlin and David Klein, *Berlin: From Symbol to Confrontation* (New York: Praeger, 1989).

The end of the cold war has brought a flood of documents from the Soviet side, the most useful of which is Anatoly Dobrynin's remarkable memoir *In Confidence* (New York: Times Books, 1995). Consult also Arkady N. Shevchenko, *Breaking with Moscow* (New York: Knopf, 1985); Georgi Arbatov, *The System: An Insider's Life in Soviet Politics* (New York: Random House, 1992); Oleg Kalugin with Fen Montaigne, *The First Directorate: My Thirty Two Years in Intelligence and Espionage against the West* (New York: St. Martin's Press, 1994); and Andrei Gromyko, *Memoirs* (New York: Doubleday, 1989). Fine secondary studies are David Holloway, *The Soviet Union and the Arms Race* (New Haven, Conn.: Yale University Press, 1983); Robin Edmonds, *Soviet Foreign Policy: The Brezhnev Years* (New York: Oxford University Press, 1983); and especially Ilya V. Gaiduk, *The Soviet Union and the Vietnam War* (Chicago: Ivan Dee, 1996).

An embittered Gerard Smith explains his role in SALT in *Doubletalk: The Story of the First Arms Limitation Talks* (New York: Doubleday, 1980) and *Disarming Diplomat: The Memoirs of Gerard C. Smith, Arms Control Negotiator* (Lanham, Md.: Madison Books, 1996). Smith's concerns are evaluated in Terry Terriff's sophisticated *The Nixon Administration and the Making of U.S. Nuclear Strategy* (Ithaca, N.Y.: Cornell University Press, 1995) and the now outmoded but still interesting John Newhouse, *Cold Dawn: The Story of SALT* (New York: Holt, Rinehart & Winston, 1973).

Other aspects of détente are the province of diplomat John J. Maresca's *To Helsinki: The Conference on Security and Cooperation in Europe, 1973–1975* (Durham, N.C.: Duke University Press, 1985); Marshall I. Goldman, *Detente and Dollars: Doing*

Business with the Soviets (New York: Basic Books, 1975); Martha Hamilton, *The Great American Grain Robbery and Other Stories* (Washington, D.C.: Washington Agribusiness Accountability Project, 1972); Dan Morgan, *Merchants of Grain* (New York: Penguin, 1980), and Sherry Sontag and Christopher Drew with Annette Lawrence Drew, *Blind Man's Bluff: The Untold Story of American Submarine Espionage* (New York: Public Affairs Press, 1998).

There are not as many sources for U.S.-China relations as for U.S.-Soviet relations, but a good place to start is Robert S. Ross, *Negotiating Cooperation: The United States and China, 1969–1989* (Stanford, Calif.: Stanford University Press, 1995); Rosemary Foot, *The Practice of Power: U.S. Relations with China since 1949* (New York: Oxford University Press, 1995); and Gordon H. Chang, *Friends and Enemies: The United States, China, and the Soviet Union, 1948–1972* (Stanford, Calif.: Stanford University Press, 1990). Three studies dealing with U.S. opinion are Leonard A. Kusnitz, *Public Opinion and Foreign Policy: America's China Policy, 1949–1979* (Westport, Conn.: Greenwood, 1984); A. Doak Barnett, *China Policy: Old Problems and New Challenges* (Washington, D.C.: Brookings, 1977); and Robert G. Sutter, *The China Quandary: Domestic Determinants of U.S. China Policy, 1972–1982* (Boulder, Colo.: Westview, 1983). John H. Holdridge describes his experiences in *Crossing the Divide: An Insider's Account of Normalization of U.S.-China Relations* (Lanham, Md.: Rowman & Littlefield, 1997). Anne Collins Walker has edited the transcripts of phone conversations from the advance team in *China Calls: Paving the Way for Nixon's Historic Journey to China* (Lanham, Md.: Madison Books, 1992). For Beijing's still murky perspective, see James W. Garver, *China's Decision for Rapprochement with the United States, 1968–1971* (Boulder, Colo.: Westview, 1982), and Robert G. Sutter, *Chinese Foreign Policy and the Cultural Revolution, 1966–77* (Boulder, Colo.: Westview, 1978). The 1972 China trip is the subject of John Adams and Alice Goodman, "Nixon in China: An Opera in Two Acts" (1987).

The literature on Middle East issues includes William B. Quandt's *Decade of Decisions: American Policy towards the Arab-Israeli Conflict, 1967–1976* (Berkeley: University of California Press, 1977); Ishaq Ghanayem and Alden Voth, *The Kissinger Legacy: American Middle Eastern Policy* (New York: Praeger, 1984); and Edward R. F. Sheehan, *The Arabs, Israelis, and Kissinger: A Secret History of American Diplomacy in the Middle East* (New York: Thomas Y. Crowell, 1976). Israeli memoirs of value are Abba Eban, *Abba Eban: An Autobiography* (New York: Random House, 1977) and *Personal Witness: Israel through My Eyes* (New York: G. P. Putnam's Sons, 1992), and Golda Meir, *My Life* (New York: G. P. Putnam's Sons, 1975). Egyptian foreign policy expert Mohamed Heikal, *The Road to Ramadan* (New York: Quadrangle, 1975), and Anwar Sadat, *In Search of Identity* (New York: Harper & Row, 1977), serve as a counterbalance.

Secondary sources include Galia Golan, *Yom Kippur and After: The Soviet Union and the Middle East Crisis* (London: Cambridge University Press, 1975); Victor Israelyan, *Inside the Kremlin during the Yom Kippur War* (University Park: Penn State University Press, 1995); Matti Golan, *The Secret Conversations of Henry Kissinger: Step-by-Step Diplomacy in the Middle East* (New York: Quadrangle, 1976); and Stephen L. Spiegel, *The Other Arab-Israeli Conflict: Making America's Middle East Policy, from Truman to Reagan* (Chicago: University of Chicago Press, 1985). Two specialized studies worth consulting are Ian Skeet, *OPEC: Twenty-five Years of Prices and Politics* (Cambridge: Cambridge University Press, 1988), and Douglas Little, "A Puppet in Search of a Puppeteer: The United States, King Hussein, and Jordan, *International History Review* 17 (August 1995): 512–44.

The administration's relations with Iran are surveyed in Barry Rubin, *Paved with Good Intentions: The American Experience and Iran* (New York: Oxford University Press, 1980), and James A. Bill, *The Eagle and the Lion: The Tragedy of American-Iranian Relations* (New Haven, Conn: Yale University Press, 1988). Among the handful of sources on Africa are Mohammad A. El-Khawas and Barry Cohen, eds., *The Kissinger Study of Southern Africa: National Security Memorandum 39* (Westport, Conn.: Lawrence Hill & Company, 1976); Odde Arne Westad, "Moscow and the Angolan Crisis, 1974–1976: A New Pattern of Intervention," *Cold War International History Project Bulletin* (winter 1996/97): 21–32; Christopher Coker, *The United States and South Africa, 1968–1985: Constructive Engagement and Its Critics* (Durham, N.C.: Duke University Press, 1986); and Anthony Lake, *The "Tar Baby" Option: American Policy toward Southern Rhodesia* (New York: Columbia University Press, 1976).

For Japan, a good place to begin is Ambassador Armin H. Meyer's *Assignment Tokyo: An Ambassador's Journal* (Indianapolis: Bobbs-Merrill, 1974), as well as his oral history in the Columbia University Oral History Project, which also covers Iran. Michael Schaller's *Altered States: The United States and Japan since the Occupation* (New York: Oxford University Press, 1997) is invaluable for the Nixon years. See also John Welfield, *An Empire in Eclipse: Japan in the Postwar American Alliance System* (London: Athlone Press, 1988), and I. M. Destler, Haruhiro Fukui, and Hideo Sato, *The Textile Wrangle: Conflict in Japanese-American Relations, 1969–1971* (Ithaca, N.Y.: Cornell University Press, 1979).

Other books on Nixon's diplomacy are Diane B. Kunz, *Butter and Guns: America's Cold War Economic Diplomacy* (New York: Free Press, 1997); Lewis Sorley, *Arms Transfers under Nixon: A Policy Analysis* (Lexington: University of Kentucky Press, 1983); Peace Corps official P. David Searles's *The Peace Corps Experience: Challenge and Change, 1969–1976* (Lexington: University of Kentucky Press, 1997); former Kissinger aide Peter Rodman's *More Precious than Peace: The Cold War and the Struggle for the Third World* (New York: Charles Scribner's Sons, 1994); Lawrence S. Kaplan, "NATO and the Nixon Doctrine Ten Years Later," *Orbis* 24 (1980): 149–61; and Robert Bothwell, *Canada and the United States: The Politics of Partnership* (New York: Twayne, 1992).

For intelligence activities during the Nixon years, of value are John Ranelagh, *The Agency: The Rise and Decline of the CIA* (New York: Simon & Schuster, 1986); Thomas Powers, *The Man Who Kept the Secrets: Richard Helms and the CIA* (New York: Knopf, 1979); William Colby with Peter Forbath, *Honorable Men: My Life in the CIA* (New York: Simon & Schuster, 1978); Mark Riebling, *Wedge: The Secret War between the FBI and the CIA* (New York: Knopf, 1994); and David Corn, *Blond Ghost: Ted Shackley and the CIA's Crusades* (New York: Simon & Schuster, 1994).

To place the administration's civil rights program in context, useful overviews include Hugh Davis Graham's splendid survey *The Civil Rights Era: Origins and Development of National Policy: 1960–1972* (New York: Oxford University Press,

1990); Harvard Sitkoff, *The Struggle for Black Equality, 1954–1992*, rev. ed. (New York: Hill & Wang, 1993); Paul Burstein, *Discrimination, Jobs, and Politics: The Struggle for Equal Employment Opportunity in the United States since the New Deal* (Chicago: University of Chicago Press, 1985); Martin Conroy, *Faded Dreams: The Politics and Economics of Race in America* (New York: Cambridge University Press, 1994); and J. Harvie Wilkinson III, *From Brown to Bakke: The Supreme Court and School Desegregation Policy: 1954–1978* (New York: Oxford University Press, 1978).

For Nixon in particular, Leon Panetta's justifiably bitter memoir (with Peter Gall) *"Bring Us Together": The Nixon Team and the Civil Rights Retreat* (Philadelphia: Lippincott, 1971) covers the early years at HEW. Kenneth O'Reilly, *Nixon's Piano: Presidents and Racial Politics from Washington to Clinton* (New York: Free Press, 1995); Reg Murphy and Hal Gullivei, *The Southern Strategy* (New York: Scribner, 1971); and Dean J. Kotlowski, "Richard Nixon and the Origins of Affirmative Action," *The Historian* 60 (spring 1998): 523–41 are valuable. See also Kenneth O'Reilly, *Racial Matters: The FBI's Secret War on Black America, 1966–1972* (New York: Free Press, 1989).

Southern politics is the subject of Bernard Grofman, *Quiet Revolution in the South: The Impact of the Voting Rights Act* (Princeton, N.J.: Princeton University Press, 1993); Alexander P. Lamis, *The Two Party South* (New York: Oxford University Press, 1988); and Stephen F. Lawson, *In Pursuit of Power: Southern Blacks and Electoral Politics* (New York: Columbia University Press, 1985). Dan Carter links the racial issue to conservatism in *The Politics of Rage: George Wallace, the Origins of the New Conservatism, and the Transformation of American Politics* (New York: Simon & Schuster, 1995) and *From George Wallace to Newt Gingrich: Race in the Conservative Counter-Revolution* (Baton Rouge: Louisiana State University Press, 1996). Valuable for the impact of busing on local politics are Ronald P. Formisano, *Boston against Busing: Race, Class, and Ethnicity in the 1960s and 1970s* (Chapel Hill: University of North Carolina Press, 1991), and Richard David Riddle, "The Rise of the Reagan Democrats in Warren, Michigan" (Ph.D. dissertation, Wayne State University, 1998).

For the record of the Burger Supreme Court, see Herman Schwartz, ed., *The Burger Years: Rights and Wrongs in the Supreme Court* (New York: Viking, 1987), and Vincent Blasi, ed., *The Burger Court—The Counter-Revolution that Wasn't* (New Haven, Conn.: Yale University Press, 1983). Bob Woodward and Scott Armstrong penetrate the High Court's veil of secrecy in the gossipy *The Brethren: Inside the Supreme Court* (New York: Simon & Schuster, 1979). For the battle over Nixon's appointments of Haynsworth and Carswell, see John Massaro, *Supremely Political: The Role of Ideology and Presidential Management in Unsuccessful Supreme Court Nominations* (Albany: State University of New York Press, 1990) for Haynsworth, see John Paul Frank, *Clement Haynsworth, the Senate, and the Supreme Court* (Charlottesville: University of Virginia Press, 1991), and for Carswell, see Richard Harris, *Decision* (New York: E. P. Dutton, 1971).

Autobiographies and biographies of justices that shed light on Nixon's relationship to the Court are Earl Warren, *The Memoirs of Earl Warren* (Garden City, N.Y.: Doubleday, 1977); G. Edward White, *Earl Warren: A Public Life* (New York: Oxford University Press, 1982); Ed Cray, *Chief Justice: A Biography of Earl Warren* (New

York: Simon & Schuster, 1997); Bruce Allen Murphy, *Fortas: The Rise and Ruin of a Supreme Court Justice* (New York: William Morrow, 1988); Laura Kalman, *Abe Fortas: A Biography* (New Haven, Conn.: Yale University Press, 1990); William O. Douglas, *The Court Years, 1939–1975: The Autobiography of William O. Douglas* (New York: Random House, 1980); James F. Simon, *Independent Journey: The Life of William O. Douglas* (New York: Harper & Row, 1980); John C. Jeffries, *Justice Lewis F. Powell, Jr.* (New York: Charles Scribner's Sons, 1994); and Gerald T. Dunne, *Hugo Black and the Judicial Revolution* (New York: Simon & Schuster, 1977).

Nixon's relations with J. Edgar Hoover are examined in the authoritative Athan G. Theoharis and John Stuart Cox, *The Boss: J. Edgar Hoover and the Great American Inquisition* (Philadelphia: Temple University Press, 1988). One must use with care two insiders' accounts: Cartha D. DeLoach, *Hoover's FBI: The Inside Story by Hoover's Trusted Lieutenant* (Washington, D.C.: Regnery, 1995), and William C. Sullivan with Bill Brown, *The Bureau: My Thirty Years in Hoover's FBI* (New York: Norton, 1979). For domestic intelligence activities during the Nixon years, see Athan Theoharis: *Spying on Americans: Political Surveillance from Hoover to the Huston Plan* (Philadelphia: Temple University Press, 1978); John T. Elliff, *Crime, Dissent, and the Attorney General: The Justice Department in the 1960s* (Beverly Hills, Calif.: Sage, 1981); Frank J. Donner, *The Age of Surveillance: The Aims and Methods of America's Political Intelligence System* (New York: Knopf, 1980); and James Kirkpatrick Davis, *Spying on America: The FBI's Domestic Counterintelligence Program* (New York: Praeger, 1992). Using Egil Krogh's papers, Edward Jay Epstein turned up interesting material in "The Krogh File—The Politics of 'Law and Order,'" *The Public Interest* (spring 1975): 99–124. Michael Massing praises Nixon's antidrug program, particularly the use of methadone, in *The Fix* (New York: Simon & Schuster, 1998).

Curtis W. Tarr, the last director of the old Selective Service System, wrote of his experiences in *By the Numbers: The Reform of the Selective Service System, 1970–1972* (Washington, D.C.: National Defense University Press, 1981). The most important study of the draft is George Q. Flynn, *The Draft, 1940–1973* (Lawrence: University Press of Kansas, 1993). The following provide the necessary background information to understand the origins of the all-volunteer force: Lawrence M. Baskir and William A. Strauss, *Chance and Circumstance: The Draft, the War and the Vietnam Generation* (New York: Knopf, 1978); Michael Useem, *Conscription, Protest, and Social Conflict: The Life and Death of a Draft Resistance Movement* (New York: John Wiley & Sons, 1973); David Cortright, *Soldiers in Revolt: The American Military Today* (Garden City, N.Y.: Doubleday, 1975); and William A. Hauser, *America's Army in Crisis: A Study in Civil-Military Relations* (Baltimore: Johns Hopkins University Press, 1973).

John William Sayer, *Ghost Dancing: The Wounded Knee Trials* (Cambridge: Harvard University Press, 1997), offers an unusually imaginative approach to the history of Native Americans. Troy R. Johnson analyzes the Native American movement in *The Occupation of Alcatraz Island: Indian Self-Determination and the Rise of Indian Activism* (Urbana: University of Illinois Press, 1996), as does Jack D. Forbes in *Native Americans and Nixon: Presidential Politics and Minority Self-Determination, 1969–1970* (Los Angeles: American Indian Studies Center, UCLA, 1981). Susan M. Hartmann looks at the women's movement in *From Margin to Mainstream: Ameri-*

can Women and Politics since 1960 (New York: Knopf, 1989), and Tony Castro looks at "brown power" in *Chicano Power: The Emergence of Mexican-America* (New York: Saturday Review Press, 1974). David Garrow's *Liberty and Sexuality: The Right to Privacy and the Making of* Roe v. Wade, *1923–1973* (New York: Macmillan, 1993) must also be examined.

Two perceptive general discussions of Great Society programs are Irwin Unger, *The Best of Intentions: The Triumphs and Failures of the Great Society under Kennedy, Johnson, and Nixon* (New York: Doubleday, 1996), and Gareth Davies, *From Opportunity to Entitlement: The Transformation and Decline of Great Society Liberalism* (Lawrence: University Press of Kansas, 1996). Specific Great Society programs are considered in Bernard J. Frieden and Marshall Frieden, *The Politics of Neglect: Urban Aid from Model Cities to Revenue Sharing* (Cambridge: MIT Press, 1977); Charles M. Haar, *Between the Idea and the Reality: A Study in the Origins, Fate and Legacy of the Model Cities Program* (Boston: Little, Brown, 1975); Timothy Conlan, *New Federalism: Intergovernmental Reform from Nixon to Reagan* (Washington, D.C.: Brookings, 1988); Edward Ziegler and Susan Muenchow, *Head Start: The Inside Story of America's Most Successful Educational Experiment* (New York: Basic Books, 1992); and Kay Mills, *Something for My Children: The History and People of Head Start* (New York: Dutton, 1998).

The best study of Nixon's welfare reform program, despite its contemporary nature, is Vincent J. Burke and Vee Burke, *Nixon's Good Deed: Welfare Reform* (New York: Columbia University Press, 1974). Two key architects of the program have written about the subject in Daniel Patrick Moynihan, *The Politics of a Guaranteed Income: The Nixon Administration and the Family Assistance Plan* (New York: Random House, 1973), and Martin Anderson, *Welfare: The Political Economy of Welfare Reform in the United States* (Stanford, Calif.: Hoover Institution Press, 1978). See also the chapter on FAP in Barbara Kellerman, *The Political Presidency: Practice and Leadership* (New York: Oxford University Press, 1984), and, in general, James T. Patterson, *America's Struggle against Poverty, 1900–1985* (Cambridge: Harvard University Press, 1986). Margaret Weir, *Politics and Jobs: The Boundaries of Employment Policy in the United States* (Princeton, N.J.: Princeton University Press, 1992); Otis Graham, Jr., *Toward a Planned Society: From Roosevelt to Nixon* (New York: Oxford University Press, 1976); and Ardith L. Maney, *Still Hungry after All These Years: Food Assistance Policy from Kennedy to Reagan* (New York: Greenwood, 1989) are important studies in related areas.

John C. Whitaker ably defends his administration's environmental policy in *Striking a Balance: Environment and Natural Resources Policy in the Nixon-Ford Years* (Washington, D.C.: American Enterprise Institute, 1976), but a group of environmentalists trashes that same policy in James Rathelsberger, ed., *Nixon and the Environment: The Politics of Devastation* (New York: Taurus Communications, 1972). Kirkpatrick Sale provides a readable overview in *The Green Revolution: The American Environmental Movement* (New York: Hill & Wang, 1993). See also Samuel P. Hays, *Beauty, Health and Permanence: Environmental Politics in the United States, 1955–1985* (New York: Cambridge University Press, 1987). Related to environmental issues, the energy crisis is explained in Daniel Yergin's monumental *The Prize: The Epic Quest for Oil, Money, and Power* (New York: Simon & Schuster, 1991), and Robert Sherrill, *The Oil Follies of 1970–1980* (New York: Doubleday, 1983).

To understand the complicated economic problems faced by the Nixon administration, Allen J. Matusow's readable and well-reasoned *Nixon's Economy: Booms, Busts, Dollars, and Votes* (Lawrence: University Press of Kansas, 1998) is essential. Nixon's record does not look impressive in Richard J. Carroll's unique compendium *An Economic Record of Presidential Performance: From Truman to Bush* (Westport, Conn.: Praeger, 1995). Arnold R. Weber's *In Pursuit of Price Stability: The Wage-Price Freeze of 1971* (Washington, D.C.: Brookings, 1973) is an intelligent contemporary evaluation. Herbert Stein writes about his experiences working with Nixon in *Presidential Economics: The Making of Economic Policy from Roosevelt to Reagan and Beyond* (New York: Simon & Schuster, 1984). In a comparable survey, journalist Hobart Rowen evaluates Nixon in his lively *Self-Inflicted Wounds: From LBJ's Guns and Butter to Reagan's Voodoo Economics* (New York: Times Books, 1994). Helpful here as well are Erwin C. Hargrove and Samuel A. Morley, eds., *The President and the Council of Economic Advisors: Interviews with CEA Chairmen* (Boulder, Colo.: Westview, 1984); Wyatt C. Wells, *Economist in an Uncertain World: Arthur F. Burns and the Federal Reserve* (New York: Columbia University Press, 1994); and James P. Pfiffner, *The President, the Budget and Congress: Impoundment and the 1974 Budget Act* (Boulder, Colo.: Westview, 1979).

For an especially clear analysis of the international economy, begin with David P. Calleo, *The Imperious Economy* (Cambridge: Harvard University Press, 1992), supplemented with Harold James's authoritative *International Monetary Cooperation since Bretton Woods* (Washington, D.C.: International Monetary Fund, 1996). American trade policy is the subject of I. M. Destler, *Making Foreign Economic Policy* (Washington, D.C.: Brookings, 1980); Judith Goldstein, *Ideas, Interests, and American Trade Policy* (Ithaca, N.Y.: Cornell University Press, 1993); and Steve Dryden, *Trade Warriors: USTR and the American Crusade for Free Trade* (New York: Oxford University Press, 1995).

Joanne Gowa deftly handles the complicated August 1971 economic decisions in *Closing the Gold Window: Domestic Politics and the End of Bretton Woods* (Ithaca, N.Y.: Cornell University Press, 1983). See also Fred L. Block, *The Origins of International Economic Disorder: A Study of United States Monetary Policy from World War II to the Present* (Berkeley: University of California Press, 1977); Robert Charles Angel, *Explaining Economic Policy Failure: Japan in the 1969–1971 International Monetary Crisis* (New York: Columbia University Press, 1991); Gregory F. Treverton, *The Dollar Drain and American Forces in Germany: Managing the Political Economy of Alliances* (Athens: Ohio University Press, 1978); and Paul A. Volcker and Toyoo Gyohten, *Changing Fortunes: The World's Money and the Threat to American Leadership* (New York: Times Books, 1992).

Studies of politics and culture during the Nixon presidency include former NEA official Michael Straight's *Nancy Hanks: An Intimate Portrait: The Creation of a National Commitment to the Arts* (Durham, N.C.: Duke University Press, 1988), and former NEH chief Ronald Berman's *Culture and Politics* (Lanham, Md.: University Press of America, 1984). See also Alice Goldfarb Marquis, *Art Lessons: Learning from the Rise and Fall of Public Arts Funding* (New York: Basic Books, 1995); Joseph Wesley Zieger, *Arts in Crisis: The National Endowment for the Arts versus America* (Chicago: Acapella Books, 1990); David M. Stone, *Nixon and the Politics of*

Television (New York: Garland, 1985); Ralph Engleman, *Public Radio and Television in America: A History* (Beverly Hills, Calif.: Sage, 1996); and Michael Kammen, "Culture and the State in America," *Journal of American History* 83 (December 1996): 791–814.

Nixon was not the only president to have problems with the media, as seen in John Tebbel and Sarah Miles Watts, *The Press and the Presidency: From George Washington to Ronald Reagan* (New York: Oxford University Press, 1996); Samuel Kernell, *Going Public: New Strategies of Presidential Leadership* (Washington, D.C.: Congressional Quarterly Press, 1993); Michael Baruch Grossman and Martha Joynt Kumar, *Portraying the Press: The White House and the News Media* (Baltimore: Johns Hopkins University Press, 1981); David Halberstam, *The Powers that Be* (New York: Knopf, 1979); and John Anthony Maltese, *Spin Control: The White House Office of Communications and the Management of Presidential News*, 2d ed. (Chapel Hill: University of North Carolina Press, 1994).

Although Nixon has his defenders, namely, speechwriter James Keogh, *President Nixon and the Press* (New York: Funk & Wagnalls, 1972), and Edith Efron, *The News Twisters* (Los Angeles: Nash, 1971), most experts are critical of his assault on the press, including Fred Powledge, *The Engineering of Restraint: The Nixon Administration and the Press* (Washington, D.C.: Public Affairs Press, 1971); William E. Porter, *Assault on the Media* (Ann Arbor: University of Michigan Press, 1976); Joseph Spear, *Presidents and the Press: The Nixon Legacy* (Cambridge: MIT Press, 1984); and Marilyn A. Lashner, *The Chilling Effect in TV News: Intimidation by the Nixon White House* (New York: Praeger, 1984). For Nixon and the FCC, see Newton N. Minow, John Bartlow Martin, and Lee M. Mitchell, *Presidential Television* (New York: Basic Books, 1973), and Corydon B. Dunham, *Fighting for the First Amendment: Stanton of CBS vs. Congress and the Nixon White House* (Westport, Conn.: Praeger, 1997).

Another arena where Nixon fought to develop favorable public opinion is revealed by Lawrence R. Jacobs and Robert Y. Shapiro in "Presidential Manipulation of Polls and Public Opinion: The Nixon Administration and the Pollsters," *Political Science Quarterly* 110 (winter 1995–96): 519–38. Two fine monographs cover the *Pentagon Papers* case: David Rudenstine, *The Day the Presses Stopped: A History of the Pentagon Papers Case* (Berkeley: University of California Press, 1996), and Sanford J. Ungar, *The Papers and the Papers: An Account of the Legal and Political Battle over the Pentagon Papers* (New York: Columbia University Press, 1972).

Media figures whose memoirs offer perspectives on Nixon and the *Pentagon Papers* case and other issues are Ben Bradlee, *A Good Life: Newspapering and Other Adventures* (New York: Simon & Schuster, 1995); Katherine Graham, *Personal History* (New York: Knopf, 1997); Henry Grunwald, *One Man's America: A Journalist's Search for the Heart of His Country* (New York: Doubleday, 1997); James Reston, *Deadline: A Memoir* (New York: Random House, 1991); and Hedley Donovan, *Right Places, Right Times* (New York: Holt, 1989).

The 1972 campaign, which included the break-in at the Watergate complex, is the subject of Timothy Crouse's lively exposé of press behavior in *The Boys on the Bus* (New York: Random House, 1973). Theodore H. White continued his series with *The Making of the President: 1972* (New York: Atheneum, 1973). Writers

Norman Mailer in *St. George and the Godfather* (New York: New American Library, 1972) and Hunter J. Thompson in *Fear and Loathing: On the Campaign Trail '72* (San Francisco: Straight Arrow Press, 1973) offer far more unconventional—and amusing—views of the campaign. George McGovern explains his problems in *The Autobiography of George McGovern* (New York: Random House, 1977), as does his campaign manager, Gary Hart, in *Right from the Start: A Chronicle of the McGovern Campaign* (New York: Quadrangle, 1973). Also worth consulting are Arthur Pearl, *Landslide: The How and Why of Nixon's Victory* (Secaucus, N.J.: Citadel Press, 1973), and Ernest R. May and Janet Fraser, eds., *Campaign 72: The Managers Speak* (Cambridge: Harvard University Press, 1973). For teamster support for Nixon and Jimmy Hoffa's release from prison, see Walter Sheridan, *The Fall and Rise of Jimmy Hoffa* (New York: Saturday Review Press, 1972).

Watergate has become a cottage industry. Michael Schudson considers eighteen years of writing about the subject in *Watergate in American Memory: How We Remember, Forget, and Reconstruct the Past* (New York: Basic Books, 1992). An early bibliography is Myron J. Smith, Jr., ed., *Watergate: An Annotated Bibliography of Sources in English, 1972–1982* (Metuchen, N.J.: Scarecrow Press, 1983), and a helpful documentary history is Congressional Quarterly, *Watergate: Chronology of a Crisis* (Washington, D.C.: Congressional Quarterly Press, 1975).

The single best study of Watergate remains Stanley I. Kutler, *The Wars of Watergate: The Last Crisis of Richard Nixon* (New York: Norton, 1992). Kutler also edited the immensely valuable *Abuse of Power: The New Nixon Tapes* (New York: Free Press, 1997) (which takes its place alongside the *Washington Post*'s *The Presidential Transcripts* [New York: Dell, 1974]) and a volume of documents, *Watergate: The Fall of Richard M. Nixon* (Westbury, Conn.: Brandywine Books, 1997). Somewhat less scholarly and less critical of Nixon is Fred Emery's solid *Watergate: The Corruption of American Politics and the Fall of Richard Nixon* (New York: Times Books, 1994). The most famous Watergate book remains Carl Bernstein and Bob Woodward, *All the President's Men* (New York: Warner, 1975). The two *Washington Post* reporters (with Woodward as first author) also wrote the less convincing *The Final Days* (New York: Simon & Schuster, 1976) about the resignation decision.

Journalists who covered the story include Theodore H. White, *Breach of Faith: The Fall of Richard Nixon* (New York: Atheneum, 1975); Elizabeth Drew, *Washington Journal: The Events of 1973–1974* (New York: Vintage, 1976); James Breslin (who had unique access to Tip O'Neill), *How the Good Guys Finally Won: Notes from an Impeachment Summer* (New York: Viking, 1975); and J. Anthony Lukas, *Nightmare: The Underside of the Nixon Years*, rev. ed. (New York: Penguin, 1988). Victor Lasky scores some points when he examines the crimes of other presidents in *It Didn't Start with Watergate* (New York: Dial, 1977).

Two studies that identify conspiracies to explain how Nixon became entrapped in Watergate are Jim Hougan, *Secret Agenda: Watergate, Deep Throat and the CIA* (New York: Random House, 1984), and Len Colodny and Robert Gettlin, *Silent Coup: The Removal of a President* (New York: St. Martin's Press, 1991). The leader of one of those alleged conspiracies, John Dean, tells his side of the story in *Blind Ambition: The White House Years* (New York: Simon & Schuster, 1976) and *Lost Honor* (Los Angeles: Stratford Press, 1982); his wife, Maureen (with Hays Gorey), tells hers in *"Mo": A Woman's View of Watergate* (New York: Simon & Schuster, 1975). Among others involved in the break-in who have written about their experiences are G. Gordon Liddy, *Will: The Autobiography of G. Gordon Liddy* (New York: St. Martin's Press, 1980); H. Maurice Stans, *The Terrors of Justice: The Untold Side of Watergate* (Chicago: Regnery, 1984); and James W. McCord, Jr., *A Piece of Tape: The Watergate Story: Fact and Fiction* (Rockville, Md.: Washington Media Sources Ltd., 1974). Baruch Korff, Nixon's chief public supporter during the crisis, describes his campaign in *The President and I: Richard Nixon's Rabbi Reveals His Role in the Saga that Traumatized the Nation* (Providence, R.I.: Baruch Korff Foundation, 1995).

Most of the key lawyers and judges involved in the investigations have written about the affair. The best are Leon Jaworski, *The Right and the Power: The Prosecution of Watergate* (New York: Reader's Digest Press, 1976); John J. Sirica, *To Set the Record Straight: The Break-in, the Tapes, the Conspirators, the Pardon* (New York: Norton, 1979); Sam J. Ervin, Jr., *The Whole Truth: The Watergate Conspiracy* (New York: Random House, 1980); Richard Ben Veniste and George Frampton, Jr., *Stonewall: The Real Story of the Watergate Prosecution* (New York: Simon & Schuster, 1977); Sam Dash, *Chief Counsel: Inside the Ervin Committee—The Untold Story of Watergate* (New York: Random House, 1976); and James Doyle, *Not above the Law: The Battles of Watergate Prosecutors Cox and Jaworski* (New York: William Morrow, 1977). Ervin committee minority counsel Fred D. Thompson presents a rare partial defense of Nixon in *At that Point in Time: The Inside Story of the Watergate Committee* (New York: Quadrangle, 1975). Ken Gormley's biography, *Archibald Cox: Conscience of a Nation* (Reading, Mass.: Addison-Wesley, 1997), is well done if hagiographic.

Legal issues are the concern of Mark J. Rozell, *Executive Privilege: The Dilemma of Secrecy and Democratic Accountability* (Baltimore: Johns Hopkins University Press, 1994); Philip B. Kurland, *Watergate and the Constitution* (Chicago: University of Chicago Press, 1978); and Howard Ball, *"We Have a Duty": The Supreme Court and the Watergate Tapes Litigation* (New York: Greenwood, 1990).

Gerald Ford explains his pardon of Nixon in *A Time to Heal: The Autobiography of Gerald R. Ford* (New York: Harper & Row, 1979). Also covering the controversial matter are Ford's chief biographer James Cannon, *Time and Chance: Gerald Ford's Appointment with History* (New York: HarperCollins, 1994), and two of Ford's aides—Robert T. Hartmann, *Palace Politics: An Inside Account of the Ford Years* (New York: McGraw-Hill, 1980), and Ron Nessen, *It Sure Looks Different from the Inside* (Chicago: Playboy Press, 1978). John Robert Greene presents a judicious analysis of the pardon (as well as Ford's activities in the White House) in *The Presidency of Gerald R. Ford* (Lawrence: University Press of Kansas, 1995). Representative Robert McClory answers the question, "Was the Fix in between Ford and Nixon," with a resounding no in *National Review*, 14 October 1983, pp. 1264–66, 1272, while Seymour M. Hersh paints a more complicated picture in "The Pardon: Nixon, Ford, Haig, and the Transfer of Power," *Atlantic* 252 (August 1983): 55–79.

Bill Gulley, the White House liaison with San Clemente, had a unique perspective of Nixon in "exile" in *Breaking Cover* (New York: Simon & Schuster, 1980). Journalists David Frost and Robert Sam Anson also reported on the disgraced president in *"I Gave Them a Sword": Behind the Scenes of the Nixon Interviews* (New York: William Morrow, 1978) and *Exile: The Unquiet Oblivion of Richard M. Nixon*

(New York: Simon & Schuster, 1984). Nixon's ablility to influence foreign policy in the early nineties is the subject of Marvin Kalb's intriguing *The Nixon Memo: Political Responsibility, Russia, and the Press* (Chicago: University of Chicago Press, 1994). The eulogies delivered at graveside in Yorba Linda and in Congress are printed in Joint Committee on Printing, U.S. Congress, *Memorial Services in the Congress of the United States and Tributes in Eulogy of Richard M. Nixon, Late a President of the United States* (Washington, D.C.: U.S. Government Printing Office, 1996).

INDEX

371

INDEX

375

INDEX